And I Quote

And I Quote

The Definitive Collection of
Quotes, Sayings, and Jokes
for the Contemporary Speechmaker

Ashton Applewhite

William R. Evans, III

Andrew Frothingham

St. Martin's Press
New York

Design by Maura Fadden Rosenthal

Library of Congress Cataloging-in-Publication Data

Applewhite, Ashton.
    And I quote : the definitive collection of quotes, sayings, and
jokes for the contemporary speechmaker / Ashton Applewhite, Tripp
Evans, Andrew Frothingham.
        p.   cm.
    "A Thomas Dunne book."
    ISBN 0-312-06897-2
    1. Public speaking.   2. American wit and humor.   I. Evans,
Tripp.   II. Frothingham, Andrew.   III. Title.
PN4193.I5A6   1992
808.5'1—dc20
                                                        91-36742
                                                        CIP

First Edition: February 1992

10 9 8 7 6 5 4 3 2 1

We dedicate this book to Tom Dunne, without whom it never would have come about, and to all our sources, thanks to whom the rest of us will never be speechless.

I N T R O D U C T I O N

WHY WE WROTE THIS BOOK

We created this book because we needed it. We write speeches, and to our surprise, very few engaging and contemporary quotation reference books are available. It's hard to find intelligent material on topics such as computers, birth control, ecology, and nuclear power. Women are underrepresented. So are minorities. Until now.

We've got Tammy Faye Bakker on women's rights ("I believe in keeping the male ego intact"); Arthur C. Clarke on the media ("I have a fantasy where Ted Turner is elected president but refuses because he doesn't want to give up power"); and Eldridge Cleaver on accountability ("If you're not part of the solution, you're part of the problem").

But don't think the time-honored, quotable masters have been left out. They're all here, from Aesop to Zola. There's Louis XIV on hiring practices ("Every time I fill a vacant office, I make ten malcontents and one ingrate"). And Catherine the Great on peace ("Peace is necessary to this vast empire. We need population, not devastation."); or William Shakespeare on parenting ("How sharper than a serpent's tooth it is to have a thankless child"). We've gone one step further, including at least one anonymous saying and one joke for each category in the book. This makes interesting maxims and witty quips easily accessible, so you can spice up an otherwise dull topic or soften up the most jaded listener.

The material in this book is suitable for every occasion from sales training ("When you stop talking, you've lost your customer."—Estée Lauder) to awards dinners ("I don't deserve this, but then I have arthritis and I don't deserve that either."—Jack Benny), from life ("Life is either a daring adventure or nothing."—Helen Keller) to death ("It's not that I'm afraid to die, I just don't want to be there when it happens."—Woody Allen).

HOW THIS BOOK IS ORGANIZED

Creating an up-to-date quotation reference book is one thing; making it "user-friendly" is something else. We know that time is money. Most people are in a hurry and don't have the opportunity to do extensive reading and research. To help you locate material quickly and without jockeying back and forth, the book begins with two reference lists to direct you. Here's how they work:

THE SUBJECT LIST

This list, which begins on p. xvii of this Introduction, essentially a Table of Contents, shows the overall structure of the book. The material is grouped by subject, as follows:

I)   The Individual
II)   Business and Politics
III) The Community
IV)   Relationships
V)   The World
VI)   Science and Technology

Each heading incorporates categories and subcategories, growing more and more specific. For example: Under the heading "IV) Relationships" there are three sub-headings: "Relationships," "Rites of Passage," and "The Sexes." Each subheading is broken down into specific categories. For example, "The Sexes" is divided into Bachelors, Women's Rights, Mankind, Men and Women, Men, Men—The Female View, Women, Women—The Male View, and Sex.

THE ALPHABETICAL LIST

The second list, the one you will probably use most often, lists every category in alphabetical order. It includes synonyms. (All categories in the book are in upper-case letters; synonyms are in lower case.) If you want to look up a specific topic, this list tells you what page(s) to turn to. For example, if you were to look up "Skill," you would be directed to ABILITY, page 2, or TALENT, page 42, the categories that come closest.

Note: Where appropriate, material appears in more than one section. It's more efficient; you won't have to waste time rummaging through lists of cross-references.

HOW TO USE QUOTES, JOKES, AND SAYINGS IN SPEECHES

If you're nervous about speaking (and a surprising number of people are), it can be particularly comforting to let other people's words carry part of your message. Using a good quote, joke, or saying is like using a good picture in a book. It adds interest and authority to the point that you are making.

When choosing a quote, ask:

- Is it relevant to what I am saying?
- Is it appropriate to my audience?
- Do I like it?

Incidentally, a quote on the right topic, but which expresses the wrong point of view is often still quite useful. We once wrote a speech for the head of a sales force that began:

I have been thinking about Alfred, Lord Tennyson's famous lines about the Charge of the Light Brigade: "Theirs not to make reply / Theirs not to reason why / Theirs but to do and die." I realized that this is the dumbest set of orders I've ever heard. It's no wonder the Light Brigade got slaughtered. My charge to you is the exact opposite. I want you to reason why—and I want you to live and thrive, not die.

SOME POINTERS WHEN USING QUOTES

- Use a quote to reinforce your message, *not* to show off your knowledge.
- Cite the author only if you know how to pronounce his or her name.
- If the audience is not likely to recognize the author's name, or if you're not sure how to pronounce it, don't fake it. You can always introduce the quote with a phrase like "An author once wrote . . ." or "It's been said that. . . ."
- When you use a quote, be careful to get it right. Even if you abbreviate your own notes, it is still a good idea to write out any quotes intact and unabbreviated.

We have included dates and situations only when that context makes a quote more meaningful. For example, this quote: "Advertisements are now so numerous that they are very negligently perused, and it is therefore become necessary to gain attention by magnificence of promises, and by eloquence sometimes sublime and sometimes pathetic. Promise—large promise—is the soul of advertising" becomes much more interesting when you know that Samuel Johnson said it in 1759.

THE SPEECH

USE THE "3-T" STRUCTURE

For a great speech all you have to know is the "3 Ts"—the classic three-part format on which most successful speeches and presentations are based:

- Tell 'em what you're going to tell 'em.
- Tell 'em.
- Tell 'em what you told 'em.

Listening to a speech is very different from reading a book. Since your listeners can't go back and review a point it's important for you to provide a clear structure, and to repeat your central points. In the first part of your speech, tell the audience your theme and preview your major points. ("Tell 'em what you're going to tell 'em.") Then proceed to fill out your outline, making and illustrating all of the points that support your theme. ("Tell 'em.") Then recap. ("Tell 'em what you told 'em.") It's simple and it works. If you use this structure, you will sound clear, directed, and organized—and you will communicate powerfully. Keeping this structure in mind, read through the next couple of pages as we illustrate how the 3-T format should work.

HOW TO GIVE AN EFFECTIVE SPEECH

"WHAT YOU'RE GOING TO TELL THEM."

We're going to tell you how to prepare yourself to give a speech, and some tips on how to make that speech great.

"TELL 'EM."

1. Be Yourself

All the great speakers were bad speakers at first.   —*Ralph Waldo Emerson*

Dr. Benjamin Spock helped legions of anxious mothers with this legendary assurance: "You know more than you think you do." In other words, if you follow your instincts, the odds are that you will do a fine job. Use your common sense and do what is most comfortable.

2. Know Your Audience

- *Find out everything you can about your audience in advance:* their vocabulary, their experience level, their mood, how many are expected to be present, and, most important, what they're in the room to learn.
- *Speak to their concerns.*
- *Bridge the gap between the audience and yourself.* Make sure what you have to say is relevant, understandable, and genuinely helpful.
- *Adjust your speech to the size of your audience.* If your audience is small (fifteen people or fewer), make your points stronger with personal references to audience members ("Obstacles can be overcome despite a bad start, as Jim found out when he managed to win back the XYZ account").
- *Listen to the speeches which precede yours.* If you are one of a number of speakers, notice what it feels like to be a member of the audience, and keep it in mind as you speak.

  Part of knowing your audience is acknowledging that they're part of the television generation: they're used to getting their messages in thirty-, fifteen-, or even ten-second commercials, and to getting the news in short, punchy soundbites. You had better be interesting, and, whenever possible, you'd better be brief. Try to avoid long, complicated anecdotes or case histories. TV-conditioned audiences tend to be somewhat passive, so even if you open with an incredibly funny story, don't count on big laughs. These are particularly unlikely before the audience is warmed up.

3. Have Something to Say

Before I speak, I have something important to say.   —*Groucho Marx*

There is an implied contract between speaker and audience. The audience's obligation is to be there and to listen. As the speaker, it is your job to have something to say, something you want to communicate. Believe what you are saying: if you don't, your audience certainly won't either. Let your audience know why you are addressing them. If you are giving a sales speech, for example, don't forget to ask for the order.

You should have a central point. When planning your speech, ask yourself, "What is the one thing that I want my audience to take away from this speech?" That's your theme. Everything in your speech should relate to that theme. Once you have the theme, you can go on and ask what is "second most important" and then "third most important" for you to communicate. Make these points only if you can make them without taking away from the impact of your main theme.

4. Don't Panic

A speech is like an airplane engine. It may sound like hell, but you've got to go on.
                    —*William Thomas Piper*

An important element of staying in charge is taking problems in stride. Few speeches ever run completely smoothly, but we've never seen an audience fail to be sympathetic and attentive to a speaker who acknowledges problems as they occur, and keeps going. If you know your speech well, and try to anticipate any problems (from noisy waiters to burned-out slide projector bulbs), you will increase the odds for a successful, interruption-free speech.

Some typical problems and solutions:

- If the speaker just before you preempts half of your subject matter, don't repeat the material. Instead, shorten your speech and refer back to hers: "As Amy has just pointed out, the economy in Asia is dangerously volatile. . . ."
- If the speaker before you uses up too much time and you get cut short, go straight to your wrap-up: "Tell 'em what you told 'em."
- If someone asks you a question that you can't answer, tell the questioner you'll find out and get back to him or her. Then do.

5. Take Charge Immediately

The human brain starts working the moment you are born and never stops until you stand up to speak in public.   —*George Jessel*

. . . You can't go wrong if you think of the first two minutes of your speech as an audition. It's a 120-second sample that has to convince your listeners that the remaining twenty minutes are worth their time and attention.   —*Roy Orben*

Relax and follow the simple guidelines that follow, use the wealth of materials in this book, and your speech will go well.

- **The first minute of a speech is crucial;** that's when you have to grab your audience's attention.
- **Know your first three sentences cold.** This will allow you to look straight into your audience's eyes as you deliver your opening.
- **Get the audience hooked.** Start right into your speech with a strong opening that grabs your audience's attention.
- **Choose a phrase and use it as a refrain.** To repeat what we said earlier, reiterate your main point.
- **Don't apologize.** Don't start with a hackneyed apology such as "I'm not much of a speaker . . ." or "Unaccustomed as I am to public speaking. . . ."
- **Show confidence.** Exhibit poise about what you have to say and your ability to say it. Don't invite your audience to doubt you; for example, if you cite a surprising statistic, acknowledge that fact and say that it's already been double-checked.
- **Reinforce your point.** "If you have an important point to make, don't try to be subtle or clever. Use a pile driver. Hit the point once. Then come back and hit it again. Then hit it a third time—a tremendous whack."—Winston Churchill

    Use quotes, sayings, anecdotes, and jokes wherever appropriate to illustrate, support, and reinforce your points.
- **Choose the simple word.** Don't use overlong words or overly complicated sentences.
- **Stay in charge.** Once you've made a strong start, communicate what you have to say in the most cogent way possible.

6. Don't Pad Your Speech

Many attempts to communicate are nullified by saying too much.

—Robert Greenleaf

Few audiences object to a good, short speech, but all will resent a waste of time. Length does not make a speech memorable or effective. The Gettysburg Address, after all, was only 269 words. If you have successfully communicated a maximum of three points in a speech, you have done well. Try to communicate too many points, and it's possible—in fact, probable—that your audience will remember none of them clearly.

Finally, a great way to undo the effects of a wonderful and rousing speech is to exceed your allotted time or to keep talking after you've covered the given topic.

7. Close Your Speech with a Bang

Your "close" is the last chance to reach your audience; it's the part they're most likely to remember. Make it memorable. After you have "told 'em what you told 'em," make a powerful personal appeal, use a good, relevant quote, or tell a strong, appropriate anecdote.

8. Shut Up and Sit Down

Be sincere; be brief; be seated.   *—Franklin D. Roosevelt*

Once you've finished making the points you've set out to make, stop.

WHAT WE'VE TOLD YOU

1. Be Yourself.
2. Know Your Audience.
3. Have Something to Say.
4. Don't Panic.
5. Take Charge Immediately.
6. Don't Pad Your Speech.
7. Close Your Speech with a Bang.
8. Shut Up and Sit Down.

QUOTES ON QUOTES

Before you start your journey into the world of quotes, take a look at what some of the more quotable masters think about the topic.

I hate quotations.   —*Ralph Waldo Emerson*

I love [quotations] because it is a joy to find thoughts one might have, beautifully expressed with much authority by someone recognizedly wiser than oneself.
                                                                       —*Marlene Dietrich*

I often quote myself; it adds spice to my conversation.   —*George Bernard Shaw*

The devil can cite Scripture for his purpose.   —*William Shakespeare*

A book that furnishes no quotations is, *me judice*, no book—it is a plaything.
                                                                       —*Thomas Love Peacock*

It is a good thing for an uneducated man to read books of quotations.
                                                                       —*Winston Churchill*

A quote is a personal possession and you have no right to change it.   —*Ray Cave*

QUOTES ON PUBLIC SPEAKING

No speechmaker's compendium would be complete without a section of quotes, anonymous sayings, and jokes on the subject of public speaking. Below is some advice, wit, wisdom, and humor on this entertaining, frightening, engaging, and essential discipline.

"Where shall I begin, please your majesty?" she asked.
   "Begin at the beginning," the king said, very gravely, "and go on till you come to the end: then stop."   —*Lewis Carroll,* **Alice in Wonderland**

I am rather like a mosquito in a nudist camp: I know what I ought to do, but I don't know where to begin.   —*Stephen Bayne*

I have never seen an ass who talked like a human being, but I have met many human beings who talked like asses.   —*Heinrich Heine*

Beware of the conversationalist who adds "In other words."   —*Robert Morley*

The easiest way to stay awake during an after-dinner speech is to deliver it.
                                                                       —*Herman Herst, Jr.*

A speech is a solemn responsibility. The man who makes a bad thirty-minute speech to two hundred people wastes only a half hour of his own time. But he wastes one hundred hours of the audience's time—more than four days—which should be a hanging offense.   —*Jenkin Lloyd Jones*

He missed an invaluable opportunity to hold his tongue.   —*Andrew Lang*

If you have to make an unpopular speech, give it all the sincerity you can muster; that's the only way to sweeten it.   —*Cardinal de Retz*

Once you get 'em laughing and their mouths open, you can stuff something in.

—Francis Harvey Green

An orator can hardly get beyond commonplaces: if he does he gets beyond his hearers.

—William Hazlitt

Churchill wrote his own speeches. When a leader does that, he becomes emotionally invested with his utterances. . . . If Churchill had had a speech writer in 1940, Britain would be speaking German today.

—James C. Humes

Only constant repetition will finally succeed in imprinting an idea on the memory of the crowd.

—Adolf Hitler

Every man is eloquent once in his life.

—Ralph Waldo Emerson

A man never becomes an orator if he has anything to say.

—Finley Peter Dunne

What orators lack in depth they make up for in length.

—Baron de Montesquieu

My method is to take the utmost trouble to find the right thing to say, and then to say it with the utmost levity.

—George Bernard Shaw

Accustomed as I am to public speaking, I know the futility of it.

—Franklin Pierce Adams

You have been giving your full attention to a turkey stuffed with sage; it is now time to consider a sage stuffed with turkey.

—William M. Evarts, addressing a group on Thanksgiving Day

I served with General Washington in the Legislature of Virginia . . . and . . . with Doctor Franklin in Congress. I never heard either of them speak ten minutes at a time, nor to any but the main point.

—Thomas Jefferson

I have always considered applause at the beginning of a lecture a manifestation of faith. If it comes in the middle, it is a sign of hope. And if it comes at the end, it is always charity.

—Abraham R. Besdin

Sayings

Great speakers listen to the audience with their eyes.

Public speaking is an audience participation event; if it weren't, it would be private speaking.

A good speech is like a pencil; it has to have a point.

Exhaust neither the topic nor the audience.

No good speech ever came to a bad end.

Caution: Do not open mouth until brain is in gear.

Jokes

Definition of a good speech:

• A good beginning and a good end—preferably close together.

• "Oh, no!" cried the politician. "I'm on now, but I can't find the speech I use when I abandon my prepared speech!"

- The best after-dinner speech to hear is, "Waiter, hand me the check."

- "Sir," the aide began, "I've just read through your speech and I don't have the foggiest idea where you stand on the issue."

  "Why, thank you very much, my boy," the politician beamed. "Do you know how long it took me to get the speech just that way?"

- Speeches are like steer horns—a point here, a point there, and a lot of bull in between.

- "I have just got a new theory of eternity."
  —Comment following a lengthy after-dinner speech

- Why doesn't the fellow who says "I'm no speechmaker" let it go at that instead of giving a demonstration?

- After speaking for more than two hours without a pause, the eminent scholar finally looked up from the podium and sheepishly apologized for going on for so long. "You see, I haven't got a watch with me," he explained.

  "Okay, fine," shouted a heckler from the audience, "but there's a calendar in back of you."

- The speaker was getting tired of being interrupted, and finally addressed his listeners with some irritation. "We seem to have a great many fools here tonight," he noted. "Wouldn't it be advisable to hear one at a time?"

  "You bet," a voice responded. "Get on with your speech."

- Being asked to speak to you is like being the javelin competitor who won the coin toss and elected to receive.

- I feel like Liz Taylor's fourth husband: I know what I am supposed to do, but I am at a loss as to how to make it different.

- The featured speaker listened with growing trepidation as the person introducing her lauded her every achievement since birth, lavishly praising her public service and professional milestones, her beauty, her brains, her experience and splendid reputation, and on and on. When it was finally her turn to address the audience, the speaker took a deep breath. "After an introduction like that," she began, "I can hardly wait to hear what I'm going to say."

- Most speakers don't need an introduction—just a conclusion.

- In Japan, to relieve the speaker's nervous tension and limit the length of a speech, the traditional "after-dinner" speeches come before the meal.

- On her way back from the ladies' room, the executive ran into another member of the audience. Wondering whether to reenter the lecture hall, she asked, "Has the speaker finished what he had to say yet?"

  "Oh yeah, he finished that five minutes ago," came the reply, "but he's still talking."

THE SUBJECT LIST

THE ALPHABETICAL LIST

*(Words in capital letters indicate existing headings in the text;
words in lower case indicate synonyms.)*

E

part one

The Individual

A C H I E V E M E N T

ABILITY

If initiative is the ability to do the right thing, then efficiency is the ability to do the thing right.
                                                                    —*Kelly Miller*

Our ability to create has outreached our ability to use wisely the products of our invention.
                                                                    —*Whitney Moore Young, Jr.*

The superior man is distressed by his want of ability.
                                                                    —*Confucius*

It is a great ability to be able to conceal one's ability.
                                                                    —*François de La Rochefoucauld*

Don't let your will roar when your power only whispers.
                                                                    —*Thomas Fuller*

You cannot fly like an eagle with the wings of a wren.
                                                                    —*William Henry Hudson*

One good head is better than a hundred strong hands.
                                                                    —*Thomas Fuller*

Martyrdom is the only way in which a man can become famous without ability.
                                                                    —*George Bernard Shaw*

The ability to get to the verge without getting into the war is the necessary art. If you cannot master it, you inevitably get into war. If you try to run away from it, if you are scared to go to the brink, you are lost.
                                                                    —*John Foster Dulles*

The single most exciting thing you encounter in government is competence, because it's so rare.
                                                                    —*Daniel Patrick Moynihan*

What another would have done as well as you, do not do it. What another would have said as well as you, do not say it; what another would have written as well, do not write it. Be faithful to that which exists nowhere but in yourself—and thus make yourself indispensable.
                                                                    —*André Gide*

Competence, like truth, beauty, and contact lenses, is in the eye of the beholder.
                                                                    —*Laurence J. Peter*

Any jackass can kick down a barn, but it takes a good carpenter to build one.
                                                                    —*Sam Rayburn*

Don't wish me happiness—I don't expect to be happy . . . it's gotten beyond that somehow. Wish me courage and strength and a sense of humor—I will need them all.
                                                                    —*Anne Morrow Lindbergh*

The race is not always to the swift, nor the battle to the strong, but that's the way to bet.
                                                                    —*Damon Runyon*

Saying

Native ability without education is like a tree without fruit.

Joke

• "You must be the worst caddie in the world," said the dejected golfer after a disastrous afternoon on the links.

"I doubt it, sir," replied the caddie. "That would be too much of a coincidence."

ACCOUNTABILITY

When a man points a finger at someone else, he should remember that four of his fingers are pointing at himself.
—*Louis Nizer*

If you can't stand the heat, you'd better get out of the kitchen.
—*Harry S Truman (attrib.)*

A person may cause evil to others not only by his action but by his inaction, and in either case he is justly accountable to them for the injury.
—*John Stuart Mill*

No snowflake in an avalanche ever feels responsible.
—*Stanislaw Lec*

He that is good for making excuses is seldom good for anything else.
—*Benjamin Franklin*

There can be no true response without responsibility; there can be no responsibility without response.
—*Arthur Vogel*

A memorandum is written not to inform the reader but to protect the writer.
—*Dean Acheson*

If you let other people do it *for* you, they will do it *to* you.
—*Robert Anthony*

The way to get things done is not to mind who gets the credit of doing them.
—*Benjamin Jowett*

The irony of the matter is that the future generations do not have a vote. In effect, we hold their proxy.
—*Charles J. Hitch, regarding the environment*

. . . if a man is not faithful to his own individuality, he cannot be loyal to anything.
—*Claude McKay*

I gave her life, I can take life away.
—*Mary Beth Whitehead, on her role as surrogate mother to Baby M*

People think responsibility is hard to bear. It's not. I think that sometimes it is the absence of responsibility that is harder to bear. You have a great feeling of impotence.
—*Henry Kissinger*

Sayings

God gave burdens, also shoulders.
—*Yiddish proverb*

Everyone, in the final analysis, is in business for himself.

Silence = Death.
—*Slogan of AIDS activists*

Jokes

• "Gee, Mr. Schmertz, we'd really like to give you that loan," said the bank officer to the rather seedy character, "but your credit rating isn't exactly . . . uh . . . superlative. What assurance can you offer that it'll be paid back on schedule?"

"Won't a gentleman's word of honor be sufficient?" he asked, in an injured tone.

"Certainly," she said brightly. "When will you be bringing him in?"

• The Six Phases of a Project

1. Enthusiasm
2. Disillusionment
3. Panic and hysteria
4. Search for the guilty
5. Punishment of the innocent
6. Praise and honor for the nonparticipants

ACHIEVEMENT

No matter what accomplishments you make, somebody helps you.

—*Althea Gibson Darben*

The only way to enjoy anything in this life is to earn it first.   —*Ginger Rogers*

It is sobering to consider that when Mozart was my age he had already been dead for a year.

—*Tom Lehrer*

Men too involved in details usually become unable to deal with great matters.

—*François de La Rochefoucauld*

Luck is not something you can mention in the presence of self-made men.

—*E. B. White*

There may now exist great men for things that do not exist.   —*Samuel Burchardt*

Noise proves nothing. Often a hen who has merely laid an egg cackles as if she had laid an asteroid.

—*Mark Twain*

Restlessness is discontent—and discontent is the first necessity of progress. Show me a thoroughly satisfied man and I will show you a failure.   —*Thomas Alva Edison*

The key to everything is patience. You get the chicken by hatching the egg—not by smashing it.

—*Ellen Glasgow*

Originality is not seen in single words or even sentences. Originality is the sum total of a man's thinking and writing.

—*Isaac Bashevis Singer*

Competence, like truth, beauty, and contact lenses, is in the eye of the beholder.

—*Laurence J. Peter*

Any jackass can kick down a barn, but it takes a good carpenter to build one.

—*Sam Rayburn*

To achieve great things, we must live as though we are never going to di.

—*Luc de Clapiers de Vauvenargues*

Everything that enlarges the sphere of human powers, that shows man he can do what he thought he could not do, is valuable.   —*Samuel Johnson*

We judge ourselves by what we feel capable of doing, while others judge us by what we have already done.   —*Henry Wadsworth Longfellow*

The way to get things done is not to mind who gets the credit of doing them.
                                                            —*Benjamin Jowett*

For a man to achieve all that is demanded of him he must regard himself as greater than he is.   —*Johann Wolfgang von Goethe*

Ye are the light of the world. A city that is set on a hill cannot be hid. Neither do men light a candle, and put it under a bushel, but on a candlestick; and it giveth light unto all that are in the house. Let your light so shine before men, that they may see your good works, and glorify your Father which is in heaven.
                                                            —*Matthew 5:14–16*

No man knows what he can do till he tries.   —*Publilius Syrus*

There are only two ways of getting on in the world: by one's own industry, or by the weaknesses of others.   —*Jean de La Bruyère*

None climbs so high as he who knows not whither he is going.
                                                            —*Oliver Cromwell*

The higher a monkey climbs, the more you see of his ass.
                                                    —*General Joseph Stillwell*

How many cares one loses when one decides not to be something but to be someone.
                                                    —*Gabrielle (Coco) Chanel*

If you practice an art, be proud of it and make it proud of you. . . . It may break your heart, but it will fill your heart before it breaks it: it will make you a person in your own right.   —*Maxwell Anderson*

In this world there are only two tragedies: one is not getting what one wants, and the other is getting it.   —*Oscar Wilde*

The reward of a thing well done is to have done it.   —*Ralph Waldo Emerson*

What we call results are beginnings.   —*Ralph Waldo Emerson*

Well done is better than well said.   —*Benjamin Franklin*

If moderation is a fault, then indifference is a crime.
                                                    —*Georg Christoph Lichtenberg*

He who can, does. He who cannot, teaches.   —*George Bernard Shaw*

Sayings

The cards you hold in the game of life mean very little—it's the way you play them that counts.

A man's deeds are his life.   —*West African saying*

Aiming isn't hitting.   —*East African saying*

The difficult we do immediately; the impossible takes a little longer.
—*Slogan of the United States Army Service Forces*

Getting something done is an accomplishment; getting something done right is an achievement.

They said it couldn't be done, but we did it.

Those who dare do; those who dare not, do not.

Jokes

• When her formal education was over, a young woman went out into the world to start her own business. After a year, she reported that she was worth $5,000, but her parents merely smiled. After a few more years her net worth had grown to some $15,000, and each year it increased by modest amounts, but her parents never had more than a smile or pat on the back for her.

Then one year she came home and announced that in order to keep the business going, she'd had to borrow a million dollars. At this her father bounded up from the sofa, clapped her on the back, and crowed, "Now *that's* an achievement!"

• "What a superb performance," gushed the woman when the recital was over. "I'd give half my life to be able to play the piano like that."

"Madam," responded the pianist with a little bow, "that is exactly what it took."

ACTION

As I grow older, I pay less attention to what men say. I just watch what they do.
—*Andrew Carnegie*

The best way to make your dreams come true is to wake up.   —*Paul Valéry*

Be willing to make decisions. That's the most important quality in a good leader. Don't fall victim to what I call the "ready-aim-aim-aim-aim syndrome." You must be willing to fire.   —*T. Boone Pickens*

The world's great men have not commonly been great scholars, nor great scholars great men.   —*Oliver Wendell Holmes*

Everything comes to him who hustles while he waits.   —*Thomas Alva Edison*

One must act in painting as in life, directly.   —*Pablo Picasso*

The bitterest tears shed over graves are for words left unsaid and deeds left undone.
—*Harriet Beecher Stowe*

Be not simply good; be good for something.   —*Henry David Thoreau*

It is difficult to keep quiet if you have nothing to do.   —*Arthur Schopenhauer*

No one is more liable to make mistakes than the man who acts only on reflection.
—*Luc de Clapiers de Vauvenargues*

An artist is a man of action, whether he creates a personality, invents an expedient, or finds the issue of a complicated situation.   —*Joseph Conrad*

You don't learn to hold your own in the world by standing on guard, but by attacking and getting well hammered yourself.   —*George Bernard Shaw*

The great end of life is not knowledge but action.   —*Thomas Henry Huxley*

It is better to be making the news than taking it; to be an actor rather than a critic.
     —*Winston Churchill*

Even if you are on the right track, you'll get run over if you just sit there.
     —*Will Rogers*

He who desires but acts not, breeds pestilence.   —*William Blake*

A man who has to be convinced to act before he acts is not a man of action. . . . You must act as you breathe.   —*Georges Clemenceau*

It is the mark of a good action that it appears inevitable in retrospect.
     —*Robert Louis Stevenson*

No sooner said than done—so acts your man of worth.   —*Quintus Ennius*

Be ye doers of the word, and not hearers only.   —*James 1:22*

A person may cause evil to others not only by his action but by his inaction, and in either case he is justly accountable to them for the injury.   —*John Stuart Mill*

We have petitioned and our petitions have been disregarded; we have entreated and our entreaties have been scorned. We beg no more, we petition no longer, we now defy.   —*William Jennings Bryan*

Everybody talks about the weather but nobody does anything about it.
     —*Charles Dudley Warner*

I have always thought the actions of men the best interpreters of their thoughts.
     —*John Locke*

Every normal man must be tempted at times to spit on his hands, hoist the black flag, and begin slitting throats.   —*H. L. Mencken*

Don't just do something, stand there.
     —*Daniel Berrigan, on the importance of thought as well as action during the 1960s war protests*

Genius is the ability to put into effect what is in your mind.
     —*F. Scott Fitzgerald*

Talk without effort is nothing.   —*Maria W. Stewart*

Violence of language leads to violence of action. Angry men seldom fight if their tongues do not lead the fray.   —*Charles Victor Roman*

Each generation must, out of relative obscurity, discover its mission, fulfill it, or betray it.   —*Frantz Fanon*

Always behave like a duck—keep calm and unruffled on the surface but paddle like the devil underneath.   —*Lord Barbizon*

If you are not part of the solution, you are part of the problem.
     —*Eldridge Cleaver*

Sayings

Just do it.   —*Nike slogan*

You miss 100 percent of the shots you never take.

Excuses interest no one except the competition.

Actions speak louder than words.

Only people who do things get criticized.

He who waits for a roast duck to fly into his mouth must wait a very, very long time.
                                                              —*Chinese proverb*

Your food is close to your stomach, but you must put it in your mouth first.
                                                              —*West African saying*

When the snake is in the house, one need not discuss the matter at length.
                                                              —*West African saying*

Joke

• Husband, lounging in recliner, to wife: "I'll think about cleaning out the garage in a little while, hon. Right now, I'm thinking about mowing the lawn."

ADMIRATION

Admiration is as indispensable to life as oxygen.   —*Genevieve Antoine Dariaux*

We always like those who admire us.   —*François de La Rochefoucauld*

Admiration, like love, wears out.   —*Luc de Clapiers de Vauvenargues*

Sayings

It is only an auctioneer who can equally and impartially admire all schools of art.

Never be too big to look up to someone.

Admiration: acknowledgment of another's similarity to oneself.

Joke

• The combat-hardened general was reviewing an elite squadron of paratroopers. "How do you like jumping?" he asked one soldier gruffly.
    "I love it, sir," was the reply.
    "And you?" asked the general of the next guy in line.
    "It's the most exhilarating thing I've ever done, sir."
    And so on down the line, until one soldier replied, "I hate it, sir."
    "Then why do you jump?" asked the startled officer.
    "Because I like being around the kind of men who want to."

AMBITION

Every man believes that he has a greater possibility.   —*Ralph Waldo Emerson*

Nothing great will ever be achieved without great men, and men are great only if they are determined to be so.   —*Charles de Gaulle*

As he was valiant, I honor him; but as he was ambitious, I slew him.
                                                        —*William Shakespeare*

Ambition is but avarice on stilts, and masked.   —*Walter Savage Landor*

Ambition is the last refuge of the failure.   —*Oscar Wilde*

Nothing arouses ambition so much in the heart as the trumpet-clang of another's fame.
                                                        —*Baltasar Gracian*

Ambition makes more trusty slaves than need.   —*Ben Jonson*

A wise man is cured of ambition by ambition itself; his aim is so exalted that riches, office, fortune and favour cannot satisfy him.   —*Samuel Johnson*

A man's worth is no greater than the worth of his ambitions.
                                                    —*Marcus Aurelius Antoninus*

A slave has but one master; an ambitious man has as many masters as there are people who may be useful in bettering his position.   —*Jean de La Bruyère*

Ambition hath no mean, it is either upon all fours or upon tiptoes.
                                                        —*George Savile*

Ambition is the grand enemy of all peace.   —*John Cowper Powys*

Ah, but a man's reach should exceed his grasp, or what's a heaven for?
                                                        —*Robert Browning*

The world owes all its onward impulses to men ill at ease. The happy man inevitably confines himself within ancient limits.   —*Nathaniel Hawthorne*

Everything comes to him who hustles while he waits.   —*Thomas Alva Edison*

Nothing is so commonplace as to wish to be remarkable.
                                                    —*Oliver Wendell Holmes, Sr.*

In Man, Ambition is the common'st thing:/ Each one, by nature, loves to be a King.
                                                        —*Robert Herrick*

One often goes from love to ambition, but one rarely returns from ambition to love.
                                                    —*François de La Rochefoucauld*

Most people would succeed in small things if they were not troubled with great ambitions.   —*Henry Wadsworth Longfellow*

The treacheries of ambition never cease.   —*Rubén Dario*

Sayings

A woman who strives to be like a man lacks ambition.

Ambition lubricates the mind.

There's always room at the top.

Where there's a will there's a way (or a beneficiary).

The way to go from rags to riches is to start by getting a decent set of rags.

Most people want to improve themselves, but not many want to work at it.

Ambitious people don't make excuses.

Jokes

• Judge: "Mr. Corbin, the police report says you've committed six burglaries in one week!"

   Defendant: "That's right, Your Honor—and if everyone worked as hard as I do, this recession would be behind us."

• The banker Salomon Rothschild was strolling down a crowded street in Vienna when he was jostled by a pickpocket. "Watch out!" warned his companion. "That fellow's trying to steal your silk handkerchief."

   "So what?" said Rothschild with a shrug. "We all had to start somewhere."

AWARDS

People with honorary awards are looked upon with disfavor. Would you let an honorary mechanic fix your brand-new Mercedes?   —*Neil Simon*

God will not look you over for medals, degrees or diplomas, but for scars.

—*Elbert Hubbard*

Let us now praise famous men, and our fathers that begat us.

—*Ecclesiasticus 44:1*

Only mediocrity can be trusted to be always at its best.   —*Max Beerbohm*

Whenever the occasion arose, he rose to the occasion.

—*Jonathan Brown, on Diego Velázquez*

Sayings

One does not give a gift without a motive.   —*West African saying*

Never look a gift horse in the mouth.

Jokes

• I don't deserve this, but then again, I have arthritis and I don't deserve that either.

—*Jack Benny, accepting an award*

• Hearing all this praise makes me feel like the soul on Judgment Day who rose, looked at the words on his tombstone, and remarked, "Either I'm in the wrong hole or someone is a terrible liar."

CHANCE

Human life, its growth, its hopes, fears, loves, et cetera, are the result of accidents.

—*Bertrand Russell*

He that leaveth nothing to chance will do few things ill, but he will do very few things.
—*George Savile*

There is danger in reckless change, but greater danger in blind conservatism.
—*Henry Glasgow*

God does not play dice with the universe.   —*Albert Einstein*

We must believe in luck. For how else can we explain the success of those we don't like?   —*Jean Cocteau*

Today even our *clocks* are not made of clockwork—so why should our world be? With the advent of quantum mechanics, the clockwork world has become a cosmic lottery. Fundamental events, such as the decay of a radioactive atom, are held to be determined by chance, not law.   —*Ian Stewart*

Saying
The cards you hold in the game of life mean very little—it's the way you play them that counts.

Joke
• The problem with chance is that while you're outside looking for a horseshoe or rabbit's foot, you may miss opportunity knocking.

COURAGE

Courage is not simply one of the virtues, but the form of every virtue at the testing point.   —*C. S. Lewis*

Courage is resistance to fear, mastery of fear—not absence of fear.
—*Mark Twain*

The man who knows when not to act is wise. To my mind, bravery is forethought.
—*Euripides*

To bear other people's afflictions, everyone has courage and enough to spare.
—*Benjamin Franklin*

It is better to die on your feet than to live on your knees.   —*Dolores Ibarruri*

A coward is a hero with a wife, kids, and a mortgage.   —*Marvin Kitman*

Courage is grace under pressure.   —*Ernest Hemingway*

If God wanted us to be brave, why did he give us legs?   —*Marvin Kitman*

Have the courage to act instead of react.   —*Earlene Larson Jenks*

A timid person is frightened before a danger, a coward during the time, and a courageous person afterwards.   —*Jean Paul Friedrich Richter*

None but a coward dares to boast that he has never known fear.
—*Marshal Ferdinand Foch*

Once more unto the breach, dear friends, once more; or close the wall up with our
English dead.   —*William Shakespeare*

Fear always springs from ignorance.   —*Ralph Waldo Emerson*

The last thing a woman will consent to discover in a man whom she loves, or on whom
she simply depends, is want of courage.   —*Joseph Conrad*

True bravery is shown by performing without witness what one might be capable of
doing before all the world.   —*François de La Rochefoucauld*

He was a bold man that first ate an oyster.   —*Jonathan Swift*

Some have been thought brave because they were afraid to run away.
                                                        —*Thomas Fuller*

Heroes may not be braver than anyone else. They're just braver five minutes longer.
                                                        —*Ronald Reagan*

Courage is very important. Like a muscle, it is strengthened by use.
                                                        —*Ruth Gordon*

It is a brave act of valor to contemn death; but where life is more terrible than death, it
is then the truest valor to dare to live.   —*Thomas Browne*

No one can prove his courage when he has never been in danger.
                                                        —*François de La Rochefoucauld*

But screw your courage to the sticking place, and you'll not fail.
                                                        —*William Shakespeare*

What counts is not necessarily the size of the dog in the fight—it's the size of the fight
in the dog.   —*Dwight D. Eisenhower*

A man of courage never needs weapons, but he may need bail.
                                                        —*Ethel Watts Mumford*

. . . what cannot be cured must be endured.   —*Ignatius Sancho*

Don't be afraid to take a big step if one is indicated. You can't cross a chasm in two
small jumps.   —*David Lloyd George*

I have not yet begun to fight. (Sometimes quoted as "I have just begun to fight.")
    —*Captain John Paul Jones, aboard the* **Bonhomme Richard**, *when asked whether he was
                            prepared to surrender to the British, September 23, 1779*

If you can keep your head when all about you are losing theirs and blaming it on
you, . . . you'll be a Man, my son!   —*Rudyard Kipling*

If you can keep your head when all about are losing theirs, it's just possible you
haven't grasped the situation.   —*Jean Kerr*

The first and great commandment is, Don't let them scare you.   —*Elmer Davis*

If blood be shed, let it be our blood. Cultivate the quiet courage of dying without
killing. For man lives freely only by his readiness to die, if need be, at the hands of
his brother, never by killing him.   —*Mohandas K. Gandhi*

Sayings

It does not take a very brave dog to bark at the bones of a lion.

When the going gets tough, the tough get going.

When the going gets tough, the tough go shopping.

If a thing is worth having, it's worth fighting for.

Stand up and fight.

Stand up and be counted.

No guts, no glory.

Jokes

• The Texan was trying to impress on the New Englander the valor of the heroes of the Alamo. "I bet they were braver than any man from your part of the States," he declared.

"I suppose you've never heard of Paul Revere?" countered the New Englander.

"Sounds familiar," said the Texan. "Isn't he the guy who ran for help?"

• The new employee had been with the firm for only a few months when she went in to ask for a raise.

"So soon!" The boss was taken aback. "Certainly not. In this company you have to work yourself up."

"I *have*!" she insisted. "Look at me—I'm trembling all over."

DECISION

Soon after a hard decision something inevitably occurs to cast doubt. Holding steady against that doubt usually proves that decision.   —*R. I. Fitzhenry*

Be willing to make decisions. That's the most important quality in a good leader. Don't fall victim to what I call the "ready-aim-aim-aim-aim syndrome." You must be willing to fire.   —*T. Boone Pickens*

Decision is a sharp knife that cuts clean and straight; indecision, a dull one that hacks and tears and leaves ragged edges behind it.   —*Gordon Graham*

At the last moment there is always a reason not existing before—namely, the impossibility of further vacillation.   —*George Eliot*

The man who sees both sides of a question is a man who sees absolutely nothing.
                    —*Oscar Wilde*

We know what happens to people who stay in the middle of the road. They get run over.   —*Aneurin Bevan*

The man who knows when not to act is wise. To my mind, bravery is forethought.
                    —*Euripides*

Equivocation is halfway to lying, and lying the whole way to hell.
                    —*William Penn*

If someone tells you he is going to make a "realistic decision," you immediately understand that he has resolved to do something bad.   —*Mary McCarthy*

He would come in and say he changed his mind—which was a gilded figure of speech, because he didn't have any.   —*Mark Twain*

A decision is the action an executive must take when he has information so incomplete that the answer does not suggest itself.   —*Arthur W. Radford*

We'll jump off that bridge when we come to it.   —*Lester B. Pearson*

When you do say Yes, say it quickly. But always take a half hour to say No, so you can understand the other fellow's side.   —*Francis Cardinal Spellman*

When a person tells you "I'll let you know"—you know.   —*Olin Miller*

Sir Stafford has a brilliant mind until it is made up.
—*Margot Asquith (attrib.), regarding Sir Stafford Cripps*

Sayings
His indecision is final.

He who hesitates is lost.

He who hesitates buys the stock two points higher.

Joke
• Wendy found that her difficulty making even the simplest decisions was causing her problems on the job. Finally she decided to seek professional help.

"Tell me, Wendy," the psychiatrist began gently, "I understand you have trouble making decisions. Is that so?"

Wendy's brow furrowed. "Well," she finally answered, "yes . . . and no."

DETERMINATION

Each generation must, out of relative obscurity, discover its mission, fulfill it, or betray it.   —*Frantz Fanon*

The best way out is always through.   —*Robert Frost*

Our greatest glory is not in never falling but in rising every time we fall.
—*Confucius*

An unfulfilled vocation drains the color from a man's entire existence.
—*Honoré de Balzac*

To generalize is to be an idiot.   —*William Blake*

One can never consent to creep when one feels an impulse to soar.
—*Helen Keller*

Ours is a world where people don't know what they want and are willing to go through hell to get it.   —*Don Marquis*

The human heart refuses to believe in a universe without a purpose.

—*Immanuel Kant*

More men fail through lack of purpose than lack of talent.   —*Billy Sunday*

My life has no purpose, no direction, no aim, no meaning, and yet I'm happy. I can't figure it out. What am I doing right?   —*Charles M. Schulz*

When people talk to me about the weather, I always feel they mean something else.

—*Oscar Wilde*

None climbs so high as he who knows not whither he is going.

—*Oliver Cromwell*

We succeed only as we identify in life, or in war, or in anything else, a single overriding objective, and make all other considerations bend to that one objective.

—*Dwight D. Eisenhower*

Blessed is he who has found his work; let him ask no other blessedness.

—*Thomas Carlyle*

Not snow, no, nor rain, nor heat, nor night keeps them from accomplishing their appointed courses with all speed.   —*Herodotus*

It is best not to swap horses while crossing the river.   —*Abraham Lincoln*

Never give in! Never give in! Never, never, never. Never—in anything great or small, large or petty—never give in except to convictions of honor and good sense.

—*Winston Churchill*

Great works are performed not by strength but by perseverance.

—*Samuel Johnson*

I take a simple view of living. It is keep your eyes open and get on with it.

—*Laurence Olivier*

To have a grievance is to have a purpose in life.   —*Eric Hoffer*

We must not, in trying to think about how we can make a big difference, ignore the small daily differences we can make which, over time, add up to big differences that we often cannot foresee.   —*Marian Wright Edelman*

There is nothing like a dream to create the future.   —*Victor Hugo*

The will is the strong blind man who carries on his shoulders the lame man who can see.   —*Arthur Schopenhauer*

I am an idealist. I don't know where I am going but I'm on my way.

—*Carl Sandburg*

The will to succeed is important, but what's even more important is the will to prepare.

—*Bobby Knight*

Man is a stubborn seeker of meaning.   —*John Gardner*

If I am building a mountain and stop before the last basketful of earth is placed on the summit, I have failed.   —*Confucius*

Some examples of persistence:

The Coca-Cola company sold only four hundred Cokes in its first year of business.
Dr. Seuss's first book was rejected by twenty-three publishers.
Henry Ford went bankrupt twice before hitting it big in the automotive industry.

Sayings
Just do it.
—*Nike slogan*

Perseverance is everything.
—*West African saying*

Today's mighty oak is just yesterday's little acorn that held its ground.

Joke
• After much persistence, the young woman managed to land an interview with the personnel director of a prestigious company, and asked if she could be considered for their excellent training program.
"Impossible," snapped the personnel director, already flooded with applications. "Try again in five years."
"Fine," replied the young woman calmly. "Would morning or afternoon be better?"

DISCIPLINE AND SELF-DISCIPLINE

A genius? Perhaps, but before I was a genius, I was a drudge.
—*Ignace Jan Paderewski*

There is no course of life so weak and sottish as that which is managed by orders, method, and discipline.
—*Michel Eyquem de Montaigne*

Self-respect is the fruit of discipline: the sense of dignity grows with the ability to say no to oneself.
—*Abraham J. Heschel*

Discipline is the soul of an army.
—*George Washington*

If I don't practice one day, I know it; two days, the critics know it; three days, the public knows it.
—*Jascha Heifetz*

Theirs not to make reply, theirs not to reason why, theirs but to do and die.
—*Alfred Lord Tennyson*

In his later years, Winston Churchill was asked to give the commencement address at Oxford University. Following his introduction, he rose, went to the podium, and said, "Never, never, never give up." Then he took his seat.

Order marches with weighty and measured strides; disorder is always in a hurry.
—*Napoleon Bonaparte*

No man is fit to command another that cannot command himself.
—*William Penn*

Show me an orchestra that likes its conductor and I'll show you a lousy conductor.
—*Goddard Lieberson*

Example   17

Nothing I do can't be done by a ten-year-old . . . with fifteen years of practice.
—Harry Blackstone, Jr., on being a magician

Most people would succeed in small things if they were not troubled with great ambitions.   *—Henry Wadsworth Longfellow*

He that leaveth nothing to chance will do few things ill, but he will do very few things.
—George Savile

There is no such thing as a great talent without great willpower.
—Honoré de Balzac

I am a great believer in luck, and I find the harder I work the more I have of it.
—Stephen Butler Leacock

It is a very bad thing to become accustomed to good luck.   *—Publilius Syrus*

Minds, like bodies, will often fall into a pimpled, ill-conditioned state from mere excess of comfort.   *—Charles Dickens*

The man who does something under orders is not unhappy; he is unhappy who does something against his will.   *—Seneca the Younger*

Man's many desires are like the small metal coins he carries about in his pocket. The more he has the more they weight him down.   *—Satya Sai Baba*

I never give them hell. I just tell the truth and they think it's hell.

—Harry S Truman

Sayings
This hurts me more than it hurts you.

Show them death and they will accept the fever.   *—Arab saying*

Joke
- "Excuse me, but can you tell me how to get to Carnegie Hall?" the tourist asked a New York City cop.
  "Practice, practice, practice," he replied.

EXAMPLE

Children have never been very good at listening to their elders, but they have never failed to imitate them.   *—James Baldwin*

He or she is greatest who contributes the greatest original practical example.
—Walt Whitman

Few things are harder to put up with than the annoyance of a good example.
—Mark Twain

Setting an example is not the main means of influencing another, it is the only means.
—Albert Einstein

Practice yourself what you preach.   *—Titus Maccius Plautus*

Sayings

No one is completely worthless—they can always serve as a bad example.

The best way to give advice is to set a good example.

Example is better than precept.

Joke

• Two dimwitted ditchdiggers got upset by the fact that they did all the hard work and received only one-tenth of the pay of the crew boss. Finally deciding to confront his boss, one guy climbed out of the ditch and went over to the foreman, who was leaning against a tree reading the racing form. "How come we do all the hard work while you sit here and earn ten times as much?" he demanded.

"Intelligence" was the crew boss's answer. "Let me give you an example." He put his hand in front of the tree. "See my hand? Hit it as hard as you can."

The ditchdigger took a mighty swing, the boss moved his hand at the last minute, and commented to the worker, now clutching his bruised fist, "See what I mean?"

Back in the ditch, the second guy eagerly questioned his friend. "It's a matter of intelligence" was the reply. "Let me give you an example: hit my hand as hard as you can." And he held it up in front of his face.

FAME

You can get awful famous in this country in seven days.   —*Gary Hart*

To see one's name in print! Some people commit a crime for no other reason.
—*Gustave Flaubert*

Martyrdom is the only way in which a man can become famous without ability.
—*George Bernard Shaw*

Our admiration is so given to dead martyrs that we have little time for living heroes.
—*Elbert Hubbard*

Fame is proof that the people are gullible.   —*Ralph Waldo Emerson*

Obscurity and competence—that is the life that is best worth living.
—*Mark Twain*

We're more popular than Jesus Christ now.   —*John Lennon*

My face is my passport.   —*Vladimir Horowitz*

The nice thing about being a celebrity is that when you bore people, they think it's their fault.   —*Henry A. Kissinger*

It took me fifteen years to discover I had no talent for writing, but I couldn't give it up because by that time I was too famous.   —*Robert Benchley*

. . . be not afraid of greatness: some are born great, some achieve greatness, and some have greatness thrust upon them.   —*William Shakespeare*

Some are born great, some achieve greatness, and some hire public relations officers.
—*Daniel J. Boorstin*

Neil Armstrong was the first man to walk on the moon. I am the first man to piss his pants on the moon.
—*Buzz Aldrin*

You're always a little disappointing in person because you can't be the edited essence of yourself.
—*Mel Brooks*

A man's great fame must always be measured against the means used to acquire it.
—*François de La Rochefoucauld*

I was the toast of two continents: Greenland and Australia.
—*Dorothy Parker (attrib.)*

In the future, everyone will be famous for fifteen minutes.
—*Andy Warhol*

I'm famous. That's my job.
—*Jerry Rubin*

Ah just love bein' famous, and ah think anybody who says they don't is full of shit.
—*Johnny Winter*

I don't mind if my skull ends up on a shelf as long as it's got my name on it.
—*Debbie Harry*

The only man who wasn't spoiled by being lionized was Daniel.
—*Sir Herbert Beerbohm Tree*

A modest man is usually admired—if people ever hear of him.
—*Edgar Watson Howe*

To punish me for my contempt for authority, fate made me an authority myself.
—*Albert Einstein*

Obscurity is the refuge of incompetence.
—*Robert Heinlein*

There's only one thing in the world worse than being talked about, and that is not being talked about.
—*Oscar Wilde*

The higher a monkey climbs, the more you see of his ass.
—*General Joseph Stillwell*

My God, who do they think I am—everybody?
—*Leonard Bernstein, at the end of an exceptionally busy day*

Sayings
Fools' names and fools' faces are often seen in public places.

Fame is better than fortune.

Fame is a magnifying glass.

Fame is but the breath of the people.

At twenty, we don't care what the world thinks of us; at thirty, we worry about what it's thinking of us; at forty we discover it isn't thinking about us at all.

Joke
- Three guys were sitting around talking about what being really, really famous would be like. The first guy defined it as being invited to the White House for a personal chat with the president.

"Nah," disagreed the second fellow. "Real fame would be being in there chatting when the Hot Line rings, and the president won't take the call."

The third guy said they both had it wrong. "Fame," he declared, "is when you're in the Oval Office and the Hot Line rings and the president answers it, listens for a second, and then says, 'It's for you.' "

• The story is told that Winston Churchill, scheduled to address the entire United Kingdom in an hour, hailed a cab in London's West End and told the driver to drive as fast as he could for the BBC.

"Sorry, sir," said the cabbie, shaking his head. "You'll have to find yourself another cab."

"And why is that?" asked the annoyed prime minister.

"Ordinarily it wouldn't be a problem, sir," explained the driver apologetically, "but Mr. Churchill's broadcasting at six o'clock and I want to get home in time to hear him."

Churchill was so gratified that he pulled a pound note out of his wallet and handed it over. The cabbie took one look at the bill and said, "Hop in, sir—the devil with Mr. Churchill."

FORTUNE AND FATE

Bad times have a scientific value. . . . We learn geology the morning after the earthquake.
—*Ralph Waldo Emerson*

There is only one genuine misfortune: not to be born.
—*Joaquim Maria Machado de Assis*

The man with the real sense of humor is the man who can put himself in the spectator's place and laugh at his own misfortune.
—*Bert Williams*

No one is content with his fortune, nor discontent with his intellect.
—*Madame Antoinette Deshoulières*

Heaven goes by favor. If it went by merit, you would stay out and your dog would go in.
—*Mark Twain*

Name the greatest of all the inventors. Accident.
—*Mark Twain*

I think we consider too much the good luck of the early bird, and not enough the bad luck of the early worm.
—*Franklin D. Roosevelt*

Oil is seldom found where it is most needed, and seldom most needed where it is found.
—*L. E. J. Brouwer*

To punish me for my contempt for authority, fate made me an authority myself.
—*Albert Einstein*

I do not believe in a fate that falls on men however they act; but I do believe in a fate that falls on them unless they act.
—*G. K. Chesterton*

Lots of folks confuse bad management with destiny.
—*Kin Hubbard*

With luck on your side you can do without brains.
—*Giordano Bruno*

As long as we are lucky we attribute it to our smartness; our bad luck we give the gods credit for.
—*Josh Billings*

I am a great believer in luck, and I find the harder I work the more I have of it.

—Stephen Butler Leacock

Luck is the residue of design.

—Branch Rickey

Depend upon the rabbit's foot if you will, but remember it didn't work for the rabbit!

—R. E. Shay

Luck is not something you can mention in the presence of self-made men.

—E. B. White

If all our misfortunes were laid in one common heap, whence everyone must take an equal portion, most people would be content to take their own and depart.

—Solon

Can anybody remember when the times were not hard and money not scarce?

—Ralph Waldo Emerson

It is a very bad thing to become accustomed to good luck.   *—Publilius Syrus*

Fortune gives too much to many, but enough to none.

—Martial, first century A.D.

Luck never made a man wise.   *—Seneca the Younger*

May you live all the days of your life.   *—Jonathan Swift*

A flock of blessings light upon thy back.   *—William Shakespeare*

The harder you work, the luckier you get.   *—Gary Player*

No man can escape his fate.   *—Sophocles*

Sayings

Better to be born lucky than rich.

Not all luck is good, and not all good is luck.

Lucky at cards, unlucky in love.

Many a live wire would be a dead one except for his connections.

Joke

• When Doug came in for the results of his routine physical, the doctor said gently, "Doug, you'd better sit down. I've got some good news and some bad news."

"Okay," said Doug, taking a seat, "give me the bad news first."

"Well," said the doctor, "you've got cancer. It's spreading at an unbelievable rate, it's totally inoperable, and you've only got three weeks to live."

"Jesus!" gasped Doug, wiping the sweat off his brow. "What the hell's the *good* news?"

"You know that really gorgeous receptionist out in the front office?"

"You bet!" answered Doug.

"The one with the body that won't quit?"

"Right."

"And the blond hair and big baby blues—"

"Yeah, yeah," interrupted Doug. "Where's the good news?"

Leaning forward, the doctor announced with a grin, "I'm sleeping with her!"

GOALS

Acceptance of prevailing standards often means we have no standards of our own.

—Jean Toomer

Never look down to test the ground before taking your next step; only he who keeps his eye fixed on the far horizon will find the right road.   *—Dag Hammarskjöld*

Hitch your wagon to a star.   *—Ralph Waldo Emerson*

If you would hit the mark, you must aim a little above it; every arrow that flies feels the attraction of earth.   *—Henry Wadsworth Longfellow*

Ours is a world where people don't know what they want and are willing to go through hell to get it.   *—Don Marquis*

We succeed only as we identify in life, or in war, or in anything else, a single overriding objective, and make all other considerations bend to that one objective.

—Dwight D. Eisenhower

There are two great rules of life, the one general and the other particular. The first is that everyone can, in the end, get what he wants if he only tries. This is the general rule. The particular rule is that every individual is more or less an exception to the general rule.   *—Samuel Butler*

When you reach for the stars, you may not quite get them, but you won't come up with a handful of mud either.   *—Leo Burnett*

Not failure, but low aim, is crime.   *—James Russell Lowell*

Everybody sets out to do something, and everybody does something, but no one does what he sets out to do.   *—George A. Moore*

The tragedy of life doesn't lie in not reaching your goal. The tragedy lies in having no goal to reach.   *—Benjamin E. Mays*

You don't understand! I could've been a contender. I could've had class and been somebody. Real class. Instead of a bum, let's face it, which is what I am.

—Terry in **On the Waterfront,** *screenplay by Budd Schulberg*

Sayings

An obstacle is something you see when you take your eyes off the goal.

Never look back unless you are planning to go that way.

Joke

• "Say, buddy, can you spare a hundred bucks?" asked the bum.

"Geez!" sputtered the passerby. "Ten cents, a quarter, even a dollar I'm used to hearing. But what gives you the gall to ask for $100?" "Mister," responded the panhandler seriously, "I believe in setting my goals high."

GREATNESS

To be a great champion you must believe you are the best. If you're not, pretend you are.
—*Muhammad Ali*

A great man shows his greatness by the way he treats little men.
—*Thomas Carlyle*

A certain excessiveness seems a necessary element in all greatness.
—*Harvey Cushing*

It is better to deserve honors and not have them than to have them and not deserve them.
—*Mark Twain*

The greater the man, the greater the crime.
—*Thomas Fuller*

Greatness is a zigzag streak of lightning in the brain.
—*Herbert Asquith*

. . . be not afraid of greatness: some are born great, some achieve greatness, and some have greatness thrust upon them.
—*William Shakespeare*

Some are born great, some achieve greatness, and some hire public relations officers.
—*Daniel J. Boorstin*

The first test of a truly great man is his humility.
—*John Ruskin*

Few great men could pass personnel.
—*Paul Goodman*

No man is truly great who is great only in his own lifetime. The test of greatness is the page of history.
—*William Hazlitt*

Nothing grows well in the shade of a big tree.
—*Constantin Brancusi*

To do great things is difficult, but to command great things is more difficult.
—*Friedrich Wilhelm Nietzsche*

It is not the strength, but the duration, of great sentiments that makes great men.
—*Friedrich Wilhelm Nietzsche*

There may now exist great men for things that do not exist.
—*Samuel Burchardt*

No great man ever complains of want of opportunity.
—*Ralph Waldo Emerson*

The nobler a man, the harder it is for him to suspect inferiority in others.
—*Cicero*

Men of genius do not excel in any profession because they labor in it, but they labor in it because they excel.
—*William Hazlitt*

It is the gods' custom to bring low all things of surpassing greatness.
—*Herodotus*

The superior man is distressed by his want of ability.
—*Confucius*

Greatness is a spiritual condition worthy to excite love, interest, and admiration, and the outward proof of possessing greatness is that we excite love, interest, and admiration.
—*Matthew Arnold*

There is no such thing as a little country. The greatness of a people is no more determined by their number than the greatness of a man is determined by his height.

—*Victor Hugo*

We are both great men, but I have succeeded better in keeping it a profound secret than he has.

—*Bill Nye*

To be great is to be misunderstood.

—*Ralph Waldo Emerson*

Great men are meteors designed to burn so that the earth may be lighted.

—*Napoleon Bonaparte*

Nothing great will ever be achieved without great men, and men are great only if they are determined to be so.

—*Charles de Gaulle*

Meeting Franklin Roosevelt was like opening your first bottle of champagne; knowing him was like drinking it.

—*Winston Churchill*

Saying
One does not become great by claiming greatness.

—*African saying*

Joke
- The exercise during history class one day was for each of the students to list whom they considered to be the eleven greatest Americans. After half an hour, everyone had turned in their papers except Irwin, who was still scratching his head and thinking furiously. "What's up?" asked the teacher. "Can't you come up with eleven great Americans?"

  "I've got all but one," the student explained hastily. "It's the quarterback I can't decide on."

HONESTY

Honesty is the best policy, but he who is governed by that maxim is not an honest man.

—*Richard Whateley*

Put a rogue in the limelight and he will act like an honest man.

—*Napoleon Bonaparte*

All cruel people describe themselves as paragons of frankness.

—*Tennessee Williams*

There is one way to find out if a man is honest—ask him. If he says yes, you know he is crooked.

—*Groucho Marx*

An honest God is the noblest work of man.

—*Robert G. Ingersoll*

He's an honest man—you could shoot craps with him over the telephone.

—*Earl Wilson*

Honesty's the best policy.

—*Miguel de Cervantes*

Sayings

Don't call a man honest just because he never had the chance to steal.

—Yiddish saying

Honesty is the best policy (but sometimes it has a high premium).

Jokes

- At long last the good-humored boss felt compelled to call Fitch into his office. "It has not escaped my attention," he pointed out gently, "that every time there's a big home game, you have to take your aunt to the doctor."

  "You know, you're *right*, sir," exclaimed Fitch. "I hadn't realized. You don't suppose she's faking it, now do you?"

- As he lay dying, the old codger turned to his wife and murmured softly, "When I limped home from the final campaign in 1918, you were waiting for me, Rachel. When I was released from Dachau at the end of World War II, you were by my side." Overcome with emotion, the old man stopped to snort loudly into a handkerchief, then continued. "Rachel, when we sold everything to start a business in the new world and it went bust and left us penniless, there you were. And now, here I am breathing my last, and here you still stand by the bedside. Rachel, I'm telling you—you're a jinx."

INITIATIVE AND INCENTIVE

The world is divided into people who do things and people who get the credit. Try, if you can, to belong to the first class. There's far less competition.

—Dwight Morrow

No man knows what he can do till he tries.

—Publilius Syrus

When in doubt, make a fool of yourself. There is a microscopically thin line between being brilliantly creative and acting like the most gigantic idiot on earth. So what the hell, leap.

—Cynthia Heimel

I do not believe in a fate that falls on men however they act; but I do believe in a fate that falls on them unless they act.

—G. K. Chesterton

Nothing can move a man who is paid by the hour; how sweet the flight of time seems to his calm mind.

—Charles Dudley Warner

Restlessness is discontent—and discontent is the first necessity of progress. Show me a thoroughly satisfied man and I will show you a failure.

—Thomas Alva Edison

Have the courage to act instead of react.

—Earlene Larson Jenks

To escape criticism—do nothing, say nothing, be nothing.

—Elbert Hubbard

I always do the first line well, but I have trouble doing the others.

—Molière

The only difference between a rut and a grave is their dimensions.

—Ellen Glasgow

The oldest habit in the world for resisting change is to complain that unless the remedy to the disease should be universally applied it should not be applied at all. But you must start somewhere.   —*Winston Churchill*

A horse never runs so fast as when he has other horses to catch up and outpace.

—*Ovid*

The man who does something under orders is not unhappy; he is unhappy who does something against his will.   —*Seneca the Younger*

The beginning is the most important part of the work.   —*Plato*

People are always blaming their circumstances for what they are. I don't believe in circumstances. The people who get on in this world are the people who get up and look for the circumstances they want, and, if they can't find them, make them.

—*George Bernard Shaw*

In real life, of course, it is the hare who wins. Every time. Look around you. And in any case it is my contention that Aesop was writing for the tortoise market. . . . Hares have no time to read. They are too busy winning the game.   —*Anita Brookner*

The only thing necessary for the triumph of evil is for good men to do nothing.

—*Edmund Burke*

The gods help them that help themselves.   —*Aesop*

Ask, and it shall be given you; seek, and ye shall find; knock, and it shall be opened unto you.   —**Matthew 7:7**

We must not, in trying to think about how we can make a big difference, ignore the small daily differences we can make which, over time, add up to big differences that we often cannot foresee.   —*Marian Wright Edelman*

Throughout history it has been the inaction of those who could have acted, the indifference of those who should have known better, the silence of the voice of justice when it mattered most, that has made it possible for evil to triumph.

—*Haile Selassie*

The man whose life is devoted to paperwork has lost the initiative. He is dealing with things that are brought to his notice, having ceased to notice anything for himself. He has been essentially defeated in his job.   —*C. Northcote Parkinson*

Boldness in business is the first, second, and third thing.   —*Thomas Fuller*

Every morning I take out my bankbook, stare at it, shudder—and turn quickly to my typewriter.   —*Sydney J. Harris, on incentive as a journalist*

"Where shall I begin, please your majesty?" she asked.

"Begin at the beginning," the king said, very gravely, "and go on till you come to the end: then stop."   —*Lewis Carroll*

Sayings
The early bird gets the worm.

A journey of a thousand miles begins with a single step.   —*Chinese proverb*

An American believes more than anything else in the last four letters of that title: I can.

Jokes

* At the conclusion of his lecture to a group of young recruits, the legendary paratrooper asked for questions. A hand shot up. "What made you decide to make that first jump, sir?"

  Without hesitating, the paratrooper replied, "An airplane at eighteen thousand feet with three dead engines."

* I feel like Liz Taylor's fourth husband: I know what I am supposed to do, but I am at a loss as to how to make it different.

* Two guys are being chased by a bear, when one stops to put on his sneakers. The other guy yells, "You idiot, you can't outrun a bear."

  The first guy gasps, "I don't have to outrun a bear—I just have to outrun you."

* Two skeletons used by the professor of anatomy found themselves stowed away in a dusty closet, and after several weeks of boredom one turned to the other and asked, "What are we doing shut up in here anyway?"

  "Got me," admitted his companion. "But if we had any guts we'd get out of here."

LEADERSHIP

It's a piece of cake until you get to the top. You find you can't stop playing the game the way you have always played it.
—*Richard M. Nixon*

When you soar like an eagle, you attract the hunters.
—*Milton S. Gould*

To do great things is difficult, but to command great things is more difficult.
—*Friedrich Wilhelm Nietzsche*

We can't all be heroes because somebody has to sit on the curb and clap as they go by.
—*Will Rogers*

'Tis skill, not strength that governs a ship.
—*Thomas Fuller*

When a leader is in the Democratic party he's a boss; when he's in the Republican party he's a leader.
—*Harry S Truman*

A leader is a dealer in hope.
—*Napoleon Bonaparte*

The leader must know, must know that he knows, and must be able to make it abundantly clear to those about him that he knows.
—*Clarence B. Randall*

They be blind leaders of the blind. And if the blind lead the blind, both shall fall into the ditch.
—*Matthew 15:14*

Be willing to make decisions. That's the most important quality in a good leader. Don't fall victim to what I call the "ready-aim-aim-aim-aim sydrome." You must be willing to fire.
—*T. Boone Pickens*

You do not lead by hitting people over the head—that's assault, not leadership.
—*Dwight D. Eisenhower*

The art of leadership . . . consists in consolidating the attention of the people against a single adversary and taking care that nothing will split up that attention.

—Adolf Hitler

No man is fit to command another that cannot command himself.

—William Penn

In time of peril, like the needle to the lodestone, obedience, irrespective of rank, generally flies to him who is best fitted to command.   *—Herman Melville*

I must follow them. I am their leader.   *—Andrew Bonar Law*

I never give them hell. I just tell the truth and they think it's hell.

—Harry S Truman

It is an interesting question how far men would retain their relative rank if they were divested of their clothes.   *—Henry David Thoreau*

A decision is the action an executive must take when he has information so incomplete that the answer does not suggest itself.   *—Arthur W. Radford*

Ye are the light of the world. A city that is set on a hill cannot be hid. Neither do men light a candle, and put it under a bushel, but on a candlestick; and it giveth light unto all that are in the house. Let your light so shine before men, that they may see your good works, and glorify your Father which is in heaven.

—Matthew 5:14–16

Only one man in a thousand is a leader of men—the other 999 follow women.

—Groucho Marx

Either lead, follow, or get out of the way.

—Sign on desk of broadcasting executive Ted Turner

I will do my best. That is all I can do. I ask for your help—and God's.

—Lyndon B. Johnson, on arriving in Washington, D.C., on the evening of John F. Kennedy's assassination, November 22, 1963

People ask the difference between a leader and a boss. . . . The leader works in the open and the boss in covert. The leader leads, and the boss drives.

—Theodore Roosevelt

General Dwight D. Eisenhower used a simple device to illustrate the art of leadership. Laying an ordinary piece of string on a table, he'd illustrate how you could easily pull it in any direction. "Try and push it, though," he cautioned, "and it won't go anywhere. It's just that way when it comes to leading people."

Now I don't want you to consider me as just your commanding officer. I want you to look on me like I was . . . well . . . *God.*

—Bull, in The Great Santini, *screenplay by Lewis John Carlino*

Sayings
The speed of the leader is the speed of the pack.   *—Yukon saying*

The thoughtless strong man is the chief among lazy men.   *—West African saying*

Take me to your leader.

You can always tell a leader, but you can't tell him much.

Judge a leader by the followers.

Leadership casts a long shadow.

Joke

• Part of the college application was directed to the applicant's parents, and one of the questions was, "Would you consider your child to be a leader or a follower?" After much deliberation, the father wrote that he felt his child, although very much an individual, was really more of a follower.

  Not long after, a letter of acceptance arrived from the college, accompanied by a note from the director of admissions welcoming his child. "We feel he'll fit in especially well," the letter went on, "as he will be the only follower in a class of 412 leaders."

OPPORTUNITY

A problem is a chance for you to do your best.
                                                        —*Duke Ellington*

. . . there is only one genuine misfortune: not to be born.
                                            —*Joaquim Maria Machado de Assis*

No great man ever complains of want of opportunity.   —*Ralph Waldo Emerson*

Problems are only opportunities in work clothes.
                                                        —*Henry J. Kaiser*

When one door of happiness closes, another opens; but often we look so long at the closed door that we do not see the one which has been opened for us.
                                                        —*Helen Keller*

I was seldom able to see an opportunity until it had ceased to be one.
                                                        —*Mark Twain*

Carpe diem. (Seize the day.)   —*Horace*

Next to knowing when to seize an opportunity, the most important thing in life is to know when to forgo an advantage.   —*Benjamin Disraeli*

It is not impossibilities which fill us with the deepest despair, but possibilities which we have failed to realize.   —*Robert Mallet*

Time is that wherein there is opportunity, and opportunity is that wherein there is no great time.   —*Hippocrates*

A man hath no better thing under the sun, than to eat, and to drink, and to be merry.
                                                        —*Ecclesiastes 8:15*

. . . where legitimate opportunities are closed, illegitimate opportunities are seized. Whatever opens opportunity and hope will help to prevent crime and foster responsibility.   —*Lyndon B. Johnson*

Bad times have a scientific value. . . . We learn geology the morning after the earthquake.   —*Ralph Waldo Emerson*

Sayings

When a fool has made up his mind, the market has gone by.   —*Spanish proverb*

Some people not only expect opportunity to knock, they expect it to beat the door down.

No opportunity is ever lost. Someone else seizes the ones you missed.

Opportunity knocks but once.

Jokes

- First Entrepreneur: "I've got a great idea: I'm going to open up a bar and grill in the middle of the Sahara Desert."

    Second Entrepreneur: "That's a ridiculous idea. You'll be lucky to get more than one customer a month."

    First Entrepreneur: "Okay, but just *think* how thirsty he'll be!"

- The fellow was joined at the bar by a voluptuous woman who soon made her talents and charms abundantly clear. "I'll make your dreams come true," she whispered, "for $150."

    "That's a lot of money," the guy pointed out, admiring the cleavage set forth under his nose.

    "I'm worth it," she assured him breathily. "For $150, I'll act out your wildest, hottest fantasy. In fact I can make any three words come true. Just dream them up, baby."

    "Any three words? For $150?" The man's voice grew husky as the woman's hand crept further and further up his inner thigh.

    She nodded, reaching the other hand up to caress the back of his neck while the fellow considered the offer. Finally he leaned back with a big smile and announced. "Okay, it's a deal!" He leaned over and whispered, "Paint my house."

OPTIMISM

Gray skies are just clouds passing over.   —*Duke Ellington*

Optimism is a kind of heart stimulant—the digitalis of failure.

—*Elbert Hubbard*

Let us be of good cheer, remembering that the misfortunes hardest to bear are those that will never happen.   —*James Russell Lowell*

The optimist proclaims that we live in the best of all possible worlds; and the pessimist fears this is true.   —*James Branch Cabell*

This is the best day the world has ever seen. Tomorrow will be better.

—*R. A. Campbell*

An Englishman who was wrecked on a strange shore and wandering along the coast came to a gallows with a victim hanging on it, and fell down to his knees and thanked God that he at last beheld a sign of civilization.   —*James Garfield*

The man who laughs has not yet heard the news.   —*Bertolt Brecht*

Pessimists are usually kind. The gay, bubbling over, have no time for the pitiful.

—Sean O'Faolain

The man who is a pessimist before forty-eight knows too much; if he is an optimist after it, he knows too little. *—Mark Twain*

Things are going to get a lot worse before they get worse. *—Lily Tomlin*

I've never seen a monument erected to a pessimist. *—Paul Harvey*

One must have the courage of one's pessimism. *—Ian McEwan*

Sayings

Pessimism is the art of finding bad news in a fortune cookie.

An obstacle is something you see when you take your eyes off the goal.

Save your good times till later.

Always expect the worst, and when it comes, make the best of it.

To believe a thing impossible is to make it so. *—French proverb*

Pessimism is the triumph of worry over matter.

A pessimist is someone who makes difficulties of his opportunities.

The man who says it cannot be done should not interrupt the man doing it.

—Chinese proverb

In the long run, the pessimist may be proved right, but the optimist has a better time on the trip.

An optimist is a man who starts a crossword puzzle with a fountain pen.

Let a smile be your umbrella.

Put on a happy face.

Jokes

• What's the difference between an optimist and a pessimist? An optimist created the plane; a pessimist created the seat belts.

• During his whistlestop campaign for the presidency in 1948, Harry Truman is reputed to have asked a fellow in the crowd before him how he was intending to vote.

"Mr. Truman," came the reply, "I wouldn't vote for you if yours was the only name on the ballot."

Truman turned to an aide and instructed, "Put that man down as doubtful."

• A passerby stopped to watch a Little League game in progress, and after a few minutes asked one of the boys in the dugout the score.

"Oh, we're behind twelve to nothing," was the answer.

"Gee, you must be kind of discouraged," the spectator commented.

"Discouraged? Why should I be discouraged?" asked the kid with a big grin. "Our team hasn't gotten to bat yet."

• You know those seed catalogues? I think the pictures are posed by professional flowers getting $50 an hour. I don't consider gardening so much growing flowers as burying seeds.

PRAISE

He writes so well he makes me feel like putting the quill back in the goose.

—Fred Allen

Well done is better than well said.   *—Benjamin Franklin*

I think this is the most extraordinary collection of talent, of human knowledge, that has ever been gathered together at the White House—with the possible exception of when Thomas Jefferson dined alone.   *—John F. Kennedy*

They say, "Gee, you look great." That means they thought you looked like hell before.

—Richard M. Nixon

The advantage of doing one's praising for oneself is that one can lay it on thick and exactly in the right places.   *—Samuel Butler*

His life was gentle and the elements so mixed in him that nature might stand on its feet and say to all the world—this was a man!   *—William Shakespeare*

This is a moment that I deeply wish my parents could have lived to share. My father would have enjoyed what you have so generously said of me—and my mother would have believed it.   *—Lyndon B. Johnson*

We recognize that flattery is poison, but its perfume intoxicates us.

—Charles Varlet de La Grange

Baloney is the unvarnished lie laid on so thick you hate it. Blarney is flattery laid on so thin you love it.   *—Bishop Fulton J. Sheen*

Flattery is all right—if you don't inhale.   *—Adlai E. Stevenson*

Some people pay a compliment as if they expected a receipt.   *—Kin Hubbard*

A compliment is something like a kiss through a veil.   *—Victor Hugo*

Let us now praise famous men, and our fathers that begat us.

—Ecclesiasticus 44:1

I will praise any man that will praise me.   *—William Shakespeare*

Flattery is like cologne water, to be smelt of, not swallowed.   *—Josh Billings*

I can live for two months on a good compliment.   *—Mark Twain*

It is more difficult to praise rightly than to blame.   *—Thomas Fuller*

Praise is the only gift for which people are really grateful.

—Marguerite, Countess of Blessington

Whenever the occasion arose, he rose to the occasion.

—Jonathan Brown, on Diego Velázquez

A man doesn't live by bread alone. He needs buttering up once in a while.

—Robert H. Henry

To withhold deserved praise lest it should make its object conceited is as dishonest as to withhold payment of a just debt lest your creditor should spend the money badly.

—*George Bernard Shaw*

The greatest honor that can come to a man is the appreciation and high regard of his fellow men.

—*H. G. Mendelson*

Sayings

One has only to die to be praised.

—*German proverb*

You catch more flies with honey than you do with vinegar.

If you think that praise is due, now's the time to show it, 'cause a man can't read his tombstone when he's dead.

A word of encouragement during failure is worth more than a dictionary of praise following success.

An actor is like a cigar; the more you puff him the smaller he gets.

Jokes

• Novice golfer to husband, teeing off: "Now tell me if you notice anything I'm doing right."

• The kindhearted department head was delighted when a less-than-dazzling employee decided to move on, but stumped when he was asked for a recommendation. Finally, after much head-scratching, he wrote, "Mr. Marks worked for me for a long time, and when you have known him as long as I have, you will undoubtedly share my opinion of him."

QUALITY AND EXCELLENCE

If you don't do it excellently, don't do it at all. Because if it's not excellent, it won't be profitable or fun, and if you're not in business for fun or profit, what the hell are you doing there?

—*Robert Townsend*

What the crowd requires is mediocrity of the highest order.

—*Antoine-Auguste Préault*

When I am working on a problem, I never think about beauty . . . but when I have finished, if the solution is not beautiful, I know it is wrong.

—*R. Buckminster Fuller*

As there is but one step from the sublime to the ridiculous, so also there is but one from the ridiculous to the sublime.

—*Samuel Butler*

Give me the luxuries of life and I will willingly do without the necessities.

—*Frank Lloyd Wright*

It is better to deserve honors and not have them than to have them and not deserve them.

—*Mark Twain*

Only mediocrity can be trusted to be always at its best.

—*Max Beerbohm*

Every man is entitled to be valued by his best moment.   —*Ralph Waldo Emerson*

There is no perfectly Epicurean corner; there is no perfectly irresponsible place. Everywhere men have made the way for us with sweat and submission. We may fling ourselves into a hammock in a fit of divine carelessness. But we are glad that the net-maker did not make the hammock in a fit of divine carelessness.

—*G. K. Chesterton*

Good is not good, where better is expected.   —*Thomas Fuller*

If I cannot overwhelm with my quality, I will overwhelm with my quantity.

—*Emile Zola*

There is hardly anything in the world that some man cannot make a little worse and sell a little cheaper.   —*John Ruskin*

It is a funny thing about life: if you refuse to accept anything but the best you very often get it.   —*W. Somerset Maugham*

It isn't evil that's running the earth, but mediocrity. The crime is not that Nero played while Rome burned, but that he played badly.   —*Ned Rorem*

The secret of joy in work is contained in one word—excellence. To know how to do something well is to enjoy it.   —*Pearl Buck*

All I want is the best of everything, and there's very little of that left.

—*Lucius Beebe*

The true test of civilization is not the census, not size of cities, but the kind of man that the country turns out.   —*Ralph Waldo Emerson*

Not much meat on her, but what's there is choice.

—*Spencer Tracy, about Katharine Hepburn*

A perfectionist is a man who takes infinite pains and gives them to others.

—*Alan Benner*

First-rate people hire first-rate people; second-rate people hire third-rate people.

—*Leo Rosten*

The road to business success is paved by those who continually strive to produce better products or services. It does not have to be a great technological product like television. Ray Kroc of McDonald's fame did it with a simple hamburger.

—*G. Kingsley Ward*

Quality is not an act. It is a habit.   —*Aristotle*

My parents always told me that people will never know how long it takes you to do something. They will only know how well it is done.   —*Nancy Hanks*

QSCV (Quality, Service, Cleanliness, and Value).

—*Standard imposed by Ray Kroc, founder of McDonald's fast-food chain*

Sayings
If it isn't perfect, make it better.   —*Japanese manufacturing slogan*

The bitterness of poor quality persists long after the sweetness of low price is forgotten.

To err is human; to try to prevent recurrence of error is science.

Jokes

• Sign in a New York restaurant window: "Courteous and efficient self-service."

• "What a superb performance," gushed the woman when the recital was over. "I'd give half my life to be able to play the piano like that."
  "Madam," responded the pianist with a little bow, "that is exactly what it took."

• The television factory boosted quality control with a little sign above each work station. It read: "Careful—this may be the one you get."

• A woman went into a diner one morning and ordered breakfast. "I want two eggs over easy," she instructed, "one of them runny as water and the other cooked hard enough to bounce. I want the toast burned black, the coffee cold, and the butter too hard to cut."
  "We can't do that, ma'am," protested the waitress.
  "Sure you can," said the customer. "You did yesterday."

• Customer: "Gee, if these machines are sold way under cost like you say they are, how do you make a living?"
  Salesman: "Simple. We make our money fixing them."

REPUTATION

Who has once the fame to be an early riser may sleep till noon.   —*James Howell*

Character is made by what you stand for; reputation, by what you fall for.
                                                        —*Robert Quillen*

It is easier to cope with a bad conscience than with a bad reputation.
                                              —*Friedrich Wilhelm Nietzsche*

Whom the gods wish to destroy they first call promising.   —*Cyril Connolly*

Either a good or a bad reputation outruns and gets before people wherever they go.
                                                    —*Lord Chesterfield*

Every man values himself more than all other men, but he always values others' opinion of him more than his own.   —*Marcus Aurelius Antoninus*

No man is rich enough to buy back his past.   —*Oscar Wilde*

Each man is afraid of his neighbor's disapproval—a thing which, to the general run of the race, is more dreaded than wounds and death.   —*Mark Twain*

A good name is rather to be chosen than great riches, and loving favor rather than silver and gold.   —**Proverbs** *22:1*

Until you've lost your reputation, you never realize what a burden it was or what freedom really is.   —*Margaret Mitchell*

Oh! I have lost my reputation. I have lost the immortal part of myself, and what remains is bestial.   —*William Shakespeare*

Associate yourself with men of good quality if you esteem your own reputation; for 'tis better to be alone than in bad quality.   —*George Washington*

There's only one thing in the world worse than being talked about, and that is not being talked about.   —*Oscar Wilde*

Reputation: what others are not thinking about you.   —*Tom Masson*

There are times when there is nothing more humiliating in life than the knowledge of being inferior to one's reputation.   —*Eleonora Duse*

No nation respects a beggar.   —*Elijah Muhammad*

I can ruin my reputation in five minutes; I don't need help.   —*Martha Graham*

Sayings

If you've got something worthwhile to do, don't talk about it—do it. After it's done, your friends and acquaintances will talk about it.

Your reputation precedes you.

Joke

• Mrs. Pinkham was understandably upset when the newspaper accidentally printed her obituary, but when she came in to see the managing editor she grew positively apoplectic with rage. "Just think of what your careless error will cost me: I'm completely mortified, a laughingstock already, the butt of cheap wisecracks. Why my social standing, my entire reputation is at stake!"

The harried editor attempted to apologize repeatedly, but was unable even to get a word in edgewise. Finally the dowager concluded her diatribe with the demand that the newspaper somehow make it up to her.

"Fine, lady," offered the editor wearily. "Tomorrow I'll list you in the birth announcements and give you a fresh start."

RESPONSIBILITY

It is our responsibilities, not ourselves, that we should take seriously.
    —*Peter Ustinov*

Responsibility, the high price of self-ownership.   —*Eli Schleifer*

It is easy to dodge our responsibilities, but we cannot dodge the consequences of dodging our responsibilities.   —*Josiah Stamp*

Liberty means responsibility. That is why most men dread it.
    —*Antonio de Mendoza*

Corporation: an ingenious device for obtaining individual profit without individual responsibility.   —*Ambrose Bierce*

No matter how lofty you are in your department, the responsibility for what your lowliest assistant is doing is yours.   —*Bessie James*

When Robert Fosse was replaced as director-choreographer on the short-lived Broadway show *The Conquering Hero*, he complained, "I conceived this show. I outlined it. I cast it. I choreographed it. I drew the first sketches for the design. I directed it. And the first thing that goes wrong, they blame me!"

When the grass looks greener on the other side of the fence, it may be that they take better care of it there.

—*Cecil Selig*

Sayings
A heavy burden does not kill on the day it is carried.   —*East African saying*

The absent are never without fault, nor those present without excuse.

Jokes
• Somewhat skeptical of his son's newfound determination to become Charles Atlas, the father nevertheless followed the teenager over to the weight-lifting department.

"Please, Dad," wheedled the boy, "I promise I'll use 'em every day . . ."

"I dunno, Michael. It's really a commitment on your part," his father pointed out.

"*Please*, Dad?"

"They're not cheap either."

"I'll use 'em, Dad, I promise. You'll see."

Finally won over, the father paid for the equipment and headed for the door. From the corner of the store he heard his son yelp, "What! You mean I have to carry them to the car?"

• A fellow applying for a job as a flagman with the Baltimore and Ohio Railroad was told the job was his if he could correctly answer a single question: As flagman, what would he do if he saw the Continental Express coming from the east at 100 mph and the Century Limited heading west at 90 mph on the same track?

The applicant pondered for a moment, then answered, "I'd fetch my brother-in-law."

"What good would that do?" asked the interviewer. "Has he worked on the railroad?"

"Nope—he ain't never seen a train accident."

• A passerby watched the progress of two workmen down a Leningrad street. One stopped every twenty feet to dig a hole, the second filled it in as soon as he was done, and they moved on to the next site. Finally, overcome by curiosity, the observer asked what in heaven's name they were doing. "You certainly aren't accomplishing anything," she pointed out.

"You don't understand at all," protested one worker indignantly. "We are usually a team of three: I dig the hole, Sergei plants the tree, and Vladimir packs the dirt back in. Today Sergei is home with the flu, but that doesn't mean Vladimir and I get to stop working, does it?"

• Two weeks after Paisley's transfer into the promotion department, his old boss got a phone call. "You told me Paisley was a responsible worker!" yelled the furious head of promotion.

"Oh he is," she confirmed. "In the year he worked in my department, the computer went down five times and had to be completely reprogrammed, the petty cash got misplaced six times, and I developed an ulcer. And each time, Paisley was responsible."

SELF-ESTEEM

We shall have our manhood.   *—Eldridge Cleaver*

The greatest possession is self-possession.   *—Ethel Watts Mumford*

He who despises himself esteems himself as a self-despiser.   *—Susan Sontag*

Of all the traps and pitfalls in life, self-disesteem is the deadliest, and the hardest to overcome, for it is a pit designed and dug by our own hands, summed up in the phrase, "It's no use—I can't do it."   *—Maxwell Maltz*

Nothing is so soothing to our self-esteem as to find our bad traits in our forebears. It seems to absolve us.   *—Van Wyck Brooks*

Many purchasers of self-help books are grappling with a creeping, leaden feeling that life is passing them by. . . . Why, these purchasers ask, am I not a glittering presence? Why do I not have an ostentatiously large and tastelessly furnished house full of sullen hangers-on?   *—Colin McEnroe*

Psychoanalysis shows the human infant as the passive recipient of love, unable to bear hostility. Development is learning to love actively and to bear rejection.

—Karl Stern

People often say that this or that person has not yet found himself. But the self is not something that one finds. It is something that one creates.   *—Thomas Szasz*

Every new adjustment is a crisis in self-esteem.   *—Eric Hoffer*

Justice is always violent to the offending, for every man is innocent in his own eyes.

—Daniel Defoe

The graveyards are full of people the world could not do without.

—Elbert Hubbard

Sayings
When a man falls in love with himself, it's usually the beginning of a lifelong romance.

The minute you get the idea you're indispensable, you aren't.

Jokes
• If you think nobody cares you're alive, try missing a couple of car payments.

• The trendy dresser fancied himself quite a ladykiller, and was delighted to find a note pinned inside a brand-new shirt. It contained a girl's name and address, and asked the recipient to send a photograph. "How romantic," he thought to himself, very taken with the idea of this mystery woman so eager to meet him, and promptly mailed off a note and photo.

    Heart aflutter, he opened her response. It read, "Thanks for writing. I was just curious to see what kind of guy would buy such a funny shirt."

STATUS

The difference between a man and his valet: they both smoke the same cigars, but only one pays for them.   *—Robert Frost*

All men are born equal, but quite a few eventually get over it.   —*Lord Mancroft*

Soldiers win battles and generals get the credit.   —*Napoleon Bonaparte*

Many of the quests for status symbols—the hot automobile, the best table in a restaurant or a private chat with the boss—are shadowy reprises of infant anxieties. . . . The larger office, the corner space, the extra window are the teddy bears and tricycles of adult office life.   —*Willard Gaylin*

A status symbol is anything you can't afford, but did.   —*Harold Coffin*

Status symbols are medals you buy yourself.   —*Bernhard Wicki*

Advertising promotes that divine discontent which makes people strive to improve their economic status.   —*Ralph Butler*

Sayings

It's nice to be important, but it's more important to be nice.

If they don't want to play with you, then you don't want to play with them.

Remember where you came from.

The best way to judge a teacher is to ask who his instructors were and who his students are.

Once the game is over, the king and the pawn go back into the same box.

—*Italian saying*

Jokes

• Observing a light across the water, the captain had his signalman instruct the other vessel to change her course ten degrees south.

The response was prompt: "Change your course ten degrees north."

"I am a captain," he responded testily. "Change your course ten degrees south."

The reply: "I'm a seaman first class—change your course north."

The captain was furious. "Change your course *now*. I'm on a battleship."

"Change your course ten degrees north, sir—I'm in a lighthouse."

• First employee: "So, is your job secure?"

Second employee: "Oh, yes. It's me they can do without."

• The nouveau riche real estate developer splurged on a Rolls-Royce Silver Shadow and couldn't wait to show it off. So after a meeting with the bank, he offered one of the senior bank officers a ride home. "Whaddaya think?" he couldn't resist asking his passenger after a mile or two. "Pretty snappy, eh? I bet you've never ridden in one of these before."

"Actually I have," replied the banker graciously, "but this is my first time in the front seat."

SUCCESS

The penalty of success is to be bored by the attentions of people who formerly snubbed you.

—*Mary Wilson Little*

. . . the man who succeeds is never conceded the right to fail.

—*William Pickens*

If every successful man needs a woman behind him, every successful woman needs at least three men.   —*Margot Naylor*

Success is a public affair. Failure is a private funeral.   —*Rosalind Russell*

The only place where success comes before work is in a dictionary.

—*Vidal Sassoon*

You write a hit play the same way you write a flop.   —*William Saroyan*

If A equals success, then the formula is A equals X plus Y plus Z, where X is work, Y is play, Z is keep your mouth shut.   —*Albert Einstein*

The successful people are the ones who can think up things for the rest of the world to keep busy at.   —*Don Marquis*

Success covers many blunders.   —*George Bernard Shaw*

Of course there is no formula for success except, perhaps, an unconditional acceptance of life and what it brings.   —*Arthur Rubinstein*

Behind every successful man there's a lot of unsuccessful years.   —*Bob Brown*

If you would hit the mark, you must aim a little above it; every arrow that flies feels the attraction of earth.   —*Henry Wadsworth Longfellow*

Nothing fails like success because we don't learn from it. We learn only from failure.

—*Kenneth Boulding*

How can they say my life isn't a success? Have I not for more than sixty years got enough to eat and escaped being eaten?   —*Logan Pearsall Smith*

We can't all be lions in this world. There must be some lambs, harmless, kindly, gregarious creatures for eating and shearing.   —*William Makepeace Thackeray*

We may stop ourselves when going up, never when going down.

—*Napoleon Bonaparte*

As is the case in all branches of art, success depends in a very large measure upon individual initiative and exertion, and cannot be achieved except by dint of hard work.

—*Anna Pavlova*

Never claim as a right what you can ask as a favor.   —*John Churton Collins*

The danger of success is that it makes us forget the world's dreadful injustice.

—*Jules Renard*

If a man can build a better book, preach a better sermon, or make a better mousetrap than his neighbor, though he builds his house in the woods, the world will make a beaten path to his door.   —*Ralph Waldo Emerson*

I am perfectly happy to believe that nobody likes us but the public.

—*Rudolph Bing*

The toughest thing about being a success is that you've got to keep on being a success.

—*Irving Berlin*

Eighty percent of success is showing up.   —*Woody Allen*

[Success] means that you have, as performers will call it, "fuck you" money. . . . All
that means is that I don't have to do what I don't want to do.   —*Johnny Carson*

There's no secret about success. Did you ever know a successful man that didn't tell
you all about it?   —*Kin Hubbard*

There is only one success—to be able to spend your life in your own way.
                                        —*Christopher Morley*

All you need in life is ignorance and confidence, and then success is sure.
                                        —*Mark Twain*

. . . I've always gone along with the view that, first, the surest guarantee of sexual
success is sexual success (you can't have one without the other and you can't have the
other without the one), and, second, that the trappings of sexual success are only
fleetingly distinguishable from sexual success itself.   —*Martin Amis*

Anybody can sympathize with the sufferings of a friend, but it requires a very fine
nature to sympathize with a friend's success.   —*Oscar Wilde*

The worst part of having success is trying to find someone who is happy for you.
                                        —*Bette Midler (attrib.)*

Self-made men are most always apt to be a little too proud of the job.
                                        —*Josh Billings*

Either lead, follow, or get out of the way.
                    —*Sign on desk of broadcasting executive Ted Turner*

I can't imagine a person becoming a success who doesn't give this game of life
everything he's got.   —*Walter Cronkite*

There's only one way to succeed in anything, and that is to give it everything. I do,
and I demand that my players do.   —*Vince Lombardi*

The common idea that success spoils people by making them vain, egotistic, and self-
complacent is erroneous; on the contrary, it makes them, for the most part, humble,
tolerant, and kind. Failure makes people cruel and bitter.
                                        —*W. Somerset Maugham*

Nothing succeeds like success.   —*Alexandre Dumas*

Sayings
Success is not the ability to get along with people, it's the ability to get ahead of them.

Enthusiasm is more important than any other commodity. It will find solutions when
none are apparent, and it will achieve success where none is thought possible.

If at first you don't succeed, try, try again.

If at first you don't succeed, try reading the instructions.

Jokes
• She always wanted to be successful so she could take it easy. Now she's so
  successful there's no way she can take it easy.

• Behind every successful man there stands an amazed woman.

TALENT

There are two kinds of talent, man-made talent and God-given talent. With man-made talent you have to work very hard. With God-given talent, you just touch it up once in a while.
—*Pearl Bailey*

Talent wins out.
—*Althea Gibson Darben*

Keep your talent in the dark and you'll never be insulted.
—*Elsa Maxwell*

A man possesses talent; genius possesses the man.
—*Isaac Stern*

Anything you're good at contributes to happiness.
—*Bertrand Russell*

There is no such thing as a great talent without great will power.
—*Honoré de Balzac*

An unfulfilled vocation drains the color from a man's entire existence.
—*Honoré de Balzac*

I have always thought that the surest proof of talent is its condescension to genius.
—*Vincent Sheehan*

I began to ration my writing, for fear I would dream through life as my father had done. I was afraid I had inherited a poisoned gene from him, a vocation without a gift.
—*Mavis Gallant*

Nothing I do can't be done by a ten-year-old . . . with fifteen years of practice.
—*Harry Blackstone, Jr., on being a magician*

There is no substitute for talent. Industry and all the virtues are of no avail.
—*Aldous Huxley*

Whom the gods wish to destroy they first call promising.
—*Cyril Connolly*

I think this is the most extraordinary collection of talent, of human knowledge, that has ever been gathered together at the White House—with the possible exception of when Thomas Jefferson dined alone.
—*John F. Kennedy*

Neither cast ye your pearls before swine.
—*Matthew 7:6*

After my screen test, the director clapped his hands gleefully and yelled, "She can't talk! She can't act! She's sensational!"
—*Ava Gardner*

We've all been blessed with God-given talents. Mine just happens to be beating people up.
—*Sugar Ray Leonard*

Hard work without talent is a shame, but talent without hard work is a tragedy.
—*Robert Half*

Sayings

You're not in competition with anyone but yourself.

A talent is both gift and obligation.

Joke
- "Please, Mr. Grossman, my act is really something special. Just give me a minute." Before the talent scout could object, the desperate actor climbed up on the desk, flapped his arms, and proceeded to fly around the room twice.

  "Okay," said the agent, "so you can imitate birds. What else?"

TIME AND TIMING

I am always quarreling with time! It is so short to do something and so long to do nothing.

—*Queen Charlotte*

The ultimate of being successful is the luxury of giving yourself the time to do what you want to do.

—*Leontyne Price*

We must use time creatively . . . and forever realize that the time is always ripe to do right.

—*Martin Luther King, Jr.*

When a man sits with a pretty girl for an hour, it seems like a minute. But let him sit on a hot stove for a minute—and it's longer than any hour. That's relativity.

—*Albert Einstein*

Time is that wherein there is opportunity, and opportunity is that wherein there is no great time.

—*Hippocrates*

I would willingly stand at street corners, hat in hand, begging passersby to drop their unused minutes into it.

—*Bernard Berenson*

The less one has to do, the less time one finds to do it in.

—*Lord Chesterfield*

It takes a lot of time to be sentimental.

—*Don Herold*

Life is short, and the time we waste in yawning never can be gained.

—*Stendhal*

Time is the measure of business, as money is of wares.

—*Francis Bacon*

Time goes, you say? Ah no! Alas, time stays, we go.

—*Austin Dobson*

Ah! The clock is always slow; it is later than you think.

—*Robert W. Service*

Time heals what reason cannot.

—*Seneca the Younger*

Time makes more converts than reason.

—*Thomas Paine*

Time is the greatest innovator.

—*Francis Bacon*

Whoever is in a hurry shows that the thing he is about is too big for him.

—*Lord Chesterfield*

One of the great disadvantages of hurry is that it takes such a long time.

—*G. K. Chesterton*

Time is a dressmaker specializing in alterations.

—*Faith Baldwin*

What is a ruin but time easing itself of endurance?

—*Djuna Barnes*

To every thing there is a season, and a time to every purpose under heaven.

—*Ecclesiastes 3:1*

Time—the devourer of all things.   —*Ovid*

You may delay, but Time will not.   —*Benjamin Franklin*

Time: that which man is always trying to kill, but which ends in killing him.
                                                              —*Herbert Spencer*

The ripeness is all.   —*William Shakespeare*

Time wounds all heels.   —*Jane Ace*

Time is money.   —*Benjamin Franklin*

Sayings
Tempus fugit *(Time flies)*.

Time flies when you're having fun.

If you want a job done fast, give it to a busy person.

Time heals all wounds.

Joke
- A big-time negotiator was out fishing one day when he caught a strange-looking fish. He reeled the fish in, unhooked it, and threw it on the ground next to him. The fish started writhing in agony and, to the negotiator's surprise, said, "Please throw me back into the lake and I'll grant you three wishes."

  "Any three wishes, huh?" The negotiator mused as visions of expensive fast cars and equally expensive and faster women paraded through his head. "Fish," he finally exclaimed, "give me five wishes and I'll throw you back."

  "Sorry," the fish answered while struggling for breath, "only three wishes."

  The negotiator knew his pride was at stake and after giving the matter some thought announced, "What do you take me for? A sucker? I'll settle for four wishes."

  "Only three," the fish muttered weakly.

  Fuming, the man debated the pros and cons of accepting the three wishes or continuing to bargain for that one extra wish. Finally, the negotiator decided it wasn't worth looking a gift fish in the mouth and said, "All right, fish, you win, three wishes."

  Unfortunately, the fish was dead.

VICTORY

Victory at all costs, victory in spite of all terror, victory however long and hard the road may be; for without victory there is no survival.   —*Winston Churchill*

To the victor belong the toils.   —*Adlai E. Stevenson*

The only victory over love is flight.   —*Napoleon Bonaparte*

There is no substitute for victory.   —*General Douglas MacArthur*

Who overcomes by force, hath overcome but half his foe.   —*John Milton*

An honorable defeat is better than a dishonorable victory.   —*Millard Fillmore*

I glory in conflict, that I may hereafter exult in victory.   —*Frederick Douglass*

History is written by the winners.   —*Alex Haley*

Winning is better than anything. Better than sex. Better than Christmas morning.
—*Bill Parcells, after winning Super Bowl XXV*

Saying
To the victor go the spoils.

Jokes
- The general issued a rousing battlecry: "Onward to victory!" Half an hour later, an urgent message reached him: "Need further instructions. Victory not on our maps."

- Anyone can win—unless there happens to be a second entry.   —*George Ade*

A D V E R S I T Y

ADVERSITY

The great pleasure in life is doing what people say you cannot do.

—Walter Bagehot

We become wiser by adversity; prosperity destroys our appreciation of the right.

—Seneca the Younger

Have the courage to face a difficulty lest it kick you harder than you bargained for.

—Stanislaus

The man who is swimming against the stream knows the strength of it.

—Woodrow Wilson

I don't say embrace trouble. That's as bad as treating it as an enemy. But I do say meet it as a friend, for you'll see a lot of it and had better be on speaking terms with it. *—Oliver Wendell Holmes, Jr.*

Trouble is a part of your life, and if you don't share it, you don't give the person who loves you a chance to love you enough. *—Dinah Shore*

If we had no winter, the spring would not be so pleasant; if we had not sometimes taste of adversity, prosperity would not be so welcome. *—Anne Bradstreet*

You don't learn to hold your own in the world by standing on guard, but by attacking and getting well hammered yourself. *—George Bernard Shaw*

Minds, like bodies, will often fall into a pimpled, ill-conditioned state from mere excess of comfort. *—Charles Dickens*

Adversity has the same effect on a man that severe training has on the pugilist—it reduces him to his fighting weight. *—Josh Billings*

Watch a man in times of . . . adversity to discover what kind of man he is; for then at last words of truth are drawn from the depths of his heart, and the mask is torn off.

—Lucretius

Adversity has the effect of eliciting talents which, in prosperous circumstances, would have lain dormant. *—Horace*

It is not always by plugging away at a difficulty and sticking to it that one overcomes it; often it is by working on the one next to it. Some things and some people have to be approached obliquely, at an angle. *—André Gide*

Adversity is the state in which a man most easily becomes acquainted with himself, being especially free from admirers then. *—Samuel Johnson*

The world is quickly bored by the recital of misfortune and willingly avoids the sight of distress.   —W. Somerset Maugham

I believe in getting into hot water; it keeps you clean.   —G. K. Chesterton

A woman is like a teabag; you never know how strong she is until she gets in hot water.   —Nancy Reagan

Our energy is in proportion to the resistance it meets.   —William Hazlitt

The greater the difficulty, the greater the glory.   —Cicero

Each handicap is like a hurdle in a steeplechase, and when you ride up to it, if you throw your heart over, the horse will go along, too.   —Lawrence Bixby

The course of true love never did run smooth.   —William Shakespeare

Diligence overcomes difficulties; sloth makes them.   —Benjamin Franklin

Can anybody remember when the times were not hard and money not scarce?
                                                                        —Ralph Waldo Emerson

Eagles: When they walk, they stumble. They are not what one would call graceful. They were not designed to walk. They fly. And when they fly, oh, how they fly, so free, so graceful. They see from the sky what we never see. Steve, you are an eagle.
    —Dr. Thomas C. Lee, professor of surgery, Georgetown University Medical School,
        inscription given with a painting of an eagle to a paraplegic medical student

Sayings
If at first you don't succeed, welcome to the club.

Adversity makes a man wise, not rich.

Many can bear adversity but few contempt.

No man is more unhappy than the one who is never in adversity; the greatest affliction of life is never to be afflicted.

Jokes
• By trying we can easily learn to endure adversity. Another man's, I mean.
                                                                              —Mark Twain

• If anything can go wrong, it will—at the worst possible time.   —Murphy's Law

ARGUMENT

My pappy told me never to bet my bladder against a brewery or get into an argument with people who buy ink by the barrel.   —Lane Kirkland

People are generally better persuaded by the reason which they have themselves discovered than by those which have come to the minds of others.
                                                                              —Blaise Pascal

There is no such test of a man's superiority of character as in the well-conducting of an unavoidable quarrel.   —Sir Henry Taylor

No matter what side of an argument you're on, you always find some people on your side that you wish were on the other side.   —*Jascha Heifetz*

How come nobody wants to argue with me? Is it because I'm always so right?
                                                                —*Jim Bouton*

It takes in reality only one to make a quarrel. It is useless for the sheep to pass resolutions in favor of vegetarianism while the wolf remains of a different opinion.
                                                        —*Dean William R. Inge*

When people agree with me, I always feel that I must be wrong.   —*Oscar Wilde*

Never argue at the dinner table, for the one who is not hungry always gets the best of the argument.   —*Richard Whateley*

I am not arguing with you—I am telling you.   —*James McNeill Whistler*

When people are least sure, they are often most dogmatic.
                                                    —*John Kenneth Galbraith*

My sad conviction is that people can only agree about what they're not really interested in.   —*Bertrand Russell*

The best way of answering a bad argument is to let it go on.   —*Sydney Smith*

I dislike arguments of any kind. They are always vulgar, and often convincing.
                                                                —*Oscar Wilde*

The best way I know of to win an argument is to start by being right.
                                                            —*Lord Hailsham*

My idea of a disagreeable person is a person who agrees with me.
                                                        —*Benjamin Disraeli*

I respect only those who resist me, but I cannot tolerate them.
                                                        —*Charles de Gaulle*

Discussion is an exchange of knowledge; argument an exchange of ignorance.
                                                            —*Robert Quillen*

The quiet shaft of ridicule ofttimes does more than argument.
                                                    —*William Scarborough*

Saying
Never make the mistake of arguing with people for whose opinion you have no respect.

Joke
• Keep your temper. Do not quarrel with an angry person, but give him a soft answer.
  It is commanded by the Holy Writ, and furthermore, it makes your opponent madder
  than anything else you could say.

BORES AND BOREDOM

If you can't stand solitude, maybe you bore others too.   —*Bob Gordon*

I never allow myself to be bored, because boredom is ageing. If you live in the past you grow old, and dull, and dusty. It's very nice, of course, to be young and beautiful; but there are other qualities, thank God.   —*Marie Tempest*

The basic fact about human existence is not that it is a tragedy, but that it is a bore. It is not so much a war as an endless standing in line.   —*H. L. Mencken*

A bore is a fellow talking who can change the subject back to his topic of conversation faster than you can change it back to yours.   —*Laurence J. Peter*

A man who lets himself be bored is even more contemptible than the bore.

—*Samuel Butler*

The secret of being a bore is to tell everything.   —*Voltaire*

Bore: a person who talks when you wish him to listen.   —*Ambrose Bierce*

Ennui, felt on the proper occasions, is a sign of intelligence.   —*Clifton Fadiman*

Bored people, unless they sleep a lot, are cruel.   —*Renata Adler*

She has the reputation of being outspoken—by no one.   —*Jack Paar*

Somebody's boring me—I think it's me.   —*Dylan Thomas*

Boredom: the desire for desires.   —*Leo Tolstoy*

A bore is a man who, when you ask him how he is, tells you.   —*Bert Taylor*

He never spares himself in conversation. He gives himself so generously that hardly anybody else is permitted to give anything in his presence.
—*Aneurin Bevan, on Winston Churchill (attrib.)*

No one really listens to anyone else, and if you try it for a while you'll see why.
—*Mignon McLaughlin*

Sayings
Work is the easiest activity man has invented to escape boredom.

Don't tell other people your troubles. Half of them aren't interested, and the other half'll think you deserved it.

If something is boring after two minutes, try it for four. If still boring, try it for eight, sixteen, thirty-two, and so on. Eventually one discovers that it is not boring but very interesting.   —*Zen saying*

Joke
• "Now that you've made it to the top, Mike, what's the best thing about it?" asked the executive VP.

   After a thoughtful pause, the new CEO replied, "These days when I bore people, they think it's their fault, not mine."

CRIME

Murder is always a mistake—one should never do anything one cannot talk about after dinner.   —*Oscar Wilde*

People have got to know whether or not their president is a crook. Well, I'm not a crook. I earned everything I've got.   —*Richard M. Nixon*

Starvation, not sin, is the parent of modern crime.   —*Oscar Wilde*

So long as governments set the example of killing their enemies, private individuals will occasionally kill theirs.   —*Elbert Hubbard*

A crowded police court docket is the surest of all signs that trade is brisk and money plenty.   —*Mark Twain*

It is criminal to steal a purse, daring to steal a fortune, a mark of greatness to steal a crown. The blame diminishes as the guilt increases.   —*Friedrich von Schiller*

The typical mass murderer is extraordinarily ordinary.   —*James Alan Fox*

I hate this "crime doesn't pay" stuff. Crime in the United States is perhaps one of the biggest businesses in the world today.   —*Peter Kirk*

I think crime pays. The hours are good, you travel a lot.   —*Woody Allen*

Posterity, I am sure, will justify me.   —*John Wilkes Booth*

I hear much of people's calling out to punish the guilty, but very few are concerned to clear the innocent.   —*Daniel Defoe*

The greatest incitement to crime is the hope of escaping punishment.   —*Cicero*

The greater the man, the greater the crime.   —*Thomas Fuller*

All go free when many offend.   —*Lucan*

He who does not prevent a crime when he can, encourages it.

—*Seneca the Younger*

Whoso diggeth a pit shall fall therein: and he that rolleth a stone, it will return upon him.   —**Proverbs 26:27**

Murder will out.   —*Geoffrey Chaucer*

Sayings
Evil deeds are like perfume—difficult to hide.   —*West African saying*

Crime doesn't pay.

It takes a thief to catch a thief.

Give him enough rope to hang himself.

Two wrongs don't make a right.

Jokes
• Did you hear about the practical joker who sent an anonymous telegram to the town's ten leading citizens? It read: "All has been found out. Flee before dawn."
   Seven of the ten did.

• The streets just aren't safe anymore. Yesterday I asked a cop how to get to Riverside Drive and he said, "First you go up to Seventy-second Street. If you get that far . . ."

• I wonder if somewhere there's a gangster who's owned by a syndicate of singers?

CRISIS

To extraordinary circumstances we must apply extraordinary remedies.

—*Napoleon Bonaparte*

In times of calamity, any rumor is believed.   —*Publilius Syrus*

If you've broken the eggs, you should make the omelet.   —*Anthony Eden*

There cannot be a crisis next week. My schedule is already full.

—*Henry Kissinger*

We were eyeball to eyeball and the other fellow just blinked.

—*Dean Rusk, on the Cuban missile crisis*

People who don't have nightmares don't have dreams.   —*Robert Paul Smith*

Sayings
Life doesn't do anything to you, it only reveals your spirit.

A diamond is a chunk of coal that made good under pressure.

Joke
• When the fellow in line at the bank finally made it up to the window, he was seized with a terrible case of hiccups. "Hic—hic—could you—hic—please tell me—hic—hic—the bal—hic—balance in—hic—my—account?"

The teller punched a few keys on his computer terminal and looked up at the customer. "I'm afraid your account is overdrawn by $4,585, Mr. Tive."

"What!" he yelped. "You must be joking!"

"I am," the teller replied cheerfully. "But your hiccups are cured."

DECEPTION AND LIES

Everything that deceives may be said to enchant.   —*Plato*

Falsehoods not only disagree with truths, but usually quarrel among themselves.

—*Daniel Webster*

The child is sincere, and the man when he is alone, if he be not a writer; but on the entrance of the second person, hypocrisy begins.   —*Ralph Waldo Emerson*

Of lies, false modesty is the most decent.   —*Sébastien Chamfort*

Most people have seen worse things in private than they pretend to be shocked at in public.   —*Edgar Watson Howe*

Without lies humanity would perish of despair and boredom.   —*Anatole France*

A single lie destroys a whole reputation of integrity.   —*Baltasar Gracian*

Lying is an indispensable part of making life tolerable.   —*Bergen Evans*

Those who think it is permissible to tell white lies soon grow color-blind.

—Austin O'Malley

There are three kinds of lies: lies, damned lies, and statistics.

—Benjamin Disraeli (attrib.)

A lie can be halfway round the world before the truth has got its boots on.

—James Callaghan

If the Republicans will stop telling lies about the Democrats, we will stop telling the truth about them.   *—Adlai Stevenson*

I do not mind lying, but I hate inaccuracy.   *—Samuel Butler*

Any fool can tell the truth, but it requires a man of some sense to know how to lie well.   *—Samuel Butler*

Lord, lord! How subject we old men are to this vice of lying.

—William Shakespeare

When people talk to me about the weather, I always feel they mean something else.

—Oscar Wilde

Put a rogue in the limelight and he will act like an honest man.

—Napoleon Bonaparte

It's the easiest thing in the world for a man to deceive himself.

—Benjamin Franklin

O what a tangled web we weave, when first we practice to deceive!

—Sir Walter Scott

Once the toothpaste is out of the tube, it's hard to get it back in.

—H. R. Haldeman

Sayings

The greatest liar is the one who talks most of himself.

Guile excels strength.   *—West African saying*

Lies, though many, will be caught by the truth as soon as she rises up.

—West African saying

A multitude of words cloaks a lie.   *—West African saying*

Truth came to market and could not be sold; we buy lies with ready cash.

—West African saying

One falsehood spoils a thousand truths.   *—West African saying*

Better a refusal than deception.   *—West African saying*

Bitter truth is better than sweet falsehood.   *—East African saying*

Jokes

• Seized with spring fever on a glorious April day, three high school boys played hooky from their afternoon classes. The next morning they explained to the homeroom teacher that a flat tire had prevented their return from lunch.

The teacher nodded knowingly. "Well, you missed a pop quiz yesterday afternoon," she said, "but I'm going to give you a chance to make it up." Instructing each to take a seat and a sheet of paper, she began, "Here's the first question: which tire was flat?"

- It's said that Abraham Lincoln once sized up the case of a prospective client as follows: "You have a pretty good case, technically, but in terms of justice and equity, it's got problems. So you'll have to look for another lawyer to handle the case, because the whole time I was up there talking to the jury, I'd be thinking, 'Lincoln, you're a liar!' and I just might forget myself and say it out loud."

ENEMIES

Forget your opponents; always play against par.

—Sam Snead

You can't hold a man down without staying down with him.

—Booker T. Washington

All our foes are mortal.

—Paul Valéry

The space in a needle's eye is sufficient for two friends, but the whole world is scarcely big enough to hold two enemies.

—Ibn Gabirol

The opposition is indispensable. A good statesman, like any other sensible human being, always learns more from his opposition than from his fervent supporters.

—Walter Lippmann

Man's chief enemy is his own unruly nature and the dark forces pent up within him.

—Ernest Jones

The shaft of the arrow had been feathered with one of the eagles's own plumes. We often give our enemies the means of our destruction.

—Aesop

He that is not with me is against me.

—Matthew 12:30

When my enemies stop hissing, I shall know I'm slipping.

—Maria Callas

Never contend with a man who has nothing to lose.

—Baltasar Gracian

Even a paranoid has some real enemies.

—Henry A. Kissinger

I bring out the worst in my enemies and that's how I get them to defeat themselves.

—Roy Cohn

A man cannot be too careful in the choice of his enemies.

—Oscar Wilde

As the sutra says, a parasite in the lion's bowels will devour the lion. A man of great fortune cannot be ruined by his enemies, but only by those close to him.

—Nichiren Daishonin

. . . one may smile, and smile, and smile, and be a villain.

—William Shakespeare

Love your enemies, for they tell you your faults.

—Benjamin Franklin

A man with a career can have no time to waste upon his wife and friends; he has to devote it wholly to his enemies.

—John Hobbes

We have met the enemy, and he is us.   —*Walt Kelley*

Who can refute a sneer?   —*William Paley*

I never hated a man enough to give him his diamonds back.   —*Zsa Zsa Gabor*

Pay attention to your enemies, for they are the first to discover your mistakes.
                                                        —*Antisthenes*

Do de other feller, befo' he do you.   —*James David Corrothers*

I like to have a real enemy to fight. It gives me something I can get my teeth into.
                                                        —*Baroness Phillips*

Enemies to me are the *sauce piquante* to my dish of life.   —*Elsa Maxwell*

Sayings

An enemy slaughters, a friend distributes.   —*West African saying*

A powerful friend becomes a powerful enemy.   —*East African saying*

An intelligent enemy is better than an ignorant friend.   —*North African saying*

When the cat dies, the mice rejoice.   —*West African saying*

Love your enemy as you'd love your brother.

Jokes

• Love your enemy—it'll drive him nuts.

• He hasn't an enemy in the world and none of his friends like him.
                                    —*George Bernard Shaw, about Oscar Wilde*

• A man was walking down a narrow lane in Belfast, Northern Ireland, when a shadowy figure jumped out and blocked his way with a machine gun. "Don't move!" he commanded. "Are you a Protestant or a Catholic?"

  "Neither," gasped the fellow in relief. "I'm Jewish."

  The gunman hit him with a burst of bullets, and smiled broadly as he said to himself, "I must be the luckiest Arab in Ireland tonight."

FAILURE

Success is a public affair. Failure is a private funeral.   —*Rosalind Russell*

Only those who dare to fail greatly can ever achieve greatly.
                                                        —*Robert F. Kennedy*

I cannot give you the formula for success, but I can give you the formula for failure, which is—try to please everybody.   —*Herbert Bayard Swope*

Not failure, but low aim, is crime.   —*James Russell Lowell*

I would prefer even to fail with honor than win by cheating.   —*Sophocles*

The greatest failure is the failure to try.   —*William A. Ward*

It is not a disgrace to fail. Failing is one of the greatest arts in the world.

—*Charles F. Kettering*

Flops are a part of life's menu and I've never been a girl to miss out on any of the courses.   —*Rosalind Russell*

Failure is not the only punishment for laziness: there is also the success of others.

—*Jules Renard*

The only difference between a rut and a grave is their dimensions.

—*Ellen Glasgow*

Failure is the condiment that gives success its flavor.   —*Truman Capote*

There is much to be said for failure. It is much more interesting than success.

—*Max Beerbohm*

Our greatest glory is not in never falling but in rising every time we fall.

—*Confucius*

If at first you don't succeed, try, try again. Then quit. There's no use being a damn fool about it.   —*W. C. Fields*

Good people are good because they've come to wisdom through failure. We get very little wisdom from success, you know.   —*William Saroyan*

Failure has gone to his head.

—*Wilson Mizner (attrib.), on a bankrupt businessman who remained incorrigibly optimistic*

An important task of a manager is to reduce his people's excuses for failure.

—*Robert Townsend*

Never give a man up until he has failed at something he likes.   —*Lewis E. Lawes*

If at first you don't succeed, destroy all evidence that you tried.

—*Newt Heilscher*

I was fired from my first three jobs, which in a funny way gave me the courage to go into business for myself.   —*Alfred C. Fuller*

When Winston Churchill was defeated in his bid for reelection as prime minister, his wife consoled him with the thought that the defeat was a blessing in disguise. "If so," responded Churchill, "then it is very effectively disguised."

Saying
A man can fail many times, but he isn't a failure till he gives up.

Jokes
- He's never been very successful. When opportunity knocks, he complains about the noise.

- If at first you don't succeed—welcome to the club!

- My friends all told me I'd never be anything but a failure at this business, so I decided to do something about it—I went out and made some new friends.

FAULTS

If you wish to be loved, show more of your faults than your virtues.
—*Edward Bulwer-Lytton*

It is well that there is no one without a fault; for he would not have a friend in the world.
—*William Hazlitt*

Our shortcomings are the eyes with which we see the ideal.
—*Friedrich Wilhelm Nietzsche*

When you have faults, do not fear to abandon them.   —*Confucius*

The greatest of faults, I should say, is to be conscious of none.
—*Thomas Carlyle*

People who have no faults are terrible; there is no way of taking advantage of them.
—*Anatole France*

Sayings

Deal with the faults of others as gently as with your own.   —*Chinese proverb*

The first faults are theirs that commit them, the second theirs that permit them.

Faults are thick where love is thin.

Jokes

• The way my wife finds fault with me, you'd think there was a reward.
—*Jack Lemmon*

• A nervous waiter noticed that two of his customers seated off in a corner were looking very displeased. Anticipating the worst, he went over and asked anxiously, "Was anything all right?"

• Failures have only two faults; what they say and what they do.

HUNGER

Hungry men have no respect for law, authority, or human life.   —*Marcus Garvey*

Starvation, not sin, is the parent of modern crime.   —*Oscar Wilde*

You cannot feed the hungry on statistics.   —*David Lloyd George*

A hungry man is not a free man.   —*Adlai Stevenson*

A hungry people listens not to reason, nor cares for justice, nor is bent by any prayers.
—*Seneca the Younger*

No man can worship God or love his neighbor on an empty stomach.
—*Woodrow Wilson*

Sayings

Thirst cannot be quenched by proxy.   —*Central African saying*

Hunger causes the wolves to sally from the wood.

Hunger knows no laws.

Joke
• Mrs. Rossdale was on her way to meet a friend when a bum came up to her with his hand out. "Lady, can you help me? I haven't eaten in three days."
  "So force yourself," she snapped, and walked on.

LOSING

'Tis better to have fought and lost, than never to have fought at all.
—Arthur Clough

Defeat should never be a source of discouragement but rather a fresh stimulus.
—Robert South

Fear of losing is what makes competitors so great. Show me a gracious loser and I'll show you a perennial loser. —<i>O. J. Simpson</i>

Losing is the great American sin. —<i>John Tunis</i>

Losers spend time explaining why they lost. Losers spend their lives thinking about what they're going to do. They rarely enjoy doing what they're doing.
—Eric Berne

An honorable defeat is better than a dishonorable victory. —<i>Millard Fillmore</i>

Man is not made for defeat. —<i>Heraclitus</i>

Sayings
Losers are always in the wrong.

Finders keepers, losers weepers.

Jokes
• Define loser:
  —A lightning rod salesman who gets caught outside in a storm with a handful of samples.

• How frequently does it happen that the person who remarks, "That's the way the ball bounces" is the one who dropped the ball?

MISTAKES

The greatest mistake you can make in life is to be continually fearing you will make one. —<i>Elbert Hubbard</i>

If I wasn't making mistakes, I wasn't making decisions.
—Robert W. Johnson (founder of Johnson & Johnson)

The first undertakers in all great attempts commonly miscarry, and leave the
advantages of their losses to those that come after them.   —Samuel Butler

Murder is always a mistake—one should never do anything one cannot talk about after
dinner.   —Oscar Wilde

To err is human, to forgive, divine.   —Alexander Pope

I never made a mistake in my life, at least, never one that I couldn't explain away
afterward.   —Rudyard Kipling

Don't ever take a fence down until you know why it was put up.   —Robert Frost

No one is more liable to make mistakes than the man who acts only on reflection.
                                                —Luc de Clapiers de Vauvenargues

It is the true nature of mankind to learn from mistakes, not from example.
                                                                    —Fred Hoyle

If you shut your door to all errors, truth will be shut out.   —Rabindranath Tagore

The fatal tendency of mankind to leave off thinking about a thing when no longer
doubtful is the cause of half their errors.   —John Stuart Mill

Nowadays most people die of a sort of creeping common sense, and discover when it is
too late that the only things one never regrets are one's mistakes.
                                                                    —Oscar Wilde

If only one could have two lives: the first in which to make one's mistakes, which seem
as if they have to be made; and the second in which to profit by them.
                                                                    —D. H. Lawrence

The man who makes no mistakes does not usually make anything.
                                                                —Edward John Phelps

If we had no faults, we would not take so much pleasure in noticing them in others.
                                                —François de La Rochefoucauld

When the defects of others are perceived with so much clarity, it is because one
possesses them oneself.   —Jules Renard

Xerox: a trademark for a photocopying device that can make rapid reproductions of
human error, perfectly.   —Merle L. Meacham

When you make a mistake, admit it. If you don't, you only make matters worse.
                                                                  —Ward Cleaver

I don't want to make the wrong mistake.   —Yogi Berra

Sayings
Stumbling is not falling.   —Portuguese proverb

It doesn't matter how much milk you spill so long as you don't lose the cow.

Jokes
• To err is human, but to really screw up requires a computer.

• Sign above bank teller's station: TO ERR IS HUMAN; TO FORGIVE IS NOT BANK POLICY.

- A company we know is encountering so many errors it's thinking of buying a computer to blame them on.

- I'm so smart, I never make the same mistake once!

OBSTACLES AND PROBLEMS

If the only tool you have is a hammer, you tend to see every problem as a nail.
—*Abraham Maslow*

A problem is a chance for you to do your best.   —*Duke Ellington*

Some problems are just too complicated for rational, logical solutions. They admit of insights, not answers.   —*Jerome Wiesner*

It is not always by plugging away at a difficulty and sticking to it that one overcomes it; often it is by working on the one next to it. Some things and some people have to be approached obliquely, at an angle.   —*André Gide*

It is a riddle wrapped in a mystery inside an enigma.
     —*Winston Churchill, describing the difficulties of forecasting the future of Russia*

Problems are only opportunities in work clothes.   —*Henry J. Kaiser*

Don't fix the blame, fix the problem.   —*Keith S. Pennington*

If you are able to state a problem, then the problem can be solved.
     —*Edwin Land, inventor of the instant camera*

No problem is too big to run away from.   —*Charles M. Schulz*

It is only because of problems that we grow mentally and spiritually.
—*M. Scott Peck*

I have yet to see any problem, however complicated, which, when you looked at it in the right way, did not become still more complicated.   —*Poul Anderson*

Of my two "handicaps," being female put many more obstacles in my path than being black.   —*Shirley Chisholm*

Nothing is particularly hard if you divide it into small jobs.   —*Ray Kroc*

The greatest pleasure in life is doing what people say you cannot do.
—*Walter Bagehot*

Sayings
The problem when solved will be simple.
     —*Sign on the wall of a General Motors research laboratory*

An obstacle is something you see when you take your eyes off the goal.

Do not look where you fell, but where you slipped.   —*West African saying*

Joke
- The shopkeeper was dismayed when a brand-new business much like his own opened up in the storefront to the left of him, and erected a huge sign which read BEST DEALS.

He was thunderstruck when another competitive enterprise opened up on his right, and announced its arrival with an even larger sign, reading LOWEST PRICES. The shopkeeper was panicked, until he got an idea. He put the biggest sign of all over his own shop—it read MAIN ENTRANCE.

OPPRESSION

Big Brother is watching you.   —*George Orwell*

Men are not prisoners of fate, but only prisoners of their own minds.
                                                          —*Franklin D. Roosevelt*

Disobedience: the silver lining to the cloud of servitude.   —*Ambrose Bierce*

Oppressed people are frequently very oppressive when first liberated. And why wouldn't they be? They know best two positions: somebody's foot on their neck or their foot on somebody's neck.   —*Florynce Kennedy*

But I am pigeon-liver'd and lack gall to make oppression bitter.
                                                          —*William Shakespeare*

Saying
The tyrant is only the slave turned inside out.   —*North African saying*

Jokes
• "You may as well be happy here," the drill sergeant informed his miserable, exhausted squad after their first day of boot camp, "because no one gives a damn if you aren't."

• The slave driver of the Roman galleon leered down at his galley slaves and bellowed, "I've got some good news and some bad news. The good news is that you'll be getting double rations tonight."
   The murmuring of the surprised slaves was interrupted by the bellow of the slave driver. "The bad news is that the admiral's son wants to water-ski."

POVERTY

Wars of nations are fought to change maps. But wars on poverty are fought to map change.   —*Muhammad Ali*

[Poverty is] a hellish state to be in. It is no virtue. It is a crime.
                                                          —*Marcus Garvey*

People who are homeless are not social inadequates. They are people without homes.
                                                          —*Sheila McKechnie*

I've been rich and I've been poor; rich is better.   —*Sophie Tucker*

Poverty of goods is easily cured; poverty of the mind is irreparable.
                                                    —*Michel Eyquem de Montaigne*

Whoso mocketh the poor reproacheth his Maker.   —*Proverbs 17:5*

We were poor when I was young, but the difference then was that the government didn't come around telling you you were poor.

—*Ronald Reagan*

Thousands upon thousands are yearly brought into a state of real poverty by their great anxiety not to be thought poor.

—*William Cobbett*

Poverty is the open-mouthed, relentless hell which yawns beneath civilized society.

—*Henry George*

A decent provision for the poor is the true test of civilization.

—*Samuel Johnson*

If a free society cannot help the many who are poor, it cannot save the few who are rich.

—*John F. Kennedy*

Poverty has many roots, but the tap root is ignorance.

—*Lyndon B. Johnson*

For ye have the poor always with you. . . .

—*Matthew 26:11*

Remember the poor—it costs nothing.

—*Josh Billings*

Poverty is no disgrace to a man, but it is confoundedly inconvenient.

—*Sydney Smith*

The rich get richer and the poor get poorer.

—*Raymond B. Egan*

The trouble with being poor is that it takes up all your time.

—*Willem de Kooning*

Poverty is no sin!

—*George Herbert*

I used to think I was poor. Then they told me I wasn't poor, I was needy. Then they told me it was self-defeating to think of myself as needy. I was deprived. Then they told me that underprivileged was overused. I was disadvantaged. I still don't have a dime. But I have a great vocabulary.

—*Jules Feiffer*

Sayings

Poverty makes a free man become a slave.

—*West African saying*

Borrowing is the first-born of poverty.

—*West African saying*

Poverty is "Who knows you?" Prosperity is "I am your relative."

—*West African saying*

Work is the medicine for poverty.

—*West African saying*

Poverty without debt is real wealth.

—*North African saying*

There's none so poor as he who knows not the joy of what he has.

The rich get richer and the poor get children.

It's just as easy to love a rich man or woman as a poor one.

Poverty sucks.

Joke

- The impoverished child of a hopelessly poor family was asked by a social worker how he had managed to survive in such abject poverty for so long. "Keep in mind," said the pauper with a wry smile, "I had a head start."

RISK

The safest way to double your money is to fold it over once and put it in your pocket.
—Kin Hubbard

Women do not like timid men. Cats do not like prudent mice.   *—H. L. Mencken*

Venus favors the bold.   *—Ovid*

The Wright brothers' design allowed them to survive long enough to learn how to fly.
—Michael Potts

Nothing will ever be attempted, if all possible objections must be first overcome.
—Samuel Johnson

Only those who dare to fail greatly can ever achieve greatly.
—Robert F. Kennedy

Results are often obtained by impetuosity and daring which could never have been obtained by ordinary methods.   *—Niccolò Machiavelli*

Don't be afraid to go out on a limb. That's where the fruit is.
—Arthur F. Lenehan

Sayings
Nothing ventured, nothing gained.

No guts, no glory.

Joke
• Hear about the girlfriend who loved to have sex, but refused to take birth control pills? Her boyfriend charged her with practicing license without a medicine.

THE HUMAN CONDITION

ATTITUDE

If you think you can, you can. And if you think you can't, you're right.

—*Mary Kay Ash*

Nothing is so commonplace as to wish to be remarkable.

—*Oliver Wendell Holmes*

Enjoy your ice cream while it's on your plate—that's my philosophy.

—*Thornton Wilder*

Humans can learn to like anything, that's why we are such a successful species.

—*Jeannette Desor*

The enemy is in front of us, behind us, to the left of us, and to the right of us. They can't escape us this time!   —*Marine Lieutenant Lewis B. (Chesty) Puller*

Funny is an attitude.

—*Flip Wilson*

Character is the result of two things—mental attitude and the way we spend our time.

—*Elbert Hubbard*

A much more effective and lasting method of face-lifting than surgical technique is happy thinking, new interests, and outdoor exercise.   —*Dr. Sara Murray Jordan*

Because I remember, I despair. Because I remember, I have the duty to reject despair.

—*Elie Wiesel*

I always cheer up immensely if an attack is particularly wounding because I think, well, if they attack one personally, it means they have not a single political argument left.

—*Margaret Thatcher*

The Wright brothers flew right through the smoke screen of impossibility.

—*Charles F. Kettering*

He that despises small things shall fall by little and little.   —*Ecclesiasticus 19:1*

He that is of a merry heart hath a continual feast.   —*Proverbs 15:15*

Be cheerful while you are alive.   —*Ptahhotep (c. 2350 B.C.)*

A bad attitude is the worst thing that can happen to a group of people. It's infectious.

—*Roger Allan Raby*

[Today's students] can put dope in their veins or hope in their brains. . . . If they can conceive it and believe it, they can achieve it. They must know it is not their aptitude but their attitude that will determine their altitude.   —*Jesse Jackson*

Change has considerable psychological impact on the human mind. To the fearful it is threatening because it means that things may get worse. To the hopeful it is encouraging because things may get better. To the confident it is inspiring because the challenge exists to make things better. Obviously, then, one's character and frame of mind determine how readily he brings about change and how he reacts to change that is imposed on him.
—*King Whitney, Jr.*

A man's happiness or unhappiness depends as much on his temperament as on his destiny.
—*François de La Rochefoucauld*

He who has confidence in himself will lead the rest.
—*Horace*

Until you know that life is interesting—and find it so—you haven't found your soul.
—*Archbishop Geoffrey Fisher*

If you think you're a second-class citizen, you are.
—*Ted Turner*

Some people are always grumbling because roses have thorns; I am thankful that thorns have roses.
—*Alphonse Karr*

Nobody holds a good opinion of a man who has a low opinion of himself.
—*Anthony Trollope*

A man's worth is no greater than the worth of his ambitions.
—*Marcus Aurelius Antoninus*

Of course there is no formula for success except, perhaps, an unconditional acceptance of life and what it brings.
—*Arthur Rubinstein*

Ah, but a man's reach should exceed his grasp, or what's a heaven for?
—*Robert Browning*

When you reach for the stars, you may not quite get them, but you won't come up with a handful of mud either.
—*Leo Burnett*

Not a shred of evidence occurs in favor of the idea that life is serious.
—*Brendan Gill*

I'm not happy, I'm cheerful. There's a difference. A happy woman has no cares at all. A cheerful woman has cares but has learned how to deal with them.
—*Beverly Sills*

Men are not prisoners of fate, but only prisoners of their own minds.
—*Franklin D. Roosevelt*

Sometimes you just gotta say "what the fuck."
—*The movie* **Risky Business**

One's existence should be in two parts: one should live like a bourgeois and think like a demigod.
—*Gustave Flaubert*

Sayings
The wise don't expect to find life worth living; they make it that way.

It takes seventeen muscles to smile and forty-three to frown.

The difficult we do immediately; the impossible takes a little longer.
—*Slogan of the United States Army Service Forces*

Jokes

- Two shoe salespeople were dispatched to a remote African country. In just a few days, their employer received telegrams from each. One read: "Get me out of here—no one here wears shoes." The other read: "Send more inventory—no one here owns shoes."

- "Now tell me, Miss Gundell," asked the senior partner of the very junior employee, "what is the main purpose of a holiday?"

  "To impress upon the employees that the company can get along without them," she responded promptly.

- The wedding night found Dan and Lorraine in a posh suite at the Hyatt, a bottle of champagne by the bed. Pulling a sexy negligee out of her suitcase, Lorraine was startled when Dan tossed her a pair of his pants and told her to put them on.

  They fell down in a pool around her ankles. "Honey, I can't wear your pants," she protested.

  "Damn straight, and don't you forget it," ordered the new husband. "I'm the man and I wear the pants in this family."

  Lorraine slipped out of her panties and tossed them to Dan. "Put these on, darling," she asked sweetly.

  Of course Dan couldn't pull the little scrap of lace past his knees. "I can't get into your pants," he complained.

  "That's right," she snapped. "And it's going to stay that way until you change your damn attitude!"

- What's the difference between a stumbling block and a stepping stone?

  —The way you approach it.

- The ninety-three-year-old woman astonished everyone who knew her with her unflagging optimism and good cheer. When pressed for her secret, she replied that her positive attitude was due to her enthusiasm for life. "And furthermore," she continued, "even at my age I still have four boyfriends I spend part of every single day with. I get out of bed each day with Will Power, and after breakfast I go for a stroll with Arthur Ritis. Charley Horse almost always visits me in the afternoon, and I spend the evening with Ben Gay. Need I say more?"

- A little boy had one of those days in which everything seemed to go wrong and he seemed to annoy his parents at every turn. Finally his father yelled at him and his mother ordered him to sit on the chair in the corner. The little boy stomped off to the chair, but after a minute or so he turned around and announced, "Mommy, I may be sitting down on the outside, but I'm standing up on the inside."

BELIEF

Beware of the community in which blasphemy does not exist: underneath, atheism runs rampant.
                                        —*Joaquim Maria Machado de Assis*

Conversion for me was not a Damascus Road experience. I slowly moved into an intellectual acceptance of what my intuition had always known.

                                        —*Madeleine L'Engle*

Man is what he believes.

                                        —*Anton Chekhov*

We have to believe in free will. We've got no choice.   —*Isaac Bashevis Singer*

All I have seen teaches me to trust the creator for all I have not seen.
                                                                    —*Ralph Waldo Emerson*

We are inclined to believe those whom we do not know because they have never
deceived us.   —*Samuel Johnson*

Convictions are more dangerous enemies of truth than lies.
                                                          —*Friedrich Wilhelm Nietzsche*

I'd rather be strongly wrong than weakly right.   —*Tallulah Bankhead*

A belief is not merely an idea the mind possesses; it is an idea that possesses the
mind.   —*Robert Bolton*

Whether you are really right or not doesn't matter; it's the belief that counts.
                                                                    —*Robertson Davies*

If God be for us, who can be against us?   —*Romans 8:31*

I know that my redeemer liveth, and that he shall stand at the latter day upon the
earth: and though after my skin worms destroy this body, yet in my flesh shall I see
God.   —*Job 19:25–26*

. . . when the gods wish to punish us, they answer our prayers.   —*Oscar Wilde*

Surely the Lord is in this place; and I knew it not.   —*Genesis 28:16*

I would not say I believe. I know! I have had the experience of being gripped by
something that is stronger than myself, something that people call God.
                                                                    —*Carl Jung*

I would believe only in a God that knows how to dance.
                                                          —*Friedrich Wilhelm Nietzsche*

They conquer who believe they can.   —*John Dryden*

I am proud of the revolutionary beliefs for which our forebears fought . . . the belief
that the rights of man come not from the generosity of the state but the hands of God.
                                                                    —*John F. Kennedy*

Reading made Don Quixote a gentleman, but believing what he read made him mad.
                                                                    —*George Bernard Shaw*

The only completely consistent people are the dead.   —*Aldous Huxley*

Mix a conviction with a man and something happens.
                                                          —*Adam Clayton Powell, Jr.*

Any man's a coward who won't die for what he believes.   —*Chester Bomar Himes*

"I can't believe that!" said Alice.
    "Can't you?" the queen said in a pitying tone. "Try again, draw a long breath, and
shut your eyes."
    Alice laughed. "There's no use trying," she said. "One can't believe impossible
things."
    "I daresay you haven't had much practice," said the queen. "When I was your age, I

always did it for half an hour a day. Why, sometimes I've believed as many as six impossible things before breakfast."

—*Lewis Carroll*

Saying

I sought my soul, but my soul I could not see. I sought my God, but my God eluded me. I sought my brother—and I found all three.

—*Quoted by the London Church News Service*

Jokes

• The preacher surveyed his flock gathered on the riverbank for full-immersion baptism. "Do you *believe*?" he howled, grasping the nearest convert by the collar and thrusting him beneath the muddy waters.

"I believe," gasped the fellow. Down he went again. "I *believe*," he cried, more fervently. Coming up for the third time, choking and red-faced, he yelled, "I DO BELIEVE!" Then added, "I believe that y'all are trying to drown me."

• Old Mrs. Watkins awoke one spring morning to find that the river had flooded not only her basement but the whole first floor of her house. And, looking out her bedroom window, she saw that the water was still rising. Two men passing by in a rowboat shouted up an invitation to row to safety with them.

"No, thank you," replied Mrs. Watkins tartly. "The Lord will provide." The men shrugged and rowed on.

By evening the water level forced Mrs. Watkins to climb out onto her roof, where she was spotted by a cheerful man in a motorboat. "Don't worry, lady," he called across the water. "I'll pick you right up."

"Please don't trouble yourself—the Lord will provide." Mrs. Watkins turned her back on her would-be rescuer, who buzzed off downriver.

Pretty soon Mrs. Watkins was forced to take refuge atop her chimney, the only part of the house still above water. Fortunately a Red Cross cutter came by on patrol. "Jump in, ma'am," urged a rescue worker.

Mrs. Watkins shook her head vehemently. "The Lord will provide." So the boat departed, the water rose, and the old woman drowned. Dripping wet and thoroughly annoyed, she came through the Pearly Gates and demanded to talk to God. "What happened?" she demanded. "I thought the Lord would *provide*."

"For cryin' out loud, lady," said God wearily, "I sent *three* boats."

BIRTH CONTROL AND ABORTION

Parents may feel the need to have many babies to be sure that a few survive.

—*World Bank, on high infant mortality rate in developing countries*

We deal with a right of privacy older than the Bill of Rights—older than our political parties, older than our school system.

—*William O. Douglas, on a woman's right to a legal abortion*

No woman can call herself free who does not own and control her own body.

—*Margaret Sanger*

You must strive to multiply bread so that it suffices for the tables of mankind, and not rather favor an artificial control of birth, which would be irrational, in order to diminish the number of guests at the banquet of life. — *Pope Paul VI*

Do you think someone who is about to rape you is going to stop and think about a condom? — *Eli Adorno*

The best contraception is the word *no*—repeated frequently.

— *Margaret Chase Smith*

The Catholic wife is under great pressure. . . . If she uses contraceptives, she is called wicked by her parish priest. If she follows the advice of her parish priest and refrains from sexual intercourse, she is called cold by her husband. If she doesn't take steps, she is called mad by society at large. — *Anne Biezanek*

The routine promotion of condoms through advertising has been stopped by networks who are so hypocritically priggish that they refuse to describe disease control as they promote disease transmission. — *Henry A. Waxman*

. . . there is no nonarbitrary line separating a fetus from a child or, indeed, an adult human being. — *Byron R. White*

I've noticed that everyone that is for abortion has already been born.

— *Ronald Reagan*

The states are not free, under the guise of protecting maternal health or potential life, to intimidate women into continuing pregnancies. . . . Abortion raises moral and spiritual questions over which honorable persons can disagree sincerely and profoundly. But those disagreements did not then and do not now relieve us of our duty to apply the Constitution faithfully. — *Harry A. Blackmun*

A father's interest in having a child—perhaps his only child—may be unmatched by any other interest in his life. It is truly surprising that the state must assign a greater value to a mother's decision to cut off a potential human life by abortion than to a father's decision to let it mature into a live child. — *William H. Rehnquist*

I realize that the subject of abortion is deeply divisive, with reaction felt more in the emotions than in the mind. For this reason, dispassionate factual discussions are more beneficial than the tossing about of violent slogans. I also realize that legalized abortion is far from the ideal solution to unwanted conception. Yet a lifetime of work in the field has convinced me that liberalized abortion is an absolutely essential tool to ease the lot of many women and families in a tough, tough world. — *Alan Guttmacher*

[There is an old Puerto Rican saying] that men must do three things during life: plant trees, write books, and have sons. I wish they would plant more trees and write more books. — *Luis Muñoz Marín*

Whenever I hear people discussing birth control, I always remember that I was the fifth. — *Clarence S. Darrow*

A society which practices death control must at the same time practice birth control.

— *John Rock*

One of the best things people could do for their descendants would be to sharply limit the number of them. — *Olin Miller*

Safe and effective contraception is essential in man's battle to control his environment.

—*Elizabeth Connell*

Once you pass into the utilitarianism of abortion, where do you go? Why do you kill an unborn child after six months and not old people or not criminals or not just every second person in the world?   —*Victor Heylen*

If my parents had been exposed to today's ideas of family planning, my brothers Win and David might not have made it.   —*John D. Rockefeller III*

Well, as you know, there are many things in life that are not fair, that wealthy people can afford and poor people can't. But I don't believe that the federal government should take action to try to make these opportunities exactly equal, particularly when there is a moral factor involved.

—*Jimmy Carter, on the availability of abortions*

If men could get pregnant, abortion would be a sacrament.

—*Gloria Steinem (attrib.)*

Sayings
The surest form of birth control is often a good argument.

I wouldn't give you a nickel for another child, but I wouldn't take a million for the ones I've got.

Jokes
• The phrase itself—birth control—doesn't make sense. It's nine months earlier that you need the control.

• Loop before you leap.   —*Family-planning slogan*

• The best form of contraception is a pill—held firmly between the knees.

CHANGE

Consistency is the quality of a stagnant mind.   —*John Sloan*

Progress is a nice word. But change is its motivator and change has its enemies.

—*Robert F. Kennedy*

The only completely consistent people are the dead.   —*Aldous Huxley*

There is danger in reckless change, but greater danger in blind conservatism.

—*Henry Glasgow*

Each generation criticizes the unconscious assumptions made by its parents. It may assent to them, but it brings them out into the open.

—*Alfred North Whitehead*

Love is more afraid of change than of destruction.

—*Friedrich Wilhelm Nietzsche*

. . . it behooves us to adapt oneself to the times if one wants to enjoy continued good fortune.   —*Niccolò Machiavelli*

Force is the midwife of every old society pregnant with a new one.

—*Karl Marx*

Wise and prudent men—intelligent conservatives—have long known that in a changing world worthy institutions can be conserved only by adjusting them to the changing time.   —*Franklin D. Roosevelt*

Weep not that the world changes—did it keep a stable, changeless state, it were cause indeed to weep.   —*William Cullen Bryant*

Change is constant in a progressive country.   —*Benjamin Disraeli*

Change is not progress.   —*H. L. Mencken*

Future shock [is] the shattering stress and disorientation that we induce in individuals by subjecting them to too much change in too short a time.   —*Alvin Toffler*

Nothing endures but change.   —*Heraclitus*

Change has considerable psychological impact on the human mind. To the fearful it is threatening because it means that things may get worse. To the hopeful it is encouraging because things may get better. To the confident it is inspiring because the challenge exists to make things better. Obviously, then, one's character and frame of mind determine how readily he brings about change and how he reacts to change that is imposed on him.   —*King Whitney, Jr.*

The oldest habit in the world for resisting change is to complain that unless the remedy to the disease should be universally applied it should not be applied at all. But you must start somewhere.   —*Winston Churchill*

The reason men oppose progress is not that they hate progress, but that they love inertia.   —*Elbert Hubbard*

The human tendency prefers familiar horrors to unknown delights.

—*Fred Woodworth*

You must change in order to survive.   —*Pearl Bailey*

Saying
If you wait for tomorrow, tomorrow comes. If you don't wait for tomorrow, tomorrow comes.

—*West African saying*

Jokes
- It's hard for me to get used to these changing times. I can remember when the air was clean and sex was dirty.   —*George Burns*

- The story of little Mary illustrates one way in which change brings growth. One day in Sunday school she was asked, "Who made you?"
    After a moment's reflection, the little girl replied, "well, God made a part of me."
    "*Part* of you?" The teacher was startled.
    "God made me very little," she explained, "and I grew the rest myself."

COMMITMENT

Committing yourself is a way of finding out who you are. A man finds his identity by identifying.
                                                                    —*Robert Terwilliger*

Passion is the quickest to develop, and the quickest to fade. Intimacy develops more slowly, and commitment more gradually still.
                                                                    —*Robert J. Sternberg*

The fear of making permanent commitments can change the mutual love of husband and wife into two loves of self—two loves existing side by side, until they end in separation.
                                                                    —*Pope John Paul II*

Never doubt that a small group of thoughtful, committed citizens can change the world. Indeed, it's the only thing that ever has.
                                                                    —*Margaret Mead*

In his later years, Winston Churchill was asked to give the commencement address at Oxford University. Following his introduction, he rose, went to the podium, and said, "Never, never, never give up." Then he took his seat.

He who is most slow in making a promise is the most faithful in performance of it.
                                                                    —*Jean-Jacques Rousseau*

I can't imagine a person becoming a success who doesn't give this game of life everything he's got.
                                                                    —*Walter Cronkite*

Whatever I have tried to do in life, I have tried with all my heart to do it well; whatever I have devoted myself to, I have devoted myself to completely.
                                                                    —*Charles Dickens*

Commitment unlocks the doors of imagination, allows vision, and gives us the "right stuff" to turn our dreams into reality.
                                                                    —*James Womack*

There's only one way to succeed in anything, and that is to give it everything. I do, and I demand that my players do.
                                                                    —*Vince Lombardi*

Sayings
Don't dig a foundation where you don't plan to build a house.

You can't keep a committed person from succeeding.

If you don't stand for something, you'll fall for anything.

Jokes
• Apathy is one of America's greatest problems—but who cares?

• Sometimes we think we're committed but we aren't. The chicken and the pig were discussing the matter through the barnyard fence. The chicken said proudly, "I give eggs every single morning—I'm committed."

  "Giving eggs isn't commitment, it's participation," countered the pig. "Giving *ham* is commitment!"

COMMON SENSE

Everybody gets so much information all day long that they lose their common sense.
                                                                    —*Gertrude Stein*

The time to repair the roof is when the sun is shining.   —*John F. Kennedy*

Logical consequences are the scarecrows of fools and the beacons of wise men.
—*Thomas Henry Huxley*

The only way of finding the limits of the possible is by going beyond them into the impossible.   —*Arthur C. Clarke*

Kind words will never die—neither will they buy groceries.   —*Bill Nye*

Castles in the air cost a vast deal to keep up.   —*Edward Bulwer-Lytton*

A radical is a man with both feet firmly planted in the air.
—*Franklin D. Roosevelt*

The whole of science is nothing more than a refinement of everyday thinking.
—*Albert Einstein*

It is best not to swap horses while crossing the river.   —*Abraham Lincoln*

Common sense is genius dressed in its working clothes.
—*Ralph Waldo Emerson*

Horse sense is what keeps horses from betting on what people will do.
—*Raymond Nash*

Sayings

One pound of common sense requires ten pounds of common sense to apply it.
—*Persian proverb*

No one tests the depth of the river with both his feet.   —*West African saying*

Jokes

• The kindergarten class went on a field trip to the local precinct house, where a kindly patrolman showed them about. Stopping in front of a "Ten Most Wanted" poster, he explained how citizens often help bring about arrests.

"Are those pictures of the bad guys?" asked one six-year-old.

The policeman soberly informed him they were.

"Well," pursued the kid, "why didn't you hold on to him after you took his picture?"

• Struthers was assigned to show an important stockholder around the rubber goods factory. The woman nodded approvingly when shown the giant machine which spit out an endless stream of rubber nipples. "One of our steady sellers; lotsa babies being born these days," Struthers explained.

Not much later the stockholder inquired as to the function of another huge machine spitting out little rubber disks. "Condoms," Struthers informed her. "Big sellers too."

"Understandably," she commented. "But why's that needle coming down and punching a little hole in each one?"

"Hey," he whispered conspiratorially, "we can't let the nipple business go downhill, now can we?"

COMPETITION

Don't look back. Someone might be gaining on you.

—*Leroy (Satchel) Paige*

I don't meet competition. I crush it.

—*Charles Revson*

Don't overlook the importance of worldwide thinking. A company that keeps its eye on Tom, Dick, and Harry is going to miss Pierre, Hans, and Yoshio.

—*Al Ries*

Like getting into a bleeding competition with a blood bank.

—*Richard Branson, chairman, Virgin Airlines, on competing with British Airways*

When two men in business always agree, one of them is unnecessary.

—*William Wrigley, Jr.*

"Know thyself" is a good saying, but not in all situations. In many it is better to say "Know others."

—*Menander*

Trust everybody, but cut the cards.

—*Finley Peter Dunne*

Put your trust in God; but be sure to keep your powder dry.

—*Oliver Cromwell*

Don't fight a battle if you don't gain anything by winning.

—*General George S. Patton, Jr.*

A verbal agreement isn't worth the paper it's written on.

—*Louis B. Mayer (attrib.)*

Forget your opponents; always play against par.

—*Sam Snead*

A man surprised is half beaten.

—*Thomas Fuller*

Whenever a friend succeeds, a little something in me dies.

—*Gore Vidal*

As he was valiant, I honor him; but as he was ambitious, I slew him.

—*William Shakespeare*

All our foes are mortal.

—*Paul Valéry*

The shaft of the arrow had been feathered with one of the eagles's own plumes. We often give our enemies the means of our destruction.

—*Aesop*

There are only two ways of getting on in the world: by one's own industry, or by the weaknesses of others.

—*Jean de La Bruyère*

Next to knowing when to seize an opportunity, the most important thing in life is to know when to forego an advantage.

—*Benjamin Disraeli*

There is hardly anything in the world that some man cannot make a little worse and sell a little cheaper.

—*John Ruskin*

We can't all be lions in this world. There must be some lambs, harmless, kindly, gregarious creatures for eating and shearing.

—*William Makepeace Thackeray*

We must believe in luck. For how else can we explain the success of those we don't like?

—*Jean Cocteau*

While one person hesitates because he feels inferior, the other is busy making mistakes and becoming superior.   *—Henry C. Link*

The world is divided into people who do things and people who get the credit. Try, if you can, to belong to the first class. There's far less competition.

—Dwight Morrow

Making money resembles chess in [many] ways, not least its cozy relationship with mathematics, still more in its abundance of traps, ploys, gambits, stratagems, variations, even in its recognized offensive and defensive openings. As in chess, the moneymaker gains more through his opponent's mistakes than through his own immaculate brilliance, and for every winner, there must be at least one loser.

—Robert Heller

Sayings

A diamond is a chunk of coal that made good under pressure.

When two men of equal wisdom play together, discord arises.

—West African saying

The one in front has reached there, the one behind only hears about it.

—West African saying

Rivalry is better than envy.   *—Central African saying*

The successful salesman sells his goods on their merit—not by knocking his competitors.

Jokes

• Anyone can win—unless there happens to be a second entry.

—George Ade

• Hard up for cash, Tarzan decided to go into the used-crocodile business. He spent the next day haggling over cranky crocs with nasty beasts, and barely had the energy to swing back to the treehouse. "Make me a martini, would you, Jane?" he asked. He gulped it down, then asked for another, and then a third.
    "Tarzan, honey, aren't you overdoing it a bit?" she remonstrated.
    "Jane, you don't understand," he retorted. "It's a *jungle* out there."

• The two ex-partners maintained an intensively competitive relationship, so the first person Alice called from the brand-new cellular phone in her Maserati was Walter. She was well into a speech about the virtues of the new gizmo when Walter interrupted. "Hang on a sec, would you, Alice? I'm in the Bentley, and the other phone is ringing."

• Two guys are being chased by a bear. One stops to put on his sneakers. The other guy yells back, "You idiot, you can't outrun a bear."
    The first guy gasps, "I don't have to outrun a bear—I just have to outrun you."

CONSISTENCY

Look, I don't even agree with *myself* at times.
*—Jeane Kirkpatrick, on changing her party affiliation
to register as a Republican*

Don't be "consistent," but be simply true.   *—Oliver Wendell Holmes, Jr.*

A consistent thinker is a thoughtless person, because he conforms to a pattern; he repeats phrases and thinks in a groove.   *—Jiddu Krishnamurti*

Consistency is the last refuge of the unimaginative.   *—Oscar Wilde*

An acquaintance seated next to R. J. Wrigley on a flight to Chicago asked the multimillionaire why he continued to advertise his chewing gum when it was far and away the most successful product in its field.

Wrigley replied, "For the same reason that the pilot keeps this plane's engines running even though we're already in the air."

A foolish consistency is the hobgoblin of little minds.

—Ralph Waldo Emerson

Sayings
What good is consistency, if you're consistently wrong?

Predicament: the wage of consistency.

Joke
• "I thought you said you could type eighty words per minute!" the employer complained angrily to her new assistant.
"Oh I can," maintained the assistant airily, "some minutes. Not all of them."

EGOTISM

Conceit is God's gift to little men.   *—Bruce Barton*

I am ready to meet my Maker. Whether my Maker is prepared for the ordeal of meeting me is another matter.   *—Winston Churchill*

I have never seen a greater monster or miracle in the world than myself.
—Michel Eyquem de Montaigne

If you think you're a second-class citizen, you are.   *—Ted Turner*

When a man is wrapped up in himself he makes a pretty small package.

—John Ruskin

Perhaps one should not think so much of oneself, though it is an interesting subject.
—Norman Douglas

Egotism is the anesthetic that dulls the pain of stupidity.   *—Frank Leahy*

Why can we remember the tiniest detail that has happened to us, and not remember how many times we told it to the same persons?

—François de La Rochefoucauld

You probably wouldn't worry about what people think of you if you knew how seldom they do.   —*Olin Miller*

Those who think they know it all are very annoying to those of us who do.
—*Robert K. Mueller*

An egotist is a man who thinks that if he hadn't been born, people would have wondered why.   —*Dan Post*

Don't be humble. You're not that great.   —*Golda Meir*

I never loved a person the way I loved myself.   —*Mae West*

People are generally better persuaded by the reason which they have themselves discovered than by those which have come to the minds of others.
—*Blaise Pascal*

Conceit is the finest armor a man can wear.   —*Jerome K. Jerome*

The meek shall inherit the earth.   —*Psalms 35:17*

When you're as great as I am, it's hard to be humble.
—*Muhammad Ali (attrib.)*

If only I had a little humility, I would be perfect.   —*Ted Turner (attrib.)*

Egotism: the art of seeing in yourself what others cannot see.
—*George V. Higgins*

Nobody holds a good opinion of a man who has a low opinion of himself.
—*Anthony Trollope*

He fell in love with himself at first sight, and it is a passion to which he has always remained faithful. Self-love seems so often unrequited.   —*Anthony Powell*

If there is such a thing as genius, which is just what—what the fuck is it?—I am one, you know. And if there isn't, I don't care.   —*John Lennon*

An actor's a guy who, if you ain't talking about him, ain't listening.
—*Marlon Brando*

A writer is rarely so well inspired as when he talks about himself.
—*Anatole France*

I'm not a success, I'm a sensation.   —*Van Cliburn*

This is the epitaph I want on my tomb: "Here lies one of the most intelligent animals who ever appeared on the face of the earth."   —*Benito Mussolini*

Never underestimate a man who overestimates himself.
—*Franklin D. Roosevelt, on General Douglas MacArthur*

Each morning when I awake, I experience again a supreme pleasure—that of being Salvador Dali.   —*Salvador Dali*

Sayings
A man cannot think chiefly of himself without being discouraged.

A big head is a big load.   *—West African saying*

Conceit wouldn't be so terrible if only the right people had it.

Jokes
• I think a lot of [Leonard] Bernstein—but not as much as he does.

—Oscar Levant

• There, but for the grace of God, goes God.

—Winston Churchill (attrib.), regarding Sir Stafford Cripps

• I am a sensitive writer, actor, director. Talking business disgusts me. If you want to talk business, call my disgusting personal manager.

*—Sylvester Stallone, on the card he hands out
when approached with business propositions*

EXPERIENCE

A man who carries a cat by the tail learns something he can learn in no other way.

—Mark Twain

Judgment comes from experience and great judgment comes from bad experience.

—Robert Packwood

If you shut your door to all errors, truth will be shut out.

—Rabindranath Tagore

Getting results through people is a skill that cannot be learned in the classroom.

—J. Paul Getty

A man has no ears for that to which experience has given him no access.

—Friedrich Wilhelm Nietzsche

You know more of a road by having traveled it than by all the conjectures and descriptions in the world.   *—William Hazlitt*

That which we have not been forced to decipher, to clarify by our own personal effort, that which was made clear before, is not ours.   *—Marcel Proust*

The knowledge of the world is only to be acquired in the world, and not in a closet.

—Lord Chesterfield

You cannot create experience. You must undergo it.   *—Albert Camus*

Experience is not what happens to a man. It is what a man does with what happens to him.   *—Aldous Huxley*

What we have to learn to do, we learn by doing.   *—Aristotle*

It's a wise man who profits by his own experience, but it's a good deal wiser one who lets the rattlesnake bite the other fellow.   *—Josh Billings*

Men are wise in proportion not to their experience but to their capacity for experience.

—Samuel Johnson

Experience keeps a dear school, yet fools will learn in no other.

—*Benjamin Franklin*

The follies which a man regrets most in his life are those which he didn't commit when he had the opportunity.   —*Helen Rowland*

I have but one lamp by which my feet are guided, and that is the lamp of experience. I know of no way of judging of the future but by the past.   —*Patrick Henry*

One thorn of experience is worth a whole wilderness of warning.

—*James Russell Lowell*

All genuine knowledge originates in direct experience.   —*Mao Tse-tung*

A rolling stone gathers no moss, but it gains a certain polish.

—*Oliver Herford*

√ Wisdom is not wisdom when it is derived from books alone.   —*Horace*

We should be careful to get out of an experience only the wisdom that is in it—and stop there, lest we be like the cat that sits down on a hot stove lid. She will never sit down on a hot stove lid again—and that is well; but also she will never sit down on a cold one anymore.   —*Mark Twain*

Do you know the difference between education and experience? Education is when you read the fine print; experience is what you get when you don't.

—*Pete Seeger*

√ It is the true nature of mankind to learn from mistakes, not from example.

—*Fred Hoyle*

Morals are an acquirement—like music, like a foreign language, like piety, poker, paralysis—no man is born with them.   —*Mark Twain*

It's said that Tom Watson, head of IBM, was asked if he was going to fire an employee whose recent mistake had cost the company $600,000.

Watson shook his head, and explained, "I just spent $600,000 training him. Why would I want anyone else to hire his experience?"

Sayings
A self-made man has no factory guarantee.

Experience is the dividend gained from one's mistakes.

Experience is fine if not bought too dear.

Experience is nontransferable.

It is disgraceful to stumble against the same stone twice.   —*Greek proverb*

Good judgment comes from experience, and experience comes from poor judgment.

Jokes
• Experience: A comb life gives you after you lose your hair.   —*Judith Stern*

• Trying to set up a match at the county fair for his protégé, the local boxing
  champion, the boxing promoter requested an experienced fighter. But when the day of

the fight came around, he paled at the sight of an aging fellow with a punch-drunk walk, cauliflower ears, and a nose smashed flat against his face by innumerable encounters with a boxing glove. "I asked for an *experienced* fighter," the promoter complained, "not a damaged one."

- The personnel director was interviewing a job applicant. "Given that you have no experience whatsoever in this field, you're asking for an awfully high salary," she pointed out.

  "I suppose so," replied the applicant, "but think how much harder the work's going to be if I don't know anything about it."

IDEALISM

An idealist is one who helps the other fellow to make a profit.

—*Henry Ford*

To say that a man is an idealist is merely to say that he is a man.

—*G. K. Chesterton*

An idealist is one who, on noticing that a rose smells better than a cabbage, concludes that it will also make a better soup.   —*H. L. Mencken*

Much that passes as idealism is disguised hatred or disguised love of power.

—*Bertrand Russell*

All idealism is falsehood in the face of necessity.

—*Friedrich Wilhelm Nietzsche*

It is only in marriage with the world that our ideals can bear fruit: divorced from it, they remain barren.   —*Bertrand Russell*

Ideals are like stars; you will not succeed in touching them with your hands, but like the seafaring man . . . you choose them as your guides, and following them you will reach your destiny.   —*Carl Schurz*

I am an idealist. I don't know where I am going but I'm on my way.

—*Carl Sandburg*

Idealism increases in direct proportion to one's distance from the problem.

—*John Galsworthy*

America is the only country deliberately founded on a good idea.

—*John Gunther*

Ideas are great arrows, but there has to be a bow. And politics is the bow of idealism.

—*Bill Moyers*

. . . it's a blessing to die for a cause, because you can so easily die for nothing.

—*Andrew Young*

The Peace Corps is a sort of Howard Johnson's on the main drag into maturity.

—*Paul Theroux*

Saying
Anyone's a fool who doesn't try to live up to his dreams and abilities.

Joke

- "Now there's a woman who has suffered a great deal for what she believes," declared Irma about a mutual acquaintance.

  "Really? How so?" asked the friend she was lunching with.

  "She believes she can wear size-six shoes on a size-eight foot."

MODESTY

Pocket all your knowledge with your watch, and never pull it out in company unless desired.
—*Lord Chesterfield*

The first test of a truly great man is his humility.
—*John Ruskin*

Self-made men are most always apt to be a little too proud of the job.
—*Josh Billings*

Modesty is the only sure bait when you angle for praise.
—*Lord Chesterfield*

One is vain by nature, modest by necessity.
—*Pierre Reverdy*

I don't deserve any credit for turning the other cheek as my tongue is always in it.
—*Flannery O'Connor*

The second-sweetest set of three words in English is "I don't know."
—*Carol Tavris*

I feel it is time that I also pay tribute to my four writers, Matthew, Mark, Luke, and John.
—*Bishop Fulton J. Sheen*

A modest man is usually admired—if people ever hear of him.
—*Edgar Watson Howe*

It's going to be fun to watch and see how long the meek can keep the earth after they inherit it.
—*Kin Hubbard*

Great artists are modest almost as seldom as they are faithful to their wives.
—*H. L. Mencken*

A whale is harpooned only when it spouts.
—*Henry Hillman, on why he avoids interviews*

My religion consists of a humble admiration of the illimitable superior spirit who reveals himself in the slight details we are able to perceive with our frail and feeble minds.
—*Albert Einstein*

Sayings

Modesty in delivering our opinions leaves us the liberty of changing them without embarrassment.

Modesty is the art of encouraging people to find out for themselves how wonderful you are.

Jokes

• The city slicker was fishing with a fancy new rod and all the latest lures, but hadn't had a nibble by lunchtime. Adding to his irritation was the fact that a farm boy in a rowboat not far away had pulled in a number of good-sized bass. They quit about the same time, and the man couldn't help coming over. "You caught all those fish with that old stick—and a bent pin for a hook?" he croaked disbelievingly. "What's your secret?"

The boy shrugged and hitched up his overalls. "I guess I just keep myself out of sight."

• It's like what the beaver said to the rabbit as they stared up at the immense bulk of Hoover Dam: "No, I didn't actually build it—but it's based on an idea of mine."

POTENTIAL

Never try to teach a pig to sing; it wastes your time and it annoys the pig.

—Paul Dickson

I consider a human soul without education like marble in a quarry, which shows none of its inherent beauties until the skill of the polisher sketches out the colors, makes the surface shine, and discovers every ornamental cloud, spot, and vein that runs through it.   *—Joseph Addison*

In proportion to the development of his individuality, each person becomes more valuable to himself, and is therefore capable of being more valuable to others.

—John Stuart Mill

I am not a perfect servant. I am a public servant doing my best against the odds. As I develop and serve, be patient. God is not finished with me yet.

—Jesse Jackson

Nine tenths of modern science is in this respect the same: it is the produce of men whom their contemporaries thought dreamers—who were laughed at for caring for what did not concern them—who, as the proverb went, "walked into a well from looking at the stars"—who were believed to be useless, if anyone could be such.

—Walter Bagehot

The nobler a man, the harder it is for him to suspect inferiority in others.

—Cicero

And what is a weed? A plant whose virtues have not been discovered.

—Ralph Waldo Emerson

Education is helping the child realize his potentialities.   *—Erich Fromm*

The essence of our effort to see that every child has a chance must be to assure each an equal opportunity, not to become equal, but to become different—to realize whatever unique potential of body, mind, and spirit he or she possesses.

—John Fischer

The greatest value in the world is the difference between what we are and what we could become.   *—Ben Herbster*

Every man believes that he has a greater possibility.

—*Ralph Waldo Emerson*

All of us do not have equal talent, but all of us should have an equal opportunity to develop our talent.   —*John F. Kennedy*

Everything that enlarges the sphere of human powers, that shows man he can do what he thought he could not do, is valuable.   —*Samuel Johnson*

The biggest temptation is . . . to settle for too little.   —*Thomas Merton*

Nature is often hidden, sometimes overcome, seldom extinguished.

—*Francis Bacon*

There's always room for improvement, you know—it's the biggest room in the house.
—*Louise Heath Leber, on being chosen Mother of the Year*

Man needs, for his happiness, not only the enjoyment of this or that, but hope and enterprise and change.   —*Bertrand Russell*

Loving a child doesn't mean giving in to all his whims; to love him is to bring out the best in him, to teach him to love what is difficult.   —*Nadia Boulanger*

I long to accomplish a great and noble task, but it is my chief duty to accomplish small tasks as if they were great and noble.   —*Helen Keller*

There is no meaning to life except the meaning man gives his life by the unfolding of his powers, by living productively.   —*Erich Fromm*

Kind words will never die—neither will they buy groceries.   —*Bill Nye*

Most novices picture themselves as masters—and are content with the picture. This is why there are so few masters.   —*Jean Toomer*

People mistake their limitations for high standards.   —*Jean Toomer*

When we grow old, there can only be one regret—not to have given enough of ourselves.   —*Eleonora Duse*

Sayings
Mighty oaks from little acorns grow.

Whoever spurns what is short has not trodden on a scorpion.

—*West African saying*

An American believes more than anything else in the last four letters of that title: I can.

Joke
• The farmer's son was returning from the market with the crate of chickens his father had entrusted to him, when all of a sudden the box fell and broke open. Chickens scurried off in different directions, but the determined boy chased all over the neighborhood scooping up the wayward birds and returning them to the repaired crate. Hoping he had found them all, the boy reluctantly returned home, anticipating

the worst for being so careless. "Pa, the chickens got loose," the boy confessed sadly, "but I managed to find all twelve of them."

"Well, you did real good, son," the farmer beamed. "You left with seven."

PRIORITIES

I'd rather have roses on my table than diamonds around my neck.

—*Emma Goldman*

Don't fight a battle if you don't gain anything by winning.

—*General George S. Patton, Jr.*

Few people do business well who do nothing else.   —*Lord Chesterfield*

To be able to throw oneself away for the sake of a moment, to be able to sacrifice years for a woman's smile—that is happiness.   —*Hermann Hesse*

The presidency is temporary—but the family is permanent.

—*Yvonne de Gaulle, wife of the French president*

It is not so important to be serious as it is to be serious about the important things. The monkey wears an expression of seriousness which would do credit to any college student, but the monkey is serious because he itches.

—*Robert Maynard Hutchins*

Don't ever take a fence down until you know why it was put up.

—*Robert Frost*

Most people would succeed in small things if they were not troubled with great ambitions.   —*Henry Wadsworth Longfellow*

He that leaveth nothing to chance will do few things ill, but he will do very few things.

—*George Savile*

Once you have been confronted with a life-and-death situation, trivia no longer matter. Your perspective grows and you live at a deeper level. There's no time for pettiness.

—*Margaretta (Happy) Rockefeller*

Anybody can become angry—that is easy; but to be angry with the right person, and to the right degree, and for the right purpose, and in the right way—that is not within everybody's power and is not easy.   —*Aristotle*

All of the animals except man know that the principal business of life is to enjoy it.

—*Samuel Butler*

Man is the only animal that laughs and weeps; for he is the only animal that is struck with the difference between what things are, and what they ought to be.

—*William Hazlitt*

Man is the only animal that laughs, drinks when he is not thirsty, and makes love at all seasons of the year.   —*Voltaire*

I think you should always laugh in bed—people always laugh at me when I'm in bed.

—*Boy George*

Saying
What seems so necessary today may not even be desirable tomorrow.

Joke
• Mr. Stone was in dire need of periodontal work, so Dr. Graves performed a series of operations over a three-month period. The patient, however, paid only the first third, ignoring all Dr. Graves's remittance notices and threats of collection agencies. Finally, the desperate dentist enclosed a snapshot of his three little children in a note reading, "Dear Mr. Stone—here's why I need the money you owe me."

Dr. Graves was thrilled when an envelope arrived from Stone the next week. Opening it up, he found an 8 × 10 photograph of a gorgeous woman. Scrawled on the bottom was a note from his errant patient: "Dear Dr. Graves—here's why I can't pay."

PROCRASTINATION

Minds, like bodies, will often fall into a pimpled, ill-conditioned state from mere excess of comfort.
—Charles Dickens

It is better to have loafed and lost than never to have loafed at all.
—James Thurber

Those who are late will be punished by life itself.
—Mikhail Gorbachev

To do nothing is also a good remedy.
—Hippocrates

Those who make the worst use of their time are the first to complain of its brevity.
—Jean de La Bruyère

Work is the greatest thing in the world, so we should always save some of it for tomorrow.
—Don Herold

No task is a long one but the task on which one dare not start. It becomes a nightmare.
—Charles Baudelaire

Procrastination is the thief of time.
—Edward Young

If a thing's worth doing, it's worth doing late.
—Frederick Oliver

Sayings
If it weren't for the last minute, a lot of things would never get done.

Tomorrow is often the busiest day of the week.

Going slowly does not stop one from arriving.
—West African saying

Joke
• Somebody was using the pencil.
—Dorothy Parker, on why she missed a deadline

RACE

That all men should be brothers is the dream of people who have no brothers.

—*Charles Chincholles*

America is God's Crucible, the great Melting Pot where all the races of Europe are melting and re-forming!   —*Israel Zangwill*

I have a dream that my four little children will one day live in a nation where they will not be judged by the color of their skin, but by the content of their character.

—*Martin Luther King, Jr.*

When this happens, when we let it ring, we will speed the day when all of God's children, black men and white men, Jews and Gentiles, Protestants and Catholics, will be able to join hands and sing in the words of the old Negro spiritual, "Free at last, free at last, thank God Almighty, we're free at last."

—*Martin Luther King, Jr.*

Just being a Negro doesn't qualify you to understand the race situation any more than being sick makes you an expert on medicine.   —*Dick Gregory*

Be nice to whites, they need you to rediscover their humanity.

—*Archbishop Desmond Tutu*

After four hundred years of slave labor, we have some back pay coming.

—*Malcolm X*

Apartheid is an insult to God and man whom God dignifies.

—*Archbishop Robert Runcie*

Everybody's colored or else you wouldn't be able to see them.

—*Captain Beefheart*

Every man has pride of race, and under appropriate circumstances when the rights of others, his equals before the law, are not to be affected, it is his privilege to express such pride and to take such action based upon it as to him seems proper. . . . Our Constitution is color-blind, and neither knows nor tolerates classes among citizens.

—*John Marshall Harlan*

Men are not superior by reason of the accidents of race or color. They are superior who have the best heart—the best brain.   —*Robert G. Ingersoll*

We must learn to live together as brothers or perish together as fools.

—*Martin Luther King, Jr.*

After all, there is but one race—humanity.   —*George Moore*

Morality knows nothing of geographical boundaries or distinctions of race.

—*Herbert Spencer*

The difference of race is one of the reasons why I fear war may always exist; because race implies difference, difference implies superiority, and superiority leads to predominance.   —*Benjamin Disraeli*

I want to be the white man's brother, not his brother-in-law.

—*Martin Luther King, Jr. (attrib.)*

I believe the life of the Negro race has been a life of tragedy, of injustice, of oppression. The law has made him equal, but man has not.

—*Clarence S. Darrow*

Though the colored man is no longer subject to be bought and sold, he is still surrounded by an adverse sentiment which fetters all his movements. In his downward course he meets with no resistance, but his course upward is resisted at every stop of his progress.   —*Frederick Douglass*

There are no "white" or "colored" signs on the foxholes or graveyards of battle.

—*John F. Kennedy*

I have a dream that one day in the red hills of Georgia, sons of former slaves and the sons of former slave-owners will be able to sit down together at the table of brotherhood.   —*Martin Luther King, Jr.*

We have to prove beyond the shadow of a doubt that it is talent and training, not color, that makes a ballet dancer.   —*Arthur Mitchell*

Black art has always existed. It just hasn't been looked for in the right places.

—*Romare Bearden*

Human law may know no distinction among men in respect of rights, but human practice may.   —*Frederick Douglass*

. . . the color of the skin is in no way connected with strength of the mind or intellectual powers. . . .   —*Benjamin Banneker*

We [blacks] wish to plead our own cause. Too long have others spoken for us.

—*John Browne Russwurm*

. . . it was asserted that we were "a ragged set crying for liberty." I reply to it, the whites have so long and so loudly proclaimed the theme of equal rights and privileges that our souls have caught the flame, ragged as we are.

—*Maria W. Stewart*

Black men, don't be ashamed to show your colors, and to own them.

—*William Wells Brown*

The race problem is a moral one. . . . Its solution will come especially from the domain of principles. Like all the other great battles of humanity, it is to be fought out with the weapons of truth.   —*Alexander Crummell*

The inspiration of the race is the race.   —*Edward Wilmot Blyden*

A white woman has one handicap to overcome: that of sex. I have two—both sex and race.   —*Mary Church Terrell*

No race can speak for another or give utterance to its striving goal.

—*Mary Church Terrell*

. . . pride of race is the antidote to prejudice.

—*Arthur Alfonso Schomburg*

If you will protest courageously, and yet with dignity and Christian love, when the history books are written in future generations, the historians will have to pause and say, "There lived a great people—a black people—who injected new meaning and dignity into the veins of civilization."   —*Martin Luther King, Jr.*

Mumbling obeisance to the abhorrence of apartheid [is] like those lapsed believers who cross themselves when entering a church.
—*Nadine Gordimer*

I draw the line in the dust and toss the gauntlet before the feet of tyranny, and I say segregation now, segregation tomorrow, segregation forever.
—*George C. Wallace*

Sayings
The white man lives in the castle; when he dies he lives in the ground.
—*West African saying*

Mankind consists of five races and an infinite number of heats.

Black is beautiful.

The real measure of black progress will be when they can spurn professional sports careers as easily as whites.

Jokes
• The tourists visiting the temples of southern India trekked for several miles to a remote ruin. Suddenly one tourist paled, and gasped, "Oh no! I forgot to lock the car."

  "Don't worry," the local guide assured her. "There's no white man within fifty miles."

• Frankly, if I'd been an Indian, I'd have wished Plymouth Rock had landed on the Pilgrims.

REBELLION

If Abu Nidal is a terrorist, then so is George Washington.
—*Muammar Qaddafi*

A man that does not know how to be angry does not know how to be good.
—*Henry Ward Beecher*

I am a member of the rabble in good standing.   —*Westbrook Pegler*

Remember always that all of us, and you and I especially, are descended from immigrants and revolutionists.   —*Franklin D. Roosevelt*

To be able to throw oneself away for the sake of a moment, to be able to sacrifice years for a woman's smile—that is happiness.   —*Hermann Hesse*

I am proud of the revolutionary beliefs for which our forebears fought . . . the belief that the rights of man come not from the generosity of the state but the hands of God.
—*John F. Kennedy*

An idea that is not dangerous is not worthy of being called an idea at all.
—*Oscar Wilde*

The dissenter is every human being at those moments of his life when he resigns momentarily from the herd and thinks for himself.   —*Archibald MacLeish*

The reasonable man adapts himself to the world: the unreasonable one persists in trying to adapt the world to himself. Therefore all progress depends on the unreasonable man.
                                                                    —*George Bernard Shaw*

The spirit of resistance to government is so valuable on certain occasions that I wish it to be always kept alive. It will often be exercised when wrong but better so than not to be exercised at all. I like a little rebellion now and then. It is like a storm in the atmosphere.
                                                                    —*Thomas Jefferson*

Here in America we are descended in blood and spirit from revolutionists and rebels— men and women who dared to dissent from accepted doctrine.
                                                                    —*Dwight D. Eisenhower*

Liberty has never come from the government. Liberty has always come from the subjects of it. The history of liberty is a history of resistance. The history of liberty is a history of limitations of governmental power, not the increase of it.
                                                                    —*Woodrow Wilson*

The tree of liberty grows only when watered by the blood of tyrants.
                                                                    —*Bertrand Barère de Vieuzac*

William Jennings Bryan compared the way a convention feels about demonstrations to the feeling of a big man whose wife "was in the habit of beating him. When asked why he permitted it, he replied that it seemed to please her and did not hurt him."

. . . I am as desirous of being a good neighbor as I am of being a bad subject. . . .
                                                                    —*Henry David Thoreau*

Every great advance in natural knowledge has involved the absolute rejection of authority.
                                                                    —*Aldous Huxley*

Anyone who takes it on himself, on his own authority, to break a bad law, thereby authorizes everyone else to break the good ones.
                                                                    —*Denis Diderot*

There are not enough jails, not enough policemen, not enough courts to enforce a law not supported by the people.
                                                                    —*Hubert H. Humphrey*

. . . a strict observance of the written laws is doubtless *one* of the high duties of a good citizen, but it is not the *highest*. The laws of necessity, or self-preservation, of saving our country when in danger, are of higher obligation.
                                                                    —*Thomas Jefferson*

To make laws that man cannot, and will not obey, serves to bring all law into contempt.
                                                                    —*Elizabeth Cady Stanton*

Restlessness is discontent—and discontent is the first necessity of progress. Show me a thoroughly satisfied man and I will show you a failure.
                                                                    —*Thomas Alva Edison*

We have petitioned and our petitions have been disregarded; we have entreated and our entreaties have been scorned. We beg no more, we petition no longer, we now defy.
                                                                    —*William Jennings Bryan*

Every normal man must be tempted at times to spit on his hands, hoist the black flag, and begin slitting throats.
                                                                    —*H. L. Mencken*

The world owes all its onward impulses to men ill at ease. The happy man inevitably confines himself within ancient limits. —*Nathaniel Hawthorne*

You can't mine coal without machine guns. —*Richard B. Mellon*

Hungry men have no respect for law, authority, or human life.

—*Marcus Garvey*

That only a few, under any circumstances, protest against the injustice of long-established laws and customs, does not disprove the fact of the oppressions, while the satisfaction of the many, if real, only proves their apathy and deeper degradation.

—*Elizabeth Cady Stanton*

Take away the violence and who will hear the men of peace?

—*Lorraine Hansberry*

We are the people our parents warned us against. —*Nicholas von Hoffman*

It is impossible to give a soldier a good education without making him a deserter. His natural foe is the government that drills him. —*Henry David Thoreau*

To be happy all the time is one of the most nonconformist things you can do. . . . To be always joyful is not just rebellion, it's *radical*.

—*John-Roger and Peter McWilliams*

The most radical revolutionary will become a conservative the day after the revolution.

—*Hannah Arendt*

The first duty of a revolutionary is to get away with it. —*Abbie Hoffman*

He who throws a bomb and kills a pedestrian, declares that as a victim of society he has rebelled against society. But could not the poor victim object: "Am I society?"

—*Enrico Malatesta*

If you will protest courageously, and yet with dignity and Christian love, when the history books are written in future generations the historians will have to pause and say, "There lived a great people—a black people—who injected new meaning and dignity into the veins of civilization." —*Martin Luther King, Jr.*

All art is a revolt against man's fate. —*André Malraux*

Revolutions are the locomotives of history. —*Nikita S. Khrushchev*

The time to stop a revolution is at the beginning, not the end.

—*Adlai E. Stevenson*

Inferiors revolt in order that they may be equal, and equals that they may be superior. Such is the state of mind which creates revolutions. —*Aristotle*

Those who make peaceful revolution impossible will make violent revolution inevitable.

—*John F. Kennedy*

If a house be divided against itself, that house cannot stand. —*Mark 3:25*

Agitators are a set of interfering meddling people, who come down to some perfectly contented class of the community and sow the seeds of discontent among them. That is the reason why agitators are so absolutely necessary. —*Oscar Wilde*

The people who are the most militant are often the ones who were least involved when things were tough and dangerous. —*Andrew Young*

Death is the price of revolution. —*H. Rap Brown*

Oppression makes a wise man mad. —*Frederick Douglass*

To make a contented slave you must make a thoughtless one. —*Frederick Douglass*

Revolution accelerates evolution. —*Kelly Miller*

When reform becomes impossible, revolution becomes imperative. —*Kelly Miller*

Revolutions never go backward. —*Kelly Miller*

Martyrs are needed to create incidents. Incidents are needed to create revolutions. Revolutions are needed to create progress. —*Chester Bomar Himes*

Revolutions are never peaceful. . . . —*Malcolm X*

Oppressed people are frequently very oppressive when first liberated. They know best two positions: somebody's foot on their neck or their foot on somebody's neck. —*Florynce Kennedy*

Sayings
Rebellion is a phase that all children go through.

Rebellion is the sign of a healthy ego.

During uprisings, the tendency is to throw the baby out with the bathwater.

Rebels aren't always rabble.

Hot heads and cold hearts never solve anything.

Jokes
• When the aged president of the company was out of town, half a dozen of his senior executives got together to plan some way to ease the old coot out of the driver's seat. To their horror, the executive VP's secretary buzzed him halfway through the meeting and informed him the president was back early and on his way to see him.

"If he catches us all here he'll know exactly what we're up to," cried the VP. "Quick—you five, jump out the window!"

"But we're on the thirteenth floor," protested the company treasurer.

"*Jump!*" yelled the VP. "This is no time for superstition."

• During the turbulent sixties, a very right-wing board of directors insisted that all prospective employees fill out an elaborate "loyalty form" that included the following question: "Do you support the overthrow of the United States government by subversion, violence, or insurrection?"

The recent college graduate, erstwhile hippie and veteran of many multiple-choice exams, circled "subversion."

REVENGE

Don't go looking for a fight—but if you're hit, deck the bastard.

—*Roger Ailes*

A woman's desire for revenge outlasts all her other emotions.

—*Cyril Connolly*

When a man steals your wife, there is no better revenge than to let him keep her.

—*Sacha Guitry*

Eye for eye, tooth for tooth, hand for hand, foot for foot.   —Exodus *21:24*

Revenge is often like biting a dog because the dog bit you.

—*Austin O'Malley*

Nobody ever forgets where he buried a hatchet.   —*Elbert Hubbard*

Revenge is profitable, gratitude is expensive.   —*Cicero*

The voice of thy brother's blood crieth unto me from the ground.

—Genesis *4:10*

One of the shameful chapters of this country was how many of the comfortable—especially those who profited from the misery of others—abused her. . . . But she got even in a way that was almost cruel. She forgave them.

—*Ralph McGill, about Eleanor Roosevelt*

Gentlemen: You have undertaken to cheat me. I won't sue you, for the law is too slow. I'll ruin you.   —*Cornelius Vanderbilt, in a letter to a competitor*

Sayings
If thine enemy wrong thee, buy each of his children a drum.   —*Chinese proverb*

Revenge is a dish best served cold.

Revenge is sweet.

How many times has every wayward child heard, "When you grow up I hope you have a child just like you so you'll know what I'm going through!"

Joke
• A Southern girls' school and a military academy had a long-standing tradition of helping each other on social occasions. One spring morning the headmistress called the academy to arrange for escorts for the annual cotillion. Since the military academy had a new commandant, she felt obliged to remind him that only boys of the Christian faith should be sent over to mingle with her fine young ladies.

When the bus arrived from the academy, twenty perfectly dressed, elegant black cadets emerged. Considerably distressed, the headmistress cried, "There must be some mistake!"

"I doubt it, ma'am," responded the lieutenant in charge. "Captain Goldberg doesn't make mistakes."

VARIETY

America is not like a blanket—one piece of unbroken cloth, the same color, the same texture, the same size. America is more like a quilt—many patches, many pieces, many colors, many sizes, all woven and held together by a common thread.

—*Jesse Jackson*

The great source of pleasure is variety.   —*Samuel Johnson*

Variety is the mother of enjoyment.   —*Benjamin Disraeli*

Variety is the soul of pleasure.   —*Aphra Behn*

Variety's the very spice of life that gives it all its flavor.

—*William Cowper*

Sayings
Variety means nothing to a hungry man.

Diversity, yes; perversity, no.

Better the evil known than the new unknown.

More flavors than Howard Johnson's.

Joke
• "Bless me, Father, for I have sinned," the young woman whispered into the grille of the confession booth. "I had intercourse eight times this weekend."

   "My gracious," gasped the priest. "That's serious. Was the man married?"

   "Five of them were."

MATTERS OF THE SOUL

CHARITY AND PHILANTHROPY

Sometimes give your services for nothing. . . .
—*Hippocrates*

Let us not paralyze our capacity for good by brooding over man's capacity for evil.
—*David Sarnoff*

Money is like manure. If you spread it around, it does a lot of good, but if you pile it up in one place, it stinks like hell.
—*Clint W. Murchison*

The worst sin toward our fellow creatures is not to hate them, but to be indifferent to them: that's the essence of inhumanity.
—*George Bernard Shaw*

It is easier for a camel to go through the eye of a needle, than for a rich man to enter into the kingdom of God.
—**Matthew** *19:24*

Science may have found a cure for most evils; but it has found no remedy for the worst of them all—the apathy of human beings.
—*Helen Keller*

Humanitarianism is the expression of stupidity and cowardice.
—*Adolf Hitler*

You can't take it with you. You never see a U-Haul following a hearse.
—*Ellen Glasgow*

No person was ever honored for what he received. Honor has been the reward for what he gave.
—*Calvin Coolidge*

We cannot exist without mutual help. All, therefore, that need aid have a right to ask it from their fellow men, and no one who has the power of granting can refuse it without guilt.
—*Sir Walter Scott*

Surplus wealth is a sacred trust which its possessor is bound to administer in his lifetime for the good of the community.
—*Andrew Carnegie*

Philanthropy is almost the only virtue which is sufficiently appreciated by mankind.
—*Henry David Thoreau*

No people do so much harm as those who go about doing good.
—*Mandell Creighton*

He that giveth unto the poor shall not lack.
—**Proverbs** *28:27*

A good deed never goes unpunished.
—*Gore Vidal*

Understanding human needs is half the job of meeting them.
—*Adlai E. Stevenson*

If you want to lift yourself up, lift up someone else.

—*Booker T. Washington*

To bear other people's afflictions, everyone has courage and enough to spare.

—*Benjamin Franklin*

Money-giving is a very good criterion . . . of a person's mental health. Generous people are rarely mentally ill people.   —*Karl A. Menninger*

Three passions, simple but overwhelmingly strong, have governed my life: the longing for love, the search for knowledge, and unbearable pity for the suffering of mankind.

—*Bertrand Russell*

At the Harvest Festival in church the area behind the pulpit was piled high with tins of fruit for the old-age pensioners. We had collected the tinned fruit from door to door. Most of it came from old-age pensioners.   —*Clive James*

A large part of altruism, even when it is perfectly honest, is grounded upon the fact that it is uncomfortable to have unhappy people about one.

—*H. L. Mencken*

As the purse is emptied the heart is filled.   —*Victor Hugo*

It is more blessed to give than to receive.   —*Acts 20:35*

'Tis always more blessed to give than to receive; for example, wedding presents.

—*H. L. Mencken*

Those who would administer wisely must, indeed, be wise, for one of the serious obstacles to the improvement of our race is indiscriminate charity.

—*Andrew Carnegie*

The desire for power in excess caused angels to fall; the desire for knowledge in excess caused man to fall; but in charity is no excess, neither can man or angels come into danger by it.   —*Francis Bacon*

Plenty of people despise money, but few know how to give it away.

—*François de La Rochefoucauld*

A beggar can never be bankrupt.   —*John Clarke*

Charity never faileth.   —**1 Corinthians *13:8***

And now abideth faith, hope, charity, these three; but the greatest of these is charity.

—**1 Corinthians *13:13***

God loveth a cheerful giver.   —**2 Corinthians *9:7***

For unto whomsoever much is given, of him shall be much required: and to whom men have committed much, of him they will ask the more.   —**Luke *12:48***

The dead carry with them to the grave in their clutched hands only that which they have given away.   —*DeWitt Wallace*

Beggars should be abolished entirely! It is annoying to give to them and it is annoying *not* to give to them.   —*Friedrich Wilhelm Nietzsche*

We do not quite forgive a giver. The hand that feeds us is in some danger of being bitten.   —*Ralph Waldo Emerson*

Freely ye have received, freely give.   —**Matthew** *10:8*

Let us not be weary in well doing.   —**Galatians** *6:9*

He gives twice that gives soon; that is, he will soon be called to give again.

—*Benjamin Franklin*

. . . when thou doest alms, let not thy left hand know what thy right hand doeth.

—**Matthew** *6:3*

As for charity, it is a matter in which the immediate effect on the persons directly concerned, and the ultimate consequence to the general good, are apt to be at complete war with one another.   —*John Stuart Mill*

Charity is the power of defending that which we know to be indefensible. Hope is the power of being cheerful in circumstances which we know to be desperate.

—*G. K. Chesterton*

It is with narrow-souled people as with narrow-necked bottles: the less they have in them the more noise they make in pouring it out.   —*Alexander Pope*

Cheapness characterizes almost all donations of the American people to the Negro. . . .

—*Alexander Crummell*

A pretty good test of a man's religion is how it affects his pocketbook.

—*Francis James Grimke*

Everybody wants to do something to help, but nobody wants to be first.   —*Pearl Bailey*

Giving away a fortune is taking Christianity too far.   —*Charlotte Bingham*

The Sea of Galilee and the Dead Sea are made of the same water. It flows down, clear and cool, from the heights of Hermon and the roots of the cedars of Lebanon. The Sea of Galilee makes beauty of it, for the Sea of Galilee has an outlet. It gets to give. It gathers in its riches that it may pour them out again to fertilize the Jordan plain. But the Dead Sea with the same water makes horror. But the Dead Sea has no outlet. It gets to keep.   —*Harry Emerson Fosdick*

When we grow old, there can only be one regret—not to have given enough of ourselves.   —*Eleonora Duse*

No man actually owns a fortune. It owns him.   —*A. P. Giannini*

It went beyond idealism and that ridiculous term *activism*, which basically means talking about something but doing nothing. . . . We made giving exciting.

—*Bob Geldof, on organizing fund-raising concerts for African relief*

It's really very simple, Governor. When people are hungry, they die. So spare me your politics and tell me what you need and how you're going to get it to these people.

—*Bob Geldof, discussing famine relief with a Sudanese deputy governor*

The fountain is my speech. The tulips are my speech. The grass and trees are my speech.   —*George T. Delacorte, donor of a public fountain*

I never thought God would hold someone accountable for not raising money.

—*Pat Robertson, on Oral Roberts's warning that God might*
"call him back" if contributions were inadequate

The eight grades of charity:

1. to give reluctantly
2. to give cheerfully but not adequately
3. to give cheerfully and adequately, but only after being asked
4. to give cheerfully, adequately, and of your own free will, but to put it in the recipient's hand in such a way as to make him feel lesser
5. to let the recipient know who the donor is, but not the reverse
6. to know who is receiving your charity but to remain anonymous to him
7. to have neither the donor nor the recipient be aware of the other's identity
8. to dispense with charity altogether, by enabling your fellow humans to have the wherewithal to earn their own living.

—Maimonides, twelfth-century Jewish sage

First we just gave them these surpluses. Next we agreed to pay freight on transportation to ports. Then we agreed to mill the grain and package it. The next thing [you know] we'll be asked to cook it and serve it.

—Allan J. Ellender, U.S. senator,
on complaints from charitable organizations

Karl Menninger was once asked what action he would recommend if a person were to feel a nervous breakdown coming on. "Lock up your house," the famous psychiatrist advised, "go across the railroad tracks, and find someone in need and do something for him."

No one would remember the Good Samaritan if he'd only had good intentions. He had money as well.   *—Margaret Thatcher*

Charity begins at home.   *—Terence*

Sayings
When hunger gets inside you, nothing else can.   *—West African saying*

A man's true wealth is the good he does in this world.

Give a man a fish and he will live for a day; give him a net, and he will live for a lifetime.   *—Chinese proverb*

We find our lives in losing them in the service of others.

You can't help someone uphill without getting closer to the top yourself.

There is no limit to the good you can do if you don't care who gets the credit.

A beggar has no dignity.   *—West African saying*

He that has no charity deserves none.

Giving honors the giver.

I sought my soul, but my soul I could not see. I sought my God, but my God eluded me. I sought my brother—and I found all three.
—Quoted by the London Church News Service

Jokes
• A clergyman famous for his abilities to get the collection plate filled turned his

talents to a Sunday school audience. Drawing an elaborate analogy between his role as the pastor of a congregation to that of a shepherd to his flock of sheep, he paused dramatically, and asked the children, "And who can tell me what a shepherd does for the sheep?"

A little hand shot up. "I know, Reverend—shears them!"

• The businessman was rather put off when the bum approached him with a request for five dollars to buy a cup of coffee. "You can buy coffee for sixty cents," he responded tartly.

"Right you are," conceded the bum cheerfully, "but I like to leave a big tip."

• The pig complained to the cow saying, "I know you give milk, but I give pork, pigskin, and even my bristles are used for brushes. Why are you loved so much more?"

"Maybe," the cow said sweetly, "it's because I give while I'm still alive."

• Without warning, a hurricane blew across the Caribbean. The luxurious yacht soon foundered in the huge waves and sank without a trace. Only two survivors, the boat's owner and its steward, managed to swim to the closest island. Observing that it was utterly uninhabited, the steward burst into tears, wringing his hands and moaning that they'd never be heard of again. Meanwhile, his companion leaned back against a palm tree and relaxed.

"Dr. Karpman, Dr. Karpman, how can you be so calm?" moaned the distraught steward. "We're going to *die* on this godforsaken island. Don't you see? They're never going to find us."

"Let me tell you something, Mitchell," began Karpman with a smile. "Four years ago I gave the United Way $500,000, and $500,000 to the United Jewish Appeal. Three years ago I did very well in the stock market, so I contributed $850,000 to each. Last year business was good, so both charities got a million dollars."

"So?" screamed the wretched steward.

"It's time for their annual fund drives," the yachtsman pointed out, "and I *know* they're going to find me."

• Define philanthropist.

—One who steals privately so he can give publicly.

CONSCIENCE

Living with a conscience is like driving a car with the brakes on.

—*Budd Schulberg*

It is easier to cope with a bad conscience than with a bad reputation.

—*Friedrich Wilhelm Nietzsche*

There is no witness so dreadful, no accuser so terrible as the conscience that dwells in the heart of every man.   —*Polybius*

The Anglo-Saxon conscience does not prevent the Anglo-Saxon from sinning; it merely prevents him from enjoying his sin.   —*Salvador de Madariaga y Rojo*

A guilty conscience needs to confess. A work of art is a confession.

—*Albert Camus*

A guilty conscience is the mother of invention.   —*Carolyn Wells*

Conscience is the inner voice that warns us that someone may be looking.
                                                                —*H. L. Mencken*

Even when there is no law, there is conscience.   —*Publilius Syrus*

Most people sell their souls and live with a good conscience on the proceeds.
                                                          —*Logan Pearsall Smith*

I cannot and will not cut my conscience to fit this year's fashions.
                                                            —*Lillian Hellman*

. . . conscienceless efficiency is no match for efficiency quickened by conscience.
                                                              —*Kelly Miller*

Edward Bok, the magazine publisher, was fond of flowers, and one spring planted
thousands of daffodils in his front yard. "You shouldn't waste your money planting any
beyond the fence," warned one neighbor. "People will steal them as fast as they
bloom."
    The next morning Bok nailed a sign on the fence which read, THESE FLOWERS ARE
UNDER THE PROTECTION OF THE PUBLIC.
    Not one was picked.

Unless you're ashamed of yourself now and then, you're not honest.
                                                            —*William Faulkner*

Sayings
Conscience gets a lot of credit that belongs to cold feet.

A clear conscience laughs at false accusations.

Joke
• Conscience is the one thing that hurts when everything else feels great.

DUTY

One has two duties—to be worried and not to be worried.   —*E. M. Forster*

If we believe a thing to be bad, and if we have a right to prevent it, it is our duty to
try to prevent it and damn the consequences.   —*Alfred Milner*

That dull, laden, soul-depressing sensation known as the sense of duty.
                                                                —*O. Henry*

Duty consists largely of pretending that the trivial is critical.

                                                                —*John Fowles*

A sense of duty is moral glue, constantly subject to stress.

                                                              —*William Safire*

There is no duty we so much underrate as the duty of being happy.
                                                        —*Robert Louis Stevenson*

The burning conviction that we have a holy duty toward others is often a way of attaching our drowning selves to a passing raft.   —Eric Hoffer

I long to accomplish a great and noble task, but it is my chief duty to accomplish small tasks as if they were great and noble.   —Helen Keller

It is seldom very hard to do one's duty when one knows what it is, but it is often exceedingly difficult to find this out.   —Samuel Butler

What's a man's first duty? The answer's brief: to be himself.

—Henrik Ibsen

Duty is what one expects from others.   —Oscar Wilde

When a stupid man is doing something he is ashamed of, he always declares that it is his duty.   —George Bernard Shaw

The service we render others is really the rent we pay for our room on earth.

—Wilfred Grenfell

Make it a point to do something every day that you don't want to do. This is the golden rule for acquiring the habit of doing your duty without pain.

—Mark Twain

Let us have faith that right makes right, and in that faith let us to the end dare to do our duty as we understand it.   —Abraham Lincoln

Sayings

Anytime you give up pleasure for duty, you're a stronger person.

Duty is duty.

Joke

• A Sunday school teacher was having a hard time getting her young charges to grasp the message of the Good Samaritan. Finally she pointed at one of the least attentive children and asked, "Alison, suppose on the way to church you passed a vacant lot and saw a man in ragged clothes lying on the ground, so badly beaten up that he was covered in blood. . . . What would you do?"

The eight-year-old's response: "I'd throw up!"

ETHICS AND MORALITY

Give to every human being every right that you claim for yourself.

—Robert Ingersoll

Ask yourself not if this or that is expedient, but if it is right.

—Alan Paton

It is important that people know what you stand for. It's equally important that they know what you won't stand for.   —Mary Waldrop

A [television] viewer who skips the advertising is the moral equivalent of a shoplifter.

—Nicholas Jackson

She wears her morals like a loose garment.   *—Langston Hughes*

When morality comes up against profit, it is seldom that profit loses.

—Shirley Chisholm

I believe that unarmed truth and unconditional love will have the final word in reality. This is why right, temporarily defeated, is stronger than evil triumphant.

—Martin Luther King, Jr.

When you punish someone, you pay for it later. There was a time when pickpockets were publicly hanged, but other pickpockets took advantage of the large crowds attracted to the execution to ply their trade.   *—J. Hopps Baker*

Art, like morality, consists in drawing the line somewhere.

—G. K. Chesterton

For what is a man profited, if he shall gain the whole world, and lose his own soul?
—Matthew 16:26

Indifference, to me, is the epitome of evil.   *—Elie Wiesel*

I would prefer even to fail with honor than win by cheating.   *—Sophocles*

No man is justified in doing evil on the grounds of expedience.

—Theodore Roosevelt

This above all—to thine own self be true, and it must follow, as the night the day, thou canst not then be false to any man.   *—William Shakespeare*

Those who corrupt the public mind are just as evil as those who steal from the public.
—Adlai E. Stevenson

Right is right, even if everyone is against it; and wrong is wrong, even if everyone is for it.   *—William Penn*

Men are more often bribed by their loyalties and ambitions than by money.
—Robert H. Jackson

I can only say that, while my own opinions as to ethics do not satisfy me, other people's satisfy me even less.   *—Bertrand Russell*

Standards are always out of date. That is what makes them standards.

—Alan Bennett

Expedients are for the hour, but principles are for the ages.

—Henry Ward Beecher

There is only one morality, as there is only one geometry.   *—Voltaire*

Everybody has a little bit of Watergate in him.   *—Billy Graham*

The moral sense, or conscience, is as much a part of man as his leg or his arm.
—Thomas Jefferson

When bad men combine, the good must associate; else they will fall, one by one, an unpitied sacrifice in a contemptible struggle.   *—Edmund Burke*

Man is an animal with primary instincts of survival. Consequently, his ingenuity has developed first and his soul afterward. Thus the progress of science is far ahead of man's ethical behavior.   *—Charlie Chaplin*

A moral being is one who is capable of reflecting on his past actions and their motives —of approving of some and disapproving of others.   —*Charles Darwin*

The worst sin toward our fellow creatures is not to hate them, but to be indifferent to them: that's the essence of inhumanity.   —*George Bernard Shaw*

Morals are an acquirement—like music, like a foreign language, like piety, poker, paralysis—no man is born with them.   —*Mark Twain*

Say what you want about the Ten Commandments, you must always come back to the pleasant fact that there are only ten of them.   —*H. L. Mencken*

The moral sense enables one to perceive morality—and avoid it. The immoral sense enables one to perceive immorality and enjoy it.   —*Mark Twain*

An Englishman thinks he is moral when he is only uncomfortable.
    —*George Bernard Shaw*

Moral indignation is jealousy with a halo.   —*H. G. Wells*

A hand on your cock is more moral—and more fun—than a finger on the trigger.
    —*Lawrence Lipton*

I know what I have done, and Your Honor knows what I have done. . . . Somewhere between my ambitions and my ideals, I lost my ethical compass.
    —*Jeb Magruder*

I would rather be the man who bought the Brooklyn Bridge than the man who sold it.
    —*Will Rogers*

The coming together of two laudable movements—death with dignity and cost containment—concerns me. . . . Patients have a right to die. But do they have a duty to die?   —*Mark Siegler*

I wish Bill [Schroeder, artificial-heart recipient] had written down on the consent form at what point he would want to say, "Stop this, I've had enough."
    —*Margaret Schroeder*

The use of fetuses as organ and tissue donors is a ticking time bomb of bioethics.
    —*Arthur Caplan*

I think that very soon the right to die will become the duty to die.
    —*Cecily Saunders*

All's fair in love and war.   —*Francis Edward Smedley*

Sayings
A man has to live with himself; he should see that he always has good company.

In our society, the only sin is not getting away with it.

Jokes
• The businessman decided it was time to give his daughter, a recent business school graduate, a little lecture. "In business, ethics are very important," he began. "Say, for instance, that a client comes in and settles his $100 account in cash. After he leaves, you notice a second $100 bill stuck to the first one. Immediately you are

presented with an ethical dilemma. . . ." The businessman paused for dramatic effect. "Should you tell your partner?"

• The headmaster was chatting with some of his students' parents and stated that the worst thing that could happen to a schoolboy was to be caught cheating.

"You're wrong about that," interrupted the school chaplain bluntly. "It would be much worse for the boy to cheat and not be caught."

• It's said that George Bernard Shaw was seated at dinner one night next to an attractive woman. "Madam," he asked boldly, "would you go to bed with me for a thousand pounds?"

The woman blushed scarlet and shook her head sharply.

"For ten thousand pounds?" the eminent man pursued.

"I would not," she declared.

"Then how about the sum of fifty thousand pounds?"

The colossal sum gave the woman pause. After some reflection, she replied coyly, "Perhaps."

"And if I were to offer you five pounds?"

"Mr. Shaw!" The woman was shocked. "What do you take me for?"

"We have already determined what you are," he pointed out calmly. "Now we are merely haggling over the price."

FAITH

Faith is much better than belief. Belief is when someone *else* does the thinking.
—*R. Buckminster Fuller*

You can't solve many of today's problems by straight linear thinking. It takes leaps of faith to sense the connections that are not necessarily obvious.
—*Matina Horner*

The will is the strong blind man who carries on his shoulders the lame man who can see.   —*Arthur Schopenhauer*

I could prove God statistically.   —*George Gallup*

Faith: belief without evidence in what is told by one who speaks without knowledge, of things without parallel.   —*Ambrose Bierce*

If there was no faith there would be no living in this world. We couldn't even eat hash with any safety.   —*Josh Billings*

Not truth, but faith it is that keeps the world alive.
—*Edna St. Vincent Millay*

No faith is our own that we have not arduously won.   —*Havelock Ellis*

Faith is the substance of things hoped for, the evidence of things not seen.
—*Hebrews 11:1*

Beware of the community in which blasphemy does not exist: underneath, atheism runs rampant.   —*Joaquim Maria Machado de Assis*

For with God nothing shall be impossible.   —*Luke 1:37*

The Lord is my strength and my shield.   —**Psalms** *27:1*

He only is my rock and my salvation; he is my defense; I shall not be moved.
—**Psalms 62:6**

The Lord is my strength and song, and he is become my salvation.
—**Exodus** *15:2*

A casual stroll through a lunatic asylum shows that faith does not prove anything.
—*Friedrich Wilhelm Nietzsche*

If a man really has strong faith, he can indulge in the luxury of skepticism.
—*Friedrich Wilhelm Nietzsche*

Faith may be defined briefly as an illogical belief in the occurrence of the improbable.
—*H. L. Mencken*

Conversion for me was not a Damascus Road experience. I slowly moved into an intellectual acceptance of what my intuition had always known.
—*Madeleine L'Engle*

You can do very little with faith, but you can do nothing without it.
—*Samuel Butler*

I would rather live in a world where my life is surrounded by mystery than live in a world so small that my mind could comprehend it.
—*Harry Emerson Fosdick*

I respect faith, but doubt is what gets you an education.   —*Wilson Mizner*

Skepticism is the beginning of faith.   —*George Bernard Shaw (attrib.)*

We do not pray not to be tempted, but not to be conquered.   —*Origen*

There is nothing more perplexing in life than to know at what point you should surrender your intellect to your faith.   —*Margot Asquith*

Atheism

An atheist is a man who has no invisible means of support.
—*John Buchan*

An atheist is a guy who watches a Notre Dame–SMU football game and doesn't care who wins.   —*Dwight D. Eisenhower*

It's an interesting view of atheism, as a sort of *crutch* for those who can't stand the reality of God. . . .   —*Tom Stoppard*

I once wanted to become an atheist, but I gave up—they have no holidays.
—*Henny Youngman*

There are no atheists in foxholes.   —*William Thomas Cummings*

Sayings
God gives nothing to those who keep their arms crossed.   —*West African saying*

Keep the faith.

Jokes

- What do you get when you cross an insomniac, a dyslexic, and an agnostic?
  —Someone who lies awake all night wondering if there really is a Dog.

- What's the worst thing about being an atheist?
  —You have no one to call to when you're having an orgasm.

- What do you get when you cross a Jehovah's Witness and an atheist?
  —Someone who rings your doorbell for no reason.

- The minister of an Oklahoma farming parish convened a prayer meeting to pray for rain during a serious drought. Noting that on that cloudless morning the church was full to overflowing, he came to the pulpit and posed a single question to his flock. "You all know why we're here," he said. "What I want to know is, why didn't any of you bring umbrellas?"

- As long as there are algebra exams, there will be prayer in the schools.

HOPE

Hope is delicate suffering.
—*Imamu Amiri Baraka*

Hope, deceitful as it is, serves at least to lead us to the end of our lives by an agreeable route.
—*François de La Rochefoucauld*

The miserable have no other medicine but only hope.
—*William Shakespeare*

Charity is the power of defending that which we know to be indefensible. Hope is the power of being cheerful in circumstances which we know to be desperate.
—*G. K. Chesterton*

The human body experiences a powerful gravitational pull in the direction of hope. That is why the patient's hopes are the physician's secret weapon. They are the hidden ingredients in any prescription.
—*Norman Cousins*

While there's life, there's hope.
—*Terence*

Hope is a good breakfast, but it is a bad supper.
—*Francis Bacon*

Hope springs eternal in the human breast.
—*Alexander Pope*

Thou art my hope in the day of evil.
—*Jeremiah 17:17*

Hope is generally a wrong guide, though it is good company along the way.
—*George Savile*

Hope deferred maketh the heart sick.
—**Proverbs 13:12**

Sayings

Be careful what you hope for—you might get it.

Hope lost, all lost.

Hope is cheap.

Hope for the best, but fear the worst.

Hope is the poor man's bread.

Hope keeps man alive.

What's past hope is past grief.

Nothing kills hope faster than cynicism.

Hope is insurance we take out in this life against hell's fire in the next.

Jokes

• Hope is a wonderful thing—one little nibble keeps a man fishing all day.

• It was Samuel Johnson who described an acquaintance's decision to marry for a second time as "the triumph of hope over experience."

INFIDELITY

Young men want to be faithful, and are not; old men want to be faithless, and cannot.
—*Oscar Wilde*

It is the fear of middle age in the young, of old age in the middle-aged, which is the prime cause of infidelity, that infallible rejuvenator.   —*Cyril Connolly*

Those who are faithful know only the trivial side of love; it is the faithless who know love's tragedies.   —*Oscar Wilde*

Adultery is the application of democracy to love.   —*H. L. Mencken*

Next to the pleasure of making a new mistress is that of being rid of an old one.
—*William Wycherley*

The fickleness of the women I love is only equaled by the infernal constancy of the women who love me.   —*George Bernard Shaw*

[He] has decided to take himself a wife, but he hasn't decided yet whose. . . .
—*Peter De Vries*

The trouble with marrying your mistress is that you create a job vacancy.
—*Sir James Goldsmith*

A Code of Honor: Never approach a friend's girlfriend or wife with mischief as your goal. There are just too many women in the world to justify that sort of dishonorable behavior. Unless she's *really* attractive.   —*Bruce Jay Friedman*

Extramarital sex is as overrated as premarital sex. And marital sex, come to think of it.
—*Simon Gray*

I've been in love with the same woman for forty-one years. If my wife finds out, she'll kill me.   —*Henny Youngman*

I am not faithful but I am attached.   —*Günter Grass*

There's nothing like a good dose of another woman to make a man appreciate his wife.

—*Clare Boothe Luce*

Infidelities may be forgiven, but never forgotten.   —*Madame de Lafayette*

Saying
Bigamy is having one spouse too many. Monogamy is the same thing.

Joke
• Surprisingly, more than three quarters of the mistresses surveyed say they find the mistress-executive relationship to be stimulating, honest, emotionally gratifying, financially rewarding, and in all ways preferable to marriage, although if the executive offered to marry them they'd grab it in a second.

—The Wall Street Journal

INSPIRATION

Trust your gut.   —*Barbara Walters*

Inspiration is a farce that poets have invented to give themselves importance.

—*Jean Anouilh*

Once people were driven—someday they will be inspired.

—*Walter Dill Scott*

I write when I'm inspired, and I see to it that I'm inspired at nine o'clock every morning.   —*Peter De Vries*

My sole inspiration is a telephone call from a producer.   —*Cole Porter*

He thought of something and made a U-turn, and we never did get to church.
     —*The son of Willis Carrier, inventor of air conditioning, who had been pondering the potential of the centrifugal compressor one Sunday morning*

Genius is one percent inspiration and ninety-nine percent perspiration.

—*Thomas Alva Edison*

There are one-story intellects, two-story intellects, and three-story intellects with skylights. All fact collectors with no aim beyond their facts are one-story men. Two-story men compare reason and generalize using labors of the fact collectors as well as their own. Three-story men idealize, imagine, and predict. Their best illuminations come from above through the skylight.   —*Oliver Wendell Holmes, Sr.*

Sayings
Inspiration is everywhere. If you're ready to appreciate it, an ant can be one of the wonders of the universe.

Inspiration from above is still the spark plug of the moral motor.

Joke

- "I'm leaving you, Ludwig," announced his long-suffering wife one morning. "I can't take it anymore."

    "Oh, but you can't, my darling," said the composer, looking up from the keyboard. "You are my inspiration."

    His wife snorted. "Tell me another one. Ha-ha-ha-*HA!*"

KINDNESS

If you want to lift yourself up, lift up someone else.

—Booker T. Washington

He was so benevolent, so merciful a man that, in his mistaken passion, he would have held an umbrella over a duck in a shower of rain.   *—Douglas Jerrold*

No act of kindness, no matter how small, is ever wasted.   *—Aesop*

A great man shows his greatness by the way he treats little men.

—Thomas Carlyle

All cruelty springs from weakness.   *—Seneca the Younger*

To err is human, to forgive, divine.   *—Alexander Pope*

Do not feel badly if your kindness is rewarded with ingratitude; it is better to fall from your dream clouds than from a third-story window.

—Joaquim Maria Machado de Assis

Sayings

Kindness is the oil that takes the friction out of life.

If you were paid ten cents for every kind word you ever spoke, and had to pay out five cents for every unkind word, would you be rich or poor?

When you are dog-tired at night, could it be from growling all day long?

Jokes

- "So how are things down on Earth?" asked St. Peter of the beggar who had just arrived at the Pearly Gates. "Did people treat you decently?"

    "Oh, they were kind enough," responded the beggar mournfully, "but even the kind ones never seemed to have any money."

- The self-absorbed parishioner was told by her priest to go out in her community and do something kind for a needy person. Unable to bring herself to actually approach one of the unfortunates, the woman scribbled "Best of luck" on a hundred-dollar bill and thrust it into the nearest hand.

    The next day she was startled when the same fellow approached his benefactor and handed her $1,000. "Nice work, lady," he said cheerfully. "Best of Luck paid ten to one."

- A lonely stranger went into a deserted restaurant and ordered the breakfast special.

When his order arrived, he looked up at the waitress and asked, "How about a kind word?"

She leaned over and whispered, "Don't eat the eggs."

• "Now Bruno," said the teacher to the aggressive youngster, "what do you think your classmates would think of you if you were always kind and polite?"

"They'd think they could beat me up," responded the kid promptly.

• "You've always been so good to me, Dad," the extravagant coed wrote home, "but I haven't gotten any money from you in two months. What sort of kindness is that?"

Her father wrote back, "Consider it unremitting kindness."

MERIT

The graveyards are full of people the world could not do without.

—*Elbert Hubbard*

You see, my good wenches, how men of merit are sought after; the undeserver may sleep, when the man of action is call'd on.   —**William Shakespeare**

Charm strikes the sight, but merit wins the soul.   —*Alexander Pope*

When campaigning for the Senate in 1962, Teddy Kennedy found himself talking with a blue-collar worker who said bluntly, "I understand you've never worked a day in your life." Kennedy braced himself for a resentful lecture, only to be taken by surprise when the man continued, "Let me tell you, you haven't missed a thing."

Saying
A successful salesman sells his goods on their merit—not by knocking his competitor.

Jokes
• The boss looked over the efficiency report on the new employee and added a few words of his own. "Hedges is a definite asset to the firm. She is efficient, discreet, energetic, creative, and—best of all—she makes the other people in her department very nervous."

• "So tell me, Ms. Harris," asked the interviewer, "have you any other skills you think might be worth mentioning?"

"Actually, yes," said the applicant modestly. "Last year I had two short stories published in national magazines, and finished a novel."

"Very impressive," he commented, "but I was thinking of skills you could apply during office hours."

The applicant explained brightly, "Oh, that *was* during office hours."

• The loan officer skeptically looked over the down-at-heels fellow in front of him, who had applied for a $500 loan. "Have you any collateral at all?" she asked. "A car, for example?"

"Oh yes, I have a ninety-one Mercedes coupe," he replied promptly.

The loan officer's eyebrows rose, but she continued. "Any stocks or shares?"

"Of course. I manage my own portfolio."

"I see." She made a note in his file. "And a house, I suppose."

"Certainly, up in the hills, with ten acres, a pool, and a tennis court."

That did it. The banker rose to her feet, protesting indignantly. "You must be joking!"

The applicant shrugged. "Well, you started it."

PEACE

The mere absence of war is not peace.   *—John F. Kennedy*

Give peace in our time, O Lord.   **—The Book of Common Prayer**

Could I have but a line, a century hence, crediting a contribution to the cause of peace, I would yield every honor which has been accorded by war.
                                    —General Douglas MacArthur

Peace is a journey of a thousand miles and it must be taken one step at a time.
                                            —Lyndon B. Johnson

Nothing can bring you peace but yourself.   *—Ralph Waldo Emerson*

Peace upon any other basis than national independence, peace purchased at the cost of any part of our national integrity, is fit only for slaves, and even when purchased at such a price, it is a delusion, for it cannot last.   *—William E. Borah*

They shall beat their swords into plowshares, and their spears into pruninghooks: nation shall not lift up sword against nation, neither shall they learn war anymore.
                                                —Isaiah 2:4

In this age when there can be no losers in peace and no victors in war, we must recognize the obligation to match national strength with national restraint.
                                            —Lyndon B. Johnson

Peace hath her victories, no less renown'd than war.   *—John Milton*

Peace, like charity, begins at home.   *—Franklin D. Roosevelt*

Only a peace between equals can last. . . .   *—Woodrow Wilson*

An unjust peace is better than a just war.   *—Cicero*

Peace hath higher tests of manhood than battle ever knew.
                                        —John Greenleaf Whittier

A soft answer turneth away wrath.   *—Proverbs 15:1*

Peace is the exhaustion of strife, and is only secure in her triumphs in being in instant readiness for war. . . .   *—Mifflin Wistar Gibbs*

Take away the violence and who will hear the men of peace?
                                            —Lorraine Hansberry

Peace is necessary to this vast empire. We need population, not devastation.
                                            —Catherine the Great

People want peace so badly that governments ought to get out of their way and let them have it.   *—Dwight D. Eisenhower*

If blood be shed, let it be our blood. Cultivate the quiet courage of dying without killing. For man lives freely only by his readiness to die, if need be, at the hands of his brother, never by killing him.   —*Mohandas K. Gandhi*

Sayings

Keep the peace.

Peace at all costs.

Peace makes plenty.

Better to keep peace than have to make peace.

War breaks out; peace settles in.

Better an uneasy peace than an easy war.

Peace is for the strong, subjugation for the weak.

Jokes

* Isn't it a little depressing to live in a world where if you're ninety-nine years old, you might not see another war?

* Things are bad. I saw two fellows downtown carrying those signs reading THE END IS NEAR—and they were synchronizing their watches.

* Coping with the Threat of Peace.
                                        —**New York Times** *headline, January 1991*

* The first pacifist claimed that his idealism was of the highest order. "Peace is so important to me, I'm willing to fight for it," he declared.
    "And I love peace so much," replied the second pacifist, "that I am willing not to fight for it."

RELIGION

Every great advance in natural knowledge has involved the absolute rejection of authority.   —*Thomas Henry Huxley*

The most beautiful thing we can experience is the mysterious. It is the source of all true art and science.   —*Albert Einstein*

Heresies are experiments in man's unsatisfied search for truth.

—*H. G. Wells*

The whole religious complexion of the modern world is due to the absence from Jerusalem of a lunatic asylum.   —*Havelock Ellis*

Religion is the opiate of the masses.   —*Karl Marx*

[The yarmulke] is an indication that one recognizes that there is something above you. It says, "Above my intellect is a sign of godliness."   —*Rabbi Pinchas Stolper*

I could prove God statistically.   —*George Gallup*

The task of organized religion is not to prove that God was in the first century, but that he is in the twentieth.
—*S. H. Miller*

To be religious is to have a life that flows with the presence of the extraordinary.
—*Ann Belford Ulanov*

Someday, after mastering the winds, the waves, the tides, and gravity, we shall harness for God the energies of love, and then, for a second time in the history of the world, man will have discovered fire.
—*Pierre Teilhard de Chardin*

I think it pisses God off if you walk by the color purple in a field somewhere and don't notice it.
—*Alice Walker*

God, give us grace to accept with serenity the things that cannot be changed, courage to change the things which should be changed, and the wisdom to distinguish the one from the other.
—*Reinhold Niebuhr (later adopted by Alcoholics Anonymous)*

The value of persistent prayer is not that he will hear us . . . but that we will finally hear him.
—*William McGill*

Until you know that life is interesting—and find it so—you haven't found your soul.
—*Archbishop Geoffrey Fisher*

God, it seems, is a verb, not a noun, proper or improper.
—*R. Buckminster Fuller*

My religion consists of a humble admiration of the illimitable superior spirit who reveals himself in the slight details we are able to perceive with our frail and feeble minds.
—*Albert Einstein*

Health is the state about which medicine has nothing to say; sanctity is the state about which theology has nothing to say.
—*W. H. Auden*

It is as impossible for man to demonstrate the existence of God as it would be for even Sherlock Holmes to demonstrate the existence of Arthur Conan Doyle.
—*Frederick Buechner*

You can't divorce religious belief and public service . . . and I've never detected any conflict between God's will and my political duty. If you violate one, you violate the other.
—*Jimmy Carter*

Men will wrangle for religion; write for it; fight for it; die for it; anything but live for it.
—*Charles Caleb Colton*

Be good, keep your feet dry, your eyes open, your heart at peace, and your soul in the joy of Christ.
—*Thomas Merton*

Superstition is the religion of feeble minds.
—*Edmund Burke*

I find that the nicest and best people generally profess no religion at all, but are ready to like the best men of all religions.
—*Samuel Butler*

I am one of those cliff-hanging Catholics. I don't believe in God, but I do believe that Mary was his mother.
—*Martin Sheen*

Mothers and dads that take their children to church never get into trouble.
—*J. Edgar Hoover*

A pretty good test of a man's religion is how it affects his pocketbook.

—*Francis James Grimke*

. . . every age thinks it is perfect, especially in religion.

—*William Pickens*

. . . don't pray when it rains if you don't pray when the sun shines.

—*Leroy (Satchel) Paige*

While there is almost no religion operating in race relations, there is plenty of God.

—*Jay Saunders Redding*

The government of the United States is in no sense founded upon the Christian religion. The United States is not a Christian nation any more than it is a Jewish or Mohammedan nation.   —*Treaty with Tripoli*

Isn't God a shit!   —*Randolph Churchill*

If God's got anything better than sex to offer, he's certainly keeping it to himself.

—*Sting*

The great god Ra, whose shrine once covered acres, is filler now for crossword puzzle makers.   —*Keith Preston*

Who says I am not under the special protection of God?   —*Adolf Hitler*

He was of the faith chiefly in the sense that the church he currently did not attend was Catholic.   —*Kingsley Amis*

Heresy is only another word for freedom of thought.   —*Graham Greene*

I'm a Catholic and I can't commit suicide, but I plan to drink myself to death.

—*Jack Kerouac*

There is only one religion, though there are a hundred versions of it.

—*George Bernard Shaw*

Religions die when they are proved to be true. Science is the record of dead religions.

—*Oscar Wilde*

Christ died for our sins. Are we to make his martyrdom meaningless by not committing them?   —*Jules Feiffer*

How beautiful upon the mountains are the feet of him that bringeth good tidings, that publisheth peace.   —Isaiah 52:7

The desert shall rejoice, and blossom as the rose.   —Isaiah 35:1

What hath God wrought!   —Numbers 23:23

Prayer gives a man the opportunity of getting to know a gentleman he hardly ever meets. I do not mean his maker, but himself.   —*Dean William R. Inge*

[The reason that] Orientals are better and wiser in sex and love is a manifestation of the same spirit that produced the Zen garden. Their religion is a much kinder religion than ours; it honors the forefathers, their gods are not mean-spirited, nasty, gimlet-eyed gods who'll give you a bolt of lightning in the ass if you masturbate.

—*Harlan Ellison*

Professor Charles Copeland was once asked why he chose to live in a few small dusty rooms on the top floor of Harvard's Hollis Hall. He replied that he never intended to move. "It is the only place in Cambridge where God alone is above me." He paused, then added, "He's busy, but he's quiet."

No one can say that Christianity has failed. It has never been tried.

—*Adam Clayton Powell, Jr.*

Christianity has not been tried and found wanting; it has been found difficult and not tried.   —*G. K. Chesterton*

Giving away a fortune is taking Christianity too far.   —*Charlotte Bingham*

God so loved the world that he gave his only begotten son, that whosoever believed in him should not perish, but have everlasting life.   —*John 3:16*

Father, forgive them, for they know not what they do.   —*Luke 23:34*

Thou shalt love the Lord thy God with all thy heart, and with all thy soul, and with all thy mind. This is the first and great commandment. And the second is like unto it, Thou shalt love thy neighbor as thyself. On these two commandments hang all the law and the prophets.   —*Matthew 22:37–40*

Christ does not save us by acting a parable of divine love; he acts the parable of divine love by saving us. That is the Christian faith.   —*Austin Farber*

I have learned that human existence is essentially tragic. It is only the love of God, disclosed and enacted in Christ, that redeems the human tragedy and makes it tolerable. No, more than tolerable. Wonderful.   —*Bishop Angus Dun*

The trouble with born-again Christians is that they are an even bigger pain the second time around.   —*Herb Caen*

Christianity is one beggar telling another beggar where he found bread.

—*D. T. Niles*

Two great European narcotics, alcohol and Christianity.

—*Friedrich Wilhelm Nietzsche*

The most stupendous system of organized robbery known has been that of the church toward woman, a robbery that has not only taken her self-respect but all rights of person; the fruits of her own industry; her opportunities of education; the exercise of her own judgment; her own conscience, her own will.   —*Matilda Gage*

Being an Episcopalian interferes neither with my business nor my religion.

—*John Kendrick Bangs*

Greater love hath no man than to attend the Episcopal Church with his wife.

—*Lyndon B. Johnson*

A Sunday school is a prison in which children do penance for the evil conscience of their parents.   —*H. L. Mencken*

At the Harvest Festival in church the area behind the pulpit was piled high with tins of fruit for the old-age pensioners. We had collected the tinned fruit from door to door. Most of it came from old-age pensioners.   —*Clive James*

Sayings

Religion's greatest miracle is the survival of faith.

A man's faith, more than his house, is his castle.

Work for the Lord. The pay isn't much, but the retirement plan is out of this world.

More wrongs have been committed in the name of Christ than in the name of the devil.

Our Christian duty is to be kind to our fellow man.

If Christ returned today, would he recognize Christianity?

Honk if you love Jesus!

As dead as a church on Monday.

All are not saints that go to church.

Church work goes on slowly.

Jokes

• If there is a God, give me a sign! . . . See, I told you that the klmpt smflrrt glptnruf. . . .
—*Steve Martin*

• God isn't dead. He's just waiting for us to negotiate.

• I don't see why religion and science can't cooperate. What's wrong with using a computer to count our blessings?

• Gardening brings almost as many people to their knees as religion—only the words they use are a little different.

• I do benefits for all religions—I'd hate to blow the hereafter on a technicality.
—*Bob Hope*

• My son has taken up meditation—at least it's better than sitting doing nothing.
—*Max Kauffmann*

• Not only is there no God, but try getting a plumber at weekends.   —*Woody Allen*

• Jesus was making his usual rounds in heaven when he noticed a wizened, white-haired old man sitting in a corner looking very disconsolate. The next week he was disturbed to come across him again, looking equally miserable, and a week later he stopped to talk to him.

"See here, old fellow," said Jesus kindly, "this is heaven. The sun is shining, the clouds are comfy, the heavenly orchestra is playing beautiful music—you're supposed to be blissfully happy! What's wrong?"

"I'll tell you," the old man offered sadly. "I was a carpenter on earth, and lost my only, dearly beloved son at an early age. And I was hoping more than anything that I would be reunited with him here in heaven."

Tears sprang into Jesus' eyes. "Father!" he cried ecstatically.

The old man jumped to his feet and burst into tears. "Pinocchio!"

• Three fellows die and are transported to the Pearly Gates, where St. Peter explains that admission depends on a quick quiz, a mere formality. "I'm just going to ask each of you a single question," he explains, turning to the first guy. "What, please, is Easter?"

"That's easy. Christmas is when you celebrate the Pilgrims' landing. You buy a turkey—"

"Sorry," interrupts St. Peter briskly, "you're out." And he asks the second man, "What can you tell me about Easter?"

"No problem," the fellow responded promptly. "That's when we commemorate Jesus' birth by going shopping, and decorating a tree—"

"No, no, no," St. Peter bursts out, and turns in exasperation to the last guy. "I don't suppose you know anything about Easter?"

"Certainly I do. See, Christ was crucified, and he died, and they took the body down from the cross and wrapped it in a shroud and put it in a cave and rolled this big stone across the entrance—"

"Hang on a sec," interrupts St. Peter excitedly, beckoning the other two over. "Listen up. We've got someone here who actually knows his stuff."

"And after three days they roll the stone away," continues the third guy confidently, "and if he sees his shadow, there's going to be six more weeks of winter."

• Deciding to drink his troubles away, a fellow stayed on and on until the bar closed and he was ejected onto the sidewalk. And when he woke up the next morning, who should he see walking up to him but the pastor of his church. "Oh, Reverend," he croaked, "I hate for you to see me this way."

"Remember, Jimmy, God sees you this way too," counseled the minister gently.

"I suppose so," groaned the fellow, "but he keeps it to himself."

• Hear about the new-wave church in California?
—It has three commandments and six suggestions.

• Three ministers were discussing how they divided up the money from the collection plate. The first minister explained that he drew a circle on the ground, tossed the collection in the air, and all the money that landed in the circle was for God and the rest for himself and the parish.

The second minister described a similar system: he drew a line, and everything on the right went to God, while all the money on the left was contributed to his salary and church upkeep.

The third minister said his system worked on pretty much the same lines. "I just toss the collection up in the air," he explained, "and anything God can catch, he can keep."

SILENCE

What a blessing it would be if we could open and shut our ears as easily as we do our eyes.
—*Georg Christoph Lichtenberg*

It's better to keep one's mouth shut and be thought a fool than to open it and resolve all doubt.
—*Abraham Lincoln*

Blessed is the man who, having nothing to say, abstains from giving in words evidence of the fact.
—*George Eliot*

Silence gives consent, or a horrible feeling that nobody is listening.

—Franklin P. Jones

. . . men of few words are the best men. . . .   *—William Shakespeare*

If nobody ever said anything unless he knew what he was talking about, a ghastly hush would descend upon the earth.   *—Alan Herbert*

Be silent, or speak something worth hearing.   *—Thomas Fuller*

I have noticed that nothing I have never said ever did me any harm.

—Calvin Coolidge

The innocent is the person who explains nothing.   *—Albert Camus*

Many a time have I wanted to stop talking and find out what I really believed.

—Walter Lippmann

Nothing so stirs a man's conscience or excites his curiosity as a woman's silence.

—Thomas Hardy

Sayings
Blessed are they who have nothing to say and cannot be persuaded to say it.

Silence is also speech.   *—West African saying*

Silence is the door of consent.   *—North African saying*

Silence is golden.

Jokes
* The only pay phone in sight was in use, so the woman stood off to the side politely, to wait till it was free. Minutes went by, however, and she couldn't help noticing that the man in the phone booth was just standing there silently, not saying a word. Finally she tapped him on the shoulder and asked if she could use the phone.

  "Hold your horses," responded the fellow, covering the receiver. "I'm talking to my wife."

* Women like silent men. They think they're listening.   *—Marcel Achard*

* One learns in life to keep silent and draw one's own confusions.

—Cornelia Otis Skinner

SOLITUDE

I want to be left alone.   *—Greta Garbo (attrib.)*

The dread of loneliness is greater than the fear of bondage, so we get married.

—Cyril Connolly

God created man, and finding him not sufficiently alone, gave him a companion to make him feel his solitude more.   *—Paul Valéry*

City life: millions of people being lonesome together.

—Henry David Thoreau

Be good and you will be lonesome.   —*Mark Twain*

Hell is other people.   —*Jean-Paul Sartre*

The strongest man in the world is the man who stands alone.

—*Henrik Ibsen*

Whosoever is delighted in solitude is either a wild beast or a god.

—*Francis Bacon*

The individual who has experienced solitude will not easily become a victim of mass
suggestion.   —*Albert Einstein*

Saying
It's lonely at the top.

Joke
• If you can't stand solitude, maybe you bore others too.   —*Bob Gordon*

TEMPTATION AND VICE

The vices of the rich and great are mistaken for errors, and those of the poor and
lonely for crimes.   —*Marguerite, Countess of Blessington*

Why resist temptation? There will always be more.   —*Don Herold*

Get thee behind me, Satan.   —*Matthew 16:23*

Watch and pray, that ye enter not into temptation: the spirit indeed is willing, but the
flesh is weak.   —*Matthew 26:41*

The biggest temptation is . . . to settle for too little.   —*Thomas Merton*

I can resist everything except temptation.   —*Oscar Wilde*

. . . there are terrible temptations that it requires strength, strength, and courage to
yield to.   —*Oscar Wilde*

It has been my experience that folks who have no vices have very few virtues.

—*Abraham Lincoln*

I prefer a comfortable vice to a virtue that bores.   —*Molière*

Vice is its own reward.   —*Quentin Crisp*

His face was filled with broken commandments.   —*John Masefield*

A thing moderately good is not so good as it ought to be. Moderation in temper is
always a virtue; but moderation in principle is always a vice.

—*Thomas Paine*

Man's chief enemy is his own unruly nature and the dark forces pent up within him.

—*Ernest Jones*

Vice is a coward; to be truly brave, a man must be truly good.

—*Ignatius Sancho*

Sayings

Forbidden fruits taste better than those that are allowed.

There's always free cheese in a mousetrap.

Jokes

• What's the eleventh commandment for wayward evangelists?
    —Thou shalt not use thy rod on thy staff.

• The wages of sin is alimony.

—*Carolyn Wells*

TRUST

Trust everybody, but cut the cards.   —*Finley Peter Dunne*

Put your trust in God; but be sure to keep your powder dry.

—*Oliver Cromwell*

A verbal agreement isn't worth the paper it's written on.

—*Louis B. Mayer (attrib.)*

Put not your trust in princes.   —*Psalms 146:3*

Those you trust the most can steal the most.   —*Lawrence Leif*

I wonder men dare trust themselves with men.   —*William Shakespeare*

Never put anything on paper, my boy, and never trust a man with a small black
mustache.   —*P. G. Wodehouse*

The louder he talked of his honor, the faster we counted our spoons.
                                                          —*Ralph Waldo Emerson*

You can never give complete authority and overall power to anyone until trust can be
proven.   —*Bill Cosby*

Sayings

Never trust a man who says, "Trust me."

Trust is hard earned, and easily lost.

Trust your instincts.

Every good partnership is based on trust.

In God we trust. All others pay cash.

Always look on the bright side of things—but if you're buying something, look on both
sides.

Joke

• After almost twenty years teaching kindergarten, Miss Groden had composed a note
  which she had each child carry home at the end of the first week of school. It read,
  "Dear Parents—if you promise not to believe everything your child says happens at
  school, I'll promise not to believe everything he or she says happens at home."

TRUTH

Men stumble over the truth from time to time, but most pick themselves up and hurry off as if nothing had happened.
—*Winston Churchill*

Truth burns up error.
—*Sojourner Truth*

Error moves with quick feet . . . and truth must never be lagging behind.
—*Alexander Crummell*

The race problem is a moral one. . . . Its solution will come especially from the domain of principles. Like all the other great battles of humanity, it is to be fought out with the weapons of truth.
—*Alexander Crummell*

Absolute truth is incompatible with an advanced state of society.
—*Joaquim Maria Machado de Assis*

. . . the truth should be told, though it kill.
—*Timothy Thomas Fortune*

You never find yourself until you face the truth.
—*Pearl Bailey*

It nothing profits to show virtue in words and destroy truth in deeds.
—*Cyprian*

Truthfulness with me is hardly a virtue. I cannot discriminate between truths that need and those that need not to be told.
—*Margot Asquith*

If one cannot invent a really convincing lie, it is often better to stick to the truth.
—*Angela Thirkell*

Truth, like surgery, may hurt, but it cures.
—*Han Suyin*

Art for the sake of art itself is an idle sentence. Art for the sake of truth, for the sake of what is beautiful and good—that is the creed I seek.
—*George Sand*

Truth exists, only falsehood has to be invented.
—*Georges Braque*

The truth shall make you free.
—*John 8:32*

My way of joking is to tell the truth; it's the funniest joke in the world.
—*George Bernard Shaw*

I never give them hell. I just tell the truth and they think it's hell.
—*Harry S Truman*

It has always been desirable to tell the truth, but seldom if ever necessary.
—*Arthur J. Balfour*

If you tell the truth, you don't have to remember anything.
—*Mark Twain*

Most writers regard truth as their most valuable possession, and therefore are most economical in its use.
—*Mark Twain*

It is one thing to show a man that he is in error, and another to put him in possession of truth.
—*John Locke*

It is the customary fate of new truths to begin as heresies and to end as superstitions.
—*Thomas Henry Huxley*

. . . in the end truth will out.
—*William Shakespeare*

The truth is rarely pure, and never simple.   —*Oscar Wilde*

No human being is constituted to know the truth, the whole truth, and nothing but the truth; and even the best of men must be content with fragments, with partial glimpses, never the full fruition.   —*William Osler*

It is an old maxim of mine that when you have excluded the impossible, whatever remains, however improbable, must be the truth.   —*Arthur Conan Doyle*

In all matters of opinion, our adversaries are insane.   —*Mark Twain*

It is a difference of opinion that makes horse races.   —*Mark Twain*

The obstinate insistence that tweedledum is not tweedledee is the bone and marrow of life.   —*William James*

The reader deserves an honest opinion. If he doesn't deserve it, give it to him anyhow.
    —*John Ciardi, on the role of reviewers*

There is nothing more fickle, more vague, or more powerful; yet capricious as it is, [public opinion] is nevertheless much more often true, reasonable, and just than we imagine.   —*Napoleon Bonaparte*

One often contradicts an opinion when it is really only the tone in which it has been presented that is unsympathetic.   —*Wilhelm Friedrich Nietzsche*

Popular opinions, on subjects not palpable to sense, are often true, but seldom or never the whole truth.   —*John Stuart Mill*

The degree of one's emotion varies inversely with one's knowledge of the facts—the less you know, the hotter you get.   —*Bertrand Russell*

The fact that an opinion has been widely held is no evidence whatever that it is not utterly absurd.   —*Bertrand Russell*

Opinion is ultimately determined by the feelings, and not by the intellect.
    —*Herbert Spencer*

Every man has a perfect right to his opinion, provided it agrees with ours.
    —*Josh Billings*

We should stop kidding ourselves. We should let go of things that aren't true. It's always better with the truth.   —*R. Buckminster Fuller*

The great enemy of the truth is very often not the lie—deliberate, contrived, and dishonest—but the myth—persistent, persuasive, and unrealistic.
    —*John F. Kennedy*

Sayings
Truth came to market and could not be sold; we buy lies with ready cash.
    —*West African saying*

Lies, though many, will be caught by the truth as soon as she rises up.
    —*West African saying*

Bitter truth is better than sweet falsehood.   —*East African saying*

He who tells the truth is not well liked.   —*West African saying*

Jokes

• Judge: "Now, Mr. Connolly, do you swear to tell the truth, the whole truth, and nothing but the truth?"

Connolly: "Yes, Your Honor, I do."

Judge: "Fine. Now you know why you're here; what have you to say for yourself?"

Connolly: "Judge, you have set up too many limitations."

• Then there's the matter of half-truths. A certain sailor, celebrating a long-awaited ship's leave, got very inebriated. When he staggered back up the gangway, the captain sternly entered in the log: "Mate drunk tonight."

When he saw the entry, the mate objected violently. "Captain, the boat was moored—you know I've never been drunk on board before, never drunk on duty. If this stays on the record, I'll never get work on another ship."

Stone-hearted, the captain refused to modify his entry. "It is the truth, and it shall remain on the record."

A few days later the captain was checking over the log and came across an entry written by the mate: "The captain was sober today." The outraged captain summoned the mate and accused him of creating a false impression. "Anyone reading this will think my sobriety was unusual, that I'm usually drunk!" he bellowed.

"The statement is true," the mate calmly asserted, "and it shall remain in the log."

VIRTUE

Virtue, like a dowerless beauty, has more admirers than followers.

—*Marguerite, Countess of Blessington*

Good people are good because they've come to wisdom through failure.

—*William Saroyan*

There are those who would misteach us that to stick in a rut is consistency—and a virtue, and that to climb out of the rut is inconsistency—and a vice.

—*Mark Twain*

Few men have virtue to withstand the highest bidder.

—*George Washington*

Woman's virtue is man's greatest invention.   —*Cornelia Otis Skinner*

Ask yourself not if this or that is expedient, but if it is right.

—*Alan Paton*

It used to be a good hotel, but that proves nothing—I used to be a good boy.

—*Mark Twain*

He that is without sin among you, let him first cast a stone at her.

—*John 8:7*

Resist the devil, and he will flee from you.   —*James 4:7*

Virtue has never been as respectable as money.   —*Mark Twain*

There is a limit at which forbearance ceases to be a virtue.

—*Edmund Burke*

Women are not virtuous, but they have given us the idea of virtue.

—*Paul Geraldy*

Only the young die good.   —*Oliver Herford*

The only reward of virtue is virtue; the only way to have a friend is to be one.

—*Ralph Waldo Emerson*

Be not simply good; be good for something.   —*Henry David Thoreau*

Virtue consists, not in abstaining from vice, but in not desiring it.

—*George Bernard Shaw*

The more virtuous any man is, the less easily does he suspect others to be vicious.

—*Cicero*

And what is a weed? A plant whose virtues have not been discovered.

—*Ralph Waldo Emerson*

Philanthropy is almost the only virtue which is sufficiently appreciated by mankind.

—*Henry David Thoreau*

To abstain from sin when a man cannot sin is to be forsaken by sin, not to forsake it.

—*St. Augustine*

Saying
Conscience gets a lot of credit that belongs to cold feet.

Joke
• Is it wrong to have sex before you're married?
   —Only if it makes you late for the ceremony!

E M O T I O N S

ANGER

No man thinks clearly when his fists are clenched. —*George Jean Nathan*

Let not the sun go down upon your wrath. —*Ephesians 4:26*

A soft answer turneth away wrath. —*Proverbs 15:1*

Wrath killeth the foolish man, and envy slayeth the silly one. —*Job 5:2*

Anybody can become angry—that is easy; but to be angry with the right person, and to the right degree, and for the right purpose, and in the right way—that is not within everybody's power and is not easy. —*Aristotle*

When I am angry I can write, pray, and preach well, for then my whole temperament is quickened, my understanding sharpened, and all mundane vexations and temptations depart. —*Martin Luther*

He owned and operated a ferocious temper. —*Thomas Russell Ybarra*

One man was so mad at me that he ended his letter: "Beware. You will never get out of this world alive." —*John Steinbeck*

A man that does not know how to be angry does not know how to be good. —*Henry Ward Beecher*

Whate'er's begun in anger ends in shame. —*Benjamin Franklin*

Sayings
Anger is one letter short of danger.

I am righteously indignant; *you* are annoyed; *he* is making a fuss about nothing.

Jokes
• "I pushed my wife out of the second story window," an upset husband confessed to a nearby patrolman. "Put me in jail and throw away the key."

   "Did you kill her?" the officer asked.

   "I'm not sure," the terrified man answered. "That's why you've got to put me in jail!"

• People who fly off the handle usually have a screw loose.

• People who like to blow a fuse are usually in the dark.

• I yelled at my assistant this morning. He didn't do anything wrong, but he types faster when he's mad.

ANXIETY AND FEAR

A timid person is frightened before a danger, a coward during the time, and a courageous person afterwards.   —*Jean Paul Friedrich Richter*

None but a coward dares to boast that he has never known fear.
                                          —*Marshal Ferdinand Foch*

Fear is a noose that binds until it strangles.   —*Jean Toomer*

To defend one's self against fear is simply to ensure that one will, one day, be conquered by it; fears must be faced.   —*James Baldwin*

A fool without fear is sometimes wiser than an angel with fear.
                                                    —*Nancy Astor*

Anxiety is the interest paid on trouble before it is due.
                                            —*Dean William R. Inge*

What, me worry?   —*Alfred E. Neuman*

Anxiety is the space between the "now" and the "then."   —*Richard Abell*

Sometimes I get the feeling that the whole world is against me, but deep down I know that's not true. Some of the smaller countries are neutral.   —*Robert Orben*

Many of our cares are but a morbid way of looking at our privileges.
                                                —*Sir Walter Scott*

The reason why worry kills more people than work is that more people worry than work.   —*Robert Frost*

When you don't have any money, the problem is food. When you have money, it's sex. When you have both, it's health. If everything is simply jake, then you're frightened of death.   —*J. P. Donleavy*

I have a new philosophy. I'm only going to dread one day at a time.
                                            —*Charles M. Schulz*

The only thing we have to fear is fear itself.   —*Franklin D. Roosevelt*

If you fear making anyone mad, then you ultimately probe for the lowest common denominator of human achievement.   —*Jimmy Carter*

Fear is the main source of superstition, and one of the main sources of cruelty.
                                                —*Bertrand Russell*

To conquer fear is the beginning of wisdom.   —*Bertrand Russell*

Of all base passions, fear is most accursed.   —*William Shakespeare*

There is only one universal passion: fear.   —*George Bernard Shaw*

Hate is the consequence of fear; we fear something before we hate it; a child who fears noises becomes a man who hates noise.   —*Cyril Connolly*

Anxiety seems to be the dominant fact—and is threatening to become the dominant cliché—of modern life.

— **Time** *magazine*

Sayings

Whenever he thought about his troubles, he felt terrible. And so at last he came to a fateful decision. He decided not to think about them.

No one would ever have crossed the ocean if he could have gotten off the ship during the storms.

Worry never paid a bill.

He who never worries never cares.

You can always find something to worry about.

Jokes

• The psychiatrist gently pointed out that most of the things his patient was anxious about never actually came to pass.

"I know," admitted the patient unhappily, "but then I worry about *why* they didn't happen."

• Everybody's shook up these days. Teenagers are upset because they're living in a world dominated by nuclear weapons—and adults are upset because they're living in a world dominated by teenagers.

• Nervous? I feel like a pizza on the way to Roseanne Barr!

• Listening to the radio on the way to work doesn't help either. The other morning the disk jockey asked, "Hey, what makes you so sure you locked the front door?"

• What's the difference between anxiety and panic?

—Anxiety is the first time you can't do it a second time, and panic is the second time you can't do it the first time.

CONFIDENCE

Power without a nation's confidence is nothing.

— *Catherine the Great*

If you're feeling good about you, what you're wearing outside doesn't mean a thing.

— *Leontyne Price*

If you have no confidence in self you are twice defeated in the race of life. With confidence, you have won even before you have started.

— *Marcus Garvey*

While one person hesitates because he feels inferior, the other is busy making mistakes and becoming superior.

— *Henry C. Link*

We have to learn to be our own best friends because we fall too easily into the trap of being our own worst enemies.

— *Roderick Thorpe*

For a man to achieve all that is demanded of him he must regard himself as greater than he is.

— *Johann Wolfgang von Goethe*

The leader must know, must know that he knows, and must be able to make it abundantly clear to those about him that he knows.   —*Clarence B. Randall*

The ablest man I ever met is the man you think you are.

—*Franklin D. Roosevelt*

Nobody holds a good opinion of a man who has a low opinion of himself.

—*Anthony Trollope*

The turning point in the process of growing up is when you discover the core of strength within you that survives all hurt.   —*Max Lerner*

Men despise great projects when they do not feel themselves capable of great successes.   —*Luc de Clapiers de Vauvenargues*

He who has the confidence in himself will lead the rest.   —*Horace*

If you think you can, you can. And if you think you can't, you're right.

—*Mary Kay Ash*

Every new adjustment is a crisis in self-esteem.   —*Eric Hoffer*

Men are more ready to offend one who desires to be beloved than one who wishes to be feared.   —*Niccolò Machiavelli*

Materialists and madmen never have doubts.   —*G. K. Chesterton*

The men who really believe in themselves are all in lunatic asylums.

—*G. K. Chesterton*

No one can make you feel inferior without your consent.

—*Eleanor Roosevelt*

Nothing is more humiliating than to see idiots succeed in enterprises we have failed in.
—*Gustave Flaubert*

One of the most wonderful things that happened in our *Nautilus* program was that everybody knew it was going to fail—so they let us completely alone so we were able to do the job.   —*Admiral Hyman G. Rickover, on development of the nuclear submarine*

Saying
Confidence is not trying the knob after you've locked the door.

Jokes
• Hear about the easygoing guy who was given three weeks to live?
    —He took the last two weeks of July and the week between Christmas and New Year's.

• Confidence: what you start off with before you completely understand the situation.

CURIOSITY

Millions saw the apple fall, but Newton was the one who asked why.

—*Bernard Baruch*

The important thing is not to stop questioning.   —*Albert Einstein*

Curiosity is a willing, a proud, an eager confession of ignorance.

—*Leonard Rubinstein*

Curiosity is one of the most permanent and certain characteristics of a vigorous intellect.   —*Samuel Johnson*

Saying
Curiosity killed the cat.

Jokes
• A key part of candidate Decker's reform program was the elimination of the X-rated video stores springing up on Main Street. As she stood before the crowd, her face grew red with anger at the very thought of this threat to public decency and morals. "I actually rented one of these filthy cassettes," she declared boldly, "and was disgusted to witness horrible acts of perversion: sodomy, oral sex, one man engaging in the sex act with three women, a woman accommodating four men, even sex with a *dog*! Vote for Lynn Decker, ladies and gentlemen, and I guarantee this blight on our community will be eliminated!" Catching her breath, she asked, "Any questions?"

  Twelve hands shot up. "Where'd you get the tape?"

• Observing the local farmer standing next to a deep hole and repeating, "33 . . . 33 . . . 33 . . . ," a soldier from the invading army was unable to contain his curiosity. "What are you doing?" he demanded.

  The peasant pointed down into the hole.

  Shrugging, the infantryman approached the edge to see for himself just what was so interesting. The peasant shoved him into the hole, straightened up, and began repeating, "34 . . . 34 . . . 34. . . ."

CYNICISM

The cynic is one who never sees a good quality in a man and never fails to see a bad one. He is the human owl, vigilant in darkness and blind to light, mousing for vermin, and never seeing noble game. The cynic puts all human actions into two classes— openly bad and secretly bad.   —*Henry Ward Beecher.*

We can destroy ourselves by cynicism and delusion, just as effectively as bombs.

—*Kenneth Clark*

Cynicism is the intellectual cripple's substitute for intelligence. It is the dishonest businessman's substitute for conscience. It is the communicator's substitute, whether he is advertising man or editor or writer, for self-respect.   —*Russell Lynes*

A cynic is a man who, when he smells flowers, looks around for a coffin.

—*H. L. Mencken (attrib.)*

[A cynic is] a man who knows the price of everything and the value of nothing.

—*Oscar Wilde*

It's going to be fun to watch and see how long the meek can keep the earth after they inherit it.   —*Kin Hubbard*

No matter how cynical you become, it's never enough to keep up.

—*Lily Tomlin*

Sayings

Don't raise your eyes to heaven—God won't help you.

I've heard that one before.

The day you're born is the day you draw your last peaceful breath.

An optimist is a parent who'll let his kid borrow the new car for a date. A pessimist is one who won't. A cynic is one who did.

Nothing kills hope faster than cynicism.

Joke

- First person: "Hey, it's cold outside. Could you close the window?"
   Second person: "So if I close the window, will it be warm outside?"

EMBARRASSMENT

Whoever blushes is already guilty; true innocence is ashamed of nothing.

—*Jean-Jacques Rousseau*

I never wonder to see men wicked, but I often wonder to see them not ashamed.

—*Jonathan Swift*

Man is the only animal that blushes. Or needs to.   —*Mark Twain*

Blushing fulfills a most important function in propagation of the human species and is all the more interesting because it is involuntary and shows a readiness to be courted.

—*Joseph Sandler*

Sayings

It's no disgrace to get lice, but it is to keep them.

The best way to save face is not to lose your head.

Joke

- The bathroom scale manufacturer was very proud of the new model being introduced at the trade fair. "Listen to these features: it's calibrated to one one-hundredth of a pound; it can measure your height as well, in feet or meters; it gives you a readout via an LED or human-voice simulator; and that's not all—"
   "Very impressive," interrupted a none-too-slender sales rep for a chain of home furnishings stores, "but before I place an order I'll have to try it out."
   "Be my guest," said the manufacturer graciously.
   But no sooner had the sales rep taken his place on the scale than a loud, very human voice issued forth: "One at a time, please, one at a time!"

EMOTIONS

Your heart often knows things before your mind does.

—*Polly Adler*

The emotions may be endless. The more we express them, the more we have to express.

—*E. M. Forster*

Man is the only creature whose emotions are entangled with his memory.

—*Marjorie Holmes*

To feel the right emotions is fully as important as to hold the right ideas, and the great service of religion is the development of the right emotions.

—*Geoffrey Parsons*

I have my own particular sorrows, loves, delights; and you have yours. But sorrow, gladness, yearning, hope, love, belong to all of us, in all times and in all places. Music is the only means whereby we feel these emotions in their universality.

—*Harry Overstreet*

Poetry is the spontaneous overflow of powerful feelings: it takes its origin from emotion recollected in tranquillity.

—*William Wordsworth*

Sayings

For news of the heart, ask the face.

—*West African saying*

Our homes need more electrical outlets, and more emotional outlets.

Once more—this time with feeling.

Jokes

• Mrs. Goldwyn decided to try to contact her deceased husband of many years through a medium, and sure enough, his voice was soon audible in the room. "Are you happy, sweetheart?" asked the widow, almost overcome with emotion.

"Yes," came the ghostly reply.

"Happier than you were when we were together?" she asked, a little nervously.

"Yes," replied the disembodied voice again.

"Oh, sweetheart," she quavered, "what's it like in heaven?"

"Who's in heaven?"

• A golfer choked in midswing and was overcome by emotion as a funeral procession passed by next to the fairway. "Gee, Fred, you're awfully broken up," observed another member of his party.

"Yeah, it's tough," said the first guy, turning back to his ball. "Today would've been our thirty-first anniversary."

ENTHUSIASM

No person who is enthusiastic about his work has anything to fear from life.

—*Samuel Goldwyn*

Exuberance is better than taste.

—*Gustave Flaubert*

The secret of genius is to carry the spirit of the child into old age, which means never losing your enthusiasm.   —*Aldous Huxley*

There is nothing so easy but it becomes difficult when you do it reluctantly.
                                                                              —*Terence*

Nothing is so contagious as enthusiasm; it moves stones, it charms brutes. Enthusiasm is the genius of sincerity and truth accomplishes no victories without it.
                                                                    —*Edward Bulwer-Lytton*

Lack of pep is often mistaken for patience.   —*Kin Hubbard*

It is unfortunate, considering enthusiasm moves the world, that so few enthusiasts can be trusted to speak the truth.   —*Arthur J. Balfour*

The love of life is necessary to the vigorous prosecution of any undertaking.
                                                                       —*Samuel Johnson*

What hunger is in relation to food, zest is in relation to life.
                                                                      —*Bertrand Russell*

The world belongs to the enthusiast who keeps cool.   —*William McFee*

Whatsoever thy hand findeth to do, do it with thy might; for there is no work, nor device, nor knowledge, nor wisdom in the grave, whither thou goest.
                                                                    —*Ecclesiastes 9:10*

There is real magic in enthusiasm. It spells the difference between mediocrity and accomplishment. . . .   —*Norman Vincent Peale*

Nothing great was ever achieved without enthusiasm.
                                                                  —*Ralph Waldo Emerson*

People who are unable to motivate themselves must be content with mediocrity, no matter how impressive their other talents.   —*Andrew Carnegie*

You can't sweep people off their feet if you can't be swept off yours.
                                                                       —*Clarence Day*

A certain excessiveness seems a necessary element in all greatness.
                                                                      —*Harvey Cushing*

Indifference may not wreck a man's life at any one turn, but it will destroy him with a kind of dry-rot in the long run.   —*Bliss Carman*

Fanaticism consists in redoubling your effort when you have forgotten your aim.
                                                                    —*George Santayana*

Human passion is the hallucination of a distempered mind.
                                                                    —*William Whipper*

Hard work keeps the wrinkles out of the mind and spirit.
                                                                  —*Helena Rubinstein*

Sayings
Enthusiasm is more important than any other commodity. It will find solutions when none are apparent, and it will achieve success where none is thought possible.

You will draw to yourself that which you most persistently think about.

Go for it.

You gotta want it.

No pain, no gain.

Joke

* A woman walked into a fancy dress store and announced to the owner, "I'm the greatest salesperson ever. And I want a job."

   "That's quite a claim," the owner answered back, "but unfortunately I don't have any openings."

   Undaunted the saleswoman asked, "How many dresses does your best salesperson sell in a day?"

   "Five or six," the owner answered.

   Without blinking an eye, the saleswoman claimed, "I'll sell twelve and I'll do it without pay or commission."

   The owner, knowing he couldn't lose, agreed. Just an hour before closing, the new saleswoman had sold eighteen dresses. "Do I get the job now?" she asked.

   "I've got one more test for you," the owner declared. He went back into the storeroom and returned with the most hideous dress imaginable. "Sell this dress by the time the store closes tonight and you've got a job."

   Forty-five minutes later, the saleswoman marched into the owner's office and threw down the sales receipt. "I'm impressed," the owner declared in amazement. "You've got the job. How on earth did you convince somebody to buy that thing?"

   "Getting the person to buy it wasn't a problem. Strangling the woman's seeing-eye dog was the tough part."

GRATITUDE

How sharper than a serpent's tooth it is to have a thankless child.

—William Shakespeare

If you pick up a starving dog and make him prosperous, he will not bite you; that is the principal difference between a dog and a man.   *—Mark Twain*

Some people are always grumbling because roses have thorns; I am thankful that thorns have roses.   *—Alphonse Karr*

Next to ingratitude, the most painful thing to bear is gratitude.

—Henry Ward Beecher

Every acknowledgment of gratitude is a circumstance of humiliation; and some are found to submit to frequent mortifications of this kind, proclaiming what obligations they owe, merely because they think it in some measure cancels the debt.

—Oliver Goldsmith

The public has neither shame nor gratitude.   *—William Hazlitt*

Blessed is he who expects no gratitude, for he shall not be disappointed.

—W. C. Bennett

Praise is the only gift for which people are really grateful.

—*Marguerite, Countess of Blessington*

Sayings

You'll thank me someday.

You'll thank me when I'm six feet under.

Gratefulness is the poor man's payment.

Gratitude can only be given, not taken.

Gratitude is sometimes more easily given than received.

Somebody up there likes me.

Joke

• For his fortieth birthday the dutiful son received the usual two ties from his mother, this time a paisley and a solid. When he picked her up for dinner that night wearing the solid, she took one look and snapped, "And what's wrong with the paisley?"

GRIEF

For certain is death for the born and certain is birth for the dead; therefore over the inevitable thou shalt not grieve.   —**Bhagavad Gita** *2:27*

Heavy hearts, like heavy clouds in the sky, are best relieved by the letting of a little water.   —*Antoine Rivarol*

Easy-crying widows take new husbands soonest; there's nothing like wet weather for transplanting.   —*Oliver Wendell Holmes, Sr.*

If you would have me weep, you must first of all feel grief yourself.

—*Horace*

Quiet and sincere sympathy is often the most welcome and efficient consolation to the afflicted. Said a wise man to one in deep sorrow, "I did not come to comfort you; God only can do that; but I did come to say how deeply and tenderly I feel for you in your affliction."   —*Tryon Edwards*

I am always grieved when a man of real talent dies, for the world needs such men more than heaven does.   —*Georg Christoph Lichtenberg*

Sorrow is so easy to express and yet so hard to tell.   —*Joni Mitchell*

Grief is so selfish.   —*Mary Elizabeth Braddon*

Grief and greed are as inextricably entwined as love and marriage should be.

—*Ann Kent*

There are few sorrows, however poignant, in which a good income is of no avail.

—*Logan Pearsall Smith*

Grief is itself a med'cine.   —*William Cowper*

The bitterest tears shed over graves are for words left unsaid and deeds left undone.

—*Harriet Beecher Stowe*

Saying

You cannot prevent the birds of sorrow from flying over your head, but you can prevent them from building nests in your hair.   —*Persian proverb*

Jokes

• It can be terribly difficult to find the right words, but sometimes they're not even necessary. When one of his classmates died, an eight-year-old friend visited the boy's home one day after school.

"What did you say?" asked his mother gently when the child returned.

"Nothing. I just sat on his mom's lap and cried with her."

• A guy returns from a long trip to Europe, having left his beloved cat in his brother's care. The minute he clears customs, he calls his brother and inquires after his pet.

"The cat's dead," replies his brother bluntly.

The guy is devastated. "You don't know how much that cat meant to me," he sobbed into the phone. "Couldn't you at least have given a little thought to a nicer way of breaking the news? For instance, couldn't you have said, 'Well, you know, the cat got out of the house one day and climbed up on the roof, and the fire department couldn't get her down, and finally she died of exposure . . . or starvation . . . or something'? Why are you always so thoughtless?"

"Look, I'm really really sorry," says his brother. "I'll try to do better next time, I swear."

"Okay, let's just put it behind us. How are you, anyway? How's Mom?"

There was a long pause. "Uh," the brother finally stammers, "uh . . . Mom's on the roof."

HAPPINESS

If only we'd stop trying to be happy we could have a pretty good time.

—*Edith Wharton*

It is difficult to tell which gives some couples the most happiness, the minister who marries them, or the judge who divorces them.   —*Mary Wilson Little*

Happiness, like youth and health, is rarely appreciated until it is past.

—*Marguerite, Countess of Blessington*

Happiness consists not in having much, but in being content with little.

—*Marguerite, Countess of Blessington*

There is no cosmetic for beauty like happiness.

—*Marguerite, Countess of Blessington*

Anything you're good at contributes to happiness.   —*Bertrand Russell*

Don't wish me happiness—I don't expect to be happy . . . it's gotten beyond that somehow. Wish me courage and strength and a sense of humor—I will need them all.

—*Anne Morrow Lindbergh*

The search for happiness is one of the chief sources of unhappiness.

—*Eric Hoffer*

Happiness: a good bank account, a good cook, and a good digestion.

—*Jean-Jacques Rousseau*

It is neither wealth nor splendor but tranquillity and occupation which give happiness.

—*Thomas Jefferson*

The greatest happiness you can have is knowing that you do not necessarily require happiness.   —*William Saroyan*

Happiness? A good cigar, a good meal, a good cigar, and a good woman—or a bad woman; it depends on how much happiness you can handle.

—*George Burns*

Good friends, good books, and a sleepy conscience: this is the ideal life.

—*Mark Twain*

Man needs, for his happiness, not only the enjoyment of this or that, but hope and enterprise and change.   —*Bertrand Russell*

Happiness is a mystery like religion, and should never be rationalized.

—*G. K. Chesterton*

Knowledge of what is possible is the beginning of happiness.

—*George Santayana*

The great source of pleasure is variety.   —*Samuel Johnson*

To be able to throw oneself away for the sake of a moment, to be able to sacrifice years for a woman's smile—that is happiness.   —*Hermann Hesse*

We must select the illusion which appeals to our temperament, and embrace it with passion, if we want to be happy.   —*Cyril Connolly*

Make a joyful noise unto God, all ye lands.   —*Psalms 61:1*

Happiness lies not in the mere possession of money; it lies in the joy of achievement, in the thrill of creative effort.   —*Franklin D. Roosevelt*

Those who bring sunshine to the lives of others cannot keep it from themselves.

—*James M. Barrie*

Happiness is a warm puppy.   —*Charles M. Schulz*

Happiness is a warm gun.   —*John Lennon and Paul McCartney*

A man's happiness or unhappiness depends as much on his temperament as on his destiny.   —*François de La Rochefoucauld*

The supreme happiness of life is the conviction that we are loved.

—*Victor Hugo*

A lifetime of happiness! No man alive could bear it: it would be hell on earth.

—*George Bernard Shaw*

Happiness is speechless.   —*George William Curtis*

The only really happy folk are married women and single men.

—*H. L. Mencken*

He is happy that knoweth not himself to be otherwise.   —*Thomas Fuller*

A merry heart doeth good like a medicine. . . .   —**Proverbs** *17:22*

The happiest person is the person who suffers the least pain; the most miserable who enjoys the least pleasure.   —*Jean-Jacques Rousseau*

It is the inalienable right of all to be happy.   —*Elizabeth Cady Stanton*

Happiness makes up in height for what it lacks in length.   —*Robert Frost*

When I was young, I used to think that wealth and power would bring me happiness. . . . I was right.   —*Gahan Wilson*

Sayings
Everyone has the power to make others happy; some do it by entering the room, others by leaving it.

To be happy and contented, count your blessings, not your cash.

If you wish to be happy for an hour, get intoxicated. If you wish to be happy for three days, get married. If you wish to be happy for eight days, kill your pig and eat it. But if you wish to be happy forever, become a gardener.   —*Chinese proverb*

Happiness takes no account of time.

Jokes
• There is a fable about a little orphan who was feeling particularly lonely and blue when she happened across a gorgeous butterfly trapped in the thorns of a blackberry bush. Taking great care not to tear its fragile wings, the girl's nimble fingers finally worked the insect free, whereupon, instead of fluttering away, it turned into a golden fairy who offered to grant any wish.

"I want to be happy!" the orphan cried.

The fairy smiled, leaned forward, whispered something in her ear, and vanished. And from that day forward there was no more happy spirit in the land than that child, who grew into a merry woman and a contented old lady. On her very deathbed, her neighbors crowded around, desperate that the secret of happiness not die with her. "Tell us, please tell us, what the fairy said to you," they pleaded.

The old woman smiled benevolently, and whispered, "She told me that everyone— no matter how rich or secure or self-contained or successful they might appear—had need of me."

• Happiness is having a large, loving, caring, close-knit family in another city.

—*George Burns*

Unhappiness

Men who are unhappy, like men who sleep badly, are always proud of the fact.

—*Bertrand Russell*

How bitter a thing it is to look into happiness through another man's eyes!

—*William Shakespeare*

My theory is to enjoy life, but the practice is against it.   —*Charles Lamb*

A man should always consider how much he has more than he wants, and how much more unhappy he might be than he really is.   —*Joseph Addison*

An era can be said to end when its basic illusions are exhausted.

—*Arthur Miller*

Unhappiness is best defined as the difference between our talents and our expectations.

—*Edward De Bono*

Ask yourself whether you are happy and you cease to be so.

—*John Stuart Mill*

History is the sole consolation left to the people, for it shows them that their ancestors were as unhappy as they are, or even more so.   —*Sébastien Chamfort*

We are never happy: we can only remember that we were so once.

—*Alexander Smith*

Pleasure chews and grinds us.   —*Michel Eyquem de Montaigne*

We do not believe in having happiness imposed upon us.

—*José Correa, UN representative from Nicaragua, in reply to Soviet representative*

Saying
If each hung up his pack of troubles on the wall and looked around at the troubles of others, he would quickly run back to claim his own bag.

Joke
• Wife: "You're always wishing for something you haven't got."
  Husband: "What else is there to wish for?"

HATRED

Few people can be happy unless they hate some other person, nation, or creed.

—*Bertrand Russell*

Hate is more lasting than dislike.   —*Adolf Hitler*

Everyone hates a martyr; it's no wonder martyrs were burned at the stake.

—*Edgar Watson Howe*

I shall never permit myself to stoop so low as to hate any man.

—*Booker T. Washington*

When our hatred is too keen it puts us beneath those whom we hate.

—*François de La Rochefoucauld*

Hate is the consequence of fear; we fear something before we hate it; a child who fears noises becomes a man who hates noise.   —*Cyril Connolly*

Now hatred is by far the longest pleasure; men love in haste but they detest at leisure.

—*Lord Byron*

Any man who tries to excite class hatred, sectional hate, hate of creeds, any kind of hatred in our community, though he may affect to do it in the interest of the class he is addressing, is in the long run with absolute certainty that class's own worst enemy.

—*Theodore Roosevelt*

Why is propaganda so much more successful when it stirs up hatred than when it tries to stir up friendly feeling?   —*Bertrand Russell*

Sayings
He who hates, hates himself.   —*Southern African saying*

Hate has no medicine.   —*West African saying*

Hatred is blind, as well as love.

Jokes
• The feud between the two politicians had been going on for years, but finally one day his opponent's bullying, thieving tactics caused the politician to blow his stack. He vented all his spleen in a venomous letter, but when his seasoned secretary brought it in for his signature, she ventured the opinion that it was a bit strong. So he cut a few of the most offensive bits, but the secretary still felt it should be toned down.

"All right," he grumbled as he struck out a few more choice phrases, "but at this rate that schmuck's likely to miss the point entirely."

Finally the secretary brought in the third version for his approval. "I suppose this'll have to do," said the politician, "but you've made a couple of typing errors. "There's no *c* in extortion; subpoena has an *o* in it; and his wife's name is Lucille."

• Little old lady: "Why are you sitting here all by yourself, little boy? Haven't you anyone to play with?"

Little boy: "Yes, I have one friend—but I hate him."

JEALOUSY

Nothing is more humiliating than to see idiots succeed in enterprises we have failed in.

—*Gustave Flaubert*

Men despise great projects when they do not feel themselves capable of great successes.   —*Luc de Clapiers de Vauvenargues*

Jealousy is that pain which a man feels from the apprehension that he is not equally beloved by the person whom he entirely loves.   —*Joseph Addison*

It is not love that is blind, but jealousy.   —*Lawrence Durrell*

Trifles light as air are to the jealous confirmations strong as proofs of holy writ.

—*William Shakespeare*

Love that is fed by jealousy dies hard.   —*Ovid*

In jealousy there is more of self-love than love.

—*François de La Rochefoucauld*

Whenever a friend succeeds, a little something in me dies.   —*Gore Vidal*

Nothing arouses ambition so much in the heart as the trumpet-clang of another's fame.

—*Baltasar Gracian*

Jealousy, an uncontrollable passion. The Siamese twin of love.

—*Marlene Dietrich*

It's matrimonial suicide to be jealous when you have a really good reason.

—*Clare Boothe Luce*

Jealousy is the only evil we endure without becoming accustomed to it.

—*Colette*

With jealousy, one has no time to be bored, and hardly time to grow old.

—*Colette*

Do not despise or hate your neighbor because he has been a success; take care of your own case.   —*William Tecumseh Vernon*

Saying
The man who is not jealous in love does not love.   —*North African saying*

Joke
• Sister Christen's first post as a missionary was to a remote tribal area in East Africa. She figured the first step in the conversion of the heathen would be to teach them her language, and she began with the tribal chieftain. Leading him into the countryside, she pointed out a banyan tree and said, "Tree."

"Tree," the chief repeated obligingly.

Next they came across a herd of monkeys. "Ba-boon," explained Sister Christen. "Ba-boon," he repeated.

"Very good." The nun beamed.

At the riverbank they encountered a herd of hippopotami. "Hip-po-pot-a-mus," recited the tribesman dutifully. And then what should they encounter in the rushes at the water's edge but a couple making love. Blushing scarlet, the nun blurted, "Man on bicycle."

The chief thrust his spear into the man's back. "Chief, why did you kill him?" screamed the horrified nun.

"Him on *my* bicycle," he explained with a shrug.

LOVE

Romantic

Here's to the happy man: All the world loves a lover.

—*Ralph Waldo Emerson*

To love and be loved is to feel the sun from both sides.   —*David Viscott*

Venus favors the bold.   —*Ovid*

Hell, madame, is to love no longer.   —*Georges Bernanos*

The course of true love never did run smooth.   —*William Shakespeare*

The love we give away is the only love we keep.   —*Elbert Hubbard*

Pains of love be sweeter far than all other pleasures are.   —*John Dryden*

Love reckons hours for months, and days for years; and every little absence is an age.
—*John Dryden*

It is impossible to repent of love. The sin of love does not exist.
—*Muriel Spark*

The first duty of love is to listen.   —*Paul Tillich*

It is not love, but lack of love, which is blind.   —*Glenway Wescott*

There is no surprise more magical than the surprise of being loved: it is God's finger on man's shoulder.   —*Charles Morgan*

Love commingled with hate is more powerful than love. Or hate.
—*Joyce Carol Oates*

Americans, who make more of marrying for love than any other people, also break up more of their marriages, but the figure reflects not so much the failure of love as the determination of people not to live without it.   —*Morton Hunt*

This is one of the miracles of love: it gives . . . a power of seeing through its own enchantments and yet not being disenchanted.   —*C. S. Lewis*

Love cures people, the ones who receive love and the ones who give it, too.
—*Karl A. Menninger*

Love is the only sane and satisfactory answer to the problem of human existence.
—*Erich Fromm*

If you haven't at least a slight poetic crack in the heart, you have been cheated by nature.   —*Phyllis Battelle*

Let no one who loves be called altogether unhappy. Even love unreturned has its rainbow.   —*James M. Barrie*

Greater love hath no man than this, that a man lay down his life for his friends.
—*John 15:13*

Love conquers all.   —*Virgil*

The supreme happiness of life is the conviction that we are loved.
—*Victor Hugo*

There is no fear in love, but perfect love casteth out fear. . . .
—**The First Epistle General of John** *4:18*

If you want to be loved, love and be lovable.   —*Benjamin Franklin*

It's love that makes the world go round.   —*W. S. Gilbert*

Love like ours can never die!   —*Rudyard Kipling*

To fear love is to fear life, and those who fear life are already three parts dead.

—Bertrand Russell

Love sought is good, but given unsought is better.   *—William Shakespeare*

Tis better to have loved and lost than never to have loved at all.

—Alfred, Lord Tennyson

[Love is] the river of life in this world.   *—Henry Ward Beecher*

When love is suppressed, hate takes its place.   *—Havelock Ellis*

Cooking is like love. It should be entered into with abandon or not at all.

—Harriet Van Horne

I am two fools, I know, for loving, and for saying so.   *—John Donne*

Love is not blind—it sees more, not less. But because it sees more, it is willing to see
less.   *—Rabbi Julius Gordon*

Cynical

I haven't had true love in years. My heart is empty. I fought for what I believed in. But
win or lose, I'll be okay.   *—Ivana Trump*

The one thing that I know about love for sure is that it's the only game in town and
that you must keep going back to bat again and again and again. I have no respect for
anyone who says they've given up, or that they're not looking or that they're tired. That
is to abrogate one's responsibility as a human being.   *—Harlan Ellison*

Love is like an hourglass, with the heart filling up as the brain empties.

—Jules Renard

If love is the answer, could you rephrase the question?   *—Lily Tomlin*

One is very crazy when in love.   *—Sigmund Freud*

The only victory over love is flight.   *—Napoleon Bonaparte*

Love is an ocean of emotions, entirely surrounded by expenses.

—James Dewar

Love is what happens to a man and woman who don't know each other.

—W. Somerset Maugham

He who cannot love must learn to flatter.   *—Johann Wolfgang von Goethe*

Love as a relation between men and women was ruined by the desire to make sure of
the legitimacy of children.   *—Bertrand Russell*

Reason is a weak antagonist against love.   *—Madeleine de Scudéry*

Any woman can fool a man if she wants to and if he's in love with her.

—Agatha Christie

. . . love without esteem cannot go far or reach high. It is an angel with only one wing.

—Alexandre Dumas (fils)

Love is indescribable and unconditional. I could tell you a thousand things that it is not, but not one that it is.
—*Duke Ellington*

Jealousy, an uncontrollable passion. The Siamese twin of love.
—*Marlene Dietrich*

Love is a cunning weaver of fantasies and fables.
—*Sappho*

Love is an ideal thing, marriage a real thing; a confusion of the real with the ideal never goes unpunished.
—*Johann Wolfgang von Goethe*

It is impossible to love and be wise.
—*Francis Bacon*

When a man is in love he endures more than at other times; he submits to everything.
—*Friedrich Wilhelm Nietzsche*

He that falls in love with himself will have no rivals.
—*Benjamin Franklin*

Don't threaten me with love, baby. Let's just go walking in the rain.
—*Billie Holiday*

If two people love each other, there can be no happy end to it.
—*Ernest Hemingway*

Whoso loves believes the impossible.
—*Elizabeth Barrett Browning*

There's nothing in this world so sweet as love, and next to love the sweetest thing is hate.
—*Henry Wadsworth Lonfellow*

Love is blind.
—*Geoffrey Chaucer*

True love is like a psychic experience. Everyone tells ghost stories, but few have ever seen a ghost.
—*François de La Rochefoucauld*

I love you more than yesterday, less than tomorrow.
—*Edmond Rostand*

Love is like any other luxury. You have no right to it unless you can afford it.
—*Anthony Trollope*

Men always want to be a woman's first love—women like to be a man's last romance.
—*Oscar Wilde*

If it is your time, love will track you down like a Cruise missile. If you say, "No, I don't want it right now," that's when you'll get it for sure. Love will make a way out of no way. Love is an exploding cigar which we willingly smoke.
—*Lynda Barry*

Love is like the measles—all the worse when it comes late in life.
—*Douglas Jerrold*

Love is like a war: easy to begin but very hard to stop.
—*H. L. Mencken*

I can see from your utter misery, from your eagerness to misunderstand each other, and from your thoroughly bad temper, that this is the real thing.
—*Peter Ustinov*

Love is only the dirty trick played on us to achieve continuation of the species.
—*W. Somerset Maugham*

There is always something ridiculous about the emotions of people whom one has ceased to love.   —*Oscar Wilde*

Greatness is a spiritual condition worthy to excite love, interest, and admiration, and the outward proof of possessing greatness is that we excite love, interest, and admiration.   —*Matthew Arnold*

Infatuation is when you think that he's as sexy as Robert Redford, as smart as Henry Kissinger, as noble as Ralph Nader, as funny as Woody Allen, and as athletic as Jimmy Connors. Love is when you realize that he's as sexy as Woody Allen, as smart as Jimmy Connors, as funny as Ralph Nader, as athletic as Henry Kissinger, and nothing like Robert Redford—but you'll take him anyway.   —*Judith Viorst*

Love is based on a view of women that is impossible to those who have had any experience with them.   —*H. L. Mencken*

Love, and a cough, cannot be hid.   —*George Herbert*

Sayings
All's fair in love and war.   —*Francis Edward Smedley*

The love that lasts is the love that's last.

Money can't buy love.

Make love, not war.

Jokes
• The young man staggered into the small-town bakery at the crack of dawn on a hideously cold, wet, stormy morning. "Thank God you're open," he gasped. "Do you have fresh cranberry muffins?" When the baker nodded, a huge smile broke out on the fellow's face. "It's worth the trek, then—she'll be so happy. It'll make her day."
  The baker nodded understandingly. "Are these for your mother, then?" he asked.
  "Would my mother send me out on a day like this?" returned the young man with an incredulous look. "And would I go?"

• Over dinner with his hard-hearted friend, the incurable romantic sighed and declared, "Love is the last word."
  The cynic shook his head and countered, "Only in a telegram."

PASSION

Passion is the quickest to develop, and the quickest to fade. Intimacy develops more slowly, and commitment more gradually still.   —*Robert J. Sternberg*

Mencius enumerated the three "mature virtues" of his "great man" as "wisdom, compassion, and courage." I should like to lop off one syllable and regard as the qualities of a great soul passion, wisdom, and courage.   —*Lin Yutang*

A master passion is the love of news.   —*George Crabbe*

The ruling passion, be it what it will, the ruling passion conquers reason still.
                                                        —*Alexander Pope*

Passions are vices or virtues in their highest powers.

—Johann Wolfgang von Goethe

Sayings
Passions are like fire and water, good servants, but bad masters.

The end of passion means the beginning of repentance.

Joke
• Taxi driver: "Where to, buddy?"
   Jilted lover: "Drive off a cliff—I'm committing suicide."

PLEASURE

Pleasure is like a cordial—a little of it is not injurious, but too much destroys.
—Marguerite, Countess of Blessington

The greatest pleasure in life is doing what people say you cannot do.
—Walter Bagehot

Pleasure is frail like a dewdrop, while it laughs it dies.
—Rabindranath Tagore

The rule of my life is to make business a pleasure, and pleasure my business.
—Aaron Burr

The Puritans hated bear-baiting, not because it gave pain to the bear but because it gave pleasure to the spectators.   *—Thomas Babington Macaulay*

The rapturous, wild, and ineffable pleasure of drinking at someone else's expense.
—Henry Sambrooke Leigh

I'm tired of love; I'm still more tired of rhyme. But money gives me pleasure all the time.   *—Hilaire Belloc*

Sayings
If it feels good, do it.

Business before pleasure.

There is more pleasure in loving than in being loved.

To overcome pleasure is the greatest pleasure.

The pleasure of what we enjoy is lost by coveting more.

Only uncomfortable chairs become antiques. The comfortable ones are worn out by a single generation.

Joke
• The masochist turned to the sadist and begged, "Beat me, beat me."
   The sadist smiled and said, "No."

T H E   M I N D

CREATIVITY

The best way to have a good idea is to have lots of ideas.   —*Linus Pauling*

The best ideas come from jokes. Make your thinking as funny as possible.
                                                              —*David Ogilvie*

Young men are fitter to invent than to judge.   —*Francis Bacon*

Originality is not seen in single words or even sentences. Originality is the sum total of a man's thinking and writing.   —*Isaac Bashevis Singer*

Originality is the essence of true scholarship. Creativity is the soul of the true scholar.
                                                              —*Nnamdi Azikiwe*

Ah, good taste! What a dreadful thing! Taste is the enemy of creativeness.
                                                              —*Pablo Picasso*

A foolish consistency is the hobgoblin of little minds.   —*Ralph Waldo Emerson*

When in doubt, make a fool of yourself. There is a microscopically thin line between being brilliantly creative and acting like the most gigantic idiot on earth. So what the hell, leap.   —*Cynthia Heimel*

Consistency is the last refuge of the unimaginative.   —*Oscar Wilde*

Good design keeps the user happy, the manufacturer in the black, and the aesthete unoffended.   —*Raymond Loewy*

Creative minds always have been known to survive any kind of bad training.
                                                              —*Anna Freud*

I can very well do without God both in my life and in my painting, but I cannot, suffering as I am, do without something which is greater than I, which is my life—the power to create.   —*Vincent van Gogh*

Art begins with resistance—at the point where resistance is overcome. No human masterpiece has ever been created without great labor.   —*André Gide*

I just invent, then wait until man comes around to needing what I've invented.
                                                              —*R. Buckminster Fuller*

The creative person is both more primitive and more cultivated, more destructive and more constructive, a lot madder and a lot saner, than the average person."
                                                              —*Dr. Frank Barron*

Could *Hamlet* have been written by a committee, or the *Mona Lisa* painted by a club? Could the New Testament have been composed as a conference report? Creative ideas do not spring from groups. They spring from individuals. The divine spark leaps.
—*A. Whitney Griswold*

No grand idea was ever born in a conference, but a lot of foolish ideas have died there.
—*F. Scott Fitzgerald*

Life comes before literature, as the material always comes before the work. The hills are full of marble before the world blooms with statues.   —*Rev. Phillips Brooks*

In creating, the only hard thing's to begin; a grass blade's no easier to make than an oak.   —*James Russell Lowell*

Nothing can be created out of nothing.   —*Lucretius, first century* B.C.

All good things which exist are the fruits of originality.   —*John Stuart Mill*

We want the creative faculty to imagine that which we know.
—*Percy Bysshe Shelley*

Men are like trees: each one must put forth the leaf that is created in him.
—*Henry Ward Beecher*

He or she is greatest who contributes the greatest original practical example.
—*Walt Whitman*

Every great and original writer, in proportion as he is great and original, must himself create the taste by which he is to be relished.   —*William Wordsworth*

You can do anything with a bayonet except sit on it.   —*Napoleon Bonaparte*

Sayings

Invention is the son of need and the father of prosperity.

Too many people think they are being creative when they are just being different.

Originality is not necessarily better than imitation, but it makes imitation possible.

Necessity is the mother of invention.

Jokes

- It was an elegant dinner party and the hostess had left nothing to chance—except that a little water had splashed on the marble floor outside the kitchen door. And when the waiter came out carrying the beautiful roast suckling pig, he slipped and fell flat, sending the roast flying.

  "Don't worry, Charles," said the hostess calmly. "Just take the roast back to the kitchen and bring out the other one."

- A teacher, an actor, a painter, a businessman, and a writer, friends since high school, finally set out on a safari adventure they'd been planning for years. On the eve of their departure, the five men acknowledge the risks of the trip and make a deal: if any one should die during the trip, the survivors will each pin $1,000 to the body to help his soul get to heaven.

  Alas, two weeks into the trip, the writer is mauled by a lion and dies of his wounds. The teacher sticks $400, all that he has, in the dead man's jacket. The actor, overcome with grief and sobbing loudly, tucks in another $500. The painter, inspired by their generosity, kicks in $1,000.

The businessman asks for a final moment alone with his dead friend. Quick as a wink, he pockets the cash and scrawls a check for $2,500.

FACTS

Figures won't lie, but liars will figure.   —*Charles H. Grosvenor (attrib.)*

The degree of one's emotion varies inversely with one's knowledge of the facts—the less you know, the hotter you get.   —*Bertrand Russell*

There are three kinds of lies: lies, damned lies, and statistics.
                    —*Benjamin Disraeli (attrib.)*

Truth exists, only falsehood has to be invented.   —*Georges Braque*

There are two kinds of statistics, the kind you look up and the kind you make up.
                    —*Rex Stout*

He uses statistics as a drunken man uses lampposts—for support rather than for illumination.   —*Andrew Lang*

A wise man recognizes the convenience of a general statement, but he bows to the authority of a particular fact.   —*Oliver Wendell Holmes, Sr.*

Get your facts first, and then you can distort them as much as you please.
                    —*Mark Twain*

Facts do not cease to exist because they are ignored.   —*Aldous Huxley*

All generous minds have a horror of what are commonly called "facts." They are the brute beasts of the intellectual domain.   —*Oliver Wendell Holmes, Sr.*

Facts are to the mind what food is to the body.   —*Edmund Burke*

I pass with relief from the tossing sea of cause and theory to the firm ground of result and fact.   —*Winston Churchill*

Knowing how hard it is to collect a fact, you understand why most people want to have some fun analyzing it.   —*Jesse L. Greenstein*

The trouble with facts is that there are so many of them.
                    —*Samuel McChord Crothers*

Comment is free, but facts are sacred.   —*C. P. Scott*

Every man has a right to be wrong in his opinions. But no man has a right to be wrong about his facts.   —*Bernard Baruch*

Saying
Let the facts speak for themselves.

Joke
• Of course facts are only as useful as one permits them to be. Take the example of the

fellow who was convinced he was dead. He visited his doctor with this complaint several times and the doctor was unable to change his mind. Finally, the exasperated doctor demanded whether his patient would believe otherwise in the face of physical evidence that he was alive.

"Of course," said the man calmly. "I'm a reasonable fellow."

"Now would you agree that dead men don't bleed?"

"Of course."

"Fine. Give me your hand," ordered the physician. Taking a needle, he swiftly pricked a fingertip, then squeezed until a drop of blood beaded up. He thrust it in front of the man's eyes. "Look! Is that not blood?"

"I'll be darned," said the patient after a moment's astonished reflection. "Dead men *do* bleed."

FOOLS

A fool and his money are soon married. — *Carolyn Wells*

There's no fool like a bold fool. — *Carolyn Wells*

Only those are unwise who have never dared to be fools. — *Elsie de Wolfe*

A fool without fear is sometimes wiser than an angel with fear. — *Nancy Astor*

Fools rush in where angels fear to tread. — *Alexander Pope*

Angels rush in when fools are almost dead. — *Rudolph Fisher*

It is difficult to free fools from the chains they revere. — *Voltaire*

Fine clothes may disguise, but foolish words will disclose a fool. — *Aesop*

Let us be thankful for the fools. But for them the rest of us could not succeed.
— *Mark Twain*

The fool doth think he is wise, but the wise man knows himself a fool.
— *William Shakespeare*

To make a trade of laughing at a fool is the highway to become one.
— *Thomas Fuller*

I am two fools, I know, for loving, and for saying so. — *John Donne*

He who loves not wine, woman, and song, remains a fool his whole life long.
— *John Heinrich Voss (attrib.)*

Every man has his follies—and often they are the most interesting things he has got.
— *Josh Billings*

A man may be a fool and not know it, but not if he is married.
— *H. L. Mencken*

Anybody who feels at ease in the world today is a fool. — *Robert Maynard Hutchins*

When he said we were trying to make a fool of him, I could only murmur that the Creator had beat us to it. — *Ilka Chase*

It's better to keep one's mouth shut and be thought a fool than to open it and resolve all doubt.

—*Abraham Lincoln*

I had rather have a fool to make me merry than experience to make me sad.

—*William Shakespeare*

When in doubt, make a fool of yourself. There is a microscopically thin line between being brilliantly creative and acting like the most gigantic idiot on earth. So what the hell, leap.

—*Cynthia Heimel*

I only open my mouth to change feet.

—*Emily Paine*

Sayings
The fool can no more taste the sweetness of wisdom than the man with a cold can appreciate the scent of a rose.

—*North African saying*

Everyone loves a fool, but nobody wants him for a son.

—*West African saying*

Joke
• A couple hired a repairman to fix a hole in their roof, and went to stay with some friends for the week the job would take.

A week later, in the midst of a torrential rainstorm, the couple returned. "You fool!" shouted the husband as he discovered the workman sitting in the living room on a soaked couch in two inches of water. "What the hell are you sitting here for? Get up there and fix the leak in that roof!"

"I can't," the workman responded. "It's raining cats and dogs out there."

"Then why didn't you repair it when the sun was out?"

"Don't be silly," the workman answered, "the roof wasn't leaking then."

GENIUS

Genius is the ability to put into effect what is in your mind.

—*F. Scott Fitzgerald*

To do what others cannot do is talent. To do what talent cannot do is genius.

—*Will Henry*

Genius is more often found in a cracked pot than in a whole one.

—*E. B. White*

A genius is a man who takes the lemons that fate hands him and starts a lemonade stand with them.

—*Elbert Hubbard*

There are one-story intellects, two-story intellects, and three-story intellects with skylights. All fact collectors with no aim beyond their facts are one-story men. Two-story men compare reason and generalize, using labors of the fact collectors as well as their own. Three-story men idealize, imagine, and predict. Their best illuminations come from above through the skylight.

—*Oliver Wendell Holmes, Sr.*

. . . the man of genius . . . does not steal, he conquers.

—*Alexandre Dumas*

If there is such a thing as genius, which is just what—what the fuck is it?—I am one, you know. And if there isn't, I don't care.

—*John Lennon*

Men of genius do not excel in any profession because they labor in it, but they labor in it because they excel. —*William Hazlitt*

Name the greatest of all the inventors. Accident. —*Mark Twain*

The secret of genius is to carry the spirit of the child into old age, which means never losing your enthusiasm. —*Aldous Huxley*

Patience is a necessary ingredient of genius. —*Benjamin Disraeli*

I don't think necessity is the mother of invention—invention, in my opinion, arises directly from idleness, possibly also from laziness. To save oneself trouble. —*Agatha Christie*

Genius does what it must, and talent does what it can. —*Edward Bulwer-Lytton*

Intelligence recognizes what has happened. Genius recognizes what will happen. —*John Ciardi*

Since when was genius found respectable? —*Elizabeth Barrett Browning*

Mediocrity knows nothing higher than itself, but talent instantly recognizes genius. —*Arthur Conan Doyle*

One machine can do the work of fifty ordinary men. No machine can do the work of one extraordinary man. —*Elbert Hubbard*

A harmless hilarity and a buoyant cheerfulness are not infrequent concomitants of genius; and we are never more deceived than when we mistake gravity for greatness, solemnity for science, and pomposity for erudition. —*Charles Caleb Colton*

Genius, in truth, means little more than the faculty of perceiving in an unhabitual way. —*William James*

Everyone is a genius at least once a year. The real geniuses simply have their bright ideas closer together. —*Georg Christoph Lichtenberg*

There is no great genius without a touch of madness. —*Seneca the Younger*

When a true genius appears in the world, you may know him by this sign, that the dunces are all in confederacy against him. —*Jonathan Swift*

Genius is one percent inspiration and ninety-nine percent perspiration. —*Thomas Alva Edison*

A genius? Perhaps, but before I was a genius, I was a drudge. —*Ignace Jan Paderewski*

Sayings
The line between madness and genius is a permeable membrane.

There's a thin line between madness and genius.

A genius is one who shoots at something no one else can see, and hits it.

Joke
• If Seneca the Younger said "Drunkenness is nothing but voluntary madness," and

"there is no great genius without a touch of madness," then is drunkenness a form of genius?   *—Tripp Evans*

HUMOR

Whatever you have read I have said is almost certainly untrue, except if it is funny, in which case I definitely said it.   *—Tallulah Bankhead*

Wit lives in the present, but genius survives the future.
    —Marguerite, Countess of Blessington

Make us laugh and you can pick all pockets.   *—Clemence Dane*

It is often a sign of wit not to show it, and not to see that others want it.
    —Suzanne Necker

The man with the real sense of humor is the man who can put himself in the spectator's place and laugh at his own misfortune.   *—Bert Williams*

Funny is an attitude.   *—Flip Wilson*

Impropriety is the soul of wit.   *—W. Somerset Maugham*

Wit is the rarest quality to be met with among people of education.
    —William Hazlitt

There is nothing in which people more betray their character than in what they laugh at.   *—Johann Wolfgang von Goethe*

No mind is thoroughly well organized that is deficient in a sense of humor.
    —Samuel Taylor Coleridge

Everything is funny as long as it is happening to somebody else.   *—Will Rogers*

You are not angry with people when you laugh at them. Humor teaches tolerance.
    —W. Somerset Maugham

The man who sees the consistency in things is a wit; the man who sees the inconsistency in things is a humorist.   *—G. K. Chesterton*

The man who can make others laugh secures more votes for a measure than the man who forces them to think.   *—Chazal*

You could read Kant by yourself, if you wanted to; but you must share a joke with someone else.   *—Robert Louis Stevenson*

Wit is the sudden marriage of ideas which before their union were not perceived to have any relation.   *—Mark Twain*

Humor is a painful thing told playfully.   *—Charles W. Jarvis*

The greatest advantage I know of being thought a wit by the world is that it gives one the greater freedom of playing the fool.   *—Jonathan Swift*

I don't make jokes; I just watch the government and report the facts.
    —Will Rogers

Of puns it has been said that they who most dislike them are least able to utter them.

—*Edgar Allan Poe*

I have never understood why it should be considered derogatory to the Creator to suppose that he has a sense of humor.   —*Ralph Inge*

Good taste and humor are a contradiction in terms, like a chaste whore.

—*Malcolm Muggeridge*

. . . brevity is the soul of wit.   —*William Shakespeare*

Men will let you abuse them only if you make them laugh.

—*Henry Ward Beecher*

Wit is so shining a quality that everybody admires it; most people aim at it, all people fear it, and few love it unless in themselves.   —*Lord Chesterfield*

A difference of taste in jokes is a great strain on the affections.   —*George Eliot*

Men show their characters in nothing more clearly than in what they think laughable.

—*Johann Wolfgang von Goethe*

No dignity, no learning, no force of character, can make any stand against good wit.

—*Ralph Waldo Emerson*

Humor can be dissected, as a frog can, but the thing dies in the process and the innards are discouraging to any but the pure scientific mind.   —*E. B. White*

Angels can fly because they take themselves lightly.   —*G. K. Chesterton*

Among those whom I like or admire, I can find no common denominator, but among those whom I love, I can: all of them make me laugh.   —*W. H. Auden*

We are in the world to laugh. In purgatory or in hell we shall no longer be able to do so. And in heaven it would not be proper.   —*Jules Renard*

Not by wrath does one kill but by laughter.   —*Friedrich Wilhelm Nietzsche*

We are all here for a spell; get all the good laughs you can.   —*Will Rogers*

Laughter is a tranquilizer with no side effects.   —*Arnold Glasgow*

If you don't learn to laugh at trouble, you won't have anything to laugh at when you grow old.   —*Edgar Watson Howe*

What I want to do is to make people laugh so that they'll see things seriously.

—*William K. Zinsser*

If you are not allowed to laugh in heaven, I don't want to go there.

—*Martin Luther*

Laughter is a form of internal jogging. It moves your internal organs around. It enhances respiration. It is an igniter of great expectation.   —*Norman Cousins*

He who laughs, lasts.   —*Mary Pettibone Poole*

There are few who would not rather be hated than laughed at.   —*Sydney Smith*

The best ideas come from jokes. Make your thinking as funny as possible.

—*David Ogilvie*

Laugh and the world laughs with you; weep, and you weep alone.
—*Ella Wheeler Wilcox*

Laughter is by definition healthy.   —*Doris Lessing*

The most wasted of all our days are those in which we have not laughed.
—*Sébastien Chamfort*

The man who laughs has not yet heard the news.   —*Bertolt Brecht*

My way of joking is to tell the truth; it's the funniest joke in the world.
—*George Bernard Shaw*

Humor is an affirmation of dignity, a declaration of our superiority to all that befalls
us.   —*Romain Gary*

If the cavemen had known how to laugh, history would have been different.
—*Oscar Wilde*

Sayings
Every survival kit should include a sense of humor.

He who laughs last laughs loudest.

Laughter is the best medicine.

If you can't take a joke, you'll have to take the medicine.

Laughter is contagious.

Many friends have been lost by jest, but few have been gained.

Fuck 'em if they can't take a joke.

Jokes
• Repartee is something we think of twenty-four hours too late.   —*Mark Twain*

• "Laughter is God's gift to mankind," proclaimed the preacher ponderously.
    "And mankind," responded the cynic, "is the proof that God has a sense of
   humor."

IDEAS

The thinker dies, but his thoughts are beyond the reach of destruction. Men are mortal;
but ideas are immortal.   —*Walter Lippmann*

You cannot put a rope around the neck of an idea; you cannot put an idea up against a
barrack square wall and riddle it with bullets; you cannot confine it in the strongest
prison cell that your slaves could ever build.   —*Sean O'Casey*

Generally students are the best vehicles for passing on ideas, for their thoughts are
plastic and can be molded and they can adjust the ideas of old men to the shape of
reality as they find it in the villages and hills of China or in ghettos and suburbs of
America.   —*Theodore H. White*

The cleverly expressed opposite of any generally accepted idea is worth a fortune to somebody.
—*George Francis FitzGerald*

You can't shoot an idea.
—*Thomas E. Dewey*

A man may die, nations may rise and fall, but an idea lives on. Ideas have endurance without death.
—*John F. Kennedy*

A young man must let his ideas grow, not be continually rooting them up to see how they are getting on.
—*William McFee*

A stand can be made against invasion by an army; no stand can be made against invasion by an idea.
—*Victor Hugo*

There is one thing stronger than all the armies in the world: an idea whose time has come.
—*Victor Hugo*

An idea that is not dangerous is not worthy of being called an idea at all.
—*Oscar Wilde*

An idea, to be suggestive, must come to the individual with the force of a revelation.
—*William James*

All the really good ideas I ever had came to me while I was milking a cow.
—*Grant Wood*

No grand idea was ever born in a conference, but a lot of foolish ideas have died there.
—*F. Scott Fitzgerald*

When forty million people believe in a dumb idea, it's still a dumb idea.
—*Ad run by United Technologies Corporation*

All great deeds and all great thoughts have a ridiculous beginning. Great works are often born on a street corner or in a restaurant's revolving door.
—*Albert Camus*

Saying
Many great ideas have been lost because the people who had them couldn't handle being laughed at.

Jokes
• Two Asians were angrily shouting at one another in the middle of a crowded Singapore street. An American observer asked his Asian companion when he thought the two would begin exchanging blows. "The man who strikes first," the friend answered, "admits that his ideas have come to an end."

• It's like what the beaver said to the rabbit as they stared up at the immense earthworks of Hoover Dam: "No, I didn't actually build it—but it's based on an idea of mine."

• First Entrepreneur: "I've got a great idea: I'm going to open up a bar and grill in the middle of the Sahara Desert."

Second Entrepreneur: "That's a ridiculous idea. You'll be lucky to get more than one customer a month."

First Entrepreneur: "Okay, but just *think* how thirsty he'll be!"

IDENTITY

Financially stable, mentally questionable.

—*Motto of the Gotham City Riders, an upscale New York City motorcycle gang*

It is not easy to find happiness in ourselves, and it is not possible to find it elsewhere.

—*Agnes Repplier*

How queer everything is today! And yesterday things went on just as usual. I wonder if I've been changed in the night? Let me think: was I the same when I got up this morning? I almost think I can remember feeling a little different. But if I'm not the same, the next question is, "Who in the world am I?" Ah, that's the great puzzle!

—*Lewis Carroll*

Knowing others is wisdom. Knowing the self is enlightenment.   —*Lao-tzu*

Self-respect is the fruit of discipline: the sense of dignity grows with the ability to say no to oneself.   —*Abraham J. Heschel*

How many cares one loses when one decides not to be something but to be someone.

—*Gabrielle (Coco) Chanel*

If you practice an art, be proud of it and make it proud of you. . . . It may break your heart, but it will fill your heart before it breaks it: it will make you a person in your own right.   —*Maxwell Anderson*

Every man has three characters—that which he exhibits, that which he has, and that which he thinks he has.   —*Alphonse Karr*

Conform and be dull.   —*James Frank Dobie*

Men are created different; they lose their social freedom and their individual autonomy in seeking to become like each other.   —*David Riesman*

Success, recognition, and conformity are the bywords of the modern world where everyone seems to crave the anesthetizing security of being identified with the majority.

—*Martin Luther King, Jr.*

The dissenter is every human being at those moments of his life when he resigns momentarily from the herd and thinks for himself.   —*Archibald MacLeish*

If a man does not keep pace with his companions, perhaps it is because he hears a different drummer. Let him step to the music he hears, however measured or far away.

—*Henry David Thoreau*

Everyone alters and is altered by everyone else. We are all the time taking in portions of one another or else reacting against them, and by these involuntary acquisitions and repulsions modifying our natures.   —*Gerald Brenan*

Everyone is a moon, and has a dark side which he never shows to anybody.

—*Mark Twain*

I have never seen a greater monster or miracle in the world than myself.

—*Michel Eyquem de Montaigne*

The turning point in the process of growing up is when you discover the core of strength within you that survives all hurt.   —*Max Lerner*

"Know thyself" is a good saying, but not in all situations. In many it is better to say "know others."

—*Menander*

Character is much easier kept than recovered.

—*Thomas Paine*

. . . the amount of eccentricity in a society has generally been proportional to the amount of genius, mental vigor, and moral courage it contained.

—*John Stuart Mill*

The Kingdom of God is within you.

—*Luke 17:21*

Prayer gives a man the opportunity of getting to know a gentleman he hardly ever meets. I do not mean his maker, but himself.

—*Dean William R. Inge*

In proportion to the development of his individuality, each person becomes more valuable to himself, and is therefore capable of being more valuable to others.

—*John Stuart Mill*

People often say that this or that person has not yet found himself. But the self is not something that one finds. It is something that one creates.

—*Thomas Szasz*

. . . if a man is not faithful to his own individuality, he cannot be loyal to anything.

—*Claude McKay*

One man's way may be as good as another's, but we all like our own best.

—*Jane Austen*

A man finds his identity by identifying. A man's identity is not best thought of as the way in which he is separated from his fellows but the way in which he is united with them.

—*Robert Terwilliger*

Trying to define yourself is like trying to bite your own teeth.

—*Alan Watts*

Character is made by what you stand for; reputation, by what you fall for.

—*Robert Quillen*

Character, like a photograph, develops in darkness.

—*Yousuf Karsh*

The one important thing I have learned over the years is the difference between taking one's work seriously and taking one's self seriously. The first is imperative and the second is disastrous.

—*Margot Fonteyn*

Nothing can bring you peace but yourself.

—*Ralph Waldo Emerson*

Elegance is innate. It has nothing to do with being well dressed. Elegance is refusal.

—*Diana Vreeland*

No one can make you feel inferior without your consent.

—*Eleanor Roosevelt*

No one can possibly achieve any real and lasting success or "get rich" in business by being a conformist.

—*J. Paul Getty*

When people are free to do as they please, they usually imitate each other.

—*Eric Hoffer*

The golden rule is that there are no golden rules.

—*George Bernard Shaw*

Don't compromise yourself. You're all you've got.

—*Janis Joplin*

When you've got the personality, you don't need the nudity.

—*Mae West*

Saying
I want to be what I was when I wanted to be what I am now.

Jokes
• A lot of people don't realize they're having an identity crisis until they try to cash a check in a strange town.

• The story of little Mary illustrates one way in which change brings growth. One day in Sunday school she was asked, "Who made you?"
   After a moment's reflection, the little girl replied, "Well, God made a part of me?"
   "*Part* of you?" The teacher was startled.
   "God made me very little," she explained, "and I grew the rest myself."

IGNORANCE AND STUPIDITY

No human folly can suppress the conceit of ignorance.   —*Charles Victor Roman*

The realization of ignorance is the first act of knowing.   —*Jean Toomer*

Violence is a tool of the ignorant.   —*Flip Wilson*

Fear always springs from ignorance.   —*Ralph Waldo Emerson*

I would rather have my ignorance than another man's knowledge, because I have so much of it.   —*Mark Twain*

Far more crucial than what we know or do not know is what we do not want to know.
                                                                               —*Eric Hoffer*

From ignorance our comfort flows, the only wretched are the wise.
                                                                               —*Matthew Prior*

Ignorance is the womb of monsters.   —*Henry Ward Beecher*

Ignorance is the night of the mind, a night without moon or star.   —*Confucius*

Ignorance is not bliss—it is oblivion.   —*Philip Wylie*

Nothing in all the world is more dangerous than sincere ignorance and conscientious stupidity.   —*Martin Luther King, Jr.*

He was born stupid and greatly improved his birthright.   —*Samuel Butler*

Stubborn and ardent clinging to one's opinion is the best proof of stupidity.
                                                                               —*Michel Eyquem de Montaigne*

It is dangerous to be sincere unless you are also stupid.   —*Oscar Wilde*

Stupidity often saves a man from going mad.   —*Oliver Wendell Holmes, Jr.*

The only foes that threaten America are the enemies at home, and these are ignorance, superstition, and incompetence.   —*Elbert Hubbard*

Sayings
The person who knows little is proud that she knows so much; the person who knows much is sorry that she knows so little.

What he lacks in intelligence, he makes up for in stupidity.

The opinion of the intelligent is better than the certainty of the ignorant.

—North African saying

No darkness like ignorance.

—North African saying

Jokes

• What's on your mind, if you will allow the overstatement?   *—Fred Allen*

• He would come in and say he changed his mind—which was a gilded figure of speech, because he didn't have any.   *—Mark Twain*

• (*Note*: This joke can be adapted to any group the speechmaker chooses.)

A stranger walks into a bar and announces loudly, "Hey, guys, have I got some great [Albanian] jokes for you!"

The bartender leans over and says in an ominous tone, "Listen, if I were you I'd watch your tongue. The two 250-pound bouncers are [Albanian]; I'm no midget, and I'm [Albanian]; and so is every other guy in here."

"Oh, no problem," counters the stranger cheerfully. "I'll talk v-e-r-y s-l-o-w-l-y."

IMAGINATION

A liberal mind is a mind that is able to imagine itself believing anything.

—Max Eastman

You can't depend on your judgment when your imagination is out of focus.

—Mark Twain

A lady's imagination is very rapid; it jumps from admiration to love, from love to matrimony in a moment.   *—Jane Austen*

Imagination is more important than knowledge.   *—Albert Einstein*

To give reason for fancy were to weigh the fire, and measure the wind.

—John Lyly

If we lacked imagination enough to foresee something better, life would indeed be a tragedy.   *—Laurence J. Peter*

Imagination grows by exercise, and contrary to common belief, is more powerful in the mature than in the young.   *—W. Somerset Maugham*

What is now proved was once only imagined.   *—William Blake*

Skill without imagination is craftsmanship and gives us many useful objects such as wickerwork picnic baskets. Imagination without skill gives us modern art.

—Tom Stoppard

When I examine myself and my methods of thought, I come close to the conclusion that the gift of fantasy has meant more to me than my talent for absorbing positive knowledge.   *—Albert Einstein*

Generalization is necessary to the advancement of knowledge; but particularly is indispensable to the creations of the imagination.   *—Thomas Babington Macaulay*

Imagination continually frustrates tradition; that is its function.   *—John Pfeiffer*

Dare to be naive.   *—R. Buckminster Fuller*

If wishes were horses, beggars might ride.   *—John Ray*

Saying
Imagination is a good stick but a bad crutch.

Joke
• Phyllis came into the office all aflutter about her husband. "You won't believe this, Susie, but Rick takes a fishing pole into the bathroom and tosses the hook into the tub."

"You've got to be kidding," gasped her friend. "Don't you think you should take him to a psychiatrist?"

"No time," replied Phyllis with a shrug. "I'm too busy cleaning fish."

INSANITY

Insanity is a matter of degree.   *—Joaquim Maria Machado de Assis*

One cannot be deeply responsive to the world without being saddened very often.
    —Erich Fromm

Dr. Karl Menninger was once asked what action he would recommend if a person were to feel a nervous breakdown coming on. "Lock up your house," the famous psychiatrist advised, "go across the railroad tracks, and find someone in need and do something for him."

The inmates are ghosts whose dreams have been murdered.
    —Jill Johnson, about Bellevue Hospital's psychiatric wards

We're all controlled neurotics.   *—Harry Reasoner*

There was only one catch, and that was Catch-22, which specified that a concern for one's own safety in the face of dangers that were real and immediate was the process of a rational mind. . . . Orr would be crazy to fly more missions and sane if he didn't, but if he was sane he had to fly them. If he flew them he was crazy and didn't have to; but if he didn't want to he was sane and had to.   *—Joseph Heller*

There is always some madness in love. But there is also always some reason in madness.   *—Friedrich Wilhelm Nietzsche*

Sometimes accidents happen in life from which we have need of a little madness to extricate ourselves successfully.   *—François de La Rochefoucauld*

What is madness? To have erroneous perceptions and to reason correctly from them.
    —Voltaire

Stupidity often saves a man from going mad.   *—Oliver Wendell Holmes, Jr.*

When dealing with the insane, the best method is to pretend to be sane.
    —Hermann Hesse

There is but an inch of difference between the cushioned chamber and the padded cell.

—*G. K. Chesterton*

We are all born mad. Some remain so.

—*Samuel Beckett*

The human race consists of the dangerously insane and such as are not.

—*Mark Twain*

Every man has a sane spot somewhere.

—*Robert Louis Stevenson*

Insanity is hereditary—you get it from your children.

—*Sam Levenson*

That's the truest sign of insanity—insane people are always sure they're just fine. It's only the sane people who are willing to admit they're crazy.

—*Nora Ephron*

Sayings

Just because you're paranoid doesn't mean they're not out to get you.

Sanity is relative.

Joke

• Summoning the patient into his office, the psychiatrist shot her a radiant smile. "You know, Claudia, in this profession one rarely uses the word 'cure,' but after five years of therapy it is my pleasure to pronounce you one hundred percent cured!" he announced proudly.

To his surprise, an unhappy look came over the woman's face. "What's wrong?" asked the doctor. "This is a success for me and a triumph for you—I thought you'd be thrilled."

"Oh, it's fine for you," she finally snapped, "but look at it from my point of view. Three years ago I was Joan of Arc. Now I'm nobody."

INTELLIGENCE

It has yet to be proved that intelligence has any survival value.

—*Arthur C. Clarke*

The only means of strengthening one's intellect is to make up one's mind about nothing —to let the mind be a thoroughfare for all thoughts.

—*John Keats*

There is no greater excitement than to support an intellectual wife and have her support you. Marriage is a partnership in which each inspires the other, and brings fruition to both of you.

—*Millicent Carey McIntosh*

The only difference between intelligence and education is this: intelligence will make you a good living.

—*Charles F. Kettering*

To the dull mind all nature is leaden. To the illumined mind the whole world sparkles with light.

—*Ralph Waldo Emerson*

We pay a high price for being intelligent. Wisdom hurts.

—*Euripides*

He's very clever, but sometimes his brains go to his head.

—*Margot Asquith*

The true, strong, and sound mind is the mind that can embrace equally great things and small.
—*Samuel Johnson*

The height of cleverness is to conceal one's cleverness.
—*François de La Rochefoucauld*

Every man of genius sees the world at a different angle from his fellows.
—*Havelock Ellis*

Unless one is a genius, it is best to aim at being intelligible.
—*Anthony Hope Hawkins*

No one is content with his fortune, nor discontent with his intellect.
—*Madame Antoinette Deshoulières*

A woman uses her intelligence to find reasons to support her intuition.
—*G. K. Chesterton*

Sayings

If brains were dynamite, you wouldn't have enough to blow your nose.

The opinion of the intelligent is better than the certainty of the ignorant.
—*North African saying*

If ignorance is bliss, why aren't more people happy?

Jokes

• When the none-too-bright young thing came to the line on the job questionnaire that read "Sign here," she pondered briefly, then wrote, "Sagittarius."

• Son: "Dad, I got an A in spelling!"
Dad: "You dumb turkey! There ain't no A in spelling."

• Most people have minds like concrete: mixed up or permanently set.

KNOWLEDGE

Knowledge itself is power.
—*Francis Bacon*

Knowledge is power, if you know the right person.
—*Ethel Watts Mumford*

In expanding the field of knowledge we but increase the horizon of ignorance.
—*Henry Miller*

Integrity without knowledge is weak and useless, and knowledge without integrity is dangerous and dreadful.
—*Samuel Johnson*

Discussion is an exchange of knowledge; argument an exchange of ignorance.
—*Robert Quillen*

Knowledge is the only instrument of production that is not subject to diminishing returns.
—*John Maurice Clark*

The greater our knowledge increases, the greater our ignorance unfolds.
—*John F. Kennedy*

We know accurately only when we know little; with knowledge doubt increases.

—Johann Wolfgang von Goethe

Just in ratio as knowledge increases, faith diminishes.

—Thomas Carlyle

If we value the pursuit of knowledge, we must be free to follow wherever that search may lead us. The free mind is no barking dog to be tethered on a ten-foot chain.

—Adlai E. Stevenson

The acquisition of knowledge is the mission of research, the transmission of knowledge is the mission of teaching, and the application of knowledge is the mission of public service.

—James A. Perkins

The fox knows many things, but the hedgehog knows one great thing.

—Archilochus, seventh century B.C.

The one important thing I have learned over the years is the difference between taking one's work seriously and taking one's self seriously. The first is imperative and the second is disastrous.

—Margot Fonteyn

The greatest obstacle to discovery is not ignorance—it is the illusion of knowledge.

—Daniel J. Boorstin

Knowing others is wisdom. Knowing the self is enlightenment.

—Lao-tzu

You never know what is enough unless you know what is more than enough.

—William Blake

Knowledge is of two kinds. We know a subject ourselves, or we know where we can find information upon it.

—Samuel Johnson

Knowledge which is obtained under compulsion obtains no hold on the mind.

—Plato

Tim was so learned that he could name a horse in nine languages: so ignorant that he bought a cow to ride on.

—Benjamin Franklin

The great end of life is not knowledge but action.

—Thomas Henry Huxley

Reality is a collective hunch.

—Mel Seesholtz

Sayings

He who knows not, and knows not that he knows not, is a fool; shun him. He who knows not, and knows that he knows not, is a student; teach him. He who knows, and knows not that he knows, is asleep; wake him. He who knows, and knows that he knows, is wise; follow him.

—Asian proverb

Regardless of how rich you are, wisdom has to be acquired on the installment plan.

What you don't know can hurt you.

He that knows little soon repeats it.

If you don't know, ask.

We know so many things that aren't so.

No one is without knowledge except him who asks no questions.

—West African saying

Not to know is bad; not to wish to know is worse.   —*West African saying*

Jokes
• You may lead an ass to knowledge but you cannot make him think.
                                                          —*Ethel Watts Mumford*

• Never pride yourself on knowledge. Remember, even a head of iceberg lettuce knows
  more than you do. It knows whether or not that light really does go out when the
  refrigerator door shuts.

MEMORY

Youth longs and manhood strives, but age remembers. . . .
                                                    —*Oliver Wendell Holmes, Sr.*

The true art of memory is the art of attention.   —*Samuel Johnson*

A retentive memory may be a good thing, but the ability to forget is the true token of
greatness.   —*Elbert Hubbard*

The right honorable gentleman is indebted to his memory for his jests and to his
imagination for his facts.   —*Richard Brinsley Sheridan*

Forget and forgive. This is not difficult, when properly understood. It means that you
are to forget inconvenient duties, and forgive yourself for forgetting. In time, by rigid
practice and stern determination, it comes easy.   —*Mark Twain*

Literature transmits incontrovertible condensed experience . . . from generation to
generation. In this way literature becomes the living memory of a nation.
                                                       —*Alexander Solzhenitsyn*

The nation which forgets its defenders will be itself forgotten.
                                                              —*Calvin Coolidge*

My yesterdays walk with me. They keep step, they are gray faces that peer over my
shoulder.   —*William Golding*

Because I remember, I despair. Because I remember, I have the duty to reject despair.
                                                                  —*Elie Wiesel*

I do not bring forgiveness with me, nor forgetfulness. The only ones who can forgive
are dead; the living have no right to forget.
                            —*Chaim Herzog, at the Bergen-Belsen concentration camp*

Memory is the mother of all wisdom.   —*Aeschylus*

Memory is a net; one finds it full of fish when he takes it from the brook, but a dozen
miles of water have run through it without sticking.
                                                    —*Oliver Wendell Holmes, Sr.*

Everyone complains of his lack of memory, but nobody of his want of judgment.
                                                    —*François de La Rochefoucauld*

Better by far that you should forget and smile than that you should remember and be
sad.   —*Christina Rossetti*

It is not so easy to forget.

—*Richard Brinsley Sheridan*

'Tis sweet to think on what was hard t'endure.

—*Robert Herrick*

Our memories are card indexes consulted, and then put back in disorder, by authorities whom we do not control.

—*Cyril Connolly*

Sayings

When I am right, no one remembers; when I am wrong, no one forgets.

Things that live on in memory have no visible means of support.

I'll never forget old what's-his-name.

We are apt to remember most vividly what we would most like to forget.

Memory plays strange tricks.

Jokes

• I have a memory like an elephant. In fact, elephants often consult me.

—*Noel Coward (attrib.)*

• "My teeth may be gone, my digestion a mess," remarked the old codger as he rocked back and forth on the porch, "but thank heavens I still have my memory, knock wood [he knocks on the arm of his chair]. . . . Who's there?"

• "Memory, it's overrated," complained the absentminded professor to a fellow teacher.
   "I can't say I agree with you," said his friend.
   "Agree about what?"

OBJECTIVITY

Show me a man who claims he is objective and I'll show you a man with illusions.

—*Henry R. Luce*

If I were objective or if you were objective or if anyone was, he would have to be put away somewhere in an institution because he'd be some sort of vegetable.

—*David Brinkley*

Obstinacy is the result of the will forcing itself into the place of the intellect.

—*Arthur Schopenhauer*

What was most significant about the lunar voyage was not that men set foot on the moon but that they set eye on earth.

—*Norman Cousins*

Smallness of mind is the cause of stubbornness, and we do not credit readily what is beyond our view.

—*François de La Rochefoucauld*

Many things cause pain which would cause pleasure if you regarded their advantages.

—*Baltasar Gracian*

Sayings

Far too many of us bring our prejudices along when we listen to a new idea.

Great Spirit, grant that I may not criticize my neighbor until I have walked a mile in his moccasins.

—Native American saying

Jokes

• The chairman of the board was famed for his bullheadedness and inability to listen to anyone else, let alone take their advice. Why should he, since he had never made a mistake.

One day an exasperated executive couldn't hold back any longer. "You say you're always right, Ted, but there must have been times when you goofed up. Admit it."

The chairman nodded. "Actually, it did happen once."

"Aha!"

"Some years back I made a decision I thought was the wrong one," the chairman elaborated, "but it turned out to be absolutely right."

• When the pediatrician arrived late one morning and had to wend his way to the door through a group of frazzled mothers and cranky babies, one woman remarked to another, "I suppose to him we look just like a sink full of dirty dishes."

OPINION

Let us always remember that he does not really believe his own opinions who dares not give free scope to his opponent.   *—Wendell Phillips*

It is the absolute right of the state to supervise the formation of public opinion.

—Joseph Goebbels

In all matters of opinion, our adversaries are insane.   *—Mark Twain*

It is a difference of opinion that makes horse races.   *—Mark Twain*

I am always of the opinion with the learned, if they speak first.

—William Congreve

Popular opinions, on subjects not palpable to sense, are often true, but seldom or never the whole truth.   *—John Stuart Mill*

The fact that an opinion has been widely held is no evidence whatever that it is not utterly absurd.   *—Bertrand Russell*

Opinion is ultimately determined by the feelings, and not by the intellect.

—Herbert Spencer

People think of the inventor as a screwball, but no one ever asks the inventor what he thinks of other people.   *—Charles F. Kettering*

I am free of all prejudice. I hate everyone equally.   *—W. C. Fields*

Prejudice is an opinion without judgment.   *—Voltaire*

Those who never retract their opinions love themselves more than they love the truth.

—Joseph Joubert

Nothing is more unjust or capricious than public opinion.

—William Hazlitt

Nothing is more conducive to peace of mind than not having any opinion at all.
—*Georg Christoph Lichtenberg*

Give every man thine ear, but few thy voice.   —*William Shakespeare*

They that approve a private opinion, call it opinion; but they that dislike it, heresy; and yet heresy signifies no more than private opinion.   —*Thomas Hobbes*

I hate to go on tryin' your patience like this—but—well, I'm either dead right or I'm *crazy.*
—*Jefferson, in* **Mr. Smith Goes to Washington,** *screenplay by Sidney Buchman*

One man's meat is another man's poison.   —*Oswald Dykes*

Sayings

Our own opinion is never wrong.

A lawyer's opinion is worth nothing unless it is paid for.

Public opinion is itself a matter of opinion.

A great leader molds public opinion; a wise leader listens to it.

If I wanted your opinion, I'd ask for it.

Each to his own taste.

Jokes

* Taking a break from the courtroom squabbles of a case in Rock Island, Abraham Lincoln took a walk in the countryside. He followed a stream and came to a bridge, with a young boy sitting right in the middle. Lincoln said companionably, "I suppose you know all about this river."

    "Sure I do, mister," responded the boy. "It was here when I was born and it's been here ever since."

    Lincoln smiled broadly. "It's good to be out here where there is so much fact and so little opinion."

* Running into the local attorney on a street corner, the man asked her a business question. He was startled when a bill for her services arrived a few days later, to the tune of $75.

    Not long afterward they ran into each other on the street again, and the lawyer greeted him cheerfully.

    "Good morning," he responded, "but I'm telling you, not asking you."

* Desk sign: YOU MAY NOT THINK MUCH OF WHAT I HAVE TO SAY, BUT REMEMBER, IT'S ONE FOUR-BILLION-FOUR-HUNDRED-AND-SEVENTY-SEVEN-MILLIONTH OF THE WORLD'S OPINION.

ORIGINALITY

The future of dance? If I knew, I'd want to do it first.   —*Martha Graham*

Originality exists in every individual because each of us differs from the other. We are all prime numbers divisible only by ourselves.   —*Jean Guitton*

Originality does not consist in saying what no one has ever said before, but in saying exactly what you think yourself.
—*James Stephens*

What is originality? Undetected plagiarism.
—*Dean William R. Inge*

My guess is that well over 80 percent of the human race goes through life without having a single original thought.
—*H. L. Mencken*

People who take time to be alone usually have depth, originality, and quiet reserve.
—*John Miller*

There is no new thing under the sun.
—*Ecclesiastes 1:9*

Sayings
People who claim to be "original" aren't giving their parents enough credit.

Originality is not necessarily better than imitation, but it makes imitation possible.

He stands the tallest who stands alone.

It's fine to stand out from the crowd, but not when they're shooting at you.

Jokes
• "Hendricks, your performance with our team has been so exceptional I'd like you to start up our new operation in Green Bay," said the beaming boss.

"Green Bay—nobody lives there but fat, dumb meat packers and football players," he blurted.

"I'll have you know, Hendricks, that my wife comes from Green Bay."

The bright young man recovered quickly, asking, "And what position does she play?"

• A company that sold red salmon found itself being outsold by pink salmon by a significant ratio. Finally, desperate to get a bigger share of the market, the owner hired an advertising agency. "I don't care what it takes, as long as it's legal," he instructed them.

All the agency did was change the label on the can, to read: "Authentic Norwegian Red Salmon—guaranteed not to turn pink."

• "Got that, Beth?" Finished dictating, the executive looked over at his trusty secretary.

Beth looked down at her notes and read, "Letter to old what's-his-name, look up company name and address, usual salutation followed by standard opening paragraph, etc. etc. etc., toss in a few statistics, blah blah blah, a bit of flattery and good luck with the new model, and the usual Yours truly."

"Sounds about right. Type it up, will you?"

PREJUDICE

Prejudice is the chains forged by ignorance to keep men apart.
—*Marguerite, Countess of Blessington*

It's only big enough people who can afford, occasionally, to be untrammeled by ordinary prejudice.
—*Han Suyin*

It is not the fault of the slaveholder that he is cruel, so much as it is the system under which he lives.   —*Solomon Northrup*

Prejudice is not so much dependent upon natural antipathy as upon education.
                                                          —*David Ruggles*

Oh, the length and breadth, the height and depth, the cruelty and the irony of prejudice which can so belittle human nature.   —*William G. Allen*

Race prejudice is the devil unchained.   —*Charles Waddell Chestnutt*

The ignorant are always prejudiced and the prejudiced are always ignorant.
                                                    —*Charles Victor Roman*

. . . pride of race is the antidote to prejudice.
                                              —*Arthur Alfonso Schomburg*

If prejudice could reason, it would dispel itself.   —*William Pickens*

Horrible thing, prejudice . . . does you all up. Puffs you all out of shape.
                                                          —*Rudolph Fisher*

[Bigotry's] birthplace is the sinister back room of the mind where plots and schemes are hatched for the persecution and oppression of other human beings.
                                                          —*Bayard Rustin*

Minds are like parachutes: they only function when open.
                                                       —*Thomas R. Dewar*

It is never too late to give up your prejudices.   —*Henry David Thoreau*

He prided himself on being a man without prejudice, and this itself is a very great prejudice.   —*Anatole France*

Prejudice is the child of ignorance.   —*William Hazlitt*

Our nation's long neglect of minorities whose skin is dark is perhaps only a little worse than our neglect of another minority whose hair is white.
                                                      —*Lyndon B. Johnson*

Irrational barriers and ancient prejudices fall quickly when the question of survival itself is at stake.   —*John F. Kennedy*

Ignorance is stubborn and prejudice dies hard.   —*Adlai E. Stevenson*

I'm an equal-opportunity bigot. I offend everyone!   —*Blanche Knott*

A chip on the shoulder is a sure indication that there is more wood higher up.
                                                          —*Aldous Huxley*

Sayings
Hate has no medicine.   —*West African saying*

The difference between conviction and prejudice is that you can defend a conviction without getting angry.

Joke
• A Chinese man was having a quiet drink when a Jewish guy came over and slugged

him so hard he fell off the barstool. "Wha . . . what the hell was *that* for?" asked the poor guy, pulling himself upright.

"*That* was for Pearl Harbor," was the defiant explanation.

"The *Japanese* attacked Pearl Harbor. I'm *Chinese*," he protested.

"Japanese, Chinese, they're all the same to me," snorted the aggressor, and returned to his beer.

A few minutes later, the Chinese man went over and slammed the first guy headfirst into the bar. Watching him stagger to his feet, he explained calmly, "That was for the *Titanic*."

"The *Titanic*?" Dazed and bewildered, the Jew protested, "The *Titanic* was sunk by an iceberg."

As he turned away, the Chinese man shrugged. "Iceberg, Goldberg, they're all the same to me."

PSYCHOLOGY

I prefer neurotic people. I like to hear rumblings beneath the surface.

—Stephen Sondheim

The analysis of character is the highest human entertainment.

—Isaac Bashevis Singer

Knowing your own darkness is the best method for dealing with the darknesses of other people.   *—Carl Jung*

Work and love—these are the basics. Without them, there is neurosis.

—Theodor Reik

The good writing of any age has always been the product of someone's neurosis.

—William Styron

Everything that irritates us about others can lead us to an understanding of ourselves.

—Carl Jung

When depression is stigmatized as illness and weakness, a double bind is created: if we admit to depression, we will be stigmatized by others; if we feel it but do not admit it, we stigmatize ourselves, internalizing the social judgment. . . . The only remaining choice may be truly sick behavior: to experience no emotion at all.

—Lesley Hazelton

Neurosis seems to be a human privilege.   *—Sigmund Freud*

Castles in the air—they are so easy to take refuge in. And so easy to build as well.

—Henrik Ibsen

Behavioral psychology is the science of pulling habits out of rats.

—Douglas Busch

The mind is its own place, and in itself, can make a Heaven of Hell, a Hell of Heaven.   *—John Milton*

The object of all psychology is to give us a totally different idea of the things we know best.   *—Paul Valéry*

Many of the quests for status symbols—the hot automobile, the best table in a restaurant or a private chat with the boss—are shadowy reprises of infant anxieties. . . . The larger office, the corner space, the extra window are the teddy bears and tricycles of adult office life.   **—Willard Gaylin**

We can be sure that the greatest hope for maintaining equilibrium in the face of any situation rests within ourselves. Persons who are secure with a transcendental system of values and a deep sense of moral duties are possessors of values which no man and no catastrophe can take from them.   **—Francis J. Braceland**

Psychoanalysis . . . shows the human infant as the passive recipient of love, unable to bear hostility. Development is the learning to love actively and to bear rejection.
                              —Karl Stern

Sayings
Psychology is the science of predicting how people behave—and explaining why they don't.

Was the world happier before psychology, or was that a delusion?

Joke
• What did one lab rat say to the other?
   "I've got my scientist so well trained that every time I push the buzzer, he brings me a snack."

THOUGHT AND THINKING

Nothing pains some people more than having to think.
                              —Martin Luther King, Jr.

Judgment is more than skill. It sets forth on intellectual seas beyond the shores of hard indisputable factual information.   **—Kingman Brewster**

Don't just do something, stand there.   **—Daniel Berrigan, on the**
                              importance of thought as well as action during the 1960s war protests

I have always thought the actions of men the best interpreters of their thoughts.
                              —John Locke

His words leap across rivers and mountains, but his thoughts are still only six inches long.   **—E. B. White**

Profundity of thought belongs to youth, clarity of thought to old age.
                              —Friedrich Wilhelm Nietzsche

What was once thought can never be unthought.   **—Friedrich Dürrenmatt**

Iron rusts from disuse, stagnant water loses its purity, and in cold weather becomes frozen; even so does inaction sap the vigors of the mind.
                              —Leonardo da Vinci

Intellectual activity is a danger to the building of character.
                              —Joseph Goebbels

Every man who expresses an honest thought is a soldier in the army of intellectual liberty.
—*Robert G. Ingersoll*

An intellectual is someone whose mind watches itself.
—*Albert Camus*

The feeling of "aha, that's it," which accompanies the clothing of a situation with meaning, is emotionally very satisfying, and is the major charm of scientific research, of artistic creation, and of the solution of crossword puzzles. It is why the intellectual life is fun.
—*Hudson Hoagland*

It is not enough to have a good mind; the main thing is to use it well.
—*René Descartes*

The only means of strengthening one's intellect is to make up one's mind about nothing —to let the mind be a thoroughfare for all thoughts.
—*John Keats*

Learning without thought is labor lost; thought without learning is perilous.
—*Confucius*

A man can stand a lot as long as he can stand himself. He can live without hope, without friends, without books, even without music, as long as he can listen to his own thoughts.
—*Axel Munthe*

Man is a plant which bears thoughts, just as a rose-tree bears roses and an apple-tree bears apples.
—*Antoine Fabre D'Olivet*

If I look confused it's because I'm thinking.
—*Samuel Goldwyn*

When all think alike, then no one is thinking.
—*Walter Lippmann*

Analysis kills spontaneity. The grain once ground into flour springs and germinates no more.
—*Henri Frédéric Amiel*

In the field of observation, chance favors only the prepared minds.
—*Louis Pasteur*

One must learn to think well before learning to think; afterward it proves too difficult.
—*Anatole France*

Minds are like parachutes: they only function when open.
—*Thomas R. Dewar*

If you make people think they're thinking, they'll love you. If you really make them think, they'll hate you.
—*Don Marquis*

A thought is often original, though you have uttered it a hundred times.
—*Oliver Wendell Holmes, Sr.*

When a thought is too weak to be expressed simply, it is proof that it should be rejected.
—*Luc de Clapiers de Vauvenargues*

When he who hears does not know what he who speaks means, and when he who speaks does not know what he himself means—that is philosophy.
—*Voltaire*

To be honest, what I feel really bad about is that I don't feel worse. That is the intellectual's problem in a nutshell.
—*Michael Frayn*

I too had thoughts once of being an intellectual, but I found it too difficult.

—*Albert Schweitzer*

We pay a high price for being intelligent. Wisdom hurts.   —*Euripides*

There's times when I just have to quit thinking . . . and the only way I can quit thinking is by shopping.   —*Tammy Faye Bakker*

Thought is free.   —*William Shakespeare*

Sayings

Think today and speak tomorrow.

Think with the wise, but talk to the vulgar.

Thinking is very far from knowing.

Jokes

• First manager: "Say, what happened to all those THINK signs you used to have posted on the walls?"

  Second manager: "Had to take 'em down. Everyone was sitting around thinking and no work got done."

• Einstein explained his theory to me every day, and on my arrival I was fully convinced that he understood it.   —*Chaim Weizmann, President of Israel, on transatlantic crossing with Albert Einstein*

• "We're going to play a little game today," Miss Kirk announced to the second graders. "I'm going to describe something and you see if you can guess what it is. Now the first thing is a fruit, and it's red and round."

  "A tomato?" guessed Freddie.

  "No, I was thinking of an apple—but I'm glad you're thinking," praised Miss Kirk. "How about another fruit, with a yellow, bumpy skin?"

  "A lemon?"

  "No, Ramona, but I'm glad to see you're thinking. The answer's a grapefruit," corrected Miss Kirk gently. "Who can tell what round, green vegetable I have in mind? Susie?"

  "Lettuce?"

  "No, I was thinking of a pea. But I'm glad to see you're thinking."

  Just then little Danny raised his hand from the back row. "Can I ask you one, teacher?"

  Miss Kirk nodded.

  "I got something in my pocket. It's long, and it's hard, and it's got a pink tip—"

  "Danny!" broke in Miss Kirk, "that's disgusting!"

  "It's a match," said Danny, "but I'm glad to see you're thinking."

VISION

I skate to where the puck is going to be, not where it has been.

—*Wayne Gretzky*

Fooling around with alternating current is just a waste of time. Nobody will use it, ever. It's too dangerous. Direct current is safe.   —*Thomas Edison*

What, sir, would you make a ship sail against the wind and currents by lighting a bonfire under her deck? I pray you excuse me. I have no time to listen to such nonsense.   —*Napoleon to Robert Fulton*

Necessity can set me helpless on my back, but she cannot keep me there; nor can four walls limit my vision.   —*Margaret Fairless Barber*

I have such poor vision I can date anyone.   —*Garry Shandling*

The man who radiates good cheer, who makes life happier wherever he meets it, is always a man of vision and faith.   —*Ella Wheeler Wilcox*

If you keep your eyes so fixed on heaven that you never look at the earth, you will stumble into hell.   —*Austin O'Malley*

He was so narrow-minded he could see through a keyhole with two eyes.

—*Esther Forbes*

Where there is no vision, the people perish.   —**Proverbs 29:18**

Sayings
You must scale the mountain if you would view the plain.   —*Chinese proverb*

A task without a vision is drudgery. A vision without a task is a dream. A task with a vision is victory.

What's the use of running if you're not on the right road?   —*German proverb*

Mothers know everything, except for things that change.

A genius is one who shoots at something no one else can see, and hits it.

Jokes
• A tourist visiting Italy came upon the construction site of a huge church. "What are you doing?" he asked three stonemasons who were working at their trade.
    "I'm cutting stone," answered the first tersely.
    "I'm cutting stone for twenty lire a day," the second responded.
    "I'm helping build a great cathedral," the third stonemason announced.

• The father was very proud when his son went off to college. He came to tour the school on Parents' Day, and observed his son hard at work in the chemistry lab. "What are you working on?" he asked.
    "A universal solvent," explained the son, "a solvent that'll dissolve anything."
    The father whistled, clearly impressed, then wondered aloud, "What'll you keep it in?"

WISDOM

A short saying oft contains much wisdom.   —*Sophocles*

Nowadays most people die of a sort of creeping common sense, and discover when it is too late that the only things one never regrets are one's mistakes.

—*Oscar Wilde*

The fool doth think he is wise, but the wise man knows himself a fool.

—*William Shakespeare*

Caution is the eldest child of wisdom.   —*Victor Hugo*

Wisdom comes by disillusionment.   —*George Santayana*

It is a characteristic of wisdom not to do desperate things.

—*Henry David Thoreau*

Wisdom is not wisdom when it is derived from books alone.   —*Horace*

Wisdom at times is found in folly.   —*Horace*

The beginning of wisdom is the definition of terms.   —*Socrates*

In order to act wisely it is not enough to be wise.   —*Fyodor Dostoyevsky*

Good people are good because they've come to wisdom through failure. We get very little wisdom from success, you know.   —*William Saroyan*

We do not receive wisdom, we must discover it for ourselves, after a journey through the wilderness which no one else can make for us, which no one can spare us, for our wisdom is the point of view from which we come at last to regard the world.

—*Marcel Proust*

Self-reflection is the school of wisdom.   —*Baltasar Gracian*

Reason is a weak antagonist against love.   —*Madeleine de Scudéry*

Who is wise? He that learns from everyone. Who is powerful? He that governs his passions. Who is rich? He that is content. Who is that? Nobody.

—*Benjamin Franklin*

If one is too lazy to think, too vain to do a thing badly, too cowardly to admit it, one will never attain wisdom.   —*Cyril Connolly*

We should be careful to get out of an experience only the wisdom that is in it—and stop there, lest we be like the cat that sits down on a hot stove lid. She will never sit down on a hot stove lid again—and that is well; but also she will never sit down on a cold one anymore.   —*Mark Twain*

Nine-tenths of wisdom consists in being wise in time.   —*Theodore Roosevelt*

The art of being wise is the art of knowing what to overlook.

—*William James*

It is better to be wise than to seem wise.   —*Origen*

Wisdom is greater than knowledge, for wisdom includes knowledge and the due use of it.   —*Joseph Burritt Sevelli Capponi*

To my extreme mortification, I grow wiser every day.

—*Mary Wortley Montagu*

Everyone complains of his memory, but no one complains of his judgement.

—*François de La Rochefoucauld*

Sayings

Wisdom comes with age.   —*West African saying*

Those killed by lack of wisdom are numerous. Those killed by wisdom do not amount to anything.

—*West African saying*

The fool can no more taste the sweetness of wisdom than the man with a cold can appreciate the scent of a rose.   —*North African saying*

When two men of equal wisdom play together, discord arises.

—*West African saying*

Joke

• The theology student decided his academic pursuits were a travesty and that he should go forth and seek the meaning of life for himself. And in the course of his travels, he was directed to a distant peak in the Himalayas where a great sage resided. Arriving at the sage's austere cave after a trek of many days, the student prostrated himself and asked humbly, "O revered Master, what is life?"

"Life," pronounced the wizened old man gravely, "is the scent of jasmine after a spring rain."

The student frowned. "But Master," he objected gently, "an Incan wise man I encountered on the steps of Machu Picchu told me life was a thorn like a needle of tempered steel."

The sage nodded, unperturbed, and said, "That's *his* life."

T H E   B O D Y

LIFE

The more science learns what life is, the more reluctant scientists are to define it.
—*Leila M. Coyne*

Is life worth living? This is a question for an embryo, not for a man.
—*Samuel Butler*

I would rather live in a world where my life is surrounded by mystery than live in a world so small that my mind could comprehend it.
—*Harry Emerson Fosdick*

Give me the luxuries of life and I will willingly do without the necessities.
—*Frank Lloyd Wright*

The first forty years of life give us the text; the next thirty supply the commentary.
—*Arthur Schopenhauer*

Life is ours to be spent, not to be saved.
—*D. H. Lawrence*

Life is like playing a violin in public and learning the instrument as one goes on.
—*Samuel Butler*

The basic fact about human existence is not that it is a tragedy, but that it is a bore. It is not so much a war as an endless standing in line.
—*H. L. Mencken*

Life backs up life. Nobody loves creditors and dead men.
—*Ugo Betti*

The art of life is to know how to enjoy a little and to endure very much.
—*William Hazlitt*

All life is an experiment.
—*Oliver Wendell Holmes, Jr.*

Life does not cease to be funny when people die any more than it ceases to be serious when people laugh.
—*George Bernard Shaw*

Life is a tragedy when seen in close-up, but a comedy in long-shot.
—*Charlie Chaplin*

What a fine comedy this world would be if one did not play a part in it!
—*Denis Diderot*

There is no meaning to life except the meaning man gives his life by the unfolding of his powers, by living productively.
—*Erich Fromm*

Indifference may not wreck a man's life at any one turn, but it will destroy him with a kind of dry rot in the long run.

—*Bliss Carman*

We live not as we wish to, but as we can.

—*Menander*

The unexamined life is not worth living.

—*Plato*

Man that is born of a woman is of few days, and full of trouble. He cometh forth like a flower, and is cut down: he fleeth also as a shadow, and continueth not.

—*Job 14:1–2*

Do not take life too seriously; you will never get out of it alive.

—*Elbert Hubbard*

Life is a disease; and the only difference between one man and another is the stage of the disease at which he lives. —*George Bernard Shaw*

Life is a foreign language. All men mispronounce it. —*Christopher Morley*

It does not at present look as though Nature had designed the universe primarily for life. . . . Life is the end of a chain of by-products; it seems to be the accident, and torrential deluges of life-destroying radiation the essential.

—*James Hopwood Jeans*

Life is an incurable disease. —*Abraham Cowley*

The only thing I regret about my life is the length of it. If I had to live my life again, I'd make all the same mistakes—only sooner. —*Tallulah Bankhead*

The life of every man is a diary in which he means to write one story and writes another; and his humblest hour is when he compares the volume as it is with what he vowed to make it. —*James M. Barrie*

Life's but a walking shadow, a poor player that struts and frets his hour upon the stage and then is heard no more: it is a tale told by an idiot, full of sound and fury, signifying nothing. —*William Shakespeare*

Let us endeavor to live so that when we come to die, even the undertaker will be sorry.
—*Mark Twain*

. . . this world is a comedy to those who think, a tragedy to those who feel. . . .
—*Horace Walpole*

Life is a sexually transmitted disease. —*Guy Bellamy*

Millions long for immortality who do not know what to do with themselves on a rainy Sunday afternoon. —*Susan Ertz*

Not a shred of evidence occurs in favor of the idea that life is serious.
—*Brendan Gill*

Most of the evils of life arise from man's inability to sit still in a room.
—*Blaise Pascal*

There are two great rules of life, the one general and the other particular. The first is that everyone can, in the end, get what he wants if he only tries. This is the general rule. The particular rule is that every individual is more or less an exception to the general rule. —*Samuel Butler*

Life is one long process of getting tired.   —*Samuel Butler*

Life is the art of drawing sufficient conclusions from insufficient premises.

—*Samuel Butler*

Life is either a daring adventure or nothing.   —*Helen Keller*

Life can only be understood backwards; but it must be lived forwards.

—*Søren Kierkegaard*

The mass of men lead lives of quiet desperation.   —*Henry David Thoreau*

When I hear somebody sigh, "Life is hard," I am always tempted to ask, "Compared to what?"   —*Sydney J. Harris*

Life was a lot simpler when what we honored was father and mother rather than all the major credit cards.   —*Robert Orben*

Life is not for everyone.   —*Michael O'Donoghue*

The purpose of life is living. Men and women should get the most they can out of their lives. The smallest, the tiniest intellect may be quite as valuable to itself; it may have all the capacity for enjoyment that the wisest has.   —*Clarence Darrow*

As soon as you trust yourself, you will know how to live.

—*Johann Wolfgang von Goethe*

Life appears to me too short to be spent in nursing animosity or registering wrongs.

—*Charlotte Brontë*

Life is worth living, . . . since it is what we make it.   —*William James*

You should make a point of trying every experience once—except incest and folk-dancing.   —*Arnold Bax*

Sayings
Life is a cereal.

Nobody gets out of it alive.

Life is the only thing worth living.

Life has a certain ending and uncertain timing.

Jokes
- If you want my final opinion on the mystery of life and all that, I can give it to you in a nutshell. The universe is like a safe to which there is a combination. But the combination is locked up in the safe.   —*Peter De Vries*

- The theology student decided his academic pursuits were a travesty and that he should go forth and seek the meaning of life for himself. And in the course of his travels, he was directed to a distant peak in the Himalayas where a great sage resided. Arriving at the sage's austere cave after a trek of many days, the student prostrated himself and asked humbly, "O revered Master, what is life?"
    "Life," pronounced the wizened old man gravely, "is the scent of jasmine after a spring rain."
    The student frowned. "But Master," he objected gently, "an Incan wise man I

encountered on the steps of Machu Picchu told me life was a thorn like a needle of tempered steel."

The sage nodded, unperturbed, and said, "That's *his* life."

YOUTH

To get back one's youth one has merely to repeat one's follies.

—*Oscar Wilde*

Always be nice to those younger than you, because they are the ones who will be writing about you.   —*Cyril Connolly*

Rejoice, O young man, in thy youth.   —*Ecclesiastes 11:9*

I am not young enough to know everything.   —*James M. Barrie*

Live as long as you may, the first twenty years are the longest half of your life.

—*Robert Southey*

Youth would be an ideal state if it came a little later in life.

—*Lord Asquith*

We cannot always build the future for our youth, but we can build our youth for the future.   —*Franklin D. Roosevelt*

Youth is like spring, an overpraised season.   —*Samuel Butler*

Young men think old men are fools, but old men know young men are fools.

—*George Chapman*

My salad days, when I was green in judgment, cold in blood. . . .

—*William Shakespeare*

The young are in a state like intoxication, for youth is sweet and they are growing.

—*Aristotle*

In fact, there's nothing that keeps its youth, so far as I know, but a tree and the truth.

—*Oliver Wendell Holmes, Sr.*

Happiness, like youth and health, is rarely appreciated until it is past.

—*Marguerite, Countess of Blessington*

Sayings

Youth is wasted on the young.

You're only young once.

Joke

• Sometimes we give kids information they're too young to understand. Like the seven-year-old who listened patiently to a lecture about the birds and the bees, then turned to his dad with a big smile. "I get it," he announced triumphantly. "Since I have a brother and a sister, you and Mom did it three times!"

AGE AND AGING

Middle Age

As long as a woman can look ten years younger than her own daughter, she is perfectly satisfied.   *—Oscar Wilde*

We have not passed that subtle line between childhood and adulthood until we move from the passive voice to the active voice—that is until we have stopped saying "It got lost," and say "I lost it."   *—Sydney J. Harris*

When I can look life in the eyes, grown calm and very coldly wise, life will have given me the truth, and taken in exchange—my youth.   *—Sara Teasdale*

He must have had a magnificent build before his stomach went in for a career of its own.   *—Margaret Halsey*

Forty is the old age of youth; fifty is the youth of old age.   *—Victor Hugo*

It is sobering to consider that when Mozart was my age [thirty-five], he had already been dead for a year.   *—Tom Lehrer*

No one over thirty-five is worth meeting who has not something to teach us—something more than we could learn ourselves, from a book.

—Cyril Connolly

The man who views the world at fifty the same as he did at twenty has wasted thirty years of his life.   *—Muhammad Ali*

The greatest thing about getting older is that you don't lose all the other ages you've been.   *—Madeleine L'Engle*

Middle age is the time when a man is always thinking that in a week or two he will feel as good as ever.   *—Don Marquis*

He carried his childhood like a hurt warm bird held to his middle-aged breast.

—Herbert Gold

Do not go gentle into that good night. Rage, rage against the dying of the light.

—Dylan Thomas

Age is a very high price to pay for maturity.   *—Tom Stoppard*

Litigation takes the place of sex at middle age.   *—Gore Vidal*

When I grow up, I want to be a little boy.   *—Joseph Heller*

At twenty years of age the will reigns; at thirty, the wit; at forty, the judgment.

—Benjamin Franklin

I refuse to admit that I am more than fifty-two, even if that does make my sons illegitimate.   *—Nancy Astor (attrib.)*

One should never trust a woman who tells one her real age. A woman who would tell one that, would tell one anything.   *—Oscar Wilde*

Thirty-five is a very attractive age. London society is full of women of the very highest birth who have, of their own free choice, remained thirty-five for years.

—Oscar Wilde

Middle age: when you begin to exchange your emotions for symptoms.

—Irvin Cobb

Boys will be boys, and so will a lot of middle-aged men.

—Elbert Hubbard

A woman is as old as she looks before breakfast.   *—Edgar Watson Howe*

An enthusiastic tennis player, Supreme Court Justice Hugo Black was advised by his doctor that the sport was inadvisable for someone in his forties. "In that case," rejoined the justice, "I can't wait to turn fifty so I can play again."

Discussing how old you are is the temple of boredom.   *—Ruth Gordon*

Anyone can get old. All you have to do is live long enough.

—Groucho Marx

My only fear is that I may live too long.   *—Thomas Jefferson*

All would live long, but none would be old.   *—Benjamin Franklin*

'Tis very certain the desire of life prolongs it.   *—Lord Byron*

I have been asked, "How do you grow old so easily?" I reply, "Very easily. I give all my time to it."   *—Emanuel Celler*

The four stages of man are infancy, childhood, adolescence, and obsolescence.

—Art Linkletter

Our nation's long neglect of minorities whose skin is dark is perhaps only a little worse than our neglect of another minority whose hair is white.

—Lyndon B. Johnson

When you are about thirty-five years old, something terrible always happens to music.

—Steve Race

What he hath scanted men in hair, he hath given them in wit.

—William Shakespeare

Children are a great comfort in your old age—and they help you to reach it faster, too.
—Lionel M. Kauffman

The secret to a long life is to stay busy, get plenty of exercise, and don't drink too much. Then again, don't drink too little.

—Hermann Smith-Johannson, at age 103

I don't care how old you get, I think a woman ought to stay sexy for her husband.
—Tammy Faye Bakker

Women, as they grow older, rely more and more on cosmetics. Men, as they grow older, rely more and more on a sense of humor.   *—George Jean Nathan*

One of the many things nobody ever tells you about middle age is that it's such a nice change from being young.   *—Dorothy Canfield Fisher*

Sayings

Everybody's shook up these days. Teenagers are upset because they're living in a world dominated by nuclear weapons—and adults are upset because they're living in a world dominated by teenagers.

The Gray Panthers.

Age before beauty.

You're only as old as you act.

I have socks older than she is.

At twenty, we don't care what the world thinks of us; at thirty, we worry about what it's thinking of us; at forty we discover it isn't thinking about us at all.

Jokes
- I've got everything I had twenty years ago—except now it's all lower.

—*Gypsy Rose Lee*

- Fun is like life insurance; the older you get, the more it costs.

—*Elbert Hubbard*

- I was born in 1962. True. And the room next to me was 1963. . . .

—*Joan Rivers*

- When an actress told Bob Hope she was "approaching forty," the comedian couldn't help wondering from what direction.

- My wife never lies about her age. She just tells everyone she's as old as I am. Then she lies about my age.

- Paul Putney had planned a trip to Paris for a very long time, and the day after his retirement, he was on a plane. His old friend Herb met him at the airport, and asked, "Well, Paul, how was Paris?"
  "Oh, it was fine," replied the weary traveler, "but I wish I'd gone twenty years ago."
  "When Paris was really Paris, eh?" said Herb sympathetically.
  "No, when Paul Putney was really Paul Putney."

Old Age

One of the many pleasures of old age is giving things up.

—*Malcolm Muggeridge*

If you don't learn to laugh at trouble, you won't have anything to laugh at when you grow old.   —*Edgar Watson Howe*

It is always the season for the old to learn.   —*Aeschylus*

I'll never make the mistake of bein' seventy again!   —*Casey Stengel*

Anyone who stops learning is old, whether at twenty or eighty. Anyone who keeps learning stays young. The greatest thing in life is to keep your mind young.

—*Henry Ford*

Old men are fond of giving good advice to console themselves for their inability to give bad examples.   —*François de La Rochefoucauld*

Growing old is no more than a bad habit which a busy man has no time to form.
—*André Maurois*

In old age . . . we are like a batch of letters that someone has sent. We are no longer in the past, we have arrived.   —*Knut Hamsun*

Lord, Lord! How subject we old men are to this vice of lying.
—*William Shakespeare*

Old boys have their playthings as well as young ones; the difference is only in the price.   —*Benjamin Franklin*

To me, old age is always fifteen years older than I am.
—*Bernard M. Baruch*

Growing old is like being increasingly penalized for a crime you haven't committed.
—*Anthony Powell*

The first forty years of life give us the text; the next thirty supply the commentary.
—*Arthur Schopenhauer*

I adore life but I don't fear death. I just prefer to die as late as possible.
—*Georges Simenon*

I know a man so old, he has to use axle grease to keep his legs from creakin' when he walks.   —*Jackie (Moms) Mabley*

There ain't nothin' an ol' man can do but bring me a message from a young one.
—*Jackie (Moms) Mabley*

Years ago, I thought old age would be dreadful, because I should not be able to do things I would want to do. Now I find there is nothing I want to do after all.
—*Nancy Astor*

Age wins and one must learn to grow old.   —*Diana Cooper*

Being an old maid is like death by drowning, a really delightful sensation after you cease to struggle.   —*Edna Ferber*

I'm not interested in age. People who tell their age are silly. You're as young as you feel.   —*Elizabeth Arden*

When we grow old, there can only be one regret—not to have given enough of ourselves.   —*Eleonora Duse*

I never allow myself to be bored, because boredom is aging. If you live in the past you grow old, and dull, and dusty. It's very nice, of course, to be young and beautiful; but there are other qualities, thank God.   —*Marie Tempest*

As old as the hills.   —*Sir Walter Scott*

It's later than you think.   —*Robert W. Service*

Sayings
Do not resist growing old—many are denied the privilege.

You're not as young as you used to be, but you're not as old as you're going to be—so watch it!
                                                                    —*Irish saying*

We grow too soon old and too late smart.
                                                    —*Pennsylvania Dutch saying*

Youth is wasted on the young.

You're only as old as you act/as you feel.

Age before beauty.

I have socks older than she is.

Long life is a gift that nobody gets to keep.

Life should be measured by its breadth, not its length.

The years in your life are less important than the life in your years.

Old age doesn't keep men from chasing women; they just have trouble remembering why.

Jokes

- Nowadays there's a pill for everything—to keep your nose from running, to keep you regular, to keep your heart beating, to keep your hair from falling out, to improve your muscle tone . . . Why, thanks to advances in medical science, every day people are dying who never looked better.

- At his annual checkup Bernie was given an excellent bill of health. "It must run in your family," commented the doctor. "How old was your dad when he died?"
    "What makes you think he's dead?" asked Bernie. "He's ninety and still going strong."
    "Aha! And how long did your grandfather live?"
    "What makes you think he's dead, Doc? He's a hundred and six, and getting married to a twenty-two-year-old next week," Bernie informed him.
    "At his age!" exclaimed the doctor. "Why's he want to marry such a young woman?"
    "Doc," replied Bernie, "what makes you think he wants to?"

- What's good about having Alzheimer's?
    —You're always meeting new people, and you can hide your own Easter eggs.

- A number of years after working on a film with a glamorous movie star, a certain cinematographer was asked to work with her again. This time, however, the diva was not at all pleased with the results. "This time around I look like a hag, and in our first film I looked radiantly beautiful," she complained bitterly.
    "Perhaps, madame," suggested the cinematographer tactfully, "it has something to do with the fact that I was eight years younger then."

- I may be forty, but every morning when I get up I feel like a twenty-year-old. Unfortunately, there's never one around.

- The elderly man flattered himself that he was still a ladies' man, and decided to flirt with the comely waitress. "So tell me, sweetheart, where have you been all my life?" he crooned.

"Actually, sir," she pointed out sweetly, "for the first forty-five years of it, I wasn't even around."

- I'm at that age now where just putting my cigar in its holder is a thrill.

—*George Burns*

- When in his nineties, Supreme Court Justice Oliver Wendell Holmes was out for a stroll with a friend when they happened past a lovely young woman. "Ah," sighed the justice, "what I'd give to be seventy again. . . ."

- What's the difference between the young and the old?
  —The young don't know what to do, while the old can't do what they know.

- Why are old people so wrinkled?
  —Ever try to iron one?

- When an aged woman was asked if there were to be candles on her birthday cake, she responded curtly, "No, it's a birthday party, not a torchlight procession."

- An eager-beaver real estate agent was doing his best to pitch a condominium to this old coot in Palm Beach. Having outlined its many attractions, he concluded his pitch. "And, Mr. Rosenblatt, this is an investment in the future."
  "Sonny," croaked Mr. Rosenblatt, "at my age I don't even buy green bananas."

DEATH

A single death is a tragedy, a million deaths is a statistic.   —*Joseph Stalin*

I never wanted to see anybody die, but there are a few obituary notices I have read with pleasure.   —*Clarence Darrow*

Of all escape mechanisms, death is the most efficient.   —*H. L. Mencken*

Death is the greatest evil, because it cuts off hope.   —*William Hazlitt*

I shall never act differently, even if I have to die for it many times.

—*Socrates*

If I could drop dead right now, I'd be the happiest man alive.

—*Samuel Goldwyn*

I cannot forgive my friends for dying; I do not find these vanishing acts of theirs at all amusing.   —*Logan Pearsall Smith*

But man dieth, and wasteth away: yea, man giveth up the ghost, and where is he?

—*Job 14:10*

When good men die, their goodness does not perish.   —*Euripides*

May my last breath be drawn through a pipe and exhaled in a pun.

—*Charles Lamb*

The general outlook is not that the person has died but that the person has lived.

—*William Buchanan, on writing obituaries*

Death is the sound of distant thunder at a picnic.   —*W. H. Auden*

It is a disturbing truth that even undertakers die sometimes.

—Arnold Bennett

. . . any man's death diminishes me, because I am involved in mankind; and therefore never send to know for whom the bell tolls; it tolls for thee.

—John Donne

It's not that I'm afraid to die, I just don't want to be there when it happens.

—Woody Allen

If my doctor told me I only had six minutes to live, I wouldn't brood. I'd type a little faster.
—Isaac Asimov

I am ready to meet my Maker. Whether my Maker is prepared for the ordeal of meeting me is another matter. *—Winston Churchill*

Boy, when you're dead, they really fix you up. I hope to hell when I *do* die somebody has sense enough to just dump me in the river or something. Anything except sticking me in a goddamn cemetery. People coming and putting a bunch of flowers on your stomach on Sunday and all that crap. Who wants flowers when you're dead? Nobody.

—J. D. Salinger

Eternity is a terrible thought. I mean, when's it going to end?

—Tom Stoppard

. . . in this world nothing is certain but death and taxes.

—Benjamin Franklin

Death is swallowed up in victory. O death, where is thy sting? O grave, where is thy victory? *—1 Corinthians 15:54–55*

Death be not proud, though some have called thee mighty and dreadful, for thou art not so. For those whom thou think'st thou dost overthrow die not, poor Death, nor yet canst thou kill me. *—John Donne*

Dust thou art, to dust returnest, was not spoken of the soul.

—Henry Wadsworth Longfellow

I have a rendezvous with Death at some disputed barricade. *—Alan Seeger*

. . . it's a blessing to die for a cause, because you can so easily die for nothing.

—Andrew Young

Death is the price of revolution. *—H. Rap Brown*

We know the road to freedom has always been stalked by death.

—Angela Davis

If you're afraid to die, you will not be able to live. *—James Baldwin*

The present life is naught but a diversion and a sport; surely the Last Abode is Life, did they but know? *—Koran 29:64*

Death is just a low chemical trick played on everybody except sequoia trees.

—J. J. Furnas

. . . I hope to see my Pilot face to face when I have crost the bar.

—Alfred, Lord Tennyson

. . . Adam, the first great benefactor of our race. He brought death into the world.

—*Mark Twain*

To die will be an awfully big adventure.   —*James M. Barrie*

It hath been often said that it is not death but dying which is terrible.

—*Henry Fielding*

If this is dying, I don't think much of it.   —*Lytton Strachey (attrib.)*

There's no tragedy in life like the death of a child. Things never get back to the way they were.   —*Dwight D. Eisenhower, on the death of his first son*

The reports of my death are greatly exaggerated.   —*Mark Twain*

Why fear death? It is the most beautiful adventure in life.

—*Charles Frohman, supposedly said as he was dying*
in the torpedoing of the SS **Lusitania**

How can they tell?

—*Dorothy Parker, on being informed of the death of President Calvin Coolidge*

His death was the first time that Ed Wynn ever made anyone sad.

—*Red Skelton*

Earth to earth, ashes to ashes, dust to dust.

—*Burial service,* **The Book of Common Prayer**

Sayings

To die in the flower of age is a life offered in sacrifice.   —*Madagascan saying*

Death is nature's way of telling you to slow down.

If you don't go to people's funerals, they won't come to yours.

It can be terribly difficult to find the right words, but sometimes they're not even necessary. When one of his classmates died, an eight-year-old friend visited the boy's home one day after school. "What did you say?" asked his mother gently when the child returned.

"Nothing. I just sat on his mom's lap and cried with her."

Jokes

• For three days after death, hair and fingernails continue to grow, but phone calls taper off.   —*Johnny Carson*

• I don't believe in dying. It's been done. I'm working on a new exit. Besides, I can't die now—I'm booked.   —*George Burns*

• Two old guys wonder if there's baseball in heaven, and promise each other that the first to die will somehow let the other one know. A week later, one of them dies. And a week after that, his friend recognizes his voice coming down from the clouds. "Joe, I've got some good news and some bad news," the disembodied voice reports. "The good news is that there *is* a baseball team in heaven. The bad news is that you're pitching on Friday."

• A guy returns from a long trip to Europe, having left his beloved cat in his brother's care. The minute he clears customs, he calls his brother and inquires after his pet.

"The cat's dead," replies his brother bluntly.

The guy is devastated. "You don't know how much that cat meant to me," he sobbed into the phone. "Couldn't you at least have given a little thought to a nicer way of breaking the news? For instance, couldn't you have said, 'Well, you know, the cat got out of the house one day and climbed up on the roof, and the fire department couldn't get her down, and finally she died of exposure . . . or starvation . . . or something'? Why are you always so thoughtless?"

"Look, I'm really really sorry," says his brother. "I'll try to do better next time, I swear."

"Okay, let's just put it behind us. How are you, anyway? How's Mom?"

There was a long pause. "Uh," the brother finally stammers, "uh . . . Mom's on the roof."

BEAUTY

Men ought to be more conscious of their bodies as objects of delight.

—Germaine Greer

I don't like standard beauty. There is no beauty without strangeness.

—Karl Lagerfeld

How you lose or keep your hair depends on how wisely you choose your parents.

—Edward R. Nida

Ah seen a man so ugly till they spread a sheet over his head at night so sleep could slip up on him.   *—Zora Neale Hurston*

There is no cosmetic for beauty like happiness.

—Marguerite, Countess of Blessington

Love built on beauty, soon as beauty, dies.   *—John Donne*

She walks in beauty, like the night of cloudless climes and starry skies; and all that's best of dark and bright meet in her aspect and her eyes.   *—Lord Byron*

What he hath scanted men in hair, he hath given them in wit.

—William Shakespeare

Beauty: the power by which a woman charms a lover and terrifies a husband.

—Ambrose Bierce

No object is so beautiful that, under certain conditions, it will not look ugly.

—Oscar Wilde

My wife was too beautiful for words, but not for arguments.   *—John Barrymore*

When I am working on a problem, I never think about beauty . . . but when I have finished, if the solution is not beautiful, I know it is wrong.

—R. Buckminster Fuller

It is only the shallow people who do not judge by appearance.   *—Oscar Wilde*

There is no excellent beauty that hath not some strangeness in the proportion.

—*Francis Bacon*

A thing of beauty is a joy forever.   —*John Keats*

It is amazing how complete is the delusion that beauty is goodness.   —*Leo Tolstoy*

Remember that the most beautiful things in the world are the most useless; peacocks and lilies, for instance.   —*John Ruskin*

Ask a toad what is beauty. . . . He will answer that it is a female with two great round eyes coming out of her little head, a large flat mouth, a yellow belly, and a brown back.   —*Voltaire*

A much more effective and lasting method of face-lifting than surgical technique is happy thinking, new interests, and outdoor exercise.   —*Sara Murray Jordan*

I always say beauty is only sin deep.   —*Saki (H. H. Munro)*

I'm tired of all this nonsense about beauty being only skin-deep. That's deep enough. What do you want, an adorable pancreas?   —*Jean Kerr*

Anatomically speaking, a bust is here today and gone tomorrow.   —*Isobel Barnett*

Beauty's but skin deep.   —*John Davies of Hereford*

Beauty is in the eye of the beholder.   —*Margaret Wolfe Hungerford*

None but the brave deserves the fair.   —*John Dryden*

Sayings
I am beautiful; *you* have quite good features; *she* isn't bad-looking if you like that type.

Her hair has more body than I do.

Jokes
• Adam was the perfect figure of a man, and Eve was indescribably beautiful . . . so where did all the ugly people come from?

• Sometimes I just go [to the beauty salon] for an estimate.   —*Phyllis Diller*

FACES

My face is my passport.   —*Vladimir Horowitz*

His face was filled with broken commandments.   —*John Masefield*

The features of our face are hardly more than gestures which have become permanent.

—*Marcel Proust*

Often a noble face hides filthy ways.   —*Euripides*

To be loved at first sight, a man should have at the same time something to respect and something to pity in his face.   —*Stendhal*

My comfort is that old age, that ill layer-up of beauty, can do no more spoil upon my face.   —*William Shakespeare*

Was this the face that launched a thousand ships, and burned the topless towers of Ilium?
—*Christopher Marlowe*

The eyes have one language everywhere.
—*George Herbert*

What a blessing it would be if we could open and shut our ears as easily we do our eyes.
—*Georg Christoph Lichtenberg*

Sayings

A rat is a beauty in the eyes of its mother.

If you are ugly, be winsome.
—*North African saying*

Joke

• "I've had it with my husband. He's such a clean freak," a disgruntled woman complained to her friend. "Every night he makes me wash and scrub my face."
"What's wrong with that?" her friend asked.
"Then he wants to iron it."

HEALTH

You can't talk of the dangers of snake poisoning and not mention snakes.
—*C. Everett Koop, regarding AIDS education*

I get my exercise running to the funerals of my friends who exercise.
—*Barry Gray*

We can now prove that large numbers of Americans are dying from sitting on their behinds.
—*Bruce B. Dan*

There are people who strictly deprive themselves of each and every eatable, drinkable, and smokable which has in any way acquired a shady reputation. They pay this price for health, and health is all they get for it.
—*Mark Twain*

Suffering isn't ennobling, recovery is.
—*Christiaan Barnard*

Sleep, riches, and health, to be truly enjoyed, must be interrupted.
—*Jean Paul Friedrich Richter*

There are no such things as incurables, there are only things for which man has not found a cure.
—*Bernard Baruch*

A hospital bed is a parked taxi with the meter running.
—*Groucho Marx*

For extreme illnesses extreme remedies are most fitting.
—*Hippocrates*

It is only when the rich are sick that they fully feel the impotence of wealth.
—*Charles Caleb Colton*

The patient, treated on the fashionable theory, sometimes gets well in spite of the medicine.
—*Thomas Jefferson*

Happiness, like youth and health, is rarely appreciated until it is past.
—*Marguerite, Countess of Blessington*

The miserable have no other medicine but only hope.

—*William Shakespeare*

We are so fond of one another because our ailments are the same.

—*Jonathan Swift*

Good friends are good for your health.   —*Irwin Sarason*

When we are well, we all have good advice for those who are ill.

—*Terence*

I enjoy convalescence. It is the part that makes the illness worthwhile.

—*George Bernard Shaw*

The trouble about always trying to preserve the health of the body is that it is so difficult to do without destroying the health of the mind.   —*G. K. Chesterton*

Health of body and mind is a great blessing, if we can bear it.

—*John Henry Newman*

Serious illness doesn't bother me for long because I am too inhospitable a host.

—*Albert Schweitzer*

Two things are bad for the heart—running uphill and running down people.

—*Bernard Gimbel*

Use your health, even to the point of wearing it out. That is what it is for. Spend all you have before you die; and do not outlive yourself.

—*George Bernard Shaw*

Constant attention by a good nurse may be just as important as a major operation by a surgeon.   —*Dag Hammarskjöld*

Once you have been confronted with a life-and-death situation, trivia no longer matters. Your perspective grows and you live at a deeper level. There's no time for pettiness.

—*Margaretta (Happy) Rockefeller*

Every stress leaves an indelible scar, and the organism pays for its survival after a stressful situation by becoming a little older.   —*Hans Selye*

Bodily pain affects man as a whole down to the deepest layers of his moral being. It forces him to face again the fundamental questions of his fate, of his attitude toward God and fellow man, of his individual and collective responsibility and of the sense of his pilgrimage on earth.   —*Pope Pius XII*

Rule Number 1 is, don't sweat the small stuff. Rule Number 2 is, it's all small stuff. And if you can't fight and you can't flee, flow.   —*Robert S. Eliot*

The subject no longer has to be mentioned by name. Someone is sick. Someone else is feeling better now. A friend has just gone back into the hospital. Another has died. The unspoken name, of course, is AIDS.   —*David W. Dunlap*

The more serious the illness, the more important it is for you to fight back, mobilizing all your resources—spiritual, emotional, intellectual, physical.   —*Norman Cousins*

Your heaviest artillery will be your will to live. Keep the big gun going.

—*Norman Cousins*

Health is infectious.   —*Georg Christoph Lichtenberg*

If you mean to keep as well as possible, the less you think about your health, the better.
—*Oliver Wendell Holmes, Sr.*

Coronary heart disease is a silent disease, and the first manifestation frequently is sudden death.
—*Herman Hellerstein*

Health is not a condition of matter, but of Mind. . . .
—*Mary Baker Eddy*

Look to your health; and if you have it, praise God, and value it next to a good conscience; for health is the second blessing that we mortals are capable of; a blessing that money cannot buy.
—*Izaak Walton*

Health that mocks the doctor's rules. Knowledge never learned of schools.
—*John Greenleaf Whittier*

Health is not valued till sickness comes.
—*Thomas Fuller*

If you treat a sick child like an adult and a sick adult like a child, everything usually works out pretty well.
—*Ruth Carlisle*

The only way to keep your health is to eat what you don't want, drink what you don't like, and do what you'd rather not.
—*Mark Twain*

The temple of God is holy, which temple ye are.
—**1 Corinthians 3:17**

Early to bed, early to rise, makes a man healthy, wealthy and wise.
—*Benjamin Franklin*

Sayings
Hypochondria is the only disease I haven't got.

Health is better than wealth.

Money can't buy health, but it certainly makes it easier to stay healthy.

Health doesn't ensure happiness, but it's hard to be happy without it.

Take your medicine like a man.

Jokes
* If exercise is so good for you, why do athletes have to retire by age thirty-five?

* "You're really in pretty good shape for a man of sixty-five," said the doctor reassuringly. "Of course, you're only forty-eight . . ."

* Definition of a minor operation: one performed on somebody else.

* Personally I always go to [insert name of hospital]. That's where all the truck drivers get operated on.

* What do you give to the man who has everything?
    —Penicillin.

* "Yeah, Doc, what's the news?" asked Fred when his doctor called with his test results.
    "I have some bad news and some really bad news," admitted the doctor. "The bad news is that you only have twenty-four hours to live."

"Oh my God," gasped Fred, sinking to his knees. "What could be worse news than that?"

"I couldn't get hold of you yesterday."

- The way Medicare is going, pretty soon all it'll pay for is get-well cards.

- Nowadays there's a pill for everything—to keep your nose from running, to keep you regular, to keep your heart beating, to keep your hair from falling out, to improve your muscle tone. . . . Why, thanks to advances in medical science, every day people are dying who never looked better.

- There was a terrible accident at the building site, and the construction worker rushed over to where a well-dressed woman was pinned beneath an iron girder. "Hang in there, lady," he said helplessly, "the ambulance will be here soon. Are you badly hurt?"

"How should I know?" she snapped. "I'm a doctor, not a lawyer."

DIETING

Many of us don't know what poor losers we are until we try dieting.

—*Thomas Lamance*

I'm a fat anorexic.

—*Kiri Te Kanawa*

Americans: People who laugh at African witch doctors and spend a hundred million dollars on fake reducing systems.

—*Leonard Louis Levine*

The best way to lose weight is to close your mouth—something very difficult for a politician. Or watch your food—just watch it, don't eat it.

—*Edward I. Koch*

The biggest seller is cookbooks and the second is diet books—how not to eat what you've just learned how to cook.

—*Andy Rooney*

To lengthen thy life, lessen thy meals.

—*Benjamin Franklin*

One must eat to live, not live to eat.

—*Molière*

O! that this too solid flesh would melt. . . .

—*William Shakespeare*

Everything I like is either illegal, immoral, or fattening.

—*Alexander Woollcott (attrib.)*

What some people call health, if purchased by perpetual anxiety about diet, isn't much better than disease.

—*George Dennison Prentice*

The appetite grows by eating.

—*François Rabelais*

The popular concept of a strengthening diet is a chicken wrung out in hot water.

—*Martin Fischer*

Who ever hears of fat men heading a riot, or herding together in turbulent mobs?

—*Washington Irving*

I went on a diet, swore off drinking and heavy eating, and in fourteen days I lost two weeks.

—*Joe E. Lewis*

Those magazine dieting stories always have the testimonial of a woman who wore a dress that could slipcover New Jersey in one photo and thirty days later looked like a well-dressed thermometer.
—*Erma Bombeck*

Another good reducing exercise consists in placing both hands against the table edge and pushing back.
—*Robert Quillen*

From the day on which she weighs 140, the chief excitement of a woman's life consists in spotting women who are fatter than she is.
—*Helen Rowland*

I cannot but bless the memory of Julius Caesar, for the great esteem he expressed for fat men, and his aversion to lean ones.
—*David Hume*

. . . she's so fat she's my two best friends. She wears stretch caftans. She's got more chins than the Chinese telephone directory.
—*Joan Rivers*

Americans like fat books and thin women.
—*Russell Baker*

All real men love to eat.
—*Marlene Dietrich*

The only way to keep your health is to eat what you don't want, drink what you don't like, and do what you'd rather not.
—*Mark Twain*

Sayings

Diets are for those who are thick and tired of it.

Desperation is a fellow shaving before stepping on the scales.

Jokes

• Let me put it this way. According to my girth, I should be a ninety-foot redwood.
—*Erma Bombeck*

• What does it mean to go on the Scarsdale diet?
—You shoot your doctor, then spend the rest of your life eating bread and water.

• In one of his pictures Jimmy Cagney shoved a grapefruit into a girl's face, and it was considered shocking. Now it's considered a diet.

• Is she fat? Her favorite food is seconds.
—*Joan Rivers, of Elizabeth Taylor*

• What do a fat girl and a moped have in common?
—They're both fun to ride as long as nobody sees you doing it.

• The bathroom scale manufacturer was very proud of the new model being introduced at the trade fair. "Listen to these features: it's calibrated to one one-hundredth of a pound; it can measure your height as well, in feet or meters; it gives you a readout via an LED or human-voice simulator; and that's not all—"
"Very impressive," interrupted a none-too-slender sales rep for a chain of home-furnishings stores, "but before I place an order I'll have to try it out."
"Be my guest," said the manufacturer graciously.
But no sooner had the sales rep taken his place on the scale than a loud, very human voice issued forth: "One at a time, please, one at a time!"

• I just found out about a fabulous new diet. It has two parts: 1) you can only eat bagels and lox; and 2) you have to live in Syria.

- When she ran into a friend at the supermarket, Sylvia smugly announced that she'd discovered the perfect diet. "Every other day I eat like a pig, stuff myself with anything I'm in the mood for. Then, on the alternate days, I don't touch a thing but water."

  "Interesting approach," commented her friend. "And how do you feel?"

  "Oh, just terrific," Sylvia replied cheerfully, "every other day."

- "Frankly, Mr. Schwartz, I just don't think your book has very good commercial prospects," pronounced the publisher, pushing the manuscript of *The 100-Year Diet* across his desk in the direction of its author. "See, the diet books the public wants are the ones that tell you how to lose weight *fast*."

  "Oh, my book tells you how to drop the weight fast," Schwartz maintained eagerly. "Then it goes on to explain how long you have to stay on the diet so you don't gain all of it back."

- My wife loves sweets. If she'd been Eve in the Garden of Eden, the snake would've had to use chocolate cake.

DRINK

People who drink to drown their sorrow should be told that sorrow knows how to swim.

—Ann Landers

Drink really promises you everything and gives you nothing.

—Nancy Astor

When you stop drinking, you have to deal with this marvelous personality that started you drinking in the first place.   *—Jimmy Breslin*

Drinking makes such fools of people, and people are such fools to begin with it's just compounding the felony.   *—Robert Benchley*

What contemptible scoundrel stole the cork from my lunch?   *—W. C. Fields*

An alcoholic is someone you don't like who drinks as much as you do.

—Dylan Thomas

Wonderful euphemisms for drunk: blitzed, blasted, blotto, bombed, cockeyed, crocked, ripped, looped, loaded, leveled, wasted, wiped, soused, sozzled, smashed, and schnockered. Stewed, stinko, stupid, tanked, totaled, tight, and tipsy. Not to mention feeling no pain, three sheets to the wind, in one's cups, intoxicated, addlepated, and pixilated.   *—Bruce Weber*

I am prepared to believe that a dry martini slightly impairs the palate, but think what it does for the soul.   *—Alec Waugh*

The whole world is about three drinks behind.   *—Humphrey Bogart*

Drunkenness is nothing but voluntary madness.   *—Seneca the Younger*

Alcoholism isn't a spectator sport. Eventually the whole family gets to play.

—Joyce Rebeta-Burditt

Bacchus hath drowned more men than Neptune.   *—Thomas Fuller*

Claret is the liquor for boys; port for men; but he who aspires to be a hero must drink brandy.
—*Samuel Johnson*

I don't drink any more—just the same amount.
—*Joe E. Lewis*

When you teetotal, you've got an awful feeling that everybody's your boss.
—*Will Fyffe*

You must know your limitations. I drink a bottle of Jack Daniel's a day, that's mine.
—*Lemmy, of Motörhead, a heavy-metal band*

I drink to make other people interesting.
—*George Jean Nathan*

Two reasons for drinking: one is, when you are thirsty, to cure it; the other, when you are not thirsty, to prevent it.
—*Thomas Love Peacock*

Champagne, if you are seeking the truth, is better than a lie detector. It encourages a man to be expansive, even reckless, while lie detectors are only a challenge to tell lies successfully.
—*Graham Greene*

A bottle of wine begs to be shared; I have never met a miserly wine lover.
—*Clifton Fadiman*

A woman drove me to drink and I never even had the courtesy to thank her.
—*W. C. Fields (attrib.)*

A man is never drunk if he can lie on the floor without holding on.
—*Joe E. Lewis*

I drink to forget I drink.
—*Joe E. Lewis*

I must get out of these wet clothes and into a dry martini.
—*Alexander Woollcott (attrib.)*

One reason I don't drink is that I want to know when I'm having a good time.
—*Nancy Astor*

I drink no more than a sponge.
—*François Rabelais*

I drink when I have occasion and sometimes when I have no occasion.
—*Miguel de Cervantes*

Kings it makes gods, and meaner creatures, kings.
—*William Shakespeare*

One drink is plenty; two drinks too many, and three not half enough.
—*W. Knox Haynes*

A good general rule is to state that the bouquet is better than the taste, and vice versa.
—*Stephen Potter, on wine one-upmanship*

Candy is dandy, but liquor is quicker.
—*Ogden Nash*

Wine that maketh glad the heart of man.
—*Psalms 104:15*

He has a profound respect for old age. Especially when it's bottled.
—*Gene Fowler, on W. C. Fields's fondness for aged bourbon*

Wine nourishes, refreshes, and cheers. . . . Wherever wine is lacking, medicines become necessary.
—*Talmud*

Work is the curse of the drinking class.
—*Oscar Wilde*

Sayings

I am sparkling; *you* are unusually talkative; *he* is drunk.

There are more old drunkards than old doctors.

Drink and the world drinks with you; swear off and you drink alone.

Better to pay the tavernkeeper than the druggist.   —*Spanish saying*

If you drink like a fish, drink what a fish drinks.

Jokes

• He drinks so much whiskey that he staggers in his sleep.

• The Ten Stages of Drunkenness:
    1. Witty and charming
    2. Rich and famous
    3. Benevolent
    4. Clairvoyant
    5. Fuck dinner
    6. Patriotic
    7. Crank up the *Enola Gay*
    8. Witty and charming, Part Two
    9. Invisible
    10. Bulletproof

• I once shook hands with Pat Boone and my whole right side sobered up.

—*Dean Martin*

• Why do elephants drink?
    —It helps them forget.

• This guy's not an ordinary, garden-variety drunk. Far from it. Last year he donated his body to science, and he's preserving it in alcohol till they can use it.

• Actually it only takes one drink to get me loaded. Trouble is, I can't remember if it's the thirteenth or fourteenth.   —*George Burns*

• What's the difference between a drunk and an alcoholic?
    —Drunks don't have to go to meetings.

DRUGS

Speed will turn you into your parents.   —*Frank Zappa (attrib.)*

Nobody in the United States is more than one handshake away from virtually any drug they want to get.   —*Norman Zinberg*

The irony is that as the [cocaine] user gets sicker, he is less able to see it. The magic of the powder is that every noseful tells you that you don't really have a problem.

—*Joseph Pursch*

I guess he got into what we now call designer drugs.

—*Geraldine Kidston, mother of a drug victim*

Two great European narcotics, alcohol and Christianity.

—*Friedrich Wilhelm Nietzsche*

All dope can do for you is kill you . . . the long hard way. And it can kill the people you love right along with you.   —*Billie Holiday*

The desire to take medicine is perhaps the greatest feature which distinguishes man from animals.   —*William Osler*

I hate to advocate drugs, alcohol, violence, or insanity to anyone, but they've always worked for me.   —*Hunter S. Thompson*

Now they're calling taking drugs an epidemic—that's 'cause white folks are doing it.

—*Richard Pryor*

Cocaine is just God's way of telling you you're making too much money.

—*Robin Williams*

It's easier to get people off heroin than coffee.   —*Richard T. Rappolt*

In extreme cases, marijuana can so destroy a man's character that he mixes freely with persons of another race.   —*South African textbook on criminology*

I've never had any problems with drugs, only with policemen.   —*Keith Richards*

Better living through chemistry.   —*Du Pont corporate slogan, 1960s*

Reality is just a crutch for people who can't cope with drugs.   —*Lily Tomlin*

Sayings
Smoking is pulmonary rape.

Just say No.

Why do you think they call it dope?

Jokes
• I didn't know my wife was on LSD until I suggested a weekend in Las Vegas. "Great!" she chirped. "Let's take the kids!"

• Why did the moron take two hits of mescaline?
    —So he could go round trip.

FOOD

I doubt whether the world holds for anyone a more soul-stirring surprise than the first adventure with ice cream.   —*Heywood Broun*

Strange to see how a good dinner and feasting reconciles everybody.

—*Samuel Pepys*

No man is lonely eating spaghetti; it requires so much attention.

—*Christopher Morley*

At a dinner party one should eat wisely but not too well, and talk well but not too wisely.   —*W. Somerset Maugham*

Part of the secret of success in life is to eat what you like and let the food fight it out inside.
—*Mark Twain*

And ye shall eat the fat of the land.
—**Genesis 45:18**

Life itself is the proper binge.
—*Julia Child*

When I write of hunger, I am really writing about love and the hunger for it, and warmth and the love of it . . . and it is all one.
—*M. F. K. Fisher*

To eat is human, to digest, divine.
—*Mark Twain*

My mouth is a happy place.
—*Pat Conroy*

There's someone at every party who eats all the celery.
—*Kin Hubbard*

Food is an important part of a balanced diet.
—*Fran Lebowitz*

An army marches on its stomach.
—*Napoleon Bonaparte (attrib.)*

Tell me what you eat and I will tell you what you are.
—*Anthelme Brillat-Savarin*

Life, within doors, has few pleasanter aspects than a neatly arranged and well-provisioned breakfast table.
—*Nathaniel Hawthorne*

There is no love sincerer than the love of food.
—*George Bernard Shaw*

An idealist is one who, on noticing that a rose smells better than a cabbage, concludes that it will also make a better soup.
—*H. L. Mencken*

My rule of life prescribed as an absolutely sacred rite smoking cigars and also the drinking of alcohol before, after, and if need be during all meals and in the interval between them.
—*Winston Churchill, on dining with the abstinent King Ibn Saud of Saudi Arabia*

He was a bold man that first ate an oyster.
—*Jonathan Swift*

As for butter versus margarine, I trust cows more than chemists.
—*Joan Gussow, assistant professor of nutrition and education, Columbia University*

The first thing I remember liking that liked me back was food.
—*Rhoda Morgenstern*

One man's meat is another man's poison.
—*Oswald Dykes*

The way to a man's heart is through his stomach.
—*Fanny Fern*

Saying
To think of food only as a fuel is foolish.

Jokes
- I'm at the age where food has taken the place of sex in my life. In fact, I've just had a mirror put over my kitchen table.
—*Rodney Dangerfield*

- Two elderly women are at a Catskills mountain resort and one of them says, "Boy, the food at this place is really terrible." The other one says, "Yeah, and such small portions."
—*Alvy, in* **Annie Hall,** *screenplay by Woody Allen and Marshall Brickman*

• You do not sew with a fork, and I see no reason why you should eat with knitting needles.
                                                                    —*Miss Piggy, on chopsticks*

HABITS

I am not an early riser. The self-respect which other men enjoy in rising early I feel due to me for waking up at all.   —*William Gerhardt*

Habit is habit, and not to be flung out of the window by any man, but coaxed downstairs a step at time.   —*Mark Twain*

The fixity of a habit is generally in direct proportion to its absurdity.
                                                                    —*Marcel Proust*

Curious things, habits. People themselves never knew they had them.
                                                                    —*Agatha Christie*

It is easier to prevent ill habits than to break them.   —*Thomas Fuller*

When you stop drinking, you have to deal with this marvelous personality that started you drinking in the first place.   —*Jimmy Breslin*

Habit is stronger than reason.   —*George Santayana*

A man of no conversation should smoke.   —*Ralph Waldo Emerson*

Many who wouldn't dream of having an addiction are addicted to normalcy.
                                                                    —*John-Roger and Peter McWilliams*

Saying
Habit may be likened to a cable; every day we weave a thread, and soon we cannot break it.

Jokes
• I hate mornings. They come so early!

• Instead of taking baths, I've decided to stay away from people.

• A rebel leader was finally apprehended by the military police and summarily sentenced to death. The generalissimo watched as the blindfolded man was led before the firing squad, then magnanimously came over to offer him a last cigarette.
  "No thanks," was the condemned man's answer. "I'm trying to quit."

MODERATION AND ABSTINENCE

I have learned to seek my happiness by limiting my desires, rather than in attempting to satisfy them.   —*John Stuart Mill*

Moderation is the silken string running through the pearl chain of all virtues.
                                                                    —*Bishop Holt*

If moderation is a fault, then indifference is a crime.
                                                                    —*Georg Christoph Lichtenberg*

I hate to advocate drugs, alcohol, violence, or insanity to anyone, but they've always worked for me.
—*Hunter S. Thompson*

A thing moderately good is not so good as it ought to be. Moderation in temper is always a virtue; but moderation in principle is always a vice.
—*Thomas Paine*

The main dangers in this life are the people who want to change everything—or nothing.
—*Nancy Astor*

The dinosaur's eloquent lesson is that if some bigness is good, an overabundance of bigness is not necessarily better.
—*Eric Johnston*

You must know your limitations. I drink a bottle of Jack Daniel's a day, that's mine.
—*Lemmy, of Motörhead, a heavy-metal band*

Extremism in the defense of liberty is no vice. . . . Moderation in the pursuit of justice is no virtue.
—*Barry M. Goldwater*

The secret to a long life is to stay busy, get plenty of exercise, and don't drink too much. Then again, don't drink too little.
—*Hermann Smith-Johannson, at 103 years old*

We know what happens to people who stay in the middle of the road. They get run over.
—*Aneurin Bevan*

The middle of the road is all of the usable surface. The extremes, right and left, are in the gutters.
—*Dwight D. Eisenhower*

Nothing succeeds like excess.
—*Oscar Wilde*

If a man is right, he can't be too radical; if he is wrong, he can't be too conservative.
—*Josh Billings*

An optimist is a person who sees a green light everywhere, while the pessimist sees only the red stoplight. . . . The truly wise person is color-blind.
—*Albert Schweitzer*

Give me chastity and self-restraint, but do not give it yet.
—*St. Augustine*

You never know what is enough unless you know what is more than enough.
—*William Blake*

To abstain from sin when a man cannot sin is to be forsaken by sin, not to forsake it.
—*St. Augustine*

Man's many desires are like the small metal coins he carries about in his pocket. The more he has the more they weight him down.
—*Satya Sai Baba*

Many who wouldn't dream of having an addiction are addicted to normalcy.
—*John-Roger and Peter McWilliams*

Insanity is a matter of degree.
—*Joaquim Maria Machado de Assis*

Moderation in all things.
—*Terence*

Sayings

Moderation is a tree with roots of contentment, and fruits of tranquillity and peace.

—*North African saying*

If you drink like a fish, drink what a fish drinks.

Do not use a hatchet to remove a fly from your friend's forehead.

—*Chinese proverb*

Joke

• A panhandler walked up to a woman who was just about to go into a coffee shop and exclaimed, "Lady, I haven't eaten in a week."

"Wow!" exclaimed the woman. "I wish I had your will power."

SLEEP AND DREAMS

Dreaming permits each and every one of us to be quietly and safely insane every night of our lives.   —*Dr. William C. Dement*

The best way to make your dreams come true is to wake up.

—*Paul Valéry*

People who don't have nightmares don't have dreams.

—*Robert Paul Smith*

Sleep is the best meditation.   —*Dalai Lama*

The amount of sleep required by the average person is about five minutes more.

—*Max Kauffmann*

To sleep, perchance to dream.   —*William Shakespeare*

Sleep, riches, and health, to be truly enjoyed, must be interrupted.

—*Jean Paul Friedrich Richter*

People who say they sleep like a baby usually don't have one.   —*Leo J. Burke*

[Sleep] is an eight-hour peep show of infantile erotica.   —*J. G. Ballard*

No small art is it to sleep; it is necessary to keep awake all day for that purpose.

—*Friedrich Wilhelm Nietzsche*

Bed is the perfect climate.   —*Noel Coward*

Sayings

Nothing is achieved in a dream.   —*West African saying*

Sleep, the near relative of death.   —*South African saying*

Jokes

• Hear about the guy who had such a bad case of insomnia the sheep fell asleep?

• "Doc, I had the strangest dream last night. I dreamed I was the only man in a nudist colony."

"My, my," responded the doctor. "Did you sleep well?"

"I tried," answered the patient, "but it was hard."

• Define bed.

—A place where people who are run down wind up.

part two

Business and Politics

ECONOMICS

CREDIT

We at Chrysler borrow money the old-fashioned way. We pay it back.

—Lee Iacocca

If you would know the value of money, go and try to borrow some.

—Benjamin Franklin

I can get no remedy against this consumption of the purse; borrowing only lingers and lingers it out, but the disease is incurable. *—William Shakespeare*

Credit . . . is the only enduring testimonial to man's confidence in man.

—James Blish

Debt is the worst poverty. *—Thomas Fuller*

I am dying beyond my means. *—Oscar Wilde*

It is not my interest to pay the principal, nor my principle to pay the interest.

—Richard Brinsley Sheridan

Some people use half their ingenuity to get into debt, and the other half to avoid paying it. *—George D. Prentice*

Neither a borrower nor a lender be; for a loan oft loses both itself and friend, and borrowing dulls the edge of husbandry. *—William Shakespeare*

Be not made a beggar by banqueting upon borrowing.

—Ecclesiasticus 18:33

No man's credit is as good as his money. *—Edgar Watson Howe*

The creditor hath a better memory than the debtor. *—James Howell*

Live within your income, even if you have to borrow to do so.

—Josh Billings

Credit is a system whereby a person who can't pay gets another person who can't pay to guarantee that he can pay. *—Charles Dickens*

Sayings

In God we trust; all others pay cash.

Creditors have better memories than debtors.

Jokes

- "Do you live within your income?"

  "No way! It's all I can do to live within my credit."

- If it isn't the sheriff it's the finance company. I've got more attachments on me than a vacuum cleaner.   —*John Barrymore*

ECONOMICS

Whoever perpetrated the mathematical inaccuracy "Two can live as cheaply as one" has a lot to answer for.   —*Caren Meyer*

Economics is a subject that does not greatly respect one's wishes.

—*Nikita S. Khrushchev*

If ignorance paid dividends, most Americans could make a fortune out of what they don't know about economics.   —*Luther Hodges*

Blessed are the young, for they shall inherit the national debt.

—*Herbert Hoover*

Christmas is the time when kids tell Santa what they want and adults pay for it. Deficits are when adults tell the government what they want—and their kids pay for it.

—*Richard Lamm*

If all economists were laid end to end, they would not reach a conclusion.

—*George Bernard Shaw (attrib.)*

There was a farmer who planted some corn. He said to his neighbor, "I hope I break even this year. I really need the money."   —*John F. Kennedy*

We have always known that heedless self-interest was bad morals; we know now that it is bad economics.   —*Franklin D. Roosevelt*

An economist is a guy with a Phi Beta Kappa key on one end of his watch chain and no watch on the other end.   —*Alben Barkley*

President Hoover used to quip that he was looking for a one-armed economist for his staff, so he wouldn't be able to say, "On the one hand this, but on the other hand that. . . ."

It's a recession when your neighbor loses his job, it's a depression when you lose your own.   —*Harry S Truman*

Sayings

Economists and weather forecasters are the only people who can make an abundant living without ever being right.

The purpose of studying economics is to avoid being deceived by economists.

The paradox of economics: During periods when none of the economic theories are working, all the economists are.

An economist is a man who talks about things you don't understand and makes you believe it's your fault.

If you're not confused, you're not paying attention.

No one has ever repealed the law of supply and demand.

Economics is nothing more nor less than keeping your head as far above water as possible.

Jokes

• A chemist, a physicist, and an economist were passengers on a flight that crashed in the middle of the ocean. Swimming to a tiny island, they discovered water but no food, so they were overjoyed when a crate of canned food washed up on the beach. The chemist lost no time in getting to work on a chemical formula that would dissolve the lids of the cans. The physicist picked up a boulder and set to work calculating the angle and velocity of the blow which would pierce the cans. Observing their frantic efforts, the economist simply picked up a can, scratched his chin, and said, "Let's assume we have a can opener."

• The avant-garde economist was fond of pointing out how prostitution epitomizes a tenet of modern economic theory: Don't buy, lease!

ECONOMY AND THRIFT

Budget: a mathematical confirmation of your suspicions.   —*A. A. Latimer*

I'm living so far beyond my income that we may almost be said to be living apart.
                                                                          —*e. e. cummings*

Live within your income, even if you have to borrow to do so.
                                                                          —*Josh Billings*

My problem lies in reconciling my gross habits with my net income.
                                                                          —*Errol Flynn*

Annual income twenty pounds, annual expenditure nineteen nineteen six, result happiness. Annual income twenty pounds, annual expenditure twenty pounds ought and six, result misery.   —*Charles Dickens*

Just about the time you think you can make both ends meet, somebody moves the ends.   —*Pansy Penner*

There are several ways in which to apportion the family income, all of them unsatisfactory.   —*Robert Benchley*

Saving is a very fine thing. Especially when your parents have done it for you.
                                                              —*Winston Churchill (attrib.)*

What this country needs is a good five-cent nickel.
                                                              —*Franklin Pierce Adams*

A bargain is something you have to find a use for once you have bought it.
                                                                          —*Benjamin Franklin*

The price of ability does not depend on merit, but on supply and demand.
                                                                      —*George Bernard Shaw*

A penny saved is a penny earned.   —*Benjamin Franklin*

Sayings

If you have to ask what it costs, you can't afford it.

He who hesitates . . . buys the stock two points higher.

Save Water—Shower with a Friend

If you expect to save at all, do it while your salary's small.

A bargain is something you cannot use at a price you cannot resist.

A miser isn't much fun to live with, but he makes a wonderful ancestor.

Jokes

• Halfway through the term, the freshman wrote home, "Dear Dad, I'm broke and have no friends. What should I do?"

  His father wrote back, "Make friends at once."

• A tightwad owed a wedding present and everything in the store seemed way overpriced—until he spotted a lovely porcelain vase which had unfortunately been broken. The storekeeper was delighted to part with the damaged item for a low price, and agreed to ship the item to the newlyweds.

  The next week the cheapskate received a note thanking him politely for the vase, which suited the couple's taste exactly. It concluded, "Thank you, too, for taking care to wrap each piece separately."

• "Henry Junior thinks money grows on trees," the overworked businessman complained to his secretary one day. "Tonight he's getting a talking-to that'll really get across the value of a dollar."

  "How'd it go?" asked the secretary the next morning.

  "Not so good," he admitted glumly. "Now he wants his allowance in Deutschmarks."

• "I finally snapped," the man said. "Last night while I was going over the bills, I discovered how much money my wife squanders and I hit the roof."

  "What did you do?" asked his friend.

  "I stormed into the bedroom and gave her a lecture on economy and thrift."

  "Did it help?"

  "I'll say. Tomorrow we're selling my golf clubs and fishing equipment."

INFLATION

Steel prices cause inflation like wet sidewalks cause rain.   —*Roger Blough*

A billion dollars ain't what it used to be.   —*Nelson Bunker Hunt*

When future historians look back on our way of curing inflation, they'll probably compare it to bloodletting in the Middle Ages.   —*Lee Iacocca*

It now costs more to amuse a child than it once did to educate his father.

—*Vaughan Monroe*

Among the things money can't buy is what it used to.   —*Max Kauffmann*

Time for belt tightening. You can't live on a million a year anymore.

—*Randy Newman*

Americans are getting stronger. Twenty years ago it took two people to carry ten dollars' worth of groceries. Today, a five-year-old can do it.

—*Henny Youngman*

What this country needs is a good five-cent nickel.

—*Franklin Pierce Adams*

Asked why Congress doesn't decrease deficit spending, Strom Thurmond explained, "It's awfully hard to get a hog to butcher itself."

Sayings

Inflation is a stab in the buck.

Inflation is when you never had anything and now even that's gone.

Inflation has made it possible for only the rich to afford a recession.

Inflation is being broke with a pocketful of money.

Jokes

• I'm three hundred percent against inflation.

• Inflation is when you pay cash for something and they ask to see your driver's license.

• How can you tell when inflation is bad?
   —If you drop a dollar on the street, you get a ticket for littering.

• The candidate was asked what was responsible for inflation. "I don't know," the politician replied earnestly, "but I'm willing to spend whatever it takes to find out."

• If the unions were smart, they wouldn't tie salaries up to the cost of living, but to the national debt.

• Inflation is when vegetarians aren't the only ones not eating meat.

• Inflation is when the product you overpaid for in February is a bargain by midsummer.

MONEY

Dollars not only count, they rule.   —*Charles Thomas Walker*

The great rule is not to talk about money with people who have much more or much less than you.   —*Katharine Whitehorn*

Money speaks sense in a language all nations understand.   —*Aphra Behn*

When it comes down to it, it is only money that commands respect.

—*Madeleine Bingham*

Words are like money; there is nothing so useless, unless when in actual use.

—*Samuel Butler*

I don't want money. It is only people who pay their bills who want that, and I never pay mine.   —*Oscar Wilde*

There was a time when a fool and his money were soon parted, but now it happens to everybody.   —*Adlai E. Stevenson*

Money, and not morality, is the principle of commercial nations.

—*Thomas Jefferson*

When a man says money can do anything, that settles it: he hasn't got any.

—*Edgar Watson Howe*

A man is usually more careful of his money than he is of his principles.

—*Edgar Watson Howe*

I'd like to live like a poor man—only with lots of money.   —*Pablo Picasso*

Making money resembles chess in [many] ways, not least its cozy relationship with mathematics, still more in its abundance of traps, ploys, gambits, stratagems, variations, even in its recognized offensive and defensive openings. As in chess, the moneymaker gains more through his opponent's mistakes than through his own immaculate brilliance, and for every winner, there must be at least one loser.

—*Robert Heller*

Those who have some means think that the most important thing in the world is love. The poor know that it is money.   —*Gerald Brenan*

No one would remember the Good Samaritan if he'd only had good intentions. He had money as well.   —*Margaret Thatcher*

Money, it turned out, was exactly like sex: you thought of nothing else if you didn't have it and thought of other things if you did.   —*James Baldwin*

The safest way to double your money is to fold it over once and put it in your pocket.

—*Kin Hubbard*

Money may be the husk of many things, but not the kernel. It brings you food, but not appetite; medicine, but not health; acquaintances, but not friends; servants, but not loyalty; days of joy, but not peace or happiness.   —*Henrik Ibsen*

There is nothing more demoralizing than a small but adequate income.

—*Edmund Wilson*

Money is the best bait to fish for man with.   —*Thomas Fuller*

When it is a question of money, everybody is of the same religion.

—*Voltaire*

When a fellow says, "It ain't the money but the principle of the thing," it's the money.

—*Elbert Hubbard*

Money is like muck, not good except it be spread.   —*Francis Bacon*

Money is like manure. If you spread it around, it does a lot of good, but if you pile it up in one place, it stinks like hell.   —*Clint W. Murchison*

"Resource-constrained environment" [are] fancy Pentagon words that mean there isn't enough money to go around.   —*General John W. Vessey, Jr.*

If you would know the value of money, go and try to borrow some.

—*Benjamin Franklin*

Among mankind money is far more persuasive than logical argument.

—*Euripides*

Money is the fruit of evil as often as the root of it.   —*Henry Fielding*

Money is indeed the most important thing in the world; and all sound and successful personal and national morality should have this fact for its basis.

—*George Bernard Shaw*

Money is like a sixth sense without which you cannot make a complete use of the other five.   —*W. Somerset Maugham*

Money is better than poverty, if only for financial reasons.   —*Woody Allen*

If you would know what the Lord God thinks of money, you have only to look at those to whom he gives it.   —*Maurice Baring*

Those who set out to serve both God and Mammon soon discover there is no God.

—*Logan Pearsall Smith*

I finally know what distinguishes man from the other beasts: financial worries.

—*Jules Renard*

Before we give you billions more, we want to know what you've done with the trillion you've got.

—*Les Aspin, U.S. Representative and chairman of the House Armed Services Committee in a letter to Secretary of Defense Caspar W. Weinberger*

The love of money is the root of all evil.   —*1 Timothy 6:10*

People who say money can't buy happiness just don't know where to shop.

—*Tom Shivers*

Sayings
Money kills more people than a club.   —*West African saying*

Money isn't everything; usually it isn't even enough.

Money can't buy you love.

Money can't buy happiness, but it certainly doesn't discourage it.

Joke
• There was this farmer with a two-seater outhouse, and one morning he happened to be sharing it with his none-too-bright brother-in-law. "Dammit," cursed the farmer as he pulled up his overalls. "Dropped a quarter in the dang hole."

"Don't worry, buddy, I'll get it for you," offered his companion cheerfully, pulling out a $5 bill and tossing it into the farmer's hole.

"What'd you do that for?" asked the bewildered farmer.

"Hell, you didn't think I'd go down there just for a quarter, did you?"

TAXES

The avoidance of taxes is the only pursuit that still carries any reward.
—John Maynard Keynes

I'm proud to be paying taxes in the United States. The only thing is—I could be just as proud for half the money.   *—Arthur Godfrey*

Psychiatrists say it's not good for man to keep too much to himself. The Internal Revenue Service says the same thing.   *—Harold Smith*

Youth today must be strong, unafraid, and a better taxpayer than its father.
—Harry V. Wade

Where there is an income tax, the just man will pay more and the unjust less on the same amount of income.   *—Plato*

Tax reform means, "Don't tax you, don't tax me, tax that fellow behind the tree."
—Russell B. Long

There is one difference between a tax collector and a taxidermist—the taxidermist leaves the hide.   *—Mortimer Caplan*

The current tax code is a daily mugging.   *—Ronald Reagan*

. . . in this world nothing is certain but death and taxes.
—Benjamin Franklin

The wisdom of man never yet contrived a system of taxation that would operate with perfect equality.   *—Andrew Jackson*

. . . the power to tax involves the power to destroy. . . .   *—John Marshall*

In constitutional states, liberty is compensation for heavy taxes; in dictatorships the substitute for liberty is light taxes.   *—Baron de Montesquieu*

Taxation without representation is tyranny.   *—James Otis (attrib.)*

Taxes, after all, are the dues that we pay for the privilege of membership in an organized society.   *—Franklin D. Roosevelt*

The income tax has made more liars out of the American people than golf has.
—Will Rogers (attrib.)

When Joe Louis was asked who had hit him the hardest during his boxing career, he replied, "That's easy—Uncle Sam!"

Sayings
Next to being shot at and missed, nothing is quite so satisfying as an income tax refund.

Government is an endless pursuit of new ways to tax.

Jokes
• I don't know why they couple death and taxes. You only die once.

• Responding to a burglar alarm in an IRS office, the police caught the thief red-handed. The accountant whose office had been burgled was delighted, until he got a call from the precinct office. "It's about the thief we apprehended in your office," explained the cop. "We found $150 in his pockets."

"What of it?" asked the accountant.

"He claims he had $225 on him before breaking in."

• Tax inspector to creative taxpayer: "Could you clarify how you thought it was legal to claim depreciation on your mother-in-law?"

• When Mr. Fine was audited, the IRS took exception to certain deductions, among them one for the birth of a child. "She was born in January," the auditor explained.

"So?" he protested. "It was last year's business."

• You've got to admire the IRS. Any organization that makes that much money without advertising deserves respect.

• "Now, class, who can tell me what caused the American Revolution to break out?" asked Mrs. Humphries of her freshman economics seminar.

"Taxation," replied a student in the front row.

"Very good, Sherry." The teacher turned to a boy whose hand was waving. "Yes, Andrew? Do you have a question?"

"Yeah, Mrs. Humphries. How come they teach that we won?"

• I just saw a modern-day version of *Faust*. In the first act he sells his soul to the devil. Then he spends the rest of the opera trying to convince the Internal Revenue Service it was a long-term capital gain.

• It's not whether you win or lose but how you play the game. Now, if we can only convince the IRS . . .

VALUE

A thing is worth whatever the buyer will pay for it.   —*Publilius Syrus*

Sometimes give your services for nothing. . . .   —*Hippocrates*

If you pay peanuts, you get monkeys.   —*Sir James Goldsmith*

Nothing can move a man who is paid by the hour; how sweet the flight of time seems to his calm mind.   —*Charles Dudley Warner*

The salary of the chief executive of the large corporation is not a market award for achievement. It is frequently in the nature of a warm personal gesture by the individual to himself.   —*John Kenneth Galbraith*

Michael Faraday, a pioneer in the field of electricity, was demonstrating the tremendous potential of his new invention, the dynamo, to the British Royal Scientific Society. A young politician in the audience, William Gladstone, grew bored, finally saying, "I'm sure this is all very interesting, Mr. Faraday, but what in God's earth good is it?"

"Someday," replied the brilliant inventor dryly, "you politicians will be able to tax it."

Sayings

Did you hear about the auto worker who was offered a position as president of a bank, but couldn't afford the pay cut?

There's always free cheese in a mousetrap.

The cost of living is high, but it's worth it.

My mother didn't leave me anything of value, except her wisdom.

What you have put into the kettle comes afterwards into your spoon.

—Turkestan proverb

Jokes

• After collecting her $10 fee, Madame Sylvia, the gypsy fortuneteller, informed her customer that his payment entitled him to ask her two questions. "Gee, isn't that a pretty high price for only a couple of questions?" protested the man.

"Some people think so," conceded the fortuneteller with a gracious nod. "And your last question?"

• Customer: "Gee, if these models are sold way under cost like you say they are, how do you make a living?"
Salesman: "Simple. We make our money fixing them."

• Upon learning that the store had been robbed of over $60,000 worth of clothes, the manager moaned, "If only this had happened two weeks ago, while the sale was still on—we'd have saved twenty percent."

• When the wealthy businessman choked on a fishbone at a restaurant, he was fortunate that a surgeon was seated at a nearby table. Springing up, the doctor deftly removed the bone and saved his life.

As soon as the fellow had calmed himself and could talk again, he thanked the surgeon profusely and offered to pay him for his services. "Just name the fee," he croaked gratefully.

"Okay," replied the doctor. "How about half of what you'd have offered when the bone was still stuck in your throat?"

• After concluding an impassioned sales spiel for the latest model, the car salesman paused to let it sink in. "Any questions?" he asked.

"Actually, yes," replied the prospect. "How come the $26,000 sticker price you're asking is *modest*, and the $400 rebate you're offering is *substantial*?"

WEALTH

Seek wealth, it's good.

—Ivan Boesky

The first rule [of becoming wealthy] is not to lose money. The second rule is not to forget the first rule.

—Warren Buffet

The millionaire [has] become common in numbers, common in the source of wealth, common (in the usage of bygone snobberies) in social origin, common in the continued narrowing of the gap between his fortune and that of the normally affluent middle class.

—Robert Heller

To turn $100 into $110 is work. To turn $100 million into $110 million is inevitable.
—*Edgar Bronfman*

If you can count your money, you don't have a billion dollars.
—*J. Paul Getty*

Inherited wealth is a big handicap to happiness. It is as certain death to ambition as cocaine is to morality.   —*William K. Vanderbilt*

The greatest luxury of riches is that they allow you to escape so much good advice.
—*Arthur Helps*

I am opposed to millionaires, but it would be dangerous to offer me the position.
—*Mark Twain*

Affluence means influence.   —*Jack London*

In truth, prosperity tries the souls even of the wise.   —*Sallust*

It is better to live rich than die rich.   —*Samuel Johnson*

The wretchedness of being rich is that you live with rich people.
—*Logan Pearsall Smith*

It is only when the rich are sick that they fully feel the impotence of wealth.
—*Charles Caleb Colton*

To be thought rich is as good as to be rich.
—*William Makepeace Thackeray*

Few rich men own their own property. The property owns them.
—*Robert G. Ingersoll*

It is easier for a camel to go through the eye of a needle, than for a rich man to enter into the kingdom of God.   —*Matthew 19:24*

. . . a man is rich in proportion to the number of things he can afford to let alone.
—*Henry David Thoreau*

I find all this money a considerable burden.   —*J. Paul Getty*

Only the rich are lonesome.   —*Paul Laurence Dunbar*

No man actually owns a fortune. It owns him.   —*A. P. Giannini*

The rich are different.   —*F. Scott Fitzgerald*

The rich are different—they have more money.
—*Ernest Hemingway, in response to Fitzgerald*

You can never be too rich or too thin.   —*Wallis Warfield Simpson*

Sayings
His wealth is superior to him.   —*West African saying*

Poverty is "Who knows you?"; Prosperity is "I am your relative."
—*West African saying*

Those who inherit fortunes are often more troublesome than those who make them.
—*Central African saying*

It requires a great deal of boldness and a great deal of caution to make a great fortune, and when you have got it, it requires ten times as much wit to keep it.

A fat purse never lacks friends.

It's just as easy to love a rich man/woman as a poor one.

Jokes
• [Beverly Hills] is so exclusive—it's the only town in America where [Taco Bell] has an unlisted number. And so rich—it's the only place I've seen a Salvation Army band with a string section.

• A millionaire and his wife had everything money could buy—until the fellow gambled on a few bad stock tips and lost everything. He came home that night with a heavy heart and explained their newly straitened circumstances to his wife. "Since we need to start somewhere, Myrna," he went on, "you'd better learn to cook so we can let the kitchen staff go."

  His wife thought it over for a few moments. Nodding, she suggested, "Okay, George, but you'd better learn to screw so we can fire the chauffeur."

PROFESSIONS AND PROFESSIONALS

GENERAL PROFESSIONS

It is a silly question to ask a prostitute why she does it. . . . These are the highest-paid "professional" women in America. **—Gail Sheehy**

No man can be a pure specialist without being in the strict sense an idiot. **—George Bernard Shaw**

Incomprehensible jargon is the hallmark of a profession. **—Kingman Brewster**

[An expert is] somebody who is more than fifty miles from home, has no responsibility for implementing the advice he gives, and shows slides. **—Edwin Meese**

The trouble with specialists is that they tend to think in grooves. **—Elaine Morgan**

People of the same trade seldom meet together, even for merriment and diversion, but the conversation ends in a conspiracy against the public, or in some contrivance to raise prices. **—Adam Smith**

All professions are conspiracies against the laity. **—George Bernard Shaw**

If only I had known, I should have become a watchmaker. **—Albert Einstein**

Even when all the experts agree, they may well be mistaken. **—Bertrand Russell**

Sayings
An expert is a man who makes his mistakes quietly.

Professionals built the *Titanic*; amateurs built the Ark.

An expert is like the bottom of a double boiler. It shoots off a lot of steam, but it never really knows what's cooking.

Jokes
• A plumber was called by a frantic homeowner to stop a leak in the upstairs bathroom. The plumber quickly took stock of the situation, took his hammer, and hit the pipe hard. The leak stopped.

The customer was delighted, until she received the bill for $180.35. "This is outrageous," she protested. "All you did was hit the pipe once."

By way of response, the plumber itemized the bill: "Wear and tear on the hammer, 35 cents. Knowing where to hit, $180.00."

- A builder, an electrician, and a lawyer were arguing about which profession was the oldest. The builder pointed out proudly that the first thing God had done was to *build* the earth.

  "True," said the electrician, "but before that, he said, 'Let there be light.' "

  "You're both right," said the lawyer agreeably, "but before the light there was chaos—and who do you think created the chaos?"

- Discovering a leak in the bathroom, the lawyer's secretary called the plumber, who fixed it in a matter of minutes. The bill, however, was substantial, so substantial that the lawyer called to complain. "You weren't here for more than ten minutes," he said, "and *I* don't charge that much for an hour."

  "I know," responded the plumber sympathetically. "I didn't either, when I was a lawyer."

- Definition of a statistician: Someone who, if you put his feet in the oven and his head in the freezer, would say, "On the average, I feel just fine."

- There was a terrible accident at the building site, and the construction worker rushed over to where a well-dressed woman was pinned beneath an iron girder. "Hang in there, lady," he said helplessly, "the ambulance will be here soon. Are you badly hurt?"

  "How should I know?" she snapped. "I'm a doctor, not a lawyer."

ACCOUNTING AND ACCOUNTANTS

Accountants are perpetually fighting their shiny-pants, green-eyeshades, number-cruncher image.
—*Albert Newgarden*

Did you ever hear of a kid playing accountant—even if he wanted to be one?
—*Jackie Mason*

The postwar architecture is the accountant's revenge on the prewar businessman's dreams.
—*Rem Koolhaas*

Is a certified public accountant upper lower middle class or lower upper middle class?
—*Charles Merrill Smith*

Over the long haul of life on this planet, it is the ecologists, and not the bookkeepers of business, who are the ultimate accountants.
—*Stewart L. McKinley*

Canceled checks . . . will be to future historians and cultural anthropologists what the Dead Sea Scrolls and hieroglyphics are to us.
—*Brent Staples*

Figures won't lie, but liars will figure.
—*Charles H. Grosvenor (attrib.)*

. . . keep your accounts on your thumbnail.
—*Henry David Thoreau*

Sayings
[Accountants are] bean counters.

Accountants' pocket protectors are to keep people from getting to their hearts.

When accountants hear, "How do I love thee, let me count the ways," it's the counting part that interests them.

CPA stands for Constantly Proposing Audits.

Jokes

- "I hear the company's looking for a new accountant," said one employee to another as they lingered by the water fountain.
  "Gee, I thought we hired one just last month."
  "That's the one they're looking for."

- Accountant's maxim: When you make the mistake of adding the date to the right side of the accounting statement, you must add it to the left side too.

- One of the sideshows at a circus featured a strong man who squeezed an orange until it appeared to be completely dry. When he finished, the strong man's manager came forward and challenged anybody in the audience to come forward and try to get one last drop out of the supercompressed piece of fruit. To make the offer a bit more enticing, the manager offered $1,000 to anyone who successfully eked out just one tiny drop of juice.
  A bulging-muscled weight lifter bounced up onto the stage, grabbed the orange from the manager, and pressed it with all his might. Nothing came out. Next, a big, burly construction worker sauntered up and took the orange from the exhausted weight lifter. After ten minutes of intense squeezing and a lot of grimacing, the construction worker finally admitted defeat.
  "No other takers?" the manager asked with a satisfied sneer.
  "May I try?" responded a short, skinny bespectacled man from the back row.
  The manager couldn't keep a straight face as he and the rest of the crowd watched the stranger make his way up to the front. Suddenly the laughter stopped when, to everyone's amazement, the little guy picked up the orange and squeezed a puddle of juice onto the floor.
  Flabbergasted, the manager sputtered, "How the heck did you do that?"
  "I'm an accountant."

- The company accountant once had occasion to go on a business trip with one of the vice presidents. "Look," exclaimed his companion, gazing out the window of the train, "a flock of sheep—they've just been shorn."
  Looking out to see for himself, the accountant noted, "On this side, at least."

- What's the definition of an actuary?
  —Someone who wanted to be an accountant but didn't have the personality.

- I go to the world's wealthiest accountant. I'll tell you how rich he is: he takes his vacation in March.

- Somehow the IRS auditor knew it was my first audit. "How could you tell?" I wondered.
  "For this kind of examination you don't have to undress," she explained.

ADVERTISING

One ad is worth more to a paper than forty editorials.   —*Will Rogers*

Advertising may be described as the science of arresting the human intelligence long enough to get money from it.
                                                              —*Stephen Leacock*

Advertising is a valuable economic factor because it is the cheapest way of selling goods, particularly if the goods are worthless.
                                                              —*Sinclair Lewis*

Advertising has annihilated the power of the most powerful adjectives.
                                                              —*Paul Valéry*

Advertising is the modern substitute for argument; its function is to make the worse appear the better.
                                                              —*George Santayana*

Few people at the beginning of the nineteenth century needed an adman to tell them what they wanted.
                                                              —*John Kenneth Galbraith*

Let advertisers spend the same amount of money improving their product that they do on advertising and they wouldn't need to advertise it.
                                                              —*Will Rogers*

Nothing's so apt to undermine your confidence in a product as knowing that the commercial selling it has been approved by the company that makes it.
                                                              —*Franklin P. Jones*

It used to be that people needed products to survive. Now products need people to survive.
                                                              —*Nicholas Johnson*

Advertising is the art of making whole lies out of half truths.
                                                              —*Edgar A. Shoaff*

A vice president in an advertising agency is a "molehill man" who has until five P.M. to make a molehill into a mountain. An accomplished molehill man will often have his mountain finished even before lunch.
                                                              —*Fred Allen*

Richard Nixon was just offered two million dollars by Schick to do a commercial—for Gillette.
                                                              —*Gerald Ford*

Many a small thing has been made large by the right kind of advertising.
                                                              —*Mark Twain*

Advertising is the greatest art form of the twentieth century.
                                                              —*Marshall McLuhan*

In good times, people want to advertise; in bad times, they have to.
                                                              —*Bruce Barton, former chairman of BBD&O*

You have to do a little bragging on yourself even to your relatives—man doesn't get anywhere without advertising.
                                                              —*John Nance Garner*

Advertising agency: Eighty-five percent confusion and fifteen percent commission.
                                                              —*Fred Allen*

The longest word in the English language is the one following the phrase "And now a word from our sponsor."
                                                              —*Hal Eaton*

Doing business without advertising is like winking at a girl in the dark. You know what you are doing, but nobody else does.
                                                              —*Stuart Henderson Britt*

You can tell the ideals of a nation by its advertisements.
                                                              —*Norman Douglas*

Advertisements contain the only truths to be relied on in a newspaper.

—*Thomas Jefferson*

Advertisements are now so numerous that they are very negligently perused, and it is therefore become necessary to gain attention by magnificence of promises, and by eloquences sometimes sublime and sometimes pathetic. Promise—large promise—is the soul of advertising.   —*Samuel Johnson (1759)*

Half the money I spend on advertising is wasted; the trouble is, I don't know which half.   —*John Wanamaker (attrib.)*

Advertise, or the sheriff may do it for you.   —*P. T. Barnum (attrib.)*

. . . we've got to know what we've got a choice of. This is the function of advertising.

—*Tom Dillon, former chairman of BBD&O*

Advertising promotes that divine discontent which makes people strive to improve their economic status.   —*Ralph Butler*

An acquaintance seated next to R. J. Wrigley on a flight to Chicago asked the multimillionaire why he continued to advertise his chewing gum when it was far and away the most successful product in its field.

Wrigley replied, "For the same reason that the pilot keeps this plane's engines running even though we're already in the air."

There is no such thing as a bad client. But there is such a thing as bad advertising.

—*Jerry Della Femina*

Sayings
A good thing sells itself; a bad thing advertises itself for sale.

—*East African saying*

You always buy familiar names, the ones you recognize; that's why the adman always claims it pays to advertise.

Advertising moves the goods—if it's good advertising. Bad advertising doesn't move the goods because it doesn't move the buyers.

Advertisers are the merchants of dreams.

Jokes
• A company that sold red salmon found itself being outsold by pink salmon by a significant ratio. Finally, desperate to get a bigger share of the market, the owner hired an advertising agency. "I don't care what it takes, as long as it's legal," he instructed them.

All the agency did was change the label on the can, to read "Authentic Norwegian Red Salmon—guaranteed not to turn pink."

• A good account person, when the client tells him to jump, asks, "How high and when should I come down?"

• A client looking for a new advertising agency called the head of account services at three companies and asked them what time it was.

"It's two-thirty in the afternoon," answered the first person.

"I'll research that and get back to you," promised the representative at the second company.

But the person who landed the account was the one who replied, "What time would you like it to be?"

- Madison Avenue has come up with a special perfume for their junior executives who want to appear conscientious. It smells like fear.

- Harry was a complete skeptic about the value of advertising. "There's no such thing as an expert," he claimed. "Anybody can advertise and come up with the exact same results."

  "Is that so?" His friend Jack, who happened to work in advertising, suggested they put Harry's theory to the test by advertising the same offer in the same medium on the same day.

  Harry's ad read, "Free trip to Disneyland. Driver needed to deliver new car from New York." And he was quite pleased when he got five responses the next day.

  The advertising man, however, took his phone off the hook after the one-hundredth call. His ad read, "Drive free from New York to Disneyland delivering new air-conditioned Cadillac."

- Mr. Smith emigrated to the United States as a young man and fulfilled the immigrant's dream: he started up his own nail factory in Brooklyn, bought a nice house, sent his kids to college, even put the oldest son through Harvard Business School. When the young man graduated, Smith patted him on the back and said, "Jimmy, you're the smart one. I'm turning the business over to you and retiring to Miami Beach."

  A year later he got an excited call from his son. "Dad, things are going great: I've computerized inventory, automated the factory, even got a great new ad campaign going. You've got to come see it with your own eyes." So the young man picked him up at the airport, and just before they reached the factory an enormous billboard loomed up. In huge letters, beneath a close-up of Jesus on the cross, it read, "Use Smith's Nails for the Toughest Jobs."

  "Jimmy," groaned Mr. Smith, "that's the new ad compaign? I'm telling you, the public's never gonna go for it."

  A year later Jimmy informed him that things at the factory were going very well. "Come on up and check it out, Dad," he urged. "Oh, and by the way, you were right about that ad campaign. We've got a whole new one running now." So Mr. Smith flew up again, and on the way in from the airport spotted the same huge billboard. Only this time the picture showed Jesus crumpled at the foot of the cross, and the slogan read, "You Should Have Used Smith's Nails."

ARCHITECTURE AND ARCHITECTS

The postwar architecture is the accountant's revenge on the prewar businessman's dreams.

—*Rem Koolhaas*

God is in the details.

—*Ludwig Mies van der Rohe*

If we build in the desert, let the house know the desert and the desert be proud of the house.

—*Frank Lloyd Wright*

Architect: One who drafts a plan of your house, and plans a draft of your money.
—*Ambrose Bierce*

We shape our buildings. Thereafter they shape us.   —*Winston Churchill*

Less is more.   —*Ludwig Mies van der Rohe*

Less is a bore.   *Robert Venturi, in response to Mies van der Rohe's credo*

The purpose of architecture is to shelter and enhance man's life on earth and to fulfill his belief in the nobility of his existence.   —*Eero Saarinen*

Architecture is life, or at least it is life itself taking form, and therefore it is the truest record of life as it was lived in the world yesterday, as it is lived today or ever will be lived.   —*Frank Lloyd Wright*

Architecture is the will of an epoch translated into space.
—*Ludwig Mies van der Rohe*

Architecture is the learned game, correct and magnificent, of forms assembled in the light.   —*Le Corbusier*

It is our art that has an opportunity to leave a footprint in the sand. They don't wrap fish in our work.   —*Hugh Newell Jacobsen*

The physician can bury his mistakes, but the architect can only advise his client to plant vines.   —*Frank Lloyd Wright*

Architecture begins where engineering ends.   —*Walter Gropius*

Well, back to the drawing board.   —*Peter Arno*

Saying
Architects are practical poets.

Joke
• It is the theater God would have built if he had the money.
—*Henry Geldzahler, on preservation of Radio City Music Hall*

BANKING AND BANKERS

Our banking system grew by accident; and whenever something happens by accident, it becomes a religion.   —*Walter Wriston*

This is the twilight of the banks. It would be a more cheerful spectacle if we could envision the dawn of the institutions that will replace them.
—*Martin Mayer*

I can hold a note as long as the Chase Manhattan Bank.   —*Ethel Merman*

Banking establishments are more dangerous than standing armies.
—*Thomas Jefferson*

I don't trust a bank that would lend money to such a poor risk.
—*Robert Benchley*

Except for the con men borrowing money they shouldn't get and the widows who have to visit the handsome young men in the trust department, no sane person ever enjoyed visiting a bank.
—*Martin Mayer*

A financier is a pawnbroker with imagination.
—*Arthur Pinero*

Banking may well be a career from which no man really recovers.
—*John Kenneth Galbraith*

Sayings

A banker is a man who lends you an umbrella when the weather is fair, and takes it away from you when it rains.

Sign above bank teller's stations: "To err is human; to forgive is not bank policy."

Jokes

• The loan officer skeptically looked over the down-at-the heels fellow in front of her, who had applied for a $500 loan. "Have you any collateral at all?" she asked. "A car, for example?"

"Oh yes, I have a ninety-one Mercedes coupe," he replied promptly.

The loan officer's eyebrows rose, but she continued. "Any stocks or shares?"

"Of course. I manage my own portfolio."

"I see." She made a note in his file. "And a house, I suppose."

"Certainly, up in the hills, with ten acres, a pool, and a tennis court."

That did it. The banker rose to her feet, protesting indignantly, "You must be joking!"

The applicant shrugged. "Well, you started it."

• Why doesn't money grow on trees?
—Because banks own all the branches.

BROKERS AND THE STOCK MARKET

Let Wall Street have a nightmare and the whole country has to help get them back in bed again.
—*Will Rogers*

I do not regard a broker as a member of the human race.
—*Honoré de Balzac*

We all have a stake in this economy. Everybody is hurt by inflation. If you really wanted to examine percentagewise who was hurt most in their income, it was the Wall Street brokers.
—*Alan Greenspan*

Bulls and bears aren't responsible for as many stock losses as bum steers.
—*Olin Miller*

I refuse to believe that trading recipes is silly. Tuna-fish casserole is at least as real as corporate stock.
—*Barbara Harrison*

In Wall Street the only thing that's hard to explain is—next week.
—*Louis Rukeyser*

There are only two emotions on Wall Street: fear and greed.

—*William Lefevre*

Stocks do not move unless they are pushed.   —*S. Jay Levin*

If you don't know who you are, the stock market is an expensive place to find out.

—*George Goodman*

Like the cosmetics industry, the securities business is engaged in selling illusion.

—*Paul Samuelson*

No warning can save a people determined to grow suddenly rich.

—*Lord Overstone*

There is scarcely an instance of a man who has made a fortune by speculation and kept it.   —*Andrew Carnegie*

Saying
Thanks to this man I've gone from Over-the-Counter to Over-the-Barrel.

Jokes
- Market Tips Translated:
  "Somewhat speculative issue" = They got me on this one.
  "A strong institutional favorite" = A run-of-the-mill utility.
  "Now trading at more realistic levels" = Now selling below what you paid for it.
  "Looking at a great earnings report" = Too bad you didn't buy a year ago.

- Since the crash, my broker sleeps like a baby. He wakes up every two hours and cries.

CLERGY

The priest is concerned with other people for the sake of God and with God for the sake of other people.   —*Robert Runcie, former Archbishop of Canterbury*

Generally speaking, bishops are generally speaking.   —*Dennis Nineham*

A Carmelite nun should be, by the very nature of her vocation, a specialist in prayer. Or, to give it a more modern twist, she is a career woman in the field of prayer and contemplation.   —*Mother Catherine Thomas*

Preaching is personal counseling on a group basis.

—*Harry Emerson Fosdick*

People expect the clergy to have the grace of a swan, the friendliness of a sparrow, the strength of an eagle, and the night hours of an owl—and some people expect such a bird to live on the food of a canary.   —*Rev. Edward Jeffrey*

My sister's at divinity school, studying how to become a divinity, I suppose.

—*Eric Frothingham*

Saying

Definition of the clergy: The members of the community with the highest minds and the lowest salaries.

Joke

• Coming to the pulpit, the minister apologized for the Band-Aid on his face. "This morning while I was shaving, I was thinking about my sermon and cut my face," he explained.

After church, he found a little note tucked under his windshield wiper. "Next week while you're shaving," it suggested, "why don't you think about your face and cut your sermon?"

COWBOYS

Any boy anywhere can grow up to be a cowpoke today if he wants to bad enough. One of the top wranglers on the circuit right now was born and raised in the Bronx.

—*Tom Robbins*

The classic American western look remains unchallenged as the epitome of virility in men's clothing. Derived from the cowboy's work clothes, it is part of the national heritage.

—*O. E. Schoeffler and William Gale*

Buffalo Bill's defunct.

—*E. E. Cummings*

Even cowgirls get the blues.

—*Tom Robbins*

These people are simple farmers, people of the land, the common clay of the New West. You know—morons.

—*Mel Brooks*

Saying

A real cowboy has a five-dollar horse and a forty-dollar saddle.

Joke

• A bowlegged cowboy decided he was tired of the hard life on the range and took a job at a department store. He soon learned his way around the place, and proudly took on the job of greeting customers at the elevators and directing them to the appropriate counters.

One day he approached an overweight woman, who informed him she was looking for talcum powder.

"Sure thing, ma'am," said the cowboy politely. "Walk this way."

"If I could walk that way, buddy," she snapped, "I wouldn't need the talcum powder."

DOCTORS AND DENTISTS

The great secret of doctors, known only to their wives, but still hidden from the public, is that most things get better by themselves; most things, in fact, are better in the morning.

—*Lewis Thomas*

Physician, heal thyself.   —Luke 4:23

Let no one suppose that the words doctor and patient can disguise from the parties the fact that they are employer and employee.   —George Bernard Shaw

Never go to a doctor whose office plants have died.   —Erma Bombeck

The best doctor in the world is a veterinarian. He can't ask his patients what is the matter—he's got to know.   —Will Rogers

The longer I practice medicine, the more convinced I am there are only two types of cases: those that involve taking the trousers off, and those that don't.
                                                                    —Alan Bennett

There is no greater reward in our profession than the knowledge that God has entrusted us with the physical care of his people.   —Dr. Elmer Hess

[Medicine is] the only profession that labors incessantly to destroy the reason for its own existence.   —James Bryce

God heals, and the doctor takes the fees.   —Benjamin Franklin

For there was never yet philosopher that could endure the toothache patiently.
                                                            —William Shakespeare

To the person with a toothache, even if the world is tottering, there is nothing more important than a visit to a dentist.   —George Bernard Shaw

Sayings
Why do the best doctors have the sickest patients?

Good doctors make poor patients.

The doctors can cure all sorts of ills, except the shock of doctors' bills.

Jokes
- "Your teeth are absolutely perfect, Mr. Rodgers," said the dentist to the Oklahoma oilman. "You can get up."
  "I'm feeling lucky," responded the millionaire. "Drill anyway."

- "Dr. Shimm," complained the elderly patient, "when I get up in the morning I feel very nauseated—and it lasts for up to an hour. What do you suggest?"
  "Hmmm," murmured the doctor, thoughtfully stroking his chin. "How about getting up an hour later?"

- Nobody ever feels sorry for doctors, but I heard about one who got so down and out that he tried to rob a bank. Nobody could read his hold-up note.

- A specialist is a doctor with a smaller practice and a bigger boat.

- My doctor is wonderful. Once, in 1955, when I couldn't afford an operation, he touched up the X-rays.   —Joey Bishop

- You know how these days everyone wants a second opinion? Well, this lady had been going to a psychiatrist for years and one day she decided she'd had enough of it. "Doctor," she announced, walking into his office, "I've been seeing you every week for five years now. I don't feel any better, I don't feel any worse. What's the story? I want you to level with me: what's wrong with me?"

"All right," said the doctor, "I'll tell you. You're crazy."

"Now wait just a minute," she protested. "I think I'm entitled to a second opinion."

"Fine," he responded. "You're ugly too."

FARMERS AND FARMING

The only difference between a pigeon and the American farmer today is that a pigeon can still make a deposit on a John Deere.
—*J. Hightower*

All the really good ideas I ever had came to me while I was milking a cow.
—*Grant Wood*

Burn down your cities and leave our farms, and your cities will spring up again as if by magic; but destroy our farms and the grass will grow in the streets of every city in the country.
—*William Jennings Bryan*

Farming looks mighty easy when your plow is a pencil and you're a thousand miles from the corn field.
—*Dwight D. Eisenhower*

The first farmer was the first man, and all historic nobility rests on possession and use of land.
—*Ralph Waldo Emerson*

Let us never forget that the cultivation of the earth is the most important labor of man.
—*Daniel Webster*

We must plant the sea and herd its animals . . . using the sea as farmers instead of hunters. That is what civilization is all about—farming replacing hunting.
—*Jacques Cousteau*

Farmers are now members of a capital-intensive industry that values good bookwork more than backwork. So several times a year almost every farmer must seek operating credit from the college fellow in the white shirt and tie—in effect, asking financial permission to work hard on his own land.
—*Andrew H. Malcolm*

Saying
Farmers are the salt of the earth.

Jokes
• The city kid was invited to spend a week on a farm, and was sent off to the henhouse to collect the eggs. She reported back, "No eggs, sir—but all the seats are taken."

• Asked what he would do with the millions he'd just won in the state lottery, Farmer Jones scratched his chin and answered, "Oh, I suppose I'll just keep on farming till it's all gone."

• The young woman fresh out of agricultural college looked the whole farm over and then pronounced the farmer's methods of cultivation hopelessly out-of-date and inefficient. "Why, I'd be amazed if you got even ten pounds of apples off that tree," she concluded decisively, pointing at a gnarled old fruit tree.

"It'd sure surprise me too," commented the old farmer. "It's a pear tree."

- Why did the idiot buy a farm in Alaska?
  —He wanted to grow frozen vegetables.

- A young farmer went to see the family doctor because he was having problems of a sexual nature with his wife.

  "Clem," the doctor confided, "you have to be more loving to your wife. Give her extra hugs and kisses. Show her how much you care."

  "I do the best I can, Doc," the boy moaned, "but I'm out working the field from dawn to dusk and I'm just too tired."

  "Hmmm," the doctor mused. "Take a shotgun with you next time you go out in the field and shoot it off every time you're feeling a bit frisky. When your wife hears the blast, she'll come a-runnin'."

  A month later the farmer returned to the doctor looking downright depressed.

  "What happened?" asked the doctor. "Didn't you do what I said?"

  "I sure did, and everything was going great until hunting season started last week," cried the farmer. "I haven't seen her since."

INSURANCE

What the insurance companies have done is to reverse the business so that the public at large insures the insurance companies. *—Gerry Spence*

I don't want to tell you how much insurance I carry with the Prudential, but all I can say is: when I go, *they* go. *—Jack Benny (attrib.)*

Insurance: An ingenious modern game of chance, in which the player is permitted to enjoy the comfortable conviction that he is beating the man who keeps the table. *—Ambrose Bierce*

Insurance is for people who don't have money. *—Neil Zukerman*

Saying
Life insurance is the only game you win when you die.

Jokes
- Customer: "I'd like to insure my house. Can I do it over the phone?"
  Insurance agent: "No, I'm afraid a personal inspection is necessary."
  Customer: "Okay, but you better hustle—it's on fire."

- How many doctors does it take to change a light bulb?
  —It depends on how much insurance the bulb has.

- My car insurance is with one of those companies that questions everything. I think I've got the $100 Debatable.

- The machine operator comes home from the factory and tells his wife he's got some good news and some bad news. "First the good news," he says, sitting down at the kitchen table. "The factory has great coverage: I'm getting $75,000 in severance pay."

"That's great, honey," says his wife supportively. "So what's the bad news?"

"Wait'll you hear what was severed. . . ."

• [The insurance salesman] keeps us poor all of our lives so we can die rich.

• "Don't let me pressure you, Mrs. Schmidt," said the aggressive life-insurance salesman. "Why don't you sleep on my offer and call me in the morning. If you wake up."

• "Mommy, can I swim out to where the waves are breaking?" asked the little girl.

The mother shook her head firmly.

"*Pleeeease*?" she begged. "Daddy's swimming out there."

"I know, darling, but he's insured."

• Why is sex like insurance?

—The older you get, the more it costs.

• What's the best thing about turning sixty-five?

—No more calls from insurance salesmen.

LAWYERS

I don't want a lawyer to tell me what I cannot do; I hire them to tell me how to do what I want to do.   *—J. P. Morgan*

If there were no bad people there would be no good lawyers.

—Charles Dickens

If the laws could speak for themselves, they would complain of the lawyers in the first place.   *—George Savile*

If a man dies and leaves his estate in an uncertain condition, the lawyers become his heirs.   *—Edgar Watson Howe*

Lawyers are men who hire out their words and anger.   *—Martial*

What's the first excellence in a lawyer? Tautology. What's the second? Tautology. What's the third? Tautology.   *—Richard Steele*

What we lawyers want to do is to substitute courts for carnage, dockets for rockets, briefs for bombs, warrants for warheads, mandates for missiles.

—George Rhyne

What most impresses us about great jurists is not their tenacious grasp of fine points, honed almost to invisibility; it is the moment when we are suddenly aware of the sweep and direction of the law and its place in the lives of men.

—Irving R. Kaufman

A countryman between two lawyers is like a fish between two cats.

—Benjamin Franklin

The first thing we do, let's kill all the lawyers.   *—William Shakespeare*

You cannot live without the lawyers, and certainly you cannot die without them.

—*Joseph H. Choate*

The trouble with law is lawyers.

—*Clarence Darrow*

He is no lawyer who cannot take two sides.

—*Charles Lamb*

There is no better way of exercising the imagination than the study of law. No poet ever interpreted nature as freely as a lawyer interprets the truth.

—*Jean Giraudoux*

Taking a break from the courtroom squabbles of a case in Rock Island, Abraham Lincoln took a walk in the countryside. He followed a stream and came to a bridge, with a young boy sitting right in the middle. Lincoln said companionably, "I suppose you know all about this river."

"Sure I do, mister," responded the boy. "It was here when I was born and it's been here ever since."

Lincoln smiled broadly. "It's good to be out here where there is so much fact and so little opinion."

Sayings

A lawyer's opinion is worth nothing unless it is paid for.

A lawsuit helps keep lawyers clothed.

Jokes

• It's said that Abraham Lincoln once sized up the case of a prospective client as follows: "You have a pretty good case, technically, but in terms of justice and equity, it's got problems. So you'll have to look for another lawyer to handle the case, because the whole time I was up there talking to the jury, I'd be thinking, 'Lincoln, you're a liar!' and I just might forget myself and say it out loud."

• A builder, an electrician, and a lawyer were arguing about which profession was the oldest. The builder pointed out proudly that the first thing God had done was to *build* the earth.

"True," said the electrician, "but before that, he said 'Let there be light.' "

"You're both right," said the lawyer agreeably, "but before the light there was chaos—and who do you think created the chaos?"

• Two souls waiting to be admitted into heaven got into a furious argument about who had been first in line. Unable to resolve the dispute, they marched up to St. Peter and explained the need for legal counsel to help each plead his case.

"I'm afraid you'll have to apply for a change of venue," St. Peter replied with a bemused smile. "There aren't any lawyers up here."

• At a dinner party a doctor and a lawyer were arguing about whose calling was the highest. The conversation grew fairly heated, and finally the doctor played his trump card. His chest swelling with righteousness, he proclaimed, "We doctors save *lives.*"

"And we lawyers," his opponent pointed out wryly, "probate your failures."

• A doctor, a lawyer, and an architect were arguing about whose dog was the smartest, so they agreed to stage a contest.

"Okay, Rover," said the architect, and Rover trotted over to a table and in five minutes had constructed a perfect scale model of Chartres Cathedral out of toothpicks. Pretty impressive, everyone agreed, and the architect gave Rover a cookie.

"Hit it, Spot," ordered the doctor, and Spot lost no time in performing an emergency cesarean section on a cow, delivering healthy twin calves in less than three minutes. Not bad, the observers concurred, and Spot got a cookie from the doctor.

"Your turn, Fella," said the lawyer. So Fella trotted over, screwed the other two dogs, took their cookies, and went out to lunch.

• Know why laboratories have switched from rats to lawyers for their experiments?

1. There's no shortage of lawyers.
2. You don't get so attached to them.
3. After all, there are *some* things you can't get rats to do.

MAIL CARRIERS

If you spend enough time at camp, in boarding school, or . . . in the military, the mailman becomes your main link with your family and the outside world.

—*Georgia S. Clark*

The postman always rings twice.   —*James M. Cain*

The mailman is the agent of impolite surprises.

—*Friedrich Wilhelm Nietzche*

I never received more than one or two letters in my life . . . that were worth the postage.   —*Henry David Thoreau*

Neither snow nor rain nor heat nor gloom of night stays these couriers from the swift completion of their appointed rounds.

—*Inscription on New York City's General Post Office,*
adapted from Herodotus

Saying
The mail must go through.

Jokes
• When Frederick's thirty years in the post office were almost up, his supervisor called him in. "You've been here a long time, Fred," he said sagely. "Is there anything you've learned during these years of service you'd like to share with us?"

    The mailman nodded. "Don't mail my gold watch. I'll take it with me."

• What's the fastest thing in the Postal Service?
    —The way the rates go up.

• The way it comes through, they ought to call it partial post.

• Hear about the new correspondence school for sex work?
    —Just invite the mailman in.

PSYCHIATRISTS AND PSYCHIATRY

I always say shopping is cheaper than a psychiatrist.

—*Tammy Faye Bakker*

A neurotic is a man who builds a castle in the air. A psychotic is a man who lives in it. And a psychiatrist is a man who collects the rent.   —*Lord Webb-Johnson*

Psychiatry enables us to correct our faults by confessing our parents' shortcomings.

—*Laurence J. Peter*

A psychiatrist is a fellow who asks you a lot of expensive questions your wife asks you for nothing.   —*Joey Adams*

A psychiatrist is a man who goes to the Folies Bergéres and looks at the audience.

—*Mervyn Stockwood*

In the factory we make cosmetics, but in my stores we sell hope.

—*Charles Revson*

One should only see a psychiatrist out of boredom.   —*Muriel Spark*

A vigorous five-mile walk will do more good for an unhappy but otherwise healthy adult than all the medicine and psychology in the world.

—*Paul Dudley White*

The great majority of neuroses in women have their origin in the marriage bed.

—*Sigmund Freud*

Psychiatry is the art of teaching people how to stand on their own two feet while reclining on couches.   —*Sigmund Freud*

Why should I tolerate a perfect stranger at the bedside of my mind?

—*Vladimir Nabokov*

I do not have a psychiatrist and I do not want one, for the simple reason that if he listened to me long enough, he might become disturbed.   —*James Thurber*

I finally had an orgasm and my doctor told me it was the wrong kind.

—*Woody Allen and Marshall Brickman*

Sometimes a cigar is just a cigar.   —*Sigmund Freud*

Being a good psychoanalyst, in short, has the same disadvantage as being a good parent: the children desert one as they grow up.   —*Morton Hunt*

Neurosis is always a substitute for legitimate suffering.   —*Carl Jung*

Analysts keep having to pick away at the scab that the patient tries to form between himself and the analyst to cover over his wounds. [The analyst] keeps the surface raw, so that the wound will heal properly.   —*Janet Malcolm*

Mental health problems do not affect three or four out of every five persons but one out of one.   —*Dr. William Menninger*

There is no perfect solution to depression, nor should there be. And odd as this may sound . . . we should be glad of that. It keeps us human.

—*Lesley Hazelton*

Life itself still remains a very effective therapist.

—*Karen Horney*

To say that a particular psychiatric condition is incurable or irreversible is to say more about the state of our ignorance than about the state of the patient.

—*Milton Rokeach*

Sayings
You go to a psychiatrist when you're slightly cracked and keep going until you're completely cracked.

My shrink doesn't understand me.

Psychiatrist: A Jewish boy who can't stand the sight of blood.

Anyone who consults a psychiatrist should have his head examined.

Jokes
* Two psychiatrists leave their offices in the same elevator. "Have a good evening," said one to the other as the doors opened.
  "Now why'd he say that?" mused the other.

* I had to give up masochism—I was enjoying it too much.   —*Mel Calman*

* Two psychiatrists encounter each other on the sidewalk. "Hey, Annabella, how are you?" said the first with a hearty handshake.
  "You tell me," was the reply.

* A man was attacked and left bleeding in a ditch. Two psychiatrists passed by and one said to the other, "We must find the man who did this—he needs help."

* Nerve is going to a psychiatrist because of a split personality and asking for a group rate.

* How many psychiatrists does it take to change a light bulb?
  —One. But the light bulb has to really want to change.

SALES AND SALESPEOPLE

If you don't sell, it's not the product that's wrong, it's *you*.   —*Estée Lauder*

Inequality of knowledge is the key to a sale.   —*Neil O. Gustafson*

She doesn't want to touch it. She doesn't want to smell it. She doesn't want to hear it. Lord love her. She's a Mail Order Freak.   —*Jim Fishel*

There are no dumb customers.   —*Peter Drucker*

When you stop talking, you've lost your customer.   —*Estée Lauder*

In the jungle of the marketplace, the intelligent buyer must be alert to every commercial sound, to every snapping of selling twig, to every rustle that may signal the uprising arm holding the knife pointed toward the jugular vein.

—*Dexter Masters*

[A car] for every purse and purpose.

—*Alfred P. Sloan, Jr., president of General Motors*

Everyone lives by selling something.   —*Robert Louis Stevenson*

People will buy anything that's one to a customer.   —*Sinclair Lewis*

Simon & Schuster runs a sales contest every year. The winners get to keep their jobs.

—*Jack O'Leary*

Any fool can paint a picture, but it takes a wise man to be able to sell it.

—*Samuel Butler*

There's a sucker born every minute.   —*P. T. Barnum*

There is no such thing as "hard sell" and "soft sell." There is only "smart sell" and "stupid sell."   —*Leo Burnett*

Sayings

It takes less to keep an old customer satisfied than to get a new customer interested.

Columbus was definitely the world's most amazing salesman. He started out not knowing where he was going. When he got there, he didn't know where it was, so when he got back, he couldn't say where he'd been. And he did it all on a big cash advance, and he got a repeat order.

The fish sees the bait, not the hook.   —*Chinese proverb*

Before salespeople can sell something to others, they must first sell it to themselves.

Caveat emptor *(Let the buyer beware)*.

Jokes

• Over breakfast in the corner diner, the salesman peered out at the snow piling up against the window. "Think the roads are clear enough to make some sales calls?" he mused.

  The waiter shrugged. "Depends on whether you're working on salary or commission, I suppose."

• When the legendary salesman was asked his secrets of success, he gave a humble shrug. "I'm sure you all know the cardinal rules: know your product; make lots of calls; never take no for an answer. But frankly, I owe my success to consistently missing a three-foot putt by two inches."

• The Arab sheik welcomed his son back from a tour of the United States, and was eager for the young man's impressions. "What were you the most impressed by, Fouad? The lush scenery, or the democratic system at work? Or perhaps by the Americans' energy and initiative, or their lack of class distinction?"

  "To tell you the truth, Dad," responded the prince, unpacking six pairs of snowshoes, "what impressed me the most was their salesmanship."

• Two shoe salesmen were sent to a remote island in the Pacific. One cabled back, "Come and get me. They don't wear shoes here."

  The other cabled, "Send more shoes, no one has any."

• If You Don't Buy This Magazine, We'll Kill This Dog.

—*Cover of the* National Lampoon, *January 1973*

- First salesman: "I made some very valuable contacts today."
  Second salesman: "I didn't get any orders either."

- Marveling at a certain employee's ability to sell toothbrushes, the head of the sales department decided to follow him around one day. He soon observed this particular salesman choose a busy streetcorner on which to set up an array of toothbrushes and a small bowl of brownish stuff surrounded by chips. The salesman would then select a likely customer and announce, "Good morning! We're introducing Nifty Chip Dip—would you like a free sample?"

  Tasting the dip, the bystander would invariably spit it out in disgust and howl, "It tastes like shit!"

  "It is," the salesman would inform them calmly. "Care to buy a toothbrush?"

- The banker fancied himself interested in young people, so when a young lad came in to make an eighty-dollar deposit, he came over and patted him on the shoulder. "You must be a pretty enterprising fellow," he remarked. "How did you earn the money?"

  "Selling Christmas cards," the boy replied.

  "Good for you! You must have sold them to everyone in the neighborhood."

  The boy shook his head. "No sir. One family bought them all—their dog bit me."

W O R K

BUSINESS

Business is like sex. When it's good, it's very, very good; when it's not so good, it's still good.
—*George Katona*

The trouble with the profit system has always been that it was highly unprofitable to most people.
—*E. B. White*

Business has only two functions—marketing and innovation.
—*Peter F. Drucker*

If you break 100, watch your golf. If you break 80, watch your business.
—*Joey Adams*

Never invest your money in anything that eats or needs repairing.
—*Billy Rose*

Boldness in business is the first, second, and third thing.
—*Thomas Fuller*

Don't steal; thou'lt never thus compete successfully in business. Cheat.
—*Ambrose Bierce*

We should distrust any enterprise that requires new clothes.
—*Henry David Thoreau*

The business of government is to keep the government out of business—that is, unless business needs government aid.
—*Will Rogers*

Business is the salt of life.
—*Thomas Fuller*

Business? It's quite simple. It's other people's money.
—*Alexandre Dumas (fils)*

Uncertainty kills business.
—*Michael Edwardes*

Men in business are in as much danger from those at work under them as from those that work against them.
—*George Savile*

Men of business must not break their word twice.
—*Thomas Fuller*

It is not the employer who pays wages; he only handles the money. It is the product that pays wages.
—*Henry Ford*

"Absorption of overhead" is one of the most obscene terms I have ever heard.
—*Peter F. Drucker*

Business without profit is not business any more than a pickle is candy.
—*Charles F. Abbott*

If the government was as afraid of disturbing the consumer as it is of disturbing business, this would be some democracy.   —*Kin Hubbard*

All business sagacity reduces itself in the last analysis to a judicious use of sabotage.
—*Thorstein Veblen*

It's not the bulls or the bears you need to avoid—it's the bum steers.
—*Chuck Hillis*

Buy low, sell high, collect early, and pay late.   —*Dick Levin*

He who builds a better mousetrap these days runs into material shortages, patent-infringement suits, work stoppages, collusive bidding, discount discrimination—and taxes.   —*H. E. Martz*

Before you build a better mousetrap, it helps to know if there are any mice out there.
—*Mortimer B. Zuckerman*

Xerox: A trademark for a photocopying device that can make rapid reproductions of human error, perfectly.   —*Merle L. Meacham*

Money itself doesn't interest me. But you must make money to go on building the business.   —*Rupert Murdoch*

Sometimes I get the feeling that the two biggest problems in America today are making ends meet—and making meetings end.   —*Robert Orben*

I've got to keep breathing. It'll be my worst business mistake if I don't.
—*Nathan Meyer Rothschild*

The big print giveth and the fine print taketh away.   —*Bishop Fulton Sheen*

The salary of the chief executive of the large corporation is not a market award for achievement. It is frequently in the nature of a warm personal gesture by the individual to himself.   —*John Kenneth Galbraith*

When you are skinning your customers, you should leave some skin on to grow so that you can skin them again.   —*Nikita S. Khrushchev*

Corporation: An ingenious device for obtaining individual profit without individual responsibility.   —*Ambrose Bierce*

Monopoly is business at the end of its journey.   —*Henry Demarest Lloyd*

The human being who would not harm you on an individual, face-to-face basis, who is charitable, civic-minded, loving, and devout, will wound or kill you from behind the corporate veil.   —*Morton Mintz, on the marketing of the Dalkon Shield*

The feminist surge will crest when a lady named Arabella, flounces and ruffles and all, can rise to the top of a Fortune 500 corporation.   —*Alma Denny*

Corporate identity specialists . . . spend their time rechristening other companies, [conducting] a legal search [and] a linguistic search to ensure that the name is not an insult in another language.   —*Lisa Belkin*

Two-tier tender offers, Pac-Man and poison-pill defenses, crown-jewel options, greenmail, golden parachutes, self-tenders—all have become part of our everyday business.   —*Felix G. Rohatyn*

Television is business, and business is America.

—*Bill Cosby*

Business begs. Philanthropy begs.

—*W. E. B. Du Bois*

When morality comes up against profit, it is seldom that profit loses.

—*Shirley Chisholm*

I have no friends and no enemies—only competitors.

—*Aristotle Onassis*

Under the new industrial competition, there are no frozen niches in frozen markets for which established producers compete like so many successive dictators in a banana republic. Markets and industries are themselves in flux, and to the winners belong not so much the old-fashioned spoils of victory as the right to define the terms of competition in the future.

—*William J. Abernathy, Kim B. Clark, and Alan M. Kantrow*

Business is business.

—*Franklin Pierce Adams*

Sayings
Business is what when you don't have any, you get out of.

Business before pleasure.

Jokes
- "What's this for?" asked the boss of his Midwest sales rep, pointing to an especially large item on her expense account.
   "That's my restaurant bill."
   "Hmmmm." The boss was skeptical. "Well, don't buy any more restaurants."

- The businessman decided it was time to give his daughter, a recent business-school graduate, a little lecture. "In business, ethics are very important," he began. "Say, for instance, that a client comes in and settles his hundred-dollar account in cash. After he leaves, you notice a second hundred-dollar bill stuck to the first one. Immediately you are presented with an ethical dilemma. . . ." The businessman paused for dramatic effect. "Should you tell your partner?"

- The bum rang the doorbell of a Beverly Hills mansion, and rang, and rang, undissuaded by the fact that it was the middle of the night. Finally, ten minutes later, the disheveled homeowner came to the door, pulling his silk dressing gown around him. "What are you doing leaning on my doorbell at three in the morning?" he screamed.
   "Can I have two dollars?" asked the bum.
   "Why the hell did you need to wake me out of a sound sleep for two goddamn dollars?" the millionaire raged.
   "I don't tell you how to run your business," was the cool response, "so don't tell me how to run mine."

CLIENTS

IBM is customer- and market-driven, not technology-driven.

—*Buck Rogers*

The client may be an idiot, but he's never wrong.

—*Tripp Evans*

Always be smarter than the people who hire you.   —*Lena Horne*

Dealing with more than one client at a time is the business world's equivalent of bigamy. It's so awkward to tell one client that you're working on someone else's business that you inevitably start lying. In my first year of account service, I attended three funerals for fictional relatives.   —*Andrew Frothingham*

There is no such thing as a bad client. But there is such a thing as bad advertising.
—*Jerry Della Femina*

A business relationship is like a marriage, only worse . . . You can't sleep with the client.   —*Tripp Evans*

Saying
Rule No. 1: The client is always right.
Rule No. 2: If the client is ever wrong, reread Rule No. 1.

Jokes
• A good account person, when the client tells him to jump, asks, "How high and when should I come down?"

• A client looking for a new advertising agency called the head of account services at three companies and asked them what time it was.
    "It's two-thirty in the afternoon," answered the first person.
    "I'll research that and get back to you," promised the representative at the second company.
    But the answer that convinced the client that this was the agency for him was "What time would you like it to be?"

COMMITTEES

If you ever live in a country run by a committee, be on the committee.
—*William Graham Sumner*

Having served on various committees, I have drawn up a list of rules: Never arrive on time: this stamps you as a beginner. Don't say anything until the meeting is over: this stamps you as being wise. Be as vague as possible: this avoids irritating the others. When in doubt, suggest that a subcommittee be appointed. Be the first to move for adjournment: this will make you popular—it's what everyone is waiting for.
—*Harry Chapman*

Not even computers will replace committees, because committees buy computers.
—*Edward Shepherd Mead*

A committee is a cul-de-sac down which ideas are lured and then quietly strangled.
—*Barnett Cocks*

We always carry out by committee anything in which any of us alone would be too reasonable to persist.   —*Frank Moore Colby*

To get something done, a committee should consist of no more than three men, two of whom are absent.   —*Robert Copeland*

A group of the unfit appointed by the unwilling to do the unnecessary.

—*Carl C. Byers*

Committee work is like a soft chair—easy to get into but hard to get out of.

—*Kenneth J. Shively*

A committee can't succeed if everybody's on board but nobody's at the wheel.

—*Kathy Griffith*

Sayings
A committee is a group that takes minutes and wastes hours.

A committee is a collection of the unfit chosen from the unwilling by the incompetent to do the unnecessary.

Jokes
- Charles Kettering was president of General Motors when Charles Lindbergh made his famous flight. When the news came over the radio, his secretary rushed in to declare, "Charlie Lindbergh just flew the Atlantic alone!"

  Kettering looked up from a pile of papers and snorted. "Heck, that's nothing—let him try it with a committee."

- Computers are definitely smarter than people. When's the last time you heard of six computers getting together to form a committee?

CONSULTANTS

Consultants are people who borrow your watch and tell you what time it is, then walk off with the watch.   —*Robert Townsend*

Experts should be on tap but never on top.   —*Winston Churchill*

Consult: To seek another's approval of a course already decided upon.

—*Ambrose Bierce*

No man can be a pure specialist without being in the strict sense an idiot.

—*George Bernard Shaw*

[An expert is] somebody who is more than fifty miles from home, has no responsibility for implementing the advice he gives, and shows slides.   —*Edwin Meese*

The trouble with specialists is that they tend to think in grooves.

—*Elaine Morgan*

Make three correct guesses consecutively and you will establish a reputation as an expert.   —*Laurence J. Peter*

A consultant is an ordinary man away from home giving advice.

—*Oscar Wilde*

It used to be that when all else failed, a guy went into the army; now he becomes a consultant.   —*Blackie Sherrod*

Consultants are people who come down from the hill to shoot the wounded after the battle is over.   —*Doc Blakeley*

After the ship has sunk, a consultant knows how it might have been saved.
                                            —*Newt Hielscher*

A consultant is someone who saves his client almost enough to pay his fee.
                                            —*Arnold H. Glasow*

Sayings
A consultant is someone whose opinion is sought after the decision has been made.

A consultant is a man who knows 147 ways to make love, but doesn't know any women.

Jokes
• The Fallons had a tomcat that insisted on going out every night to prowl around and chase after cats in heat. And week after week he'd return bloody and battered, ears torn, fur shredded. Finally his owners had had enough, and took him to the vet to be neutered.

  The cat lay low for a week or two, so the Fallons were delighted when one night the cat got dressed in black tie and tails, just as in the old days, and headed out the door. They were even more surprised when he was home by midnight without a spot or scratch on him. Crowding around and stroking him, they asked, "How'd you do it, old boy?"

  "Easy," responded the cat, slicking back his whiskers. "Now I'm a consultant."

• [An expert is] like the bottom of a double boiler. It shoots off a lot of steam, but it never really knows what's cooking.

CONVENTIONS

A convention is a splendid place to study human nature. Man in a crowd is quite a different creature than man acting alone.   —*William Jennings Bryan*

Of representative assemblies may not this good be said: That contending parties in a country do thereby ascertain one another's strength. They fight there, since fight they must, by petition, parliamentary eloquence, not by sword, bayonet, and bursts of military cannon.   —*Thomas Carlyle*

Conventions are like coins, an easy way of dealing with the commerce of relations.
                                            —*Freya Stark*

Saying
An individual starts off by facing his problem with resolution, but a convention saves the resolution for the end.

Jokes
• Delegate-at-large: A man at a convention whose wife didn't accompany him.

- "You keep maintaining that conventions are nothing but a waste of time," the eager young man pointed out to the veteran conventioneer. "So why do you keep attending them?"

    "If I didn't," retorted the seasoned fellow, "how could I be sure?"

- William Jennings Bryan compared the way a convention feels about demonstrations to the feeling of a big man whose wife "was in the habit of beating him." When asked why he permitted it, he replied that "it seemed to please her and did not hurt him."

LABOR

Encouraging worker ideas and participation in decision making is no longer just an option for American business. It is a necessity. Employees come to the workplace today with expectations that their recommendations will be given serious consideration.

—*Roger Smith*

Esau sold his birthright for a mess of pottage. Judas Iscariot sold his Savior for thirty pieces of silver. Benedict Arnold sold his country for a promise of a commission in the British Army. The modern strikebreaker sells his birthright, his country, his wife, his children, and his fellow men for an unfulfilled promise from his employer, trust, or corporation.

—*Jack London*

You need men, and I have all the men. What am I bid?

—*John L. Lewis, union organizer, to management at the bargaining table*

Dammit, the law is the law, and the law says they cannot strike. If they strike, they quit their jobs.

—*Ronald Reagan, on air-traffic controllers*

On the evening bus, the tense, pinched faces of young file clerks and elderly secretaries tell us more than we care to know.

—*Studs Terkel*

Our professionals miscalculated on every major point. Always their approach was "Give 'em nothing—and do it retroactively."

—*Spokesperson for the New York Publishers Association,*
commenting on four-month newspaper strike

I am a man, not a consignment of goods to be bought and sold.

—*Curtis Flood*

The strike is the weapon of the industrial jungle.

—*Sidney Hillman*

My mistake was buying stock in the company. Now I worry about the lousy work I'm turning out.

—*Marvin Townsend*

I believe in the dignity of labor, whether with head or hand; that the world owes every man the opportunity to make a living.

—*John D. Rockefeller, Jr.*

Sayings

Cut your own wood and it will warm you twice.

Orare est labore, laborare est orare. (To pray is to work, to work is to pray.)

—*Ancient motto of the Benedictine order*

Labor is the ultimate power of the people.

The real power of labor is that it works.

One man's labor is another man's capital.

Jokes

- "We don't mind the wage cut, or the faster assembly line," said the shop steward to the foreman, "but what's this new rule that you have to be sick if you want to take a sick day?"

- Employee: "I really need a raise—I've even been praying in church for one."
  Boss: "How dare you go over my head!"

- Employee: "Three other people have been promoted past me even though I have twenty years of experience in this job!"
  Boss: "No you don't. You have one year of experience twenty times—you've been making the same mistakes since you first started."

- "Hey, Mac, why'd the foreman fire you?" asked a co-worker.
  "You know how the foreman is the guy who stands around watching other people work?"
  "Yeah, but why'd you get fired?" pursued the employee.
  "The foreman got jealous—a lot of people thought I was the foreman," replied Mac with a grin.

- After days of tough negotiation, the senior shop steward emerged from behind closed doors looking very pleased with himself. Addressing the workers, he declared the results: a 25 percent wage hike, two months paid vacation, full dental coverage, and two hours for lunch. "And furthermore," he concluded triumphantly, "you only have to work one day a week—Wednesday."
  "What?" came a voice from the back of the room, "*every* Wednesday?"

MANAGEMENT AND BOSSES

Chief executives, who themselves own a few shares of their companies, have no more feeling for the average stockholder than they do for baboons in Africa.

—T. Boone Pickens

I don't want any yes-men around me. I want everybody to tell me the truth, even if it costs them their jobs.   *—Samuel Goldwyn*

Getting results through people is a skill that cannot be learned in the classroom.

—J. Paul Getty

The salary of the chief executive of the large corporation is not a market award for achievement. It is frequently in the nature of a warm personal gesture by the individual to himself.   *—John Kenneth Galbraith*

Never try to teach a pig to sing; it wastes your time and it annoys the pig.

—Paul Dickson

One of the most wonderful things that happened in our Nautilus program was that everybody knew it was going to fail—so they let us completely alone so we were able to do the job.

—Admiral Hyman G. Rickover, on development of the nuclear submarine

If my boss calls, be sure to get his name.

—Comment of ABC executive, quoted by William Rukeyser
in report on rapid personnel shifts

There's just three things I'd ever say:
   If anything goes bad, I did it.
   If anything goes semi-good, then we did it.
   If anything goes real good, then you did it.
That's all it takes to get people to win football games for you.

—Paul (Bear) Bryant

Efficiency is getting the job done *right*. Effectiveness is getting the *right job done*.

—John-Roger and Peter McWilliams

Falling in love with the boss is the cardinal sin in the office. Nothing is more boring or irritating to his friends and colleagues than an adoring and possessive secretary.

—Lady Dartmouth

I have received memos so swollen with managerial babble that they struck me as the literary equivalent of assault with a deadly weapon.   *—Peter Baida*

Men are going to learn to be managers in a world where the organization will come close to consisting of all chiefs and one Indian. The Indian, of course, is the computer.

—Thomas L. Whisler

The secret of managing is to keep the guys who hate you away from the guys who are undecided.   *—Casey Stengel*

I won't eat anything that has intelligent life, but I would gladly eat a network executive or a politician.   *—Marty Feldman*

Simon & Schuster runs a sales contest every year. The winners get to keep their jobs.

—Jack O'Leary

Lots of folks confuse bad management with destiny.   *—Kin Hubbard*

What is worth doing is worth the trouble of asking somebody to do it.

—Ambrose Bierce

The longer the title, the less important the job.   *—George McGovern*

Always mistrust a subordinate who never finds fault with his superior.

—William Collins

The shepherd always tries to persuade the sheep that their interests and his own are the same.   *—Stendhal*

On a good day, I view the job [of president of Yale] as directing an orchestra. On the dark days, it is more like that of a clutch—engaging the engine to effect forward motion, while taking greater friction.   *—A. Bartlett Giamatti*

It is difficult to get a man to understand something when his salary depends upon his not understanding it.   *—Upton Sinclair*

The conventional definition of management is getting work done through people, but real management is developing people through work.   *—Aga Hasan Abedi*

When people are highly motivated, it's easy to accomplish the impossible. And when they're not, it's impossible to accomplish the easy. So how do we motivate them? Discard the mushroom theory of management—the one that says, keep your employees in the dark and throw a lot of manure on them. If you're going to manage a growing company, you have to concentrate on managing people, not ignoring them.

—*Bob Collings*

A businessman's judgment is no better than his information.   —*R. P. Lamont*

The brand of leadership we propose has a simple base of MBWA (Managing by Wandering Around). To "wander" with customers and vendors and our own people is to be in touch with the very first vibrations of the new.

—*Thomas J. Peters and Nancy K. Austin*

A good manager is a man who isn't worried about his own career but the careers of those who work for him.   —*H. M. S. Burns*

Executives who get there and stay suggest solutions when they present the problems.

—*Malcolm S. Forbes*

One of the most important tasks of a manager is to eliminate his people's excuses for failure.   —*Robert Townsend*

No one can possibly achieve any real and lasting success or "get rich" in business by being a conformist.   —*J. Paul Getty*

Every president needs his son-of-a-bitch; I'm Nixon's.

—*H. R. (Bob) Haldeman*

By working faithfully eight hours a day, you may eventually get to be a boss and work twelve hours a day.   —*Robert Frost*

The most important aspect of the relationship between the president and the secretary of state is that they both understand who is president.   —*Dean Acheson*

In a hierarchy, every employee tends to rise to his level of incompetence.

—*Laurence J. Peter*

Management is nothing more than motivating people.   —*Lee Iacocca*

It has long since become a familiar observation that generals regularly spend their time preparing to fight the war. Managers often do the same. Whether from the force of habit or from the appeal of comfortable modes of thought and action, they often fail to see how the problems that beset them are unlike those with which they have become familiar.   —*William B. Abernathy, Kim B. Clark, and Alan M. Kantrow*

I learned in business that you had to be very careful when you told somebody who's working for you to do something, because the chances were very high he'd do it. In government, you don't have to worry about that.   —*George Shultz*

Every time I fill a vacant office, I make ten malcontents and one ingrate.

—*Louis XIV*

Of course in selecting staff I shall make a few bad decisions. After all, Jesus Christ had to make twelve appointments and one of them was a bummer.

—*Ted Turner*

Sayings

A man who works with his hands is a laborer. A man who works with his hands and his brains is a craftsman. But a man who works with his brains and the hands of others is an executive.

The players win, not the coach. The best thing a coach can do is get the best players in action and let them do their thing. The coach can lose for you, but he can't win for you.

A Short Course in Human Relations
   The six most important words: I admit that I was wrong.
   The five most important words: You did a great job.
   The four most important words: What do you think?
   The three most important words: Could you please . . . ?
   The two most important words: Thank you.
   The most important word: We.
   The least important word: I.

Jokes

- An executive is one who never puts off until tomorrow what he can get someone else to do today.

- Running into a former colleague who'd gone into business for himself, Sylvia asked him how it was going.
   "To tell you the truth," admitted her friend, "I never knew how stupid bosses could be until I became self-employed."

- An enterprising woman turned a demoralized, run-down agency into one of the top in its field. It didn't cost her a penny; she didn't have to hire any experts or consultants. Her secret? Each Monday morning, she requested a report from every department head on all of the good things that had happened in his department during the past week.

- You can't help liking the managing director—if you don't, he fires you.

- Addressing the annual sales meeting, the owner of the company loosened up the audience with a couple of jokes, as was his custom. Everyone roared except a certain fellow in the fifth row, so the boss tried a few more of his best lines. Still the guy never cracked a smile.
   Finally, the exasperated speaker looked straight at him and demanded, "What's your problem? Don't you have a sense of humor?"
   "I don't have to laugh," the guy explained. "I'm starting a new job on Monday."

- The boss, Ms. Bennett, always scheduled the weekly staff meetings for 4:30 on Fridays. When one of the employees finally got up the nerve to ask why, she explained, "I'll tell you why—I've learned that's the only time of the week when none of you seem to want to argue with me."

- A young woman made her way to the back of the restaurant to use the pay phone. "Mr. Lewis?" she inquired. "I understand you've been advertising for an account executive? Oh . . . you're quite satisfied with the person you hired six weeks ago? Well, I hope you continue to be pleased."

She hung up, and as she turned away, the bartender said, "Listen, I couldn't help overhearing your conversation. Too bad about that job."

The woman flashed him a big smile and assured him his sympathies weren't necessary. "Lewis is my boss—he hired me six weeks ago," she explained cheerfully. "I was just phoning to find out how I'm doing."

MEETINGS

Sometimes I get the feeling that the two biggest problems in America today are making ends meet—and making meetings end.
                                                            —*Robert Orben*

Meetings are indispensable when you don't want to do anything.
                                                            —*Robert Frost*

Meetings . . . are rather like cocktail parties. You don't want to go, but you're cross not to be asked.
                                                            —*Jilly Cooper*

The Law of Triviality. Briefly stated, it means that the time spent on any item of the agenda will be in inverse proportion to the sum involved.
                                                            —*C. Northcote Parkinson*

A conference is a gathering of important people who singly can do nothing but together can decide that nothing can be done.
                                                            —*Fred Allen*

Sayings
Show me a person who likes to go to meetings and I'll show you a person who doesn't have enough to do.

A meeting is no substitute for progress.

Jokes
• Business meetings are important—because they're one way of demonstrating how many people the company can operate without.

• What's the difference between an alcoholic and a drunk?
    —Drunks don't have to go to meetings.

• During a heated Senate subcomittee meeting, one man lost his temper and told another member to "go to hell." The maligned fellow appealed to Vice-President Calvin Coolidge, who was presiding, concerning the propriety of the remark.
    Coolidge, who'd been idly leafing through a book, looked and said, "I've checked the rule book, Senator—you don't have to go."

NEGOTIATION

Only free men can negotiate; prisoners cannot enter into negotiations. Your freedom and mine cannot be separated.
        —*Nelson Mandela, refusing to bargain for freedom after twenty-one years in prison*

A verbal contract isn't worth the paper it's written on.   —*Louis B. Mayer*

Never claim as a right what you can ask as a favor.   —*John Churton Collins*

There is nothing more likely to start disagreement among people or countries than an agreement.   —*E. B. White*

Neither a fortress nor a maidenhead will hold out long after they begin to parley.   —*Benjamin Franklin*

Let us never negotiate out of fear. But let us never fear to negotiate.   —*John F. Kennedy*

When a man tells me he's going to put all his cards on the table, I always look up his sleeve.   —*Lord Hore-Belisha*

Let me suggest that tragedy is not what men suffer but what they miss.
   —*Abba Eban, addressing the impulsive tendency of nations to reject diplomatic compromise*

One and one is two, and two and two is four, and five will get you ten if you know how to work it.   —*Mae West*

You need men, and I have all the men. What am I bid?
   —*John L. Lewis, union organizer, to management at the bargaining table*

Sayings
I can forget and you can forget but a piece of paper never forgets.

Don't win a battle and lose the war.

Everyone has his price.

Jokes
• Luke was small for his age but a quick thinker, which stood him in good stead when the school bully came up and demanded his lunch money.

   "Whatsamatter, you deaf?" growled the big kid as Luke looked up at him calmly. "Hand it over, runt!"

   Luke jumped back a good three feet, drew a line in the dirt with his toe, and said dramatically, "Now, you just step across that line."

   Taken by surprise, the bully actually paused for a moment before stalking across the line and glaring down at his prey once more. "So whaddaya gonna do about it?"

   Luke looked him straight in the eye with a smile and pointed out, "Now we're on the same side!"

• A certain businessman was proud of his reputation as a hard-nosed negotiator. He took a much needed vacation to fish in the Rockies, and happened to pull an extraordinary, iridescent fish into his boat. As it thrashed about frantically, the fish suddenly spoke. "Put me back in the water and I will grant you any three wishes."

   A light came into the businessman's eye. "Make it five and we've got a deal."

   "Please, I can only grant three," gasped the fish.

   The man considered the offer for a minute, then proposed four and a half.

   "Three," the fish whispered, its struggles growing feebler.

   "Okay, we'll compromise on four."

   But there was no reply. The fish lay dead in the bottom of the boat.

THE OFFICE

The person who says "I'm not political" is in great danger. . . . Only the fittest will survive, and the fittest will be the ones who understand their office's politics.

—Jean Hollands

No office anywhere on earth is so puritanical, impeccable, elegant, sterile, or incorruptible as not to contain the yeast for at least one affair, probably more. You can say it couldn't happen *here*, but just let a yeast riser into the place and first thing you know—bread!   *—Helen Gurley Brown*

Windows . . . are as essential to office prestige as Christmas is to retailing.

—Enid Nemy

The brain is a wonderful little organ. It starts working the moment you get up in the morning, and does not stop until you get into the office.   *—Robert Frost*

I yield to no one in my admiration for the office as a social center, but it's no place actually to get any work done.   *—Katherine Whitehorn*

Sayings
I gave at the office.

A salesman's office is the car.

Office romances are ill fated and inevitable.

No need to insure the office clock—everyone watches it.

Jokes
• He and I had an office so tiny that an inch smaller and it would have been adultery.

—Dorothy Parker

• What is boss spelled backwards?—Double s-o-b.

• Define boss: Someone who delegates authority, shifts all the blame, and takes all the credit. Or, someone who throws his own weight around instead of pulling it.

• I work for a good cause—'cause I need the money.

• A smart employee is someone who spends December working her fingers to the bonus.

RESEARCH

Research is four things: brains with which to think, eyes with which to see, machines with which to measure, and fourth, money.   *—Albert Szent-Gyorgyi*

One pits his wits against apparently inscrutable nature, wooing her with ardor, [but] nature is blind justice who cannot recognize personal identity.

—Charles Benton Huggins

He uses statistics as a drunken man uses lampposts—for support rather than for illumination.   *—Andrew Lang*

Knowing how hard it is to collect a fact, you understand why most people want to have some fun analyzing it.   —*Jesse L. Greenstein*

It is inexcusable for scientists to torture animals; let them make their experiment on journalists and politicians.   —*Henrik Ibsen*

Money won't buy happiness, but it will pay the salaries of a large research staff to study the problem.   —*Bill Vaughan*

It is a capital mistake to theorize before one has data.

—*Arthur Conan Doyle*

Market research can establish beyond the shadow of a doubt that the egg is a sad and sorry product and that it obviously will not continue to sell. Because after all, eggs won't stand up by themselves, they roll too easily, are too easily broken, require special packaging, look alike, are difficult to open, and won't stack on the shelf.

—*Robert Pliskin*

The trouble with research is that it tells you what people were thinking about yesterday, not tomorrow. It's like driving a car using a rearview mirror.

—*Bernard Loomis*

The latest research on polls has turned up some interesting variables. It turns out, for instance, that people will tell you any old thing that pops into their heads.

—*Charles Saxon*

The will to succeed is important, but what's even more important is the will to prepare.

—*Bobby Knight*

Every man has a right to be wrong in his opinions. But no man has a right to be wrong about his facts.   —*Bernard Baruch*

It requires a very unusual mind to undertake the analysis of the obvious.

—*Alfred North Whitehead*

Basic research is what I am doing when I don't know what I am doing.

—*Wernher von Braun*

Sayings
Answers are easy. Finding the right questions is the tricky part.

Better ask twice than lose your way once.   —*Danish proverb*

Jokes
- Developing a new process involves three steps. First, an American company announces its invention. Next, the Soviet Union announces that a Soviet scientist made the same discovery fifteen years earlier. Third, the Japanese start exporting it.

- How do researchers differentiate male chromosomes from female chromosomes?
    —They pull down their genes.

RETIREMENT

Most people spend most of their days doing what they do not want to do in order to earn the right, at times, to do what they may desire.   —*John Brown*

I'm now at the age where I've got to prove that I'm just as good as I never was.

—*Rex Harrison (attrib.)*

I have made noise enough in the world already, perhaps too much, and am now getting old, and want retirement.   —*Napoleon Bonaparte*

I am convinced that the best service a retired general can perform is to turn in his tongue along with his suit and to mothball his opinions.

—*General Omar N. Bradley*

I really think it's better to retire when you still have some snap left in your garters.

—*Russell B. Long*

Who knows whether in retirement I shall be tempted to the last infirmity of mundane minds, which is to write a book.   —*Archbishop Geoffrey Fisher*

People do not retire. They are retired by others.   —*Duke Ellington*

Saying
I'm retired. But I'm not dead yet.

Jokes
- The problem with being retired is that you never know what day it is, what time it is, where you're supposed to be, or what you're supposed to be doing. It's a lot like working for the government.

- The managing director had quite a bit to drink at Mrs. Witherspoon's retirement banquet, and it showed when he stood up to present her gift. "Mrs. Witherspoon, as a token of your contribution to our firm over the last three decades, we had a very special gold watch made up," he declared loudly. "It needs a lot of winding up, it's always late, and every day at 4:45 it stops working."

- Not known for his tact, the boss's retirement speech for old Stumpig consisted of the following: "We're really going to miss Stumpig. He's going to be hard to replace, especially at the pitiful salary we've been paying him all these years."

- I married him for better or worse, but not for lunch.
  —*Hazel Weiss, after her husband, George Weiss, retired as general manager of the New York Yankees, 1960*

- You can only hold your stomach in for so many years.
  —*Burt Reynolds, on retiring briefly from films*

WORK

There are very few jobs that actually require a penis or a vagina. All other jobs should be open to everybody.

—*Florynce Kennedy (also attributed to Gloria Steinem)*

Work makes you free.   —*Inscription over the entrance to Auschwitz*

It's an ear job, not an eye job.

—*Donald T. Regan, on his job as White House chief of staff*

As is the case in all branches of art, success depends in a very large measure upon individual initiative and exertion, and cannot be achieved except by dint of hard work.

—*Anna Pavlova*

Blessed is he who has found his work; let him ask no other blessedness.

—*Thomas Carlyle*

If you pay peanuts, you get monkeys.   —*Sir James Goldsmith*

The only way anybody'd get me to work was to make the hours from one to two with an hour off for lunch.   —*Minnesota Fats*

The best preparation for good work tomorrow is to do good work today.

—*Elbert Hubbard*

Work and love—these are the basics. Without them there is neurosis.

—*Theodor Reik*

Work is the refuge of people who have nothing better to do.

—*Oscar Wilde*

I have nothing to offer but blood, toil, tears, and sweat.

—*Winston Churchill*

A bee is never as busy as it seems; it's just that it can't buzz any slower.

—*Kin Hubbard*

I have never liked working. To me a job is an invasion of privacy.

—*Daniel McGoorty*

The harder you work, the luckier you get.   —*Gary Player*

Labor: One of the processes by which A acquires property of B.

—*Ambrose Bierce*

Well, we can't stand around here doing nothing, people will think we're workmen.

—*Spike Milligan*

Work is not a curse, it is the prerogative of intelligence, the only means to manhood, and the measure of civilization. Savages do not work.   —*Calvin Coolidge*

Work hard. There is no short cut.   —*Alfred P. Sloan, Jr.*

My father taught me to work; he did not teach me to love it.

—*Abraham Lincoln*

The world is full of willing people; some willing to work, the rest willing to let them.

—*Robert Frost*

Work is work if you're paid to do it, and it's pleasure if you pay to be allowed to do it.

—*Finley Peter Dunne*

The difference between a rut and a grave is the depth.

—*Bishop Gerald Burrill*

The more I want to get something done, the less I call it work.

—*Richard Bach*

In a hierarchy, every employee tends to rise to his level of incompetence.

—*Laurence J. Peter*

The person who knows "how" will always have a job. The person who knows "why" will always be his boss.
—*Diane Ravitch*

I like work: it fascinates me. I can sit and look at it for hours.
—*Jerome K. Jerome*

Work is accomplished by those employees who have not yet reached their level of incompetence.
—*Laurence J. Peter*

In order that people may be happy in their work, these three things are needed: they must be fit for it; they must not do too much of it; and they must have a sense of success in it.
—*John Ruskin*

Job. A low word now much in use, of which I cannot tell the etymology. (1) A low, mean lucrative busy affair. (2) Petty, piddling work: a piece of chance work.
—*Samuel Johnson*

The man whose life is devoted to paperwork has lost the initiative. He is dealing with things that are brought to his notice, having ceased to notice anything for himself. He has been essentially defeated in his job.
—*C. Northcote Parkinson*

Work is much more fun than fun.
—*Noel Coward*

I pride myself on the fact that my work has no socially redeeming value.
—*John Waters*

Work is no curse, but drudgery is.
—*Henry Ward Beecher*

Far and away the best prize that life offers is the chance to work hard at work worth doing.
—*Theodore Roosevelt*

. . . there is as much dignity in tilling a field as in writing a poem.
—*Booker T. Washington*

Work was like cats were supposed to be; if you disliked and feared it and tried to keep out of its way, it knew at once and sought you out. . . .
—*Kingsley Amis*

Anyone can do any amount of work, provided it isn't the work he is supposed to be doing at that moment.
—*Robert Benchley*

Work expands so as to fill the time available for its completion.
—*C. Northcote Parkinson*

Work is the curse of the drinking class.
—*Oscar Wilde (attrib.)*

The man with the best job in the country is the vice president. All he has to do is get up every morning and say "How's the president?"
—*Will Rogers*

Every man's work, whether it be literature or music or pictures or architecture or anything else, is always a portrait of himself.
—*Samuel Butler*

The gambling known as business looks with austere disfavor upon the business known as gambling.
—*Ambrose Bierce*

Work is the greatest thing in the world, so we should always save some of it for tomorrow.
—*Don Herold*

The reason why worry kills more people than work is that more people worry than work.
—*Robert Frost*

Many of us spend half our time wishing for things we could have if we didn't spend half our time wishing.   —*Alexander Woollcott*

If you have great talents, industry will improve them; if you have but modest abilities, industry will supply their deficiencies.   —*Joshua Reynolds*

There is no such thing as a free lunch.   —*Milton Friedman, economist*

If you don't drive your business, you will be driven out of business.
                                                                    —*B. C. Forbes*

It is an immutable law in business that words are words, explanations are explanations, promises are promises—but only performance is reality.
                                                                    —*Harold S. Geneen*

When you soar like an eagle, you attract the hunters.   —*Milton S. Gould*

When two men in business always agree, one of them is unnecessary.
                                                                    —*William Wrigley, Jr.*

Life without industry is guilt, industry without art is brutality.
                                                                    —*John Ruskin*

Few people do business well who do nothing else.   —*Lord Chesterfield*

Civilization and profits go hand in hand.   —*Calvin Coolidge*

The business of America is business.   —*Calvin Coolidge*

Keep thy shop and thy shop will keep thee.   —*Benjamin Franklin*

If you would have your business done, go; if not, send.
                                                                  —*Benjamin Franklin*

It is just as important that business keep out of government as that government keep out of business.   —*Herbert Hoover*

Put all your eggs in one basket and—*watch that basket*.   —*Mark Twain*

[The businessman] is the only man who is forever apologizing for his occupation.
                                                              —*H. L. Mencken (attrib.)*

If the government was as afraid of disturbing the consumer as it is of disturbing business, this would be some democracy.   —*Kin Hubbard*

Whenever you're sitting across from some important person, always picture him sitting there in a suit of long red underwear. That's the way I always operated in business.
                                                                  —*Joseph P. Kennedy*

Nothing is illegal if a hundred businessmen decide to do it, and that's true anywhere in the world.   —*Andrew Young*

The playthings of our elders are called business.   —*St. Augustine*

The ideal client is the very wealthy man in very great trouble.
                                                                    —*John Sterling*

Landlord of a bordello! The company's good and the mornings are quiet, which is the best time to write.   —*William Faulkner, on his ideal job*

The pay is good, and I can walk to work.

—*John F. Kennedy, on being elected president*

I am a sensitive writer, actor, director. Talking business disgusts me. If you want to talk business, call my disgusting personal manager.
   —*Sylvester Stallone, on the card he hands out when approached with business propositions*

Like getting into a bleeding competition with a blood bank.
        —*Richard Branson, Chairman, Virgin Airlines, on competing with British Airways*

Work is accomplished by those employees who have not yet reached their level of incompetence.
                                                            —*Laurence J. Peter*

Work is a necessity for man. Man invented the alarm clock.

—*Pablo Picasso*

Like every man of sense and feeling, I abominate work.   —*Aldous Huxley*

Most people spend most of their days doing what they do not want to do in order to earn the right, at times, to do what they may desire.   —*John Brown*

I go on working for the same reason that a hen goes on laying eggs.

—*H. L. Mencken*

Nobody ever drowned in his own sweat.   —*Ann Landers*

My parents always told me that people will never know how long it takes you to do something. They will only know how well it is done.   —*Nancy Hanks*

All work and no play makes Jack a dull boy.   —*James Howell*

Many hands make light work.   —*John Heywood*

Sayings

Work for the Lord. The pay isn't much, but the retirement plan is out of this world.

Everyone should be paid what he is worth, no matter how big a pay cut is involved.

Words do not make flour.   —*Italian proverb*

He who is afraid of doing too much always does too little.   —*German proverb*

Work is the easiest activity man has invented to escape boredom.

If you're willing to work, others will let you.

Nobody likes hard work better than the person who pays for it.

What more people are looking for these days is less to do, more time to do it in, and more pay for not getting it done.

A man who works with his hands is a laborer. A man who works with his hands and his brains is a craftsman. But a man who works with his brains and the hands of others is an executive.

Just about the time a woman thinks her work is done, she becomes a grandmother.

Women are flooding the work force so they can afford the labor-saving devices that make it possible for them to go to work.

First get the job; then get the job done.

Don't send a boy to do a man's job.

Don't send a boy to do a man's job these days; send a woman.

Make the best of a bad job.

A job worth doing is worth doing well.

If you want the job done fast, give it to a busy man.

Business is a two-way street.

Business before pleasure.

There's no room for sentiment in business.

The customer is always right.

Everyone, in the final analysis, is in business for himself.

Jokes

• "Now remember, Royce—your salary is confidential and should not be discussed with anyone else in the company," the manager instructed.
   "Oh, don't worry, Ms. Amorelli," the new employee assured her. "I'm just as ashamed of it as you are."

• How long have you been working here?
   —Ever since they threatened to fire me.

• According to the latest statistics, there are [current figure] million Americans who aren't working. And there are plenty more if you count the ones with jobs.

• It's no surprise that people grouse about their take-home pay. You know why you have to take it home? It's too little to go by itself.

• It's easy to tell inventory from money. Money's the stuff you can get rid of.

THE POLITICAL SCENE

POLITICS

In politics stupidity is not a handicap. — *—Napoleon Bonaparte*

Politics has got so expensive that it takes lots of money to even get beat with.
—Will Rogers

Politics is the art of looking for trouble, finding it everywhere, diagnosing it incorrectly, and applying the wrong remedies. *—Groucho Marx*

Politics is not the art of the possible. It consists in choosing between the disastrous and the unpalatable. *—John Kenneth Galbraith*

Any party which takes credit for the rain must not be surprised if its opponents blame it for the drought. *—Dwight W. Morrow*

The fact is that a reformer can't last in politics. He can make a show for a while, but he always comes down like a rocket. Politics is as much a regular business as the grocery or the drygoods or the drub business. *—George Washington Plunkett*

In politics there is no honor. *—Benjamin Disraeli*

I always cheer up immensely if an attack is particularly wounding because I think, well, if they attack one personally, it means they have not a single political argument left. *—Margaret Thatcher*

Politics is supposed to be the second-oldest profession. I have come to realize that it bears a very close resemblance to the first. *—Ronald Reagan*

I seldom think of politics more than eighteen hours a day.

—Lyndon B. Johnson

Man is by nature a political animal. *—Aristotle*

If you take yourself seriously in politics, you've had it. *—Lord Carrington*

Politics are almost as exciting as war and quite as dangerous. In war you can only be killed once, but in politics many times. *—Winston Churchill*

Politics is like being a football coach. You have to be smart enough to understand the game, and stupid enough to think it's important. *—Eugene McCarthy*

Politics is perhaps the only profession for which no preparation is thought necessary.
—Robert Louis Stevenson

An independent is the guy who wants to take the politics out of politics.
—Adlai E. Stevenson

A radical is a man with both feet firmly planted in the air.
—*Franklin D. Roosevelt*

The middle of the road is all of the usable surface. The extremes, right and left, are in the gutters.   —*Dwight D. Eisenhower*

If a man is right, he can't be too radical; if he is wrong, he can't be too conservative.
—*Josh Billings*

Doublethink means the power of holding two contradictory beliefs in one's mind simultaneously, and accepting both of them.   —*George Orwell*

You can't divorce religious belief and public service . . . and I've never detected any conflict between God's will and my political duty. If you violate one, you violate the other.   —*Jimmy Carter*

Oil is seldom found where it is most needed, and seldom most needed where it is found.   —*L. E. J. Brouwer*

In politics, as in other things, there is no such thing as one getting something for nothing. The payoff may involve compromises of various types that may strike at the ideals and principles one has held dear all his life.   —*A. Philip Randolph*

I have sometimes looked with wonder on the jargon of our times wherein those whose minds reside in the past are called "progressive" while those whose minds are vital enough to challenge and to mold the future are dubbed "reactionary."
—*Jomo Mzee Kenyatta*

Ideas are great arrows, but there has to be a bow. And politics is the bow of idealism.
—*Bill Moyers*

Michael Faraday, a pioneer in the field of electricity, was demonstrating the tremendous potential of his new invention, the dynamo, to the British Royal Scientific Society. A young politician in the audience, William Gladstone, grew bored, finally saying, "I'm sure this is all very interesting, Mr. Faraday, but what in God's earth good is it?"

"Some day," replied the brilliant inventor dryly, "you politicians will be able to tax it."

Sayings
Running for your varsity team is athletics; running for a train is exercise; running for office is work.

They keep saying that what really matters isn't whether you won but how well you played. The problem is that the best way to determine how well you played the game is by whether or not you won.

Politics is the art of the passable.

Jokes
• If you've got 'em by the balls, their hearts and minds will follow.
—*Sign in the White House office of Charles Colson, aide to Richard Nixon*

• We have the power to do any damn fool thing we want to do, and we seem to do it about every ten minutes.
—*J. William Fulbright, on the Senate's right to change its mind*

• Communism: You have two cows. The government takes both, milks them, keeps the milk, and gives you a pint.
Socialism: The government takes one of your cows and gives it to a neighbor.
Fascism: The government takes both cows and shoots one of them.
Nazism: The government takes both cows and shoots you.
Capitalism: You milk both cows, sell one of the cows, and buy a bull.
Bureaucracy: The government takes both cows, milks them, and pours the milk down the drain.

• How boring was the last election?
—When voters walked into the voting booth and pulled the lever, the machine yawned.

• What's the difference between baseball and politics?
—In baseball you're out if you're caught stealing.

CANDIDATES AND POLITICIANS

Politicians are the same all over. They promise to build a bridge even when there's no river.
—*Nikita S. Khrushchev*

Being a president is like riding a tiger . . . keep on riding or be swallowed. A president is either constantly on top of events or . . . events will soon be on top of him.
—*Harry S Truman*

A politician has spent the best years of his life in an endeavor to make the world safe for stupidity.
—*Nancy Boyd*

The first requirement of a statesman is that he be dull. This is not always easy to achieve.
—*Dean Acheson*

The politician is an acrobat. He keeps his balance by saying the opposite of what he does.
—*Maurice Barres*

Every president needs his son-of-a-bitch; I'm Nixon's.
—*H. R. (Bob) Haldeman*

The most successful politician is he who says what everybody is thinking most often and in the loudest voice.
—*Theodore Roosevelt*

An independent is the guy who wants to take the politics out of politics.
—*Adlai E. Stevenson*

I have spent much of my life fighting the Germans and fighting the politicians. It is much easier to fight the Germans.
—*Lord Montgomery*

Ninety-eight percent of the adults in this country are decent, hard-working Americans. It's the other lousy two percent that get all the publicity. But then—we elected them.
—*Lily Tomlin*

A politician is an animal that can sit on a fence and keep both ears to the ground.
—*H. L. Mencken*

An honest politician is one who, when he is bought, will stay bought.
—*Simon Cameron*

An honest politician is one who, when he is bought, will stay bought.

—*Simon Cameron*

I won't eat anything that has intelligent life, but I would gladly eat a network executive or a politician.   —*Marty Feldman*

What is the use of being elected or reelected unless you stand for something?

—*Grover Cleveland*

Frankly, I don't mind not being president. I just mind that somebody else is.

—*Edward M. Kennedy*

I like to operate like a submarine on sonar. When I am picking up noise from both the left and the right, I know my course is correct.

—*Gustavo Díaz Ordaz, while campaigning for the presidency of Mexico*

You campaign in poetry. You govern in prose.   —*Mario Cuomo*

When I was a boy, I was told that anybody could become president; I'm beginning to believe it.   —*Clarence Darrow*

You can't beat somebody with nobody.   —*Joseph Cannon (attrib.)*

The idea that you can merchandise candidates for high office like breakfast cereal is . . . I think, the ultimate indignity for the democratic process.

—*Adlai E. Stevenson*

The man with the best job in the country is the vice president. All he has to do is get up every morning and say "How's the president?"   —*Will Rogers*

Once there were two brothers. One ran away to sea, the other was elected vice president, and nothing was ever heard of either of them again.

—*Thomas R. Marshall*

I wanted to be a sports writer, but it took me too long to turn out my stuff. I found I could become vice president faster than I could become a newspaperman.

—*Richard M. Nixon*

The short memories of American voters is what keeps our politicians in office.

—*Will Rogers*

Here is an animal with a hide two feet thick and no apparent interest in politics. What a waste.   —*James C. Wright, Jr., about the rhinoceros*

Bad politicians are sent to Washington by good people who don't vote.

—*William E. Simon*

People have got to know whether or not their president is a crook. Well, I'm not a crook. I earned everything I've got.   —*Richard M. Nixon*

I am not a perfect servant. I am a public servant doing my best against the odds. As I develop and serve, be patient. God is not finished with me yet.

—*Jesse Jackson*

If you want to find a politician free of any influence, you can find Adolf Hitler, who made up his own mind.   —*Eugene McCarthy*

Since a politician never believes what he says, he is surprised when others believe him.   —*Charles de Gaulle*

Probably the most distinctive characteristic of the successful politician is selective cowardice.   —*Richard Harris*

Mothers all want their sons to grow up to be president, but they don't want them to become politicians in the process.   —*John F. Kennedy (attrib.)*

Now I know what a statesman is: he's a dead politician. We need more statesmen.
—*Bob Edwards*

Every man who takes office in Washington either grows or swells, and when I give a man an office, I watch him carefully to see whether he is swelling or growing.
—*Woodrow Wilson*

Some members of the Congress are the best actors in the world.   —*Shirley Chisholm*

America is just the country that shows how all the written guarantees in the world for freedom are no protection against tyranny and oppression of the worst kind. There the politician has come to be looked upon as the very scum of society.
—*Peter Kropotkin*

If nominated, I will not accept; if elected, I will not serve.
—*General William T. Sherman*

If it walks like a duck, and quacks like a duck, then it just may be a duck.
—*Walter Reuther, trade union leader, on how to tell a Communist*

You really have to get to know Dewey to dislike him.   —*Robert A. Taft*

Sayings
Promise them anything but get out the vote.

Elections are the way we find chosen people.

Politicians don't like to talk turkey because they hate to eat crow.

Jokes
• Why are politicians so busy?
   —When they're not spending time passing laws, they're trying to help their friends get around them.

• Why does our government get so much support?
   —Because the politicians keep holding it up.

• What do political speeches and cattle horns have in common?
   —There are some good points, but a lot of bull in the middle.

• Why do politicians stand on their records?
   —So the voters can't get a good look at them.

• Ever notice how they always place the street cleaners directly behind the politicians in a parade?

• A father wanted to find out if his son was going to be either a banker, a preacher, or a bum so he devised a little test. He put a twenty-dollar bill, a Bible, and a bottle of whiskey on the kitchen table and hid in the broom closet. A short time later, his son walked in to the kitchen and slowly walked around the table. Eventually he picked

he opened the bottle, slugged down the contents, grabbed the twenty-dollar bill and stuffed it in his pocket, stashed the Bible under his arm, and strode out of the room humming to himself. The father grinned and said, "Imagine that! My boy's going to be a politician!"

• Concluding a powerful and impassioned speech enumerating his many splendid qualities, the candidate finally asked if anyone had any questions.
  "Yes, sir," called out a voice from the crowd. "Who else is running?"

• When the candidate running for the governorship of Texas announced at a big barbecue that he was a "favorite son," one of his detractors was heard to mutter, "That's the most obvious unfinished sentence ever spoken in the state of Texas."

• It really shakes you to see one of them sign a piece of legislation, and then wipe his fingerprints off the pen.

• I know one politician who went to Washington and took the pulse of the town—and everything else that wasn't nailed down.

• The "Mona Lisa" expression looks like a reporter listening to a politician.

VOTING

If you don't vote, you're going to get a spanking.   —*Madonna*

Bad politicians are sent to Washington by good people who don't vote.
                                                    —*William E. Simon*

We go by the major vote, and if the majority are insane, the sane must go to the hospital.   —*Horace Mann*

Whenever a fellow tells me he's bipartisan I know he's going to vote against me.
                                                    —*Harry S Truman*

America is a land where a citizen will cross the ocean to fight for democracy—and won't cross the street to vote in a national election.   —*Bill Vaughan*

Voters don't decide issues, they decide who will decide issues.
                                                    —*George F. Will*

If the ballot doesn't work, we'll try something else. But let us try the ballot.
                                                    —*Malcolm X*

Vote for the man who promises least; he'll be the least disappointing.
                                                    —*Bernard Baruch*

Bad officials are elected by good citizens who do not vote.
                                                    —*George Jean Nathan*

A straw vote only shows which way the hot air blows.   —*O. Henry*

Voting is the first duty of democracy.   —*Lyndon B. Johnson*

The ballot is stronger than the bullet.   —*Abraham Lincoln*

Inside the polling booth every American man and woman stands as the equal of every other American man and woman. There they have no superiors. There they have no masters save their own minds and consciences.   —*Franklin D. Roosevelt*

Nobody will ever deprive the American people of the right to vote except the American people themselves.   —*Franklin D. Roosevelt*

Act as if the whole election depended on your single vote. . . .

—*John Wesley*

Sayings
If voting changed anything, they'd make it illegal.

The votes that count are the ones that can be counted.

Jokes
• During his whistle-stop campaign for the presidency in 1948, Harry Truman is reputed to have asked a fellow in the crowd before him how he was intending to vote.
    "Mr. Truman," came the reply, "I wouldn't vote for you if yours was the only name on the ballot."
    Truman turned to an aide and instructed, "Put that man down as doubtful."

• It was a terrific election. Ninety-five million Americans took time off from work to vote, and sixty-eight million of them did.

CONSERVATIVES

Conservative: A statesman who is enamored of existing evils, as distinguished from the liberal, who wishes to replace them with others.   —*Ambrose Bierce*

I never dared to be a radical when young for fear it would make me conservative when old.   —*Robert Frost*

A liberal is a person who believes that water can be made to run uphill. A conservative is someone who believes everybody should pay for his water. I'm somewhere in between: I believe water should be free, but that it flows downhill.

—*Theodore H. White*

A conservative is a man who will not look at the new moon, out of respect for that ancient institution, the old one.   —*Douglas Jerrold*

The modern conservative is engaged in one of man's oldest exercises in moral philosophy—that is the search for a superior moral justification for selfishness.

—*John Kenneth Galbraith*

The most radical revolutionary will become a conservative the day after the revolution.

—*Hannah Arendt*

The true conservative seeks to protect the system of private property and free enterprise by correcting such injustices and inequalities as arise from it. The most serious threat to our institutions comes from those who refuse to face the need for change. Liberalism becomes the protection for the far-sighted conservative.   —*Franklin D. Roosevelt*

Sayings

A conservative is someone who admires radicals a century after they're dead.

Conservative means small change and radical means large bills.

Joke
• A conservative believes freedom is worth any price—and if you can't afford it, you can't have it.

DEMOCRATS AND REPUBLICANS

When a leader is in the Democratic party he's a boss; when he's in the Republican party he's a leader.   *—Harry S Truman*

. . . while the Republicans are smart enough to make money, the Democrats are smart enough to get in office every two or three times a century and take it away from 'em.
—Will Rogers

If the Republicans will stop telling lies about the Democrats, we will stop telling the truth about them.   *—Adlai E. Stevenson*

I like Republicans, have grown up with them and would trust them with anything in the world except public office.   *—Adlai E. Stevenson*

Sayings

A Republican is a Democrat who got rich.

Around the world people have revolted for the right to have more than one party. Here in the United States, we settle for one and a half.

We're asked to choose between a party with a lumbering elephant as a mascot and another whose mascot is a jackass. The sad part is how appropriate the symbols genuinely are.

Jokes
• The Democrats and the Republicans seem dedicated to the idea that the real party is in Washington.

• I belong to no organized party—I am a Democrat.   *—Will Rogers (attrib.)*

• Republicans sleep in twin beds—some even in separate rooms. That is why there are more Democrats.   *—Will Stanton*

LIBERALS

A liberal is a man too broad-minded to take his own side in a quarrel.
—Robert Frost

A liberal is a person who believes that water can be made to run uphill. A conservative is someone who believes everybody should pay for his water. I'm somewhere in between: I believe water should be free, but that it flows downhill.
—Theodore H. White

You know what they say; if God had been a liberal, we wouldn't have had the Ten Commandments. We'd have had the ten suggestions.

—Malcolm Bradbury and Christopher Bigsby

What the liberal really wants is to bring about change which will not in any way endanger his position.   *—Stokeley Carmichael*

The liberals in the House strongly resemble liberals I have known through the last two decades in the civil rights conflict. When it comes time to show on which side they will be counted, they excuse themselves.   *—Shirley Chisholm*

There are no more liberals . . . They've all been mugged.

—James Q. Wilson

Radical chic invariably favors radicals who seem primitive, exotic, and romantic, such as the grape workers who are not merely radical and "of the soil" but also Latin; the Panthers, with their leather pieces, Afros, shades and shoot-outs; and the Red Indians, who, of course, had always seemed primitive, exotic, and romantic.

—Tom Wolfe

Stop the liberals from spending taxpayers' money on perverted, deviant art.

—Jesse Helms

Sayings
A liberal is a conservative who's been mugged by reality.

The liberals can understand everything but people who don't understand them.

Joke
• The two diehard liberals were walking down the street when they nearly stumbled across the prostrate form of a fellow who'd been robbed and badly beaten. "This is terrible, really terrible," said one liberal, as they kneeled down beside the victim. "The person who did this really needs help."

CIVIL RIGHTS

After four hundred years of slave labor, we have some back pay coming.

—Malcolm X

. . . it's a blessing to die for a cause, because you can so easily die for nothing.

—Andrew Young

The white man's happiness cannot be purchased by the black man's misery.

—Frederick Douglass

I glory in conflict, that I may hereafter exult in victory.

—Frederick Douglass

The haughty American nation . . . makes the Negro clean its boots and then proves the moral and physical inferiority of the Negro by the fact that he is a bootblack.

—George Bernard Shaw

America has put a tight shoe on the Negro and now he has a callus on his soul.

—*Dick Gregory*

. . . an American Negro isn't a man—he's a walking defense mechanism.

—*Frank Yerby*

The Negro was invented in America.   —*John Oliver Killens*

Some of the best pretending in the world is done in front of white folks.

—*Ossie Davis*

Of my two "handicaps," being female put many more obstacles in my path than being black.   —*Shirley Chisholm*

This [America] is the red man's country by natural right, and the black man's by virtue of his suffering and toil.   —*Robert Purvis*

Sayings
We shall overcome.

Do the right thing.

A conservative believes freedom is worth any price—and if you can't afford it, you can't have it.

Black is beautiful.

Separate but equal.

Black power.

Jokes
• Two residents of a little town in Alabama, one white and one black, went downtown to register to vote in the upcoming election. The official in charge took down their names and addresses, then held up a bar of soap. "What's this?" he asked the white guy.
  "A bar of soap."
  "Right. You're registered." Then he turned to the black man and asked, "How many bubbles in this bar of soap?"

• What do you call a black hitchhiker?
  —Stranded.

• What did the little black kid say as he walked in front of the zebra?
  "Now you see me . . . now you don't . . . now you see me . . ."

CAPITALISM

For the right amount of money, you're willing to eat Alpo.

—*Reggie Jackson*

Civilization and profits go hand in hand.   —*Calvin Coolidge*

Frankly, I'd like to see the government get out of war altogether and leave the whole field to private industry.   —*Joseph Heller*

Fascism is capitalism plus murder.   *—Upton Sinclair*

When we hang the capitalists they will sell us the rope.   *—Joseph Stalin*

Nobody ever lost money taking a profit.   *—Bernard Baruch*

The trouble with the profit system has always been that it was highly unprofitable to most people.   *—E. B. White*

The engine which drives enterprise is not thrift, but profit.

—John Maynard Keynes

Capitalism has destroyed our belief in any effective power but that of self-interest backed by force.   *—George Bernard Shaw*

The inherent vice of capitalism is the unequal sharing of blessings; the inherent virtue of socialism is the equal sharing of miseries.   *—Winston Churchill*

Not every problem someone has with his girlfriend is necessarily due to the capitalist mode of production.   *—Herbert Marcuse*

Capitalism inevitably and by virtue of the very logic of its civilization creates, educates, and subsidizes a vested interest in social unrest.

—Joseph Schumpeter

. . . racism cannot be separated from capitalism.   *—Angela Davis*

The public be damned.   *—W. H. Vanderbilt*

"The trouble with socialism," a European observer once remarked, "is socialism. The trouble with capitalism is capitalists."   *—William F. Buckley, Jr.*

The superior man understands what is right; the inferior man understands what will sell.   *—Confucius*

Capitalism without bankruptcy is like Christianity without hell.

—Frank Borman

A holding company is a thing where you hand an accomplice the goods while the policeman searches you.   *—Will Rogers*

It is just as important that business keep out of government as that government keep out of business.   *—Herbert Hoover*

Sayings
Capitalism is the best means ever found to motivate men.

Capitalism is merely economic Darwinism.

Capitalism is what makes America great.

Capitalism is the most rewarding system of government.

The carrot gets better results than the stick.

Jokes
• "My boy decided to go into business on a shoestring," said George. "He's tripled his investment, but he's still not satisfied, can you believe it?"

"Why not?" asked his friend.

"He can't think of anything to do with three shoestrings."

- Communism: You have two cows. The government takes both, milks them, keeps the milk, and gives you a pint.

  Socialism: The government takes one of your cows and gives it to a neighbor.

  Fascism: The government takes both cows and shoots one of them.

  Nazism: The government takes both cows and shoots you.

  Capitalism: You milk both cows, sell one of the cows, and buy a bull.

  Bureaucracy: The government takes both cows, milks them, and pours the milk down the drain.

COMMUNISM

Our program necessarily includes the propaganda of atheism.

—V. I. Lenin

Communism is the corruption of a dream of justice.   *—Adlai E. Stevenson*

Communism is like Prohibition. It's a good idea but it won't work.

—Will Rogers

[Communism is] a strange, a perverted creed, that has a queer attraction both for the most primitive and for the most sophisticated societies.

—Harold Macmillan

If it walks like a duck, and quacks like a duck, then it just may be a duck.
     —Walter Reuther, trade union leader, on how to tell a Communist

Communism is not love. Communism is a hammer which we use to crush the enemy.

—Mao Tse-tung

Saying

A Communist is one who has nothing and wishes to share it with the world.

Jokes

- Communism: You have two cows. The government takes both, milks them, keeps the milk, and gives you a pint.

  Socialism: The government takes one of your cows and gives it to a neighbor.

  Fascism: The government takes both cows and shoots one of them.

  Nazism: The government takes both cows and shoots you.

  Capitalism: You milk both cows, sell one of the cows, and buy a bull.

  Bureaucracy: The government takes both cows, milks them, and pours the milk down the drain.

- Under capitalism it's dog eat dog. Under Communism, it's just the opposite.

- The Eastern bloc family was visited by a Western friend, who found only the young daughter at home. "When will your father be back?" he inquired.

  "In sixteen hours, eight minutes, and twenty-seven seconds," the little girl replied crisply.

  "My goodness—where is he?"

"He is in his twenty-sixth orbit around the earth."

"I see." The visitor was clearly impressed. "And your mother, when will she be home?"

The little girl shrugged.

"Can you give me some idea when she is expected?"

The little girl shook her head.

"Come on now," persisted the visitor. "How is it that you know to the second when your father will be back but can't even manage a guess as to when I can see your mother? Where is she?"

"She's in line for meat at the market."

DEMOCRACY

Let the people think they govern and they will be governed.

—*William Penn*

We go by the major vote, and if the majority are insane, the sane must go to the hospital.   —*Horace Mann*

The death of democracy is not likely to be an assassination from ambush. It will be a slow extinction from apathy, indifference, and undernourishment.

—*Robert Maynard Hutchins*

Only a base, vile, insignificant country can be democratic.

—*Benito Mussolini*

The health of a democratic society may be measured by the quality of functions performed by private citizens.   —*Alexis de Tocqueville*

The ship of democracy, which has weathered all storms, may sink through the mutiny of those on board.   —*Grover Cleveland*

Democracy cannot be static. Whatever is static is dead.

—*Eleanor Roosevelt*

Democracy is a process, not a static condition. It is becoming, rather than being. It can easily be lost, but never is fully won.   —*William H. Hastie*

A great democracy must be progressive or it will soon cease to be a great democracy.

—*Theodore Roosevelt*

We must be thoroughly democratic and patronize everybody without distinction of class.   —*George Bernard Shaw*

Democracy is the art of running the circus from the monkey cage.

—*H. L. Mencken*

Democracy means government by the uneducated, while aristocracy means government by the badly educated.   —*G. K. Chesterton*

And so, my fellow Americans: ask not what your country can do for you—ask what you can do for your country.   —*John F. Kennedy*

Democracy substitutes elections by the incompetent many for appointment by the corrupt few.   —*George Bernard Shaw*

It has been said that democracy is the worst form of government except all those other forms that have been tried from time to time.   —*Winston Churchill*

One fifth of the people are against everything all the time.   —*Robert F. Kennedy*

The experience of democracy is like the experience of life itself—always changing, infinite in its variety, sometimes turbulent and all the more valuable for having been tested by adversity.   —*Jimmy Carter*

If the government was as afraid of disturbing the consumer as it is of disturbing business, this would be some democracy.   —*Kin Hubbard*

I am a member of the rabble in good standing.   —*Westbrook Pegler*

Democracy is good. I say this because other systems are worse.

—*Jawaharlal Nehru*

If this nation is not truly democratic, then she must die.

—*Alexander Crummell*

A democracy cannot long endure with the head of a god and the tail of a demon.
—*Josephine Silone Yates*

Democracy is not tolerant. Democracy is a prescribed way of life erected on the premise that all men are created equal.   —*Chester Bomar Himes*

The unhealthy gap between what we preach in America and what we often practice creates a moral dry rot that eats at the very foundation of our democratic ideals and values.   —*Whitney Moore Young, Jr.*

Saying
When people start standing in line to get out of this country instead of standing in line to get in, then we can start worrying about our system.

Joke
• Sign in a corporate boardroom: "Thank heavens this is a free country where you can do exactly as the government pleases."

SOCIALISM

The function of socialism is to raise suffering to a higher level.

—*Norman Mailer*

We should have had socialism already, but for the socialists.

—*George Bernard Shaw (attrib.)*

You can be socially minded without being a socialist.   —*Charles E. Wilson*

"The trouble with socialism," a European observer once remarked, "is socialism. The trouble with capitalism is capitalists."   —*William F. Buckley, Jr.*

Socialism is nothing but capitalism for the lower classes.

—*Oswald Spengler*

Socialism is workable only in heaven, where it isn't needed, and in hell, where they've got it.   —*Cecil Palmer*

Socialism, or any other alternative to private enterprise, would inevitably mean a vast expansion of federal government. General Motors would disappear; it would be lumped with Ford, Chrysler, Boeing, Pan American and so on in a vast Ministry of Transportation. And bureaucracy would conquer all.   —*John W. Gardner*

From each according to his abilities, to each according to his needs.

—*Karl Marx*

Saying
A socialist is someone who has nothing and wants to divide it with you.

Jokes
* Communism: You have two cows. The government takes both, milks them, keeps the milk, and gives you a pint.
  Socialism: The government takes one of your cows and gives it to a neighbor.
  Fascism: The government takes both cows and shoots one of them.
  Nazism: The government takes both cows and shoots you.
  Capitalism: You milk both cows, sell one of the cows, and buy a bull.
  Bureaucracy: The government takes both cows, milks them, and pours the milk down the drain.

* Would it be possible to import socialism into the Sahara?
  —Yes, but after the first five-year plan, the Sahara will have to import sand.

DIPLOMACY AND TACT

What the United States does best is to understand itself. What it does worst is understand others.   —*Carlos Fuentes*

[The] American temptation [is] to believe that foreign policy is a subdivision of psychiatry.   —*Henry A. Kissinger*

Neither conscience nor sanity itself suggests that the United States is, should or could be the global gendarme.   —*Robert S. McNamara*

I thought using the Ayatollah's money to support the Nicaraguan resistance . . . was a neat idea.   —*Oliver North*

The aim of an argument or discussion should not be victory, but progress.

—*Joseph Joubert*

This is the very devilish thing about foreign affairs: they are foreign and will not always conform to our whim.   —*James Reston*

The well bred contradict other people. The wise contradict themselves.

—*Oscar Wilde*

There is nothing more likely to start disagreement among people or countries than an agreement.   —*E. B. White*

It has always been desirable to tell the truth, but seldom if ever necessary.
—*Arthur J. Balfour*

Tact is the art of convincing people that they know more than you do.
—*Raymond Mortimer*

Some people mistake weakness for tact. If they are silent when they ought to speak and so feign an agreement which they do not feel, they call it being tactful. Cowardice would be a much better name.
—*Frank Medlicott*

The ability to get to the verge without getting into the war is the necessary art. If you cannot master it, you inevitably get into war. If you try to run away from it, if you are scared to go to the brink, you are lost.
—*John Foster Dulles*

Watching foreign affairs is sometimes like watching a magician; the eye is drawn to the hand performing the dramatic flourishes, leaving the other hand—the one doing the important job—unnoticed.
—*David K. Shipler*

We shall be judged more by what we do at home than what we preach abroad.
—*John F. Kennedy*

Sincere diplomacy is no more possible than dry water or wooden iron.
—*Joseph Stalin*

To say nothing, especially when speaking, is half the art of diplomacy.
—*Will Durant*

Diplomacy is to do and say the nastiest thing in the nicest way.
—*Isaac Goldberg*

A diplomat is a man who always remembers a woman's birthday but never remembers her age.
—*Robert Frost*

Diplomacy is the art of fishing tranquilly in troubled waters.
—*J. Christopher Herold*

I despise the pleasure of pleasing people whom I despise.
—*Lady Mary Wortley Montagu*

An ambassador is an honest man sent to lie abroad for the good of his country.
—*Henry Wotton*

Living next to you [the United States] is in some ways like sleeping with an elephant. No matter how friendly and even tempered is the beast, if I can call it that, one is affected by every twitch and grunt.
—*Pierre Trudeau, former Canadian prime minister*

You can safely appeal to the United Nations in the comfortable certainty that it will let you down.
—*Conor Cruise O'Brien*

All diplomacy is a continuation of war by other means.
—*Chou En-lai*

You cannot shake hands with a clenched fist.
—*Indira Gandhi*

Diplomats are useful only in fair weather. As soon as it starts to rain, they drown in every drop.
—*Charles de Gaulle*

A diplomat is a person who can tell you to go to hell in such a way that you actually look forward to the trip.
—*Caskie Stinnett*

A diplomat is a man who thinks twice before he says nothing.

—Frederick Sawyer

It takes in reality only one to make a quarrel. It is useless for the sheep to pass resolutions in favour of vegetarianism while the wolf remains of a different opinion.

—Dean William R. Inge

Diplomacy, *n.*, is the art of letting somebody else have your way.

—David Frost

Saying
You catch more flies with honey than you do with vinegar.

Jokes
• Definition of a diplomat: A man who can convince his wife that a fur coat will make her look fat.

• The aging film star was furious when she saw the new photographs. "I look wretched, Clive, positively ancient!" she shrieked at the hapless photographer. "Why, they're nowhere near as good as the last set you took."

"Indeed," he observed tactfully. "It must be because I was ten years younger then."

• The newly appointed ambassador to a tiny Central American country was delighted when her first speech was followed by enthusiastic chants of "Yopapa, yopapa!" from the sizable crowd. In fact, "Yopapa!" rang out after every public appearance, and the ambassador grew more and more gratified—until, stepping out of her limousine in a tiny rural village, she was warned, "Don't step in the yopapa!"

• Interviewing candidates for a position as a shoe salesman, the store manager asked each one how they would handle a customer who had one foot much larger than the other. The fellow who got the job was the one who said he would say, "Why, ma'am, your left foot is even smaller than your right!"

GOVERNMENT

There can be no truer principle than this—that every individual of the community at large has an equal right to the protection of government.

—Alexander Hamilton

That all men are equal is a proposition to which, in ordinary times, no sane individual has ever given his assent.   *—Aldous Huxley*

Nothing appears more surprising to those who consider human affairs with a philosophical eye than the easiness by which the many are governed by the few.

—David Hume

Fear and hope are the two great instruments for the governance of men. . . .

—Jean-Jacques Rousseau

In general, the art of government consists in taking as much money as possible from one class of citizens to give to the other.   *—Voltaire*

If you ever live in a country run by a committee, be on the committee.

—*William Graham Sumner*

Every country has the government it deserves.   —*Joseph de Maistre*

If you're going to sin, sin against God, not the bureaucracy. God will forgive you, but the bureaucracy won't.   —*Admiral Hyman G. Rickover*

Government, even in its best state, is but a necessary evil; in its worst state, an intolerable one.   —*Thomas Paine*

No government can be long secure without a formidable opposition.

—*Benjamin Disraeli*

The less government we have, the better—the fewer laws, and the less confided power.

—*Ralph Waldo Emerson*

. . . *all* government, whatever its forms or pretenses, is a dead weight that paralyzes the free spirit and activities of the masses.   —*Emma Goldman*

The government solution to a problem is usually as bad as the problem.

—*Milton Friedman (attrib.)*

No man is good enough to govern another man without that other's consent.

—*Abraham Lincoln*

There's no trick to being a humorist when you have the whole government working for you.   —*Will Rogers*

You can fool too many of the people too much of the time.

—*James Thurber*

The only good government . . . is a bad one in a hell of a fright.

—*Joyce Cary*

Hell hath no fury like the bureaucrat scorned.   —*Milton Friedman*

We are willing to spend the least amount of money to keep a kid at home, more to put him in a foster home, and the most to institutionalize him.

—*Marian W. Edelman*

Bad administration, to be sure, can destroy good policy; but good administration can never save bad policy.   —*Adlai E. Stevenson*

Bureaucracy defends the status quo long past the time when the quo has lost its status.

—*Laurence J. Peter*

I don't mind how much my ministers talk—as long as they do what I say.

—*Margaret Thatcher*

The stakes . . . are too high for government to be a spectator sport.

—*Barbara Jordan*

It is error alone which needs the support of government. Truth can stand by itself.

—*Thomas Jefferson*

[Congress is] functioning the way the Founding Fathers intended—not very well. They understood that if you move too quickly, our democracy will be less responsible to the majority.   —*Barber Conable, Jr.*

The nine [sic] most terrifying words in the English language are "I'm from the government and I'm here to help you."   —*Ronald Reagan*

In constitutional states, liberty is compensation for heavy taxes; in dictatorships the substitute for liberty is light taxes.   —*Baron de Montesquieu*

The art of governing consists in not allowing men to grow old in their jobs.
     —*Napoleon Bonaparte*

Govern a great nation as you would cook a small fish. (Don't overdo it.)   —*Lao-tzu*

All free governments are managed by the combined wisdom and folly of the people.
     —*James A. Garfield*

It is perfectly true that the government is best which governs least. It is equally true that the government is best that provides the most.   —*Walter Lippmann*

It's a piece of cake until you get to the top. You find you can't stop playing the game the way you have always played it.   —*Richard M. Nixon*

Some of us are like a shovel brigade that follow a parade down Main Street cleaning up.   —*Donald T. Regan*

It is the absolute right of the state to supervise the formation of public opinion.
     —*Joseph Goebbels*

The oppressed are allowed once every few years to decide which particular representatives of the oppressing class are to represent and repress them.
     —*Karl Marx*

There are two periods when Congress does no business: one is before the holidays, and the other after.   —*George D. Prentice*

Fleas can be taught nearly everything a congressman can.   —*Mark Twain*

Our government sprang from and was made for the people—not the people for the government. To them it owes an allegiance; from them it must derive its courage, strength, and wisdom.   —*Andrew Johnson*

The spirit of resistance to government is so valuable on certain occasions that I wish it to be always kept alive. It will often be exercised when wrong but better so than not to be exercised at all. I like a little rebellion now and then. It is like a storm in the atmosphere.   —*Thomas Jefferson*

Britain has invented a new missile. It's called the civil servant—it doesn't work and it can't be fired.   —*Walter Walker*

The single most exciting thing you encounter in government is competence, because it's so rare.   —*Daniel Patrick Moynihan*

A government which robs Peter to pay Paul can always depend on the support of Paul.
     —*George Bernard Shaw*

The biggest lesson I learned from Vietnam is not to trust [our own] government statements. I had no idea until then that you could not rely on [them].
     —*J. William Fulbright*

I learned in business that you had to be very careful when you told somebody that's working for you to do something, because the chances were very high he'd do it. In government, you don't have to worry about that. —*George P. Shultz*

The state has no business in the bedrooms of the nation.
—*Pierre Trudeau, appealing for revised divorce laws in Canada*

Sayings

Government should not interfere with any business capable of failing by itself.

Most people would be glad to tend their own business if the government would give it back.

Government never shrinks.

The people's government is always run by the government's people.

Government gets the best people—one way or another.

Jokes

• He who builds a better mousetrap will soon find the government spending $850,000 to build a better mouse.

• Guidelines for Bureaucrats: 1) When in charge, ponder. 2) When in trouble, delegate. 3) When in doubt, mumble. —*James H. Boren*

• My dog can bark like a congressman, fetch like an aide, beg like a press secretary, and play dead like a receptionist when the phone rings. —*Gerald P. Solomon*

• Working for a federal agency was like trying to dislodge a prune skin from the roof of the mouth. More enterprise went into the job than could be justified by the result.
—*Caskie Stinnett*

• Trying to make things work in government is sometimes like trying to sew a button on a custard pie. —*Admiral Hyman G. Rickover*

• When they call the roll in the Senate, the senators do not know whether to answer "present" or "not guilty." —*Theodore Roosevelt*

THE MILITARY

I think women are too valuable to be in combat. —*Caspar W. Weinberger*

To enlist native help . . . treat natives like human beings. . . . Respect personal property, especially their women. —*1969 U.S. Army Field Manual*

They talk about conscription as a democratic institution. Yes; so is a cemetery.
—*Meyer London*

Military intelligence is a contradiction in terms. —*Groucho Marx (attrib.)*

It is impossible to give a soldier a good education without making him a deserter. His natural foe is the government that drills him. —*Henry David Thoreau*

I am convinced that the best service a retired general can perform is to turn in his tongue along with his suit and to mothball his opinions.

—*General Omar N. Bradley*

Discipline is the soul of an army.   —*George Washington*

"Resource-constrained environment" [are] fancy Pentagon words that mean there isn't enough money to go around.   —*General John W. Vessey, Jr.*

Military justice is to justice what military music is to music.

—*Georges Clemenceau*

The first virtue in a soldier is endurance of fatigue; courage is only the second virtue.

—*Napoleon Bonaparte*

Soldiers ought more to fear their general than their enemy.

—*Michel Eyquem de Montaigne*

When I first went into the active army, you could tell someone to move a chair across the room—now you have to tell him why.   —*Major Robert Lembke*

The professional military mind is by necessity an inferior and unimaginative mind; no man of high intellectual quality would willingly imprison his gifts in such a calling.

—*H. G. Wells*

The atomic bomb will not go off—and I speak as an expert in explosives.
—*Admiral William D. Leahy (to President Truman, 1945)*

No nation ever had an army large enough to guarantee it against attack in time of peace or ensure it victory in time of war.   —*Calvin Coolidge*

Cogito ergo boom.   —*Susan Sontag*

Praise the Lord and pass the ammunition.

—*Chaplain Howell M. Forgy, at Pearl Harbor*

Retreat, hell! We're just advancing in another direction.
—*Marine General P. O. Smith, during the Korean War*

Saying
There are three ways of doing it: the right way, the wrong way, and the army way.

Jokes
• New recruit: "Colonel Santer always says, 'Never take a drink when you feel as if you need one' and old Nettelfield says, 'Never take a drink except when you need one.' Now what is a fellow going to do?"
Seasoned soldier: "Follow both rules, and you'll be all right."

• There's this to recommend army life: you never have to decide what to wear.

• Frankly, instead of considering it as the armed forces, I think of it as prep school for the American Legion.

• Lieutenant Bremmer was given a twenty-four-hour pass on the condition that he get a haircut before leaving the base. And on his way to the barber, he was to drop off the Commander's golf clubs at the officers' mess.

Just as he was entering the mess, the soldier encountered the Regimental CO, who inquired, "Off to play golf?"

"No, sir," replied the soldier, "going to get my hair cut."

He spent the weekend confined to barracks for insubordination.

POWER

We must guard against the acquisition of unwarranted influence . . . by the military-industrial complex. The potential for the disastrous rise of misplaced power exists and will persist.   —*Dwight D. Eisenhower*

The secret of the demagogue is to make himself as stupid as his audience so that they believe they are as clever as he.   —*Karl Kraus*

Men of power have no time to read; yet the men who do not read are unfit for power.
                                                        —*Michael Foot*

Ecological devastation is the excrement, so to speak, of man's power worship.
                                                        —*Ernest Becker*

Power without a nation's confidence is nothing.   —*Catherine the Great*

Art is interested in life at the moment when the ray of power is passing through it.
                                                        —*Boris Pasternak*

Knowledge is power if you know it about the right person.
                                                        —*Ethel Watts Mumford*

Power is not merely shouting aloud. Power is to act positively with all the components of power.   —*Gamal Abdel Nasser*

Nearly all men can stand adversity, but if you want to test a man's character, give him power.   —*Abraham Lincoln*

He who loves the world as his body may be entrusted with the empire.
                                                        —*Lao-tzu*

Lack of something to feel important about is almost the greatest tragedy a man may have.   —*Arthur E. Morgan*

The urge to save humanity is almost always a false front for the urge to rule.
                                                        —*H. L. Mencken*

Power is the ultimate aphrodisiac.   —*Henry A. Kissinger*

He who has his thumb on the purse has the power.   —*Otto von Bismarck*

Power tends to corrupt, and absolute power corrupts absolutely.
                                                        —*Lord Acton*

Power corrupts, but lack of power corrupts absolutely.
                                                        —*Adlai E. Stevenson*

Being powerful is like being a lady. If you have to tell people you are, you ain't.
                                                        —*Jesse Carr*

Everyone has an influence on public affairs if he will take the trouble to exert it.

—*Calvin Coolidge*

You can get much further with a kind word and a gun than you can with a kind word alone.   —*Al Capone*

I have a fantasy where Ted Turner is elected president but refuses because he doesn't want to give up power.   —*Arthur C. Clarke*

Gentlemen: You have undertaken to cheat me. I won't sue you, for the law is too slow. I'll ruin you.   —*Cornelius Vanderbilt, in a letter to a competitor*

Knowledge is power.

—*Francis Bacon*

Sayings
It's not what you know, it's who you know.

Power to the people.

Jokes
* Important Guest: "Could I have another piece of chicken, please?"
  Server: "I'm sorry, only one piece per person."
  Important Guest: "But I'm starving."
  Server: "I'm sorry, sir."
  Important Guest: "Do you know who I *am*? I'm the guest of honor!"
  Server: "Do you know who *I* am? I'm the person in charge of the chicken."

* The boss, Ms. Bennett, always scheduled the weekly staff meetings for 4:30 on Fridays. When one of the employees finally got up the nerve to ask why, she explained, "I'll tell you why—I've learned that's the only time of the week when none of you seem to want to argue with me."

* Definition of a power struggle: When your boss has the power and you have the struggle.

PROPAGANDA

All animals are equal, but some animals are more equal than others.

—*George Orwell*

It is the absolute right of the state to supervise the formation of public opinion.

—*Joseph Goebbels*

Doublethink means the power of holding two contradictory beliefs in one's mind simultaneously, and accepting both of them.   —*George Orwell*

The propagandist's purpose is to make one set of people forget that certain other sets of people are human.   —*Aldous Huxley*

Our program necessarily includes the propaganda of atheism.

—*V. I. Lenin*

You can fool too many of the people too much of the time.

—*James Thurber*

There isn't any way for the people of Nicaragua to find out what's happening in
Nicaragua.   —*Elliot Abrams, announcing U.S. aid to Nicaraguan rebels for new anti-*
Sandinista radio station

We must never forget that art is not a form of propaganda; it is a form of truth.
—*John F. Kennedy*

He who has a message and no propaganda will not get very far.
—*Joel Augustus Rogers*

Why is propaganda so much more successful when it stirs up hatred than when it tries
to stir up friendly feeling?   —*Bertrand Russell*

Propaganda is the art of persuading others of what you don't believe yourself.
—*Abba Eban*

Never believe anything until it has been officially denied.

—*Claud Cockburn*

Sayings

Propaganda can often be deflated by wit.

In the modern world, propaganda is as important as ammunition.

Wars are now fought for the hearts and minds of nations.

Jokes

• Slogans subject to graffiti often take on a whole new meaning. For example:
    —"Join the Military, see foreign lands, and meet interesting people" was turned
into "Join the Military, see foreign lands, meet interesting people, and kill them."
    —"Support the right to bear arms" was turned into "Support the right to arm
bears."
    —"Make love, not war" was turned into "Make love, not war, but be ready for
both."

• At an international engineering conference a Russian asked the man seated next to
him where he hailed from.
    "Why, I'm from the greatest country on earth," replied the American proudly.
    "Funny," commented his puzzled companion, "you don't sound Russian."

THE PUBLIC

Consider the public. . . . Never fear it nor despise it. Charm it, interest it, stimulate
it, shock it now and then if you must, make it laugh, make it cry, but above all . . .
never, never bore the living hell out of it.   —*Noel Coward*

The public is like a piano.   —*Al Capp*

What the crowd requires is mediocrity of the highest order.

—*Antoine-Auguste Préault*

Learn from the masses, and then teach them.   —*Mao Tse-tung*

To succeed in chaining the multitude you must seem to wear the same fetters.

—*Voltaire*

Since the masses are always eager to believe something, for their benefit nothing is so easy to arrange as facts.   —*Charles-Maurice de Talleyrand*

I love the people with their straightforward minds. It's just that their smell brings on my migraine.   —*Bertolt Brecht*

Ten persons who speak make more noise than ten thousand who are silent.

—*Napoleon Bonaparte*

It is an easy and vulgar thing to please the mob, and no very arduous task to astonish them.   —*Charles Caleb Colton*

The acquisition of knowledge is the mission of research, the transmission of knowledge is the mission of teaching, and the application of knowledge is the mission of public service.   —*James A. Perkins*

I do not know the method of drawing up an indictment against an whole people.

—*Edmund Burke*

God must have loved the common people because he made so many of them.

—*Abraham Lincoln (attrib.)*

Blessed are the common people. God loves them, that is why he made millions of them.   —*Nnamdi Azikiwe*

Just remember this, Mr. Potter, that this rabble you're talking about . . . they do most of the working and paying and living and dying in this community.

—*George Bailey, in* It's a Wonderful Life, *screenplay by Frances Goodrich, Albert Hackett, and Frank Capra*

Sayings
Everybody knows better than anybody.

What the public thinks depends on what the public hears.

Joke
• You give the people what they want, they'll turn out.

—*A rival producer, observing the crowd at Louis B. Mayer's funeral*

WAR

You will kill ten of our men, and we will kill one of yours, and in the end it will be you who tire of it.   —*Ho Chi Minh*

War never leaves a nation where it found it.   —*Edmund Burke*

I look upon the whole world as my fatherland, and every war has to me the horror of a family feud.   —*Helen Keller*

It is forbidden to kill, therefore all murderers are punished unless they kill in large number and to the sound of trumpets.   —*Voltaire*

The grass-roots support is not there. And we have to prevent it from developing again.
—*Brigadier General Jack Farris, about the Vietnam War*

Terrorism has become the systematic weapon of a war that knows no borders or seldom has a face.
—*Jacques Chirac*

War is a poor chisel to carve out tomorrows.
—*Martin Luther King, Jr.*

Wars of nations are fought to change maps. But wars on poverty are fought to map change.
—*Muhammad Ali*

The spirit of war can never be destroyed by all the butcheries and persecutions the human mind can invent.
—*William Whipper*

Peace is the exhaustion of strife, and is only secure in her triumphs in being in instant readiness for war. . . .
—*Mifflin Wistar Gibbs*

A life without fighting is a dead sea in the universal organism.
—*Joaquim Maria Machado de Assis*

Make wars unprofitable and you make them impossible.
—*A. Philip Randolph*

Violence seldom accomplishes permanent and desired results. Herein lies the futility of war.
—*A. Philip Randolph*

War is never fatal but always lost.
—*Gertrude Stein*

Ambition is the grand enemy of all peace.
—*John Cowper Powys*

Trees, though they are cut and lopped, grow up again quickly, but if men are destroyed, it is not easy to get them again.
—*Pericles*

You can't say civilizations don't advance . . . for in every war they kill you a new way.
—*Will Rogers*

The law is silent during war.
—*Cicero*

Once more unto the breach, dear friends, once more; or close the wall up with our English dead.
—*William Shakespeare*

I have nothing to offer but blood, toil, tears, and sweat.
—*Winston Churchill*

War is the business of barbarians.
—*Napoleon Bonaparte*

God is always on the side of the heaviest battalions.
—*Voltaire*

The right of conquest has no foundation other than the right of the strongest.
—*Jean-Jacques Rousseau*

How are the mighty fallen in the midst of the battle!
—*2 Samuel 1:25*

Ideas are the great warriors of the world, and a war that has no ideas behind it is simply brutality.
—*James A. Garfield*

Soldiers win battles and generals get the credit.
—*Napoleon Bonaparte*

Every gun that is made, every warship launched, every rocket fired, signifies in the final sense a theft from those who hunger and are not fed, those who are cold and are not clothed.
—*Dwight D. Eisenhower*

. . . war can only be abolished through war, and in order to get rid of the gun it is necessary to take up the gun.   —*Mao Tse-tung*

Frankly, I'd like to see the government get out of war altogether and leave the whole field to private industry.   —*Joseph Heller*

In peace the sons bury their fathers and in war the fathers bury their sons.
—*Francis Bacon*

Older men declare war. But it is youth that must fight and die.
—*Herbert Hoover*

It is well that war is so terrible—we would grow too fond of it.
—*General Robert E. Lee*

It is always easy to begin a war, but very difficult to stop one, since its beginning and end are not under the control of the same man.   —*Sallust, first century* B.C.

The quickest way of ending a war is to lose it.   —*George Orwell*

There is many a boy here today who looks on war as all glory, but boys, it is all hell.
—*General William T. Sherman*

. . . it is all too obvious that if we do not abolish war on this earth, then surely, one day, war will abolish us from the earth.   —*Harry S Truman*

Nothing in life is so exhilarating as to be shot at without result.
—*Winston Churchill*

History is filled with wars which everybody knew would never happen.
—*Enoch Powell*

It is not merely cruelty that leads men to love war, it is excitement.
—*Henry Ward Beecher*

A general and a bit of shooting . . . takes your mind off the cost of living.
—*Brendan Behan*

But that was war. Just about all he could find in its favor was that it paid well and liberated children from the pernicious influence of their parents.
—*Joseph Heller*

War may make a fool of man, but it by no means degrades him; on the contrary, it tends to exalt him, and its net effects are much like those of motherhood on women.
—*H. L. Mencken*

The nation which forgets its defenders will be itself forgotten.
—*Calvin Coolidge*

My yesterdays walk with me. They keep step, they are gray faces that peer over my shoulder.   —*William Golding, on the influence of his wartime naval service*

A hand on your cock is more moral—and more fun—than a finger on the trigger.
—*Lawrence Lipton*

There are no "white" or "colored" signs on the foxholes or graveyards of battle.
—*John F. Kennedy*

In this age when there can be no losers in peace and no victors in war, we must recognize the obligation to match national strength with national restraint.

—*Lyndon B. Johnson*

I have a rendezvous with Death at some disputed barricade.   —*Alan Seeger*

You're not here to die for your country. You're here to make those so-and-so's die for theirs.   —*General John H. (Iron Mike) Michaelis, in Korea*

Sayings

A war without headquarters is an expedition.   —*West African saying*

Self-defense is not fear.   —*East African saying*

War ends nothing.   —*Central African saying*

In the next war there will be no rear echelon.

Jokes

• The missionary located a primitive tribe of cannibals and settled into trying to convert them to Western ways of thought and behavior. He spent many evenings around the fire conversing with the cannibal chieftain, who was considered quite a sage and reminisced at length about his many victorious campaigns and all the people he had eaten in the process.

"Ah, but our wars are fought for a higher purpose," expounded the missionary. "For religious freedom, for democracy, for truth . . ."

The cannibal nodded. "You must eat many, many people," he commented admiringly.

"Oh, no!" The missionary was shocked. "We don't eat humans."

"Then," the chieftain pointed out, "you have no reason to kill each other."

• Private Richie was a brave soldier, but all his worst fears about combat came true when he stepped on a land mine and woke in a hospital to see his lower legs a mass of plaster and gauze. "Doc, what's the story?" he asked anxiously.

"Private, I have some good news and some bad news," the doctor gravely informed him. "The bad news is that both your legs had to be amputated below the knee.

Richie groaned. "And the good news?"

"See the fellow in that bed across the aisle?" asked the doctor brightly.

Richie nodded.

"He wants to buy your boots!"

part three

The Community

T H E   A R T S

ART

We look too much to museums. The sun coming up in the morning is enough.
—*Romare Bearden*

Art is like a border of flowers along the course of civilization.
—*Lincoln Steffens*

Art for the sake of art itself is an idle sentence. Art for the sake of truth, for the sake of what is beautiful and good—that is the creed I seek.   —*George Sand*

I like to know what a picture represents without being told by the artist. Ladies with no mouth and six arms; gentlemen with eyes in their stomachs and legs of grand pianos; landscapes with wardrobe trunks overflowing with human limbs and peopled by alarm clocks with black silk-stockinged feet, only make me laugh, and anyone who can take them seriously has my undying admiration.   —*Hermione Gingold*

One cannot remain the same. Art is a mirror which should show many reflections, and the artist should not always show the same face, or the face becomes a mask.
—*Yvette Guilbert*

We must carry the arts to the people, not wait for the people to come to the arts.
—*Arthur Mitchell*

Art . . . cannot be an egotistic activity engulfed in the limits of pure creation, free of all human contamination.   —*Nicolas Guillen*

Black art has always existed. It just hasn't been looked for in the right places.
—*Romare Bearden*

He knows all about art, but he doesn't know what he likes.
—*James Thurber*

The greatness of art is not to find what is common but what is unique.
—*Isaac Bashevis Singer*

It is very good advice to believe only what an artist does, rather that what he says about his work.   —*David Hockney*

All art is a revolt against man's fate.   —*André Malraux*

Art for art's sake makes no more sense than gin for gin's sake.
—*W. Somerset Maugham*

Art flourishes where there is a sense of adventure.

—*Alfred North Whitehead*

I shut my eyes in order to see.

—*Paul Gauguin*

In a work of art the intellect asks questions; it does not answer them.

—*Friedrich Hebbel*

Art is the signature of civilizations.

—*Jean Sibelius*

Art is interested in life at the moment when the ray of power is passing through it.

—*Boris Pasternak*

The new job of art is to sit on the wall and get more expensive.

—*Robert Hughes*

Life is very nice, but it lacks form. It's the aim of art to give it some.

—*Jean Anouilh*

In art, as in life, instinct is enough.

—*Anatole France*

All day long I add up columns of figures and make everything balance. I come home. I sit down. I look at a Kandinsky and it's wonderful! It doesn't mean a damn thing!

—*Solomon Guggenheim*

Less is more.

—*Ludwig Mies van der Rohe*

I don't believe less is more. I believe that less is less, fat fat, thin thin, and enough is enough.

—*Stanley Elkin*

Art is a jealous mistress.

—*Ralph Waldo Emerson*

We must never forget that art is not a form of propaganda; it is a form of truth.

—*John F. Kennedy*

Art must be parochial in the beginning to become cosmopolitan in the end.

—*George Moore*

The essence of all art is to have pleasure in giving pleasure.

—*Mikhail Baryshnikov*

I think of art, at its most significant, as a DEW line, a Distant Early Warning system that can always be relied on to tell the old culture what is beginning to happen to it.

—*Marshall McLuhan*

Art, like morality, consists in drawing the line somewhere.

—*G. K. Chesterton*

If you ask me what I came to do in this world, I, an artist, I will answer you: "I am here to live out loud."

—*Emile Zola*

A guilty conscience needs to confess. A work of art is a confession.

—*Albert Camus*

Life without industry is guilt, industry without art is brutality.

—*John Ruskin*

Art is essentially the affirmation, the blessing, and the deification of existence.

—*Friedrich Wilhelm Nietzsche*

Art imitates nature in this: not to dare is to dwindle.

—*John Updike*

Art is not a pastime but a priesthood.

—*Jean Cocteau*

Religion and art spring from the same root and are close kin. Economics and art are strangers.   —*Willa Cather*

There is an inherent truth which must be disengaged from the outward appearance of the object to be represented. This is the only truth that matters. . . . Exactitude is not truth.   —*Henri Matisse*

The people who make art their business are mostly imposters.

—*Pablo Picasso*

Art is the most intense mode of individualism that the world has known.

—*Oscar Wilde*

You must have the devil in you to succeed in any of the arts.   —*Voltaire*

One must act in painting as in life, directly.   —*Pablo Picasso*

Art teaches nothing, except the significance of life.   —*Henry Miller*

Painting isn't an aesthetic operation; it's a form of magic designed as a mediator between this strange hostile world and us, a way of seizing the power by giving form to our terrors as well as our desires.   —*Pablo Picasso*

You use a glass mirror to see your face; you use works of art to see your soul.

—*George Bernard Shaw*

The work of art may have a moral effect, but to demand moral purpose from the artist is to make him ruin his work.   —*Johann Wolfgang von Goethe*

Without art, the crudeness of reality would make the world unbearable.

—*George Bernard Shaw*

The most beautiful thing we can experience is the mysterious. It is the source of all true art and science.   —*Albert Einstein*

Art is meant to disturb.   —*Georges Braque*

All of the arts, poetry, music, ritual, the visible arts, the theatre, must singly and together create the most comprehensive art of all, a humanized society, and its masterpiece, free man.   —*Bernard Berenson*

If art is to nourish the roots of our culture, society must set the artist free to follow his vision wherever it takes him.   —*John F. Kennedy*

True art selects and paraphrases, but seldom gives a verbatim translation.

—*Thomas Bailey Aldrich*

One of the best things about paintings is their silence—which prompts reflection and random reverie.   —*Mark Stevens, decrying guided tours by headphone*

I think art is a great big river that just flows and it's been flowing for thousands of years. . . . Art doesn't win wars, but it's the only thing that remains after the civilizations go. Nobody knows much about the politics of certain Egyptian dynasties but people remember the art, the great things that were created.

—*Robert Scull*

Art hath an enemy called ignorance.   —*Ben Jonson*

Sayings

Art lies in concealing art.

Art may be regarded as a luxury, but to the artist, it is a necessity.

Art is what separates man from beast.

Jokes

• The penniless artist was cornered by her landlord, who demanded several months past rent. "Just think," she pleaded, "someday tourists will be pointing at this building, and saying 'The great abstract painter Susan Krechevsky used to live here.' "

  The landlord shrugged. "And if you don't pay up, they can come by tomorrow and say that."

• I saw some things at the auction labeled Art Objects: considering what they looked like, I'd object too.

• A sad thing happened at the museum the other day. They replaced that statue *The Thinker*—with a computer.

• Abstract art: A product of the untalented, sold by the unprincipled to the utterly bewildered.

—*Al Capp*

ARTISTS

An artist is his own fault.

—*John O'Hara*

An artist is a man of action, whether he creates a personality, invents an expedient, or finds the issue of a complicated situation.

—*Joseph Conrad*

Every artist writes his own autobiography.

—*Havelock Ellis*

The artist, like the God of the creation, remains within or behind or beyond or above his handiwork, invisible, refined out of existence, indifferent, paring his fingernails.

—*James Joyce*

Great artists are modest almost as seldom as they are faithful to their wives.

—*H. L. Mencken*

The aim of every artist is to arrest motion, which is life, by artificial means and hold it fixed so that a hundred years later, when a stranger looks at it, it moves again since it is life.

—*William Faulkner*

The great artists of the world are never puritans, and seldom even ordinarily respectable.

—*H. L. Mencken*

An artist should be well read in the best books, and thoroughly high bred, both in heart and bearing. In a word, he should be fit for the best society, and should keep out of it.

—*John Ruskin*

The artist is the seismograph of his age.

—*Robert W. Corrigan*

Every time an artist dies, part of the vision of mankind passes with him.
—*Franklin D. Roosevelt*

The refusal to rest content, the willingness to risk excess on behalf of one's obsessions, is what distinguishes artists from entertainers, and what makes some artists adventurers on behalf of us all.   —*John Updike*

I never practice; I always play.   —*Wanda Landowska*

Copy nature and you infringe on the work of our Lord. Interpret nature and you are an artist.   —*Jacques Lipchitz*

Every child is an artist. The problem is how to remain an artist once he grows up.
—*Pablo Picasso*

The first quality that is needed [in an artist] is audacity.
—*Winston Churchill*

Aesthetics is to the artist what ornithology is to the birds.
—*Barnett Newman*

Artists must be sacrificed to their art. Like bees, they just put their lives into the sting they give.   —*Ralph Waldo Emerson*

In other countries, art and literature are left to a lot of shabby bums living in attics and feeding on booze and spaghetti, but in America the successful writer or picture-painter is indistinguishable from any other decent business man.
—*Sinclair Lewis*

Anyone who sees and paints a sky green and pastures blue ought to be sterilized.
—*Adolf Hitler*

The artistic temperament is a disease that afflicts amateurs.
—*G. K. Chesterton*

He always did have that "touch of madness" that marks the true artists and breaks the hearts of young girls from fine homes.   —*Robert Crumb*

The artist is a lucky dog. . . . In any community of a thousand souls there will be nine hundred doing the work, ninety doing well, nine doing good, and one lucky dog painting or writing about the other nine hundred and ninety-nine.
—*Tom Stoppard*

No great artist ever sees things as they really are. If he did he would cease to be an artist.   —*Oscar Wilde*

Immature artists imitate. Mature artists steal.   —*Lionel Trilling*

Journeys, like artists, are born and not made. A thousand differing circumstances contribute to them, few of them willed or determined by the will—whatever we may think.   —*Lawrence Durrell*

One cannot remain the same. Art is a mirror which should show many reflections, and the artist should not always show the same face, or the face becomes a mask.
—*Yvette Guilbert*

Saying
Often they hang the painting when they should hang the artist instead.

Jokes
- An artist who'd had considerable success selling his work to hotel chains was asked his secret. "Simple," he admitted cheerfully. "I make all my paintings too big to fit in a suitcase."

- I was on my way to becoming an artist, but they booted me out of drawing class when I wanted to trace the nudes.

T H E   S T A G E

ACTORS AND ACTING

I think acting is the biggest drag of all time for a girl.
—*Jackie Collins*

I got all the schooling any actress needs. That is, I learned to write well enough to sign contracts.
—*Hermione Gingold*

Comedians on the stage are invariably suicidal when they get home.
—*Elsa Lanchester*

Lead the audience by the nose to the thought.
—*Laurence Olivier*

On the stage he was natural, simple, affecting; 'twas only that when he was off he was acting.
—*Oliver Goldsmith*

When an actor has money he doesn't send letters, he sends telegrams.
—*Anton Chekhov*

If you really want to help the American theater, don't be an actress, dahling. Be an audience.
—*Tallulah Bankhead*

Playing Shakespeare is so tiring. You never get a chance to sit down unless you're a king.
—*Josephine Hull*

Acting is merely the art of keeping a large group of people from coughing.
—*Ralph Richardson*

Know your lines and don't bump into the furniture.
—*Spencer Tracy*

Acting is all about honesty. If you can fake that, you've got it made.
—*George Burns (attrib.)*

Your motivation is your pay packet on Friday. Now get on with it.
—*Noel Coward (attrib.)*

Acting is standing up naked and turning around slowly.
—*Rosalind Russell*

Some of the greatest love affairs I've known involved one actor, unassisted.
—*Wilson Mizner (attrib.)*

Anyone who works is a fool. I don't work—I merely inflict myself on the public.
—*Robert Morley (attrib.)*

After my screen test, the director clapped his hands gleefully and yelled, "She can't talk! She can't act! She's sensational!"
—*Ava Gardner*

Sayings

An actor is like a cigar; the more you puff him the smaller he gets.

Don't quit your day job.

Jokes

• An aspiring actor called home to announce with great pride that he'd been cast in an off-Broadway play. "It's a real opportunity, Dad," he said, "I play this guy who's been married for twenty-five years."

"That's great, son," enthused his father. "And one of these days you'll work up to a speaking part."

• You should be on the stage . . . the next one leaves in five minutes.

• How many actors does it take to change a light bulb?
   —One hundred. One to change the bulb, and ninety-nine to say, "I could've done that."

THEATER

The theater is so endlessly fascinating because it's so accidental. It's so much like life.
                                                                            —Arthur Miller

Consider the public. . . . Never fear it nor despise it. Charm it, interest it, stimulate it, shock it now and then if you must, make it laugh, make it cry, but above all . . . never, never bore the living hell out of it.   *—Noel Coward*

The first rule of the theater—give the best lines to yourself.

                                                                            —Robert Bloch

It's one of the tragic ironies of the theater that only one man in it can count on steady work—the night watchman.   *—Tallulah Bankhead*

Show me a congenital eavesdropper with the instincts of a Peeping Tom and I will show you the makings of a dramatist.   *—Kenneth Tynan*

Judge not the play before the play is done: her plot hath many changes. . . .
                                                                            —Francis Quarles

The business of the dramatist is to keep out of sight and let nothing appear but his characters.   *—Thomas Babington Macaulay*

The play's the thing wherein I'll catch the conscience of the king.
                                                                            —William Shakespeare

All the world's a stage and all the men and women merely players: they have their exits and their entrances; and one man in his time plays many parts. . . .
                                                                            —William Shakespeare

It is an extremely difficult thing to put on the stage anything which runs contrary to the opinions of a large body of people.   *—George Bernard Shaw*

Whoever condemns the theater is an enemy of his country.   *—Voltaire*

Opening night: The night before the play is ready to open.

—*George Jean Nathan*

Sayings

There's a broken heart for every light on Broadway.

Real life isn't necessarily good theater.

The show must go on.

The stars may be on stage, but the audience is king.

Jokes

• A showman who'd been asked for a definition of theater gave the following example: "When a person falls down in the middle of the sidewalk and a crowd gathers around, that's an event," he explained. "But when someone falls down in the middle of a stage, and people pay money to see it, that's theater."

• Danny Kaye noted the difference between comedy and tragedy in Russian drama. In both, everybody dies; but in the comedy, they die happy.

DANCE

Dance is the only art of which we ourselves are the stuff of which it is made.

—*Ted Shawn*

The universe lies before you on the floor, in the mysterious bodies of your dancers, in your mind. From this voyage no one returns poor or weary.

—*Agnes de Mille*

Dancing is the loftiest, the most moving, the most beautiful of the arts, because it is no mere translation or abstraction from life; it is life itself.   —*Havelock Ellis*

I would believe only in a God that knows how to dance.

—*Friedrich Wilhelm Nietzsche*

We have to prove beyond the shadow of a doubt that it is talent and training, not color, that makes a ballet dancer.   —*Arthur Mitchell*

Movement never lies.   —*Martha Graham*

Dance is the landscape of man's soul.   —*Martha Graham*

Sayings

Dance like corks upon the water.

Dance like popcorn over a hot fire.

Joke

• Dancing is the perpendicular expression of a horizontal desire.

AUDIENCES

I see their souls, and I hold them in my hands, and because I love them they weigh nothing.   *—Pearl Bailey, on audiences*

The best audience is intelligent, well educated, and a little drunk.
—Alben W. Barkley

If they liked you, they didn't applaud—they just let you live.   *—Bob Hope*

I am perfectly happy to believe that nobody likes us but the public.
—Rudolf Bing, director of the Metropolitan Opera

I never failed to convince an audience that the best thing they could do was to go away.   *—Thomas Love Peacock*

Every crowd has a silver lining.   *—P. T. Barnum*

If you really want to help the American theater, don't be an actress, dahling. Be an audience.   *—Tallulah Bankhead*

A painter paints his pictures on canvas. But musicians paint their pictures on silence. We provide the music, and you provide the silence.
—Leopold Stokowski, reprimanding a talkative audience

The play was a great success but the audience was a failure.
—Oscar Wilde

Saying
The stars may be on stage, but the audience is king.

Jokes
- Now they've got a stereo that gives real concert-hall sound. Every two minutes it coughs and rattles a program.

- The great pianist Liszt was asked by Nicholas I of Russia to perform at court. Right in the middle of his first sonata, however, Liszt noticed the czar talking to an aide. Irritated, he continued to play, but when Nicholas continued to converse, the composer finally put his hands in his lap.
   The czar swiftly sent an aide to inquire as to the reason for the interruption. "When the czar speaks, everyone should be silent," said Liszt.
   There were no further interruptions.

THE MOVIES

I dream for a living.   *—Steven Spielberg*

The movies enable an actor not only to act but also to sit down in the theater and clap for himself.   *—Will Rogers*

There's nothing funnier than the human animal.   *—Walt Disney*

An actor entering through the door, you've got nothing. But if he enters through the window, you've got a situation.   *—Billy Wilder*

Movies are fun, but they're not a cure for cancer.   —*Warren Beatty*

If my fanny squirms, it's bad. If my fanny doesn't squirm, it's good. It's as simple as that.   —*Harry Cohn*

I didn't know the whole world was wired to Harry Cohn's ass.

—*Herman Manckiewicz*

Most arts appeal to the mature. This art appeals at once to every class: mature, immature, developed, undeveloped, law abiding, criminal. . . .
        —*Production Code of the Motion Picture Association of America, early 1960s*

Over in Hollywood they almost made a great picture, but they caught it just in time.
                                    —*Wilson Mizner*

Hollywood was born schizophrenic. For seventy-five years it has been both a town and a state of mind, an industry and an art form.   —*Richard Corliss*

You can take all the sincerity in Hollywood, place it in the navel of a fruit fly, and still have room enough for three caraway seeds and a producer's heart.

—*Fred Allen*

No one ever went broke in Hollywood underestimating the intelligence of the public.
                                    —*Elsa Maxwell*

Hollywood—an emotional Detroit.   —*Lillian Gish*

They know only one word of more than one syllable here, and that is *fillum*.
                                    —*Louis Sherwin*

Sayings
America's most popular export.

The mythology of modern times.

Movie theaters are the cathedrals of the twentieth century.

Everything's always all right at the movies.

The only "ism" Hollywood believes in is plagiarism.

Read the book, see the movie.

The Silver Screen.

Jokes
• An intellectual in Hollywood is anyone who can read freeway signs without moving his lips.

• In one of his pictures Jimmy Cagney shoved a grapefruit into a girl's face, and it was considered shocking. Now it's considered a diet.

• An adult Western is where the hero still kisses his horse at the end, only now he worries about it.   —*Milton Berle*

M   U   S   I   C

COMPOSERS

In order to compose, all you need to do is remember a tune that nobody else has
thought of.
                                                              —*Robert Schumann*

Keep it simple, keep it sexy, keep it sad.

                                              —*Mitch Miller, on popular music*

You compose because you want to somehow summarize in some permanent form your
most basic feelings about being alive, to set down . . . some sort of permanent
statement about the way it feels to live now, today. So that when it's all gone, people
will be able to go to the artwork of the time and get some sense of what it felt like to
be alive in this year.
                                                              —*Aaron Copland*

Ah, Mozart! He was happily married—but his wife wasn't.   —*Victor Borge*

I like Beethoven, especially the poems.   —*Ringo Starr*

Music is not written in red, white, and blue. It is written in the heart's blood of the
composer.
                                                              —*Nellie Melba*

Wagner's music is better than it sounds.   —*Mark Twain*

Saying
Composers can *see* music.

Jokes
- The great pianist Liszt was asked by Nicholas I of Russia to perform at court. Right
  in the middle of his first sonata, however, Liszt noticed the czar talking to an aide.
  Irritated, he continued to play, but when Nicholas continued to converse, the
  composer finally put his hands in his lap.
      The czar swiftly sent an aide to inquire as to the reason for the interruption.
  "When the czar speaks, everyone should be silent," said Liszt.
      There were no further interruptions.

- At a party to celebrate the success of the musical *Showboat*, Mrs. Kern, the wife of
  the composer, was approached by a gushing fan. "And to think your husband wrote
  that fabulous song 'Old Man River'! It's absolutely my favorite—"
      "No, you've got it wrong," interrupted Mrs. Hammerstein. "*My* husband wrote 'Old
  Man River.' Her husband wrote, 'Dum dum *dum*-dum, da-dum dum *dum*-dum . . .' "

• What's Beethoven doing now?
  —Decomposing!

MUSIC AND MUSICIANS

To produce music is also in a sense to produce children.

—*Friedrich Wilhelm Nietzsche*

When people hear good music, it makes them homesick for something they never had, and never will have.   —*Edgar Watson Howe*

If I don't practice one day, I know it; two days, the critics know it; three days, the public knows it.   —*Jascha Heifetz*

Nothing soothes me more after a long and maddening course of pianoforte recitals than to sit and have my teeth drilled.   —*George Bernard Shaw*

Music is the universal language of mankind.

—*Henry Wadsworth Longfellow*

Jazz will endure as long as people hear it through their feet instead of their brains.

—*John Philip Sousa*

Song is the pen of the soul.   —*Rabbi Chaim Drizin*

Show me an orchestra that likes its conductor and I'll show you a lousy conductor.

—*Goddard Lieberson*

If music could be translated into human speech, it would no longer need to exist.

—*Ned Rorem*

Keep it simple, keep it sexy, keep it sad.   —*Mitch Miller*

Music and silence . . . combine strongly because music is done with silence, and silence is full of music.   —*Marcel Marceau*

Chaos is a friend of mine.

—*Bob Dylan, defining his musical style in the mid-1960s*

Playing "bop" is like playing Scrabble with all the vowels missing.

—*Duke Ellington*

The popular song is America's greatest ambassador.   —*Sammy Cahn*

I don't know anything about music—in my line, you don't have to.

—*Elvis Presley*

I can hold a note as long as the Chase Manhattan Bank.   —*Ethel Merman*

Music is well said to be the speech of angels; in fact, nothing among the utterances allowed to man is felt to be so divine. It brings us near to the Infinite.

—*Thomas Carlyle*

Music hath charms to soothe a savage breast. . . .   —*William Congreve*

And the night shall be filled with music, / And the cares that infest the day, / Shall fold their tents like the Arabs, / And silently steal away.

—*Henry Wadsworth Longfellow*

Extraordinary how potent cheap music is.   *—Noel Coward*

Classical music is the kind we keep thinking will turn into a tune.

—Kin Hubbard

It is quite untrue that the English people don't appreciate music. They may not understand it but they absolutely love the sound it makes.

—Sir Thomas Beecham

Without music, life would be a mistake.   *—Friedrich Wilhelm Nietzsche*

When you are about thirty-five years old, something terrible always happens to music.

—Steve Race

Music is essentially useless, as life is.   *—George Santayana*

It was loud in spots and less loud in other spots, and it all had that quality which I have noticed in all violin solos of seeming to last much longer than it actually did.

—P. G. Wodehouse

Hell is full of musical amateurs. Music is the brandy of the damned.

—George Bernard Shaw

. . . music is perpetual, and only hearing is intermittent.

—Henry David Thoreau

If you have to ask what jazz is, you'll never know.   *—Louis Armstrong*

If you're in jazz and more than ten people like you, you're labeled "commercial."

—Wally Stott

Music played at weddings always reminds me of the music played for soldiers before they go into battle.   *—Heinrich Heine*

Music is not written in red, white, and blue. It is written in the heart's blood of the composer.   *—Nellie Melba*

Music is my mistress, and she plays second fiddle to no one.

—Duke Ellington

Music is either good or bad, and it's got to be learned. You got to have balance.

—Louis Armstrong

Music is the only language in which you cannot say a mean or sarcastic thing.

—John Erskine

I have my own particular sorrows, loves, delights; and you have yours. But sorrow, gladness, yearning, hope, love, belong to all of us, in all times and in all places. Music is the only means whereby we feel these emotions in their universality.

—Harry Overstreet

I have no pleasure in any man who despises music. It is no invention of ours: it is the gift of God. I place it next to theology. Satan hates music: he knows how it drives the evil spirit out of us.   *—Martin Luther*

Sayings
If thine enemy wrong thee, buy each of his children a drum.

—Chinese proverb

The song is ended but the melody lingers on.

Face the music.

Jokes
• "Excuse me, but can you tell me how I can get to Carnegie Hall?" the tourist asked a New York City cop.

    "Practice, practice, practice," he replied.

• When the orchestra began playing Tchaikovsky's *Romeo and Juliet* overture, a woman noticed tears beginning to run down the cheeks of the elderly man she was seated next to. Before long he was sobbing outright, so she turned and said gently, "You must be an incurable romantic."

    "Not at all," he gulped. "I'm a musician."

OPERA

Oh how wonderful, really wonderful, opera would be if there were no singers!

—*Gioacchino Rossini*

The opera is like a husband with a foreign title: expensive to support, hard to understand, and therefore a supreme social challenge.   —*Cleveland Amory*

I do not mind what language an opera is sung in so long as it is a language I do not understand.   —*Edward Appleton*

People are wrong when they say that opera is not what it used to be. It *is* what it used to be. That is what is wrong with it.   —*Noel Coward*

An unalterable and unquestioned law of the musical world required that the German text of French operas sung by Swedish artists should be translated into Italian for the clearer understanding of English-speaking audiences.   —*Edith Wharton*

No good opera plot can be sensible, for people do not sing when they are feeling sensible.   —*W. H. Auden*

Opera in English is, in the main, just about as sensible as baseball in Italian.

—*H. L. Mencken*

The opera's never over until the fat lady sings.   —*W. T. Tyler*

Saying
Opera attendance is a penance that the rich have imposed upon themselves.

Joke
• Opera is when a guy gets stabbed in the back and instead of bleeding, he sings.

—*Ed Gardner*

ROCK AND ROLL

Rock 'n' roll is trying to convince girls to pay money to be near you.

—*Richard Hell*

Rock journalism is people who can't write interviewing people who can't talk for people who can't read.   *—Frank Zappa*

Rock 'n' roll might best be summed up as monotony tinged with hysteria.

—Vance Packard

I'm the Connie Francis of rock and roll.   *—Elton John*

I bit the head off a bat the other night. It was like eating a Crunchie wrapped in chamois leather.   *—Ozzy Osborne*

For most rockers, the only thing standing between them and total illiteracy is the need to get through their Mercedes-Benz owner's manuals.   *—Garry Trudeau*

It will be gone by June.   *—1955 statement on rock 'n' roll by* **Variety**

Rock and roll is a communicable disease.   **—New York Times,** *1956*

Sayings

Rock 'n' roll has a beat that can't be beat.

Rock till you drop.

Jokes

• I heard some rock 'n' roll yesterday; it sounded exactly like labor pains with a beat.

• I'm not knocking rock and roll, but if Van Gogh had lived to hear it, he'd have cut off the other ear.

• You know you're going out with someone too young for you when they say, "Did you know Paul McCartney was in a band before Wings?"

• Why can't you go to the bathroom at a Beatles reunion concert?
    —There's no John.

PROSE AND POETRY

BOOKS AND READING

People say that life is the thing, but I prefer reading.
—*Logan Pearsall Smith*

Temples fall, statues decay, mausoleums perish, eloquent phrases declaimed are forgotten, but good books are immortal. —*William Tecumseh Vernon*

. . . it often requires more courage to read some books than it does to fight a battle.
—*Sutton Elbert Griggs*

Literature is my Utopia. Here I am not disfranchised. No barrier of the sense shuts me out from the sweet, gracious discourse of my book friends. They talk to me without embarrassment or awkwardness. —*Helen Keller*

Language is the soul of intellect, and reading is the essential process by which that intellect is cultivated beyond the commonplace experiences of everyday life.
—*Charles Scribner*

Men of power have no time to read; yet the men who do not read are unfit for power.
—*Michael Foot*

Literature transmits incontrovertible condensed experience . . . from generation to generation. In this way literature becomes the living memory of a nation.
—*Alexander Solzhenitsyn*

When I am not walking I am reading; I cannot sit and think. Books think for me.
—*Charles Lamb*

What I like in a good author is not what he says, but what he whispers.
—*Logan Pearsall Smith*

Reading made Don Quixote a gentleman, but believing what he read made him mad.
—*George Bernard Shaw*

Read no history: nothing but biography, for that is life without theory.
—*G. K. Chesterton*

Until I feared I would lose it, I never loved to read. One does not love breathing.
—*Harper Lee*

Reading is sometimes an ingenious device for avoiding thought.
—*Arthur Helps*

Reading is thinking with someone else's head instead of one's own.
—*Arthur Schopenhauer*

The chief knowledge that a man gets from reading books is the knowledge that very few of them are worth reading.   —*H. L. Mencken (attrib.)*

Don't read science fiction books. It'll look bad if you die in bed with one on the nightstand. Always read stuff that will make you look good if you die in the middle of the night.   —*P. J. O'Rourke*

A man's library is a sort of harem.   —*Ralph Waldo Emerson*

Beware of the man of one book.   —*St. Thomas Aquinas*

It is with books as with men: a very small number play a great part.

—*Voltaire*

Some books are to be tasted, others to be swallowed, and some few to be chewed and digested.   —*Francis Bacon*

"What is the use of a book," thought Alice, "without pictures or conversation?"

—*Lewis Carroll*

The multitude of books is making us ignorant.   —*Voltaire*

Books are the collective memory of mankind.   —*Herbert Bailey Smith*

A man loses contact with reality if he is not surrounded by his books.

—*François Mitterrand*

An art book is a museum without walls.   —*André Malraux*

A good novel tells us the truth about its hero; but a bad novel tells us the truth about its author.   —*G. K. Chesterton*

A book that is shut is but a block.   —*Thomas Fuller*

A book is what they make a movie out of for television.

—*Leonard Louis Levinson*

A classic is something that everybody wants to have read and nobody wants to read.

—*Mark Twain*

The chief glory of every people arises from its authors. . . .

—*Samuel Johnson*

Life comes before literature, as the material always comes before the work. The hills are full of marble before the world blooms with statues.   —*Phillips Brooks*

Books are the quietest and most constant of friends; they are the most accessible and wisest of counselors, and the most patient of teachers.   —*Charles W. Eliot*

In the highest civilization, the book is still the highest delight. He who has once known its satisfaction is provided with a resource against calamity.

—*Ralph Waldo Emerson*

I cannot live without books.   —*Thomas Jefferson*

. . . who kills a man kills a reasonable creature, God's image; but he who destroys a good book kills reason itself, kills the image of God, as it were, in the eye.

—*John Milton*

Books are good enough in their way, but they are a mighty bloodless substitute for life.
—*Robert Louis Stevenson*

We're drowning in information and starving for knowledge.
—*Rutherford D. Rogers, librarian, Yale University,*
on the massive amount of matter printed each year

How many a man has dated a new era in his life from the reading of a book.
—*Henry David Thoreau*

There is no such thing as a moral or an immoral book. Books are well written or badly written. That is all.
—*Oscar Wilde*

Sayings

You can't tell a book by its cover.

Books and friends should be few and good.

There is no worse robber than a bad book.
—*Italian saying*

Joke

• "Enough about me," said the newly published woman. "Have you read my book?"

AUTOBIOGRAPHY

Nobody can write the life of a man, but those who have eat and drunk and lived in social intercourse with him.
—*Samuel Johnson*

Every man's work, whether it be literature or music or pictures or architecture or anything else, is always a portrait of himself.
—*Samuel Butler*

Every artist writes his own autobiography.
—*Havelock Ellis*

Autobiography is now as common as adultery—and hardly less reprehensible.
—*Lord Altrincham*

An autobiography is an obituary in serial form with the last installment missing.
—*Quentin Crisp*

Next to the writer of real estate advertisements, the autobiographer is the most suspect of prose artists.
—*Donal Henahan*

When you put down the good things you ought to have done, and leave out the bad things you did do—that's Memoirs.
—*Will Rogers*

Only when one has lost all curiosity about the future has one reached the age to write an autobiography.
—*Evelyn Waugh (attrib.)*

Keep a diary and one day it'll keep you.
—*Mae West*

Saying

Autobiography is a writer's dream—you never have to leave the house to do research.

Joke
• Looking down sternly from the bench, the judge asked the defendant why, after a blameless six decades, she had turned to a life of crime.

"Your Honor, I began working on my memoirs," she explained, "and they were just too damn boring."

EDITORS

Only presidents, editors, and people with tapeworms have the right to use the editorial "we."   —*Mark Twain*

For better or worse, editing is what editors are for: and editing is selection and choice of material. That editors—newspapers or broadcast—can and do abuse this power is beyond doubt, but that is no reason to deny the discretion Congress provided.
     —*Warren E. Burger, in a Supreme Court majority ruling that allowed radio and TV*
          stations to refuse to sell time for political or controversial advertisements

Editing is the same as quarreling with writers.   —*Harold Ross*

No passion in the world is equal to the passion to alter someone else's draft.
     —*H. G. Wells*

An editor is one who separates the wheat from the chaff and prints the chaff.
     —*Adlai E. Stevenson*

The editor doesn't make the news . . . but he does interpret it and shape it, as the conductor does. . . . Above all, he selects what's going to be on the program, which is one hell of a power.   —*Hedley Donovan*

Sayings
Book Doctors.

Editors read books with scissors.

The voice of reason reining in the writer.

An editor knows a beautiful sentence when she reads it—then she simplifies it.

The urge to edit someone else's copy is stronger than the urge to eat, sleep, or procreate.

Joke
• When Peters, the star fullback, was injured the week before the homecoming game, the *Campus Gazette* ran the story with the headline "Team to Play Without Peters."

The dean was less than pleased, and ordered the editor to revise the headline for the next week's edition. The editor cheerfully obliged, and the second story ran with the headline "Team Will Play with Peters Out."

PUBLISHING

There are three difficulties in authorship: to write anything worth the publishing, to find honest men to publish it, and to get sensible men to read it.
     —*Charles Caleb Colton*

The profession of book writing makes horse racing seem like a solid, stable business.

—*John Steinbeck*

To write a book is a task needing only one pen, ink, and paper; to print a book is rather more difficult, because genius often expresses itself illegibly; to read a book is more difficult still, for one has to struggle with sleep; but to sell a book is the most difficult task of all.   —*Frank Mumny*

I am a publisher—a hybrid creature: one part stargazer, one part gambler, one part businessman, one part midwife, and three parts optimist.   —*Cass Canfield*

In a world where the time it takes to travel (supersonic) or to bake a potato (microwave) or to process a million calculations (microchip) shrinks inexorably, only three things have remained constant and unrushed: the nine months it takes to have a baby, the nine months it takes to untangle a credit card dispute, and the nine months it takes to publish a hardcover book.   —*Andrew Tobias*

Saying
After a while, you get ink in your blood.

Jokes
- Do you realize what would happen if Moses were alive today? He'd come down from Mount Sinai with the Ten Commandments and spend the next five years trying to get them published.

- I just heard about the greatest book club. You send in $15 a month for a year—and they leave you completely alone!

- First guy: "Hey, did you hear Joe's writing a book?"
  Second guy: "Why doesn't he buy one—it's faster."

POETS AND POETRY

Genuine poetry can communicate before it is understood.   —*T. S. Eliot*

A poet can write about a man slaying a dragon, but not about a man pushing a button that releases a bomb.   —*W. H. Auden*

Poetry is man's rebellion on being what he is.   —*James Branch Cabell*

A poet never takes notes. You never take notes in a love affair.

—*Robert Frost*

You don't have to suffer to be a poet. Adolescence is enough suffering for anyone.

—*John Ciardi*

Writing free verse is like playing tennis with the net down.   —*Robert Frost*

There is no money in poetry; but then, there is no poetry in money, either.

—*Robert Graves*

A poet in history is divine, but a poet in the next room is a joke.

—*Max Eastman*

I know that poetry is indispensable, but to what I couldn't say.

—*Jean Cocteau*

A poet looks at the world as a man looks at a woman.   —*Wallace Stevens*

Poets utter great and wise things which they do not themselves understand.

—*Plato*

A poem is a form of refrigeration that keeps language from going bad.

—*Peter Porter*

Poetry is a synthesis of hyacinths and biscuits.   —*Carl Sandburg*

Poets are born, not paid.   —*Wilson Mizner*

Inspiration is a farce that poets have invented to give themselves importance.

—*Jean Anouilh*

Poetry is the spontaneous overflow of powerful feelings: it takes its origin from emotion recollected in tranquillity.   —*William Wordsworth*

Saying
Poets are like birds: the least thing makes them sing.

Joke
• Rose are red/ Violets are blue/ Some poems rhyme/ This one doesn't.

WRITERS AND WRITING

A professional writer is an amateur who didn't quit.   —*Richard Bach*

Every book has an intrinsic impossibility, which its writer discovers as soon as his first excitement dwindles.   —*Annie Dillard*

The profession of book writing makes horse racing seem like a solid, stable business.

—*John Steinbeck*

The good writing of any age has always been the product of *someone's* neurosis.

—*William Styron*

Biography, like big-game hunting, is one of the recognized forms of sport, and it is [as] unfair as only sport can be.   —*Philip Guedalla*

People who write fiction, if they had not taken it up, might have become very successful liars.   —*Ernest Hemingway*

Anybody can make history; only a great man can write it.   —*Oscar Wilde*

Reading makes a full man, conference a ready man, and writing an exact man.

—*Francis Bacon*

Perversity is the muse of modern literature.   —*Susan Sontag*

Literature is the human activity that takes the fullest and most precise account of variousness, possibility, complexity, and difficulty.   *—Lionel Trilling*

Without knowing the force of words, it is impossible to know men.

—Confucius

What is so wonderful about great literature is that it transforms the man who reads it towards the condition of the man who wrote it.   *—E. M. Forster*

A writer is rarely so well inspired as when he talks about himself.

—Anatole France

An author who speaks about his own books is almost as bad as a mother who talks about her own children.   *—Benjamin Disraeli*

What no wife of a writer can ever understand is that a writer is working when he's staring out the window.   *—Burton Rascoe*

Nothing a man writes can please him as profoundly as something he does with his back, shoulders, and hands, for writing is an artificial activity. It is a lonely and private substitute for conversation.   *—Brooks Atkinson*

If you want to get rich from writing, write the sort of thing that's read by persons who move their lips when they're reading to themselves.   *—Don Marquis*

In composing, as a general rule, run your pen through every other word you have written; you have no idea what vigor it will give your style.   *—Sydney Smith*

Writing is the only profession where no one considers you ridiculous if you earn money.   *—Jules Renard*

Writers should be read, but neither seen nor heard.   *—Daphne Du Maurier*

It's not the college degree that makes a writer. The great thing is to have a story to tell.   *—Polly Adler*

Life can't defeat a writer who is in love with writing, for life itself is a writer's lover until death.   *—Edna Ferber*

You write a hit play the same way you write a flop.   *—William Saroyan*

Writing is easy. All you have to do is stare at a blank sheet of paper until drops of blood form on your forehead.   *—Gene Fowler*

I have made this a rather long letter because I haven't had time to make it shorter.

—Blaise Pascal

I'm not happy when I'm writing, but I'm more unhappy when I'm not.

—Fannie Hurst

To see one's name in print! Some people commit a crime for no other reason.

—Gustave Flaubert

If writing must be a precise form of communication, it should be treated like a precision instrument. It should be sharpened and it should not be used carelessly.

—Theodore M. Bernstein

One of the signs of Napoleon's greatness is that he once had a publisher shot.

—Siegfried Unseld

The career of a writer is comparable to that of a woman of easy virtue. You write first for pleasure, later for the pleasure of others, and finally for money.

—Marcel Achard

I am an obsessive rewriter, doing one draft and then another and another, usually five. In a way, I have nothing to say but a great deal to add.   *—Gore Vidal*

I've been to a lot of places and done a lot of things, but writing was always first. It's a kind of pain I can't do without.   *—Robert Penn Warren*

The writer must believe that what he is doing is the most important thing in the world. And he must hold to this illusion even when he knows it is not true.

—John Steinbeck

A writer is somebody for whom writing is more difficult than it is for other people.

—Thomas Mann

The most essential gift for a good writer is a built-in, shockproof shit detector. This is the writer's radar and all great writers have had it.   *—Ernest Hemingway*

I am a camera with its shutter open, quite passive, recording, not thinking.

—Christopher Isherwood

Everything goes by the board: honor, pride, decency . . . to get the book written.

—William Faulkner

Sit down and put down everything that comes into your head and then you're a writer. But an author is one who can judge his own stuff's worth, without pity, and destroy most of it.   *—Colette*

Literature is the art of writing something that will be read twice.

—Cyril Connolly

Planning to write is not writing. Outlining . . . researching . . . talking to people about what you're doing, none of that is writing. Writing is writing.

—E. L. Doctorow

Writing is the great vocation of the dispossessed.   *—Mary Gordon*

If you wish to be a writer, write.   *—Epictetus*

A writer should have the precision of a poet and the imagination of a scientist.

—Vladimir Nabokov

Writing a book is an adventure: it begins as an amusement, then it becomes a mistress, then a master, and finally a tyrant.   *—Winston Churchill*

The novelist, afraid his ideas may be foolish, slyly puts them in the mouth of some other fool and reserves the right to disavow him.   *—Diane Johnson*

There's nothing to writing. All you do is sit down at a typewriter and open a vein.

—Red Smith

All a writer has to do to get a woman is to say he's a writer. It's an aphrodisiac.

—Saul Bellow

Finishing a book is just like you took a child out in the yard and shot it.

—Truman Capote

What a writer wants to do is not what he does.   *—Jorge Luis Borges*

There are three rules for writing the novel. Unfortunately, no one knows what they are.
                                        —W. Somerset Maugham (attrib.)

It's a damn good story. If you have any comments, write them on the back of a check.
                            —Erle Stanley Gardner, note on submitted manuscript

Will the reader turn the page?
                        —Catherine Drinker Bowen, note posted in her study

That's not writing—that's typing.   *—Truman Capote on Jack Kerouac*

It is not my experience that society hates and fears the writer, or that society adulates
the writer. Instead my experience is the common one, that society places the writer so
far beyond the pale that society does not regard the writer at all.
                                                    —Annie Dillard

The pen is mightier than the sword.   *—Edward Bulwer-Lytton*

Saying
Many writers create worlds in which the wrongs they suffered as children are finally
righted.

Jokes
• I never think at all when I write. Nobody can do two things at the same time and do
  them both well.   *—Don Marquis*

• He writes so well he makes me feel like putting the quill back in the goose.
                                                        —Fred Allen

• I love being a writer. What I can't stand is the paperwork.   *—Peter De Vries*

• Getting a phone message from one of his authors, the editor called back. "What can I
  do for you Tom?" she asked cordially.
     "It's about my manuscript," said the writer. "The one I sent you a couple of
  months ago?"
     "Uh, yes . . . yes. Can't wait to read it," managed the editor, unable to summon
  up the slightest memory. "But remind me, Tom, is it a historical novel?"
     "No," replied the writer dryly, "or at least it wasn't when I sent it in."

CRITICS AND CRITICISM

CRITICS—GENERAL

I am perfectly happy to believe that nobody likes us but the public.
—*Rudolf Bing, director of the Metropolitan Opera*

Two and two continue to make four, in spite of the whine of the amateur for three, or the cry of the critic for five.   —*James McNeill Whistler*

A critic is a legless man who teaches running.   —*Channing Pollock*

It is much easier to be critical than to be correct.   —*Benjamin Disraeli*

Impersonal criticism is like an impersonal fist fight or an impersonal marriage, and as successful.   —*George Jean Nathan*

In judging others, folks will work overtime for no pay.
—*Charles Edwin Carruthers*

To escape criticism—do nothing, say nothing, be nothing.
—*Elbert Hubbard*

Nature fits all her children with something to do,/ He who would write and can't write, can surely review.   —*James Russell Lowell*

Since we have to speak well of the dead, let's knock them while they're alive.
—*John Sloan*

A critic is a man who knows the way but can't drive the car.
—*Kenneth Tynan*

Criticism comes easier than craftsmanship.   —*Zeuxis, fifth century B.C.*

I like criticism, but it must be my way.   —*Mark Twain*

You explain how it went, and as far as you can figure out how it got that way.
—*Virgil Thomson, on his role as critic*

Pay no attention to what the critics say; no statue has ever been put up to a critic.
—*Jean Sibelius*

There is a certain justice in criticism. The critic is like a midwife—a tyrannical midwife.   —*Stephen Spender*

Honest criticism is hard to take, particularly from a friend, an acquaintance, or a stranger.   —*Franklin P. Jones*

A good writer is not, per se, a good critic. No more than a good drunk is automatically a good bartender.   —*Jim Bishop*

A critic is a bunch of biases held loosely together by a sense of taste.
                                                          —*Whitney Balliett*

The good critic is he who relates the adventures of his soul among masterpieces.
                                                          —*Anatole France*

A man must serve his time to every trade/ Save censure—critics are all ready made.
                                                          —*Lord Byron*

Critics are like eunuchs in a harem: they know how it's done, they've seen it done every day, but they're unable to do it themselves.
                                                          —*Brendan Behan (attrib.)*

A critic is a man created to praise greater men than himself, but he is never able to find them.   —*Richard Le Gallienne*

What a blessed thing it is that Nature, when she invented, manufactured, and patented her authors, contrived to make critics out of the chips that were left!
                                                          —*Oliver Wendell Holmes, Sr.*

If you can't stand the heat, you'd better get out of the kitchen.
                                                          —*Harry S. Truman (attrib.)*

Playboy interviewer: "You've been accused of vulgarity."
Mel Brooks: "Bullshit!"

Sayings
Nobody throws stones at a fruitless tree.

The person who can't dance says the band can't play.

Do not use a hatchet to remove a fly from your friend's forehead.
                                                          —*Chinese proverb*

One survives all wounds except those of critics.   —*North African saying*

Joke
• The eight-year-old was talking to her grandmother, and when the subject happened to come around to spanking, the girl announced that her father didn't spank her anymore.
    "And what does he do instead?" inquired Granny.
    "Oh, when I'm bad he just makes a speech about it."
    "And just what does he say?" pursued Granny.
    "Search me," said the girl breezily. "I never listen."

CRITICS—ART

You know who critics are?—the men who have failed in literature and art.

—Benjamin Disraeli

Writing about art is like dancing about architecture.   *—Steve Martin*

Pop art is the inedible raised to the unspeakable.   *—Leonard Baskin*

Hair like black ice cream.   *—Robert Hughes, on Caravaggio's painting*

What makes people the world over stand in line for Van Gogh is not that they will see beautiful pictures [but] that in an indefinable way they will come away feeling better human beings. And that is exactly what Van Gogh hoped for.

—John Russell

A painting is like a man. If you can live without it, then there isn't much point in having it.   *—Lila Acheson Wallace*

Three men riding on a bicycle which has only one wheel, I guess that's surrealist.

—Don Kingman

The protein of our cultural imagination.

—Robert Hughes, on exhibits in new gallery of the Museum of Modern Art

Saying
Critics are the kind of people who'd memorize the menu at an orgy.

Jokes
• "I know great art when I see it," pronounced the snooty critic.
  Responded the artist: "And I know great art when I feel it."

• I may not know anything about art, but I know what's suitable for framing.

—New Yorker *cartoon caption*

CRITICS—BOOKS

Your manuscript is both good and original; but the part that is good is not original, and the part that is original is not good.   *—Samuel Johnson*

Asking a writer what he thinks about critics is like asking a lamppost what it feels about dogs.   *—John Osborne*

From the moment I picked it [a book] up until I laid it down, I was convulsed with laughter. Some day I intend reading it.   *—Groucho Marx (attrib.)*

This is not a novel to be tossed aside lightly. It should be thrown with great force.

—Dorothy Parker

I never read a book before reviewing it—it prejudices a man so.

—Sydney Smith

As for Mrs. May, I must have named her that because I knew some English teacher would write and ask me why. I think you folks sometimes strain the soup too thin. . . .

—*Flannery O'Connor*

Sayings

A critic should be able to tell you all about a book without giving any of it away.

Critics are the writers whom writers fear most.

Joke

• A famous literary critic got drunk and confused at a cocktail party, and ended up in his host's pantry, reading the phone book. After about seventy-five pages, he looked up and murmured, "Plenty of characters, but the plot's weak."

CRITICS—MOVIES

Everybody has two businesses—his own and the movies.   —*Will Hayes*

Through the magic of motion pictures, someone who's never left Peoria knows the softness of a Paris spring, the color of a Nile sunset, the sorts of vegetation one will find along the upper Amazon, and that Big Ben has not yet gone digital.

—*Vincent Canby*

Hollywood grew to be the most flourishing factory of popular mythology since the Greeks.   —*Alistair King*

Hollywood was born schizophrenic. For seventy-five years, it has been both a town and a state of mind, an industry and an art form.   —*Richard Corliss*

During the years when the barely educated immigrants were being replaced by barely educated native sons, Hollywood . . . proved a more reliable, cost-effective means of securing world domination than any nuclear arsenal or diplomatic démarche.

—*Frederic Raphael*

It was one of history's great love stories, the mutually profitable romance which Hollywood and bohunk America conducted almost in the dark, a tapping of fervent messages through the wall of the San Gabriel Range.   —*John Updike*

Sam Goldwyn is credited with devising the all-purpose critical response to a new film: "What a picture!"

This long but tiny film . . .   —*Stanley Kauffmann, reviewing* Isadora

This film needs a certain something. Possibly burial.

—*David Lardner, reviewing* Panama Hattie

If my fanny squirms, it's bad. If my fanny doesn't squirm, it's good. It's as simple as that.   —*Harry Cohn*

I didn't know the whole world was wired to Harry Cohn's ass.

—*Herman Manckiewicz*

I pride myself on the fact that my work has no socially redeeming value.

—*John Waters*

Saying

Being a movie critic is every child's dream—you get to watch movies and somebody *pays* you to do it!

Jokes

• Movie critics are always suggesting they shoot fewer movies and more actors.

• Movie critics must be slow learners—they're always reviewing the material.

• Movie reviewers think they're enlightened—even though they're always in the dark.

CRITICS—THEATER

To many people dramatic criticism must seem like an attempt to tattoo soap bubbles.
—*John Mason Brown*

The day I shall begin to worry is when the critics declare: "This is Noel Coward's greatest play." But I know they bloody well won't.   —*Noel Coward (attrib.)*

A drama critic is a person who surprises the playwright by informing him what he meant.   —*Wilson Mizner*

I love every bone in their heads.   —*Eugene O'Neill, on critics*

One of us is obviously mistaken.
—*William Saroyan, to a British critic who had panned his latest play*

It seems not to have been written. It is the quintessence of life. It is the basic truth.
—*Brooks Atkinson on Tennessee Williams's* Cat on a Hot Tin Roof

I saw this show under adverse circumstances—my seat was facing the stage.
—*John David Klein, on* Three Guys Naked from the Waist Down

I have seen stronger plots than this in a cemetery.
—*Stewart Klein, on* Break a Leg

Go to the Martin Beck Theater and watch Katharine Hepburn run the gamut of emotions from A to B.   —*Dorothy Parker, reviewing* The Lake

All through the five acts . . . he played the King as though under momentary apprehension that someone else was about to play the Ace.
—*Eugene Field, reviewing Creston Clarke's* King Lear

Miss Stapleton played the part as though she had not yet signed the contract with the producer.   —*George Jean Nathan, reviewing* The Emperor's Clothes

The play was a great success but the audience was a failure.
—*Oscar Wilde*

Saying

Definition of a critic: Someone who likes to hiss and tell.

Jokes

• There's a story about the theater critic Heywood Broun and the actor Geoffrey Steyne. It seems Steyne sued Broun after one of Broun's reviews skewered Steyne and called him the worst actor on the American stage. Eventually, the suit was thrown out of court, but it was not forgotten.

Steyne subsequently appeared in a new play which Broun was sent to review. Being as politic as possible, Broun refrained from mentioning the actor's name until the last sentence, which read, "Mr. Steyne's performance was not up to his usual standard."

• Define theater critic.
  —One who stones the first cast.

A S S O C I A T I O N S

CLUBS

You're either on the bus or off the bus.
                                                                    —*Ken Kesey*

I don't want to belong to any club that would have me as a member.
                                                            —*Groucho Marx (attrib.)*

All men seek the society of those who think and act somewhat like themselves.
                                                                —*William Cobbett*

A convention is a splendid place to study human nature. Man in a crowd is quite a different creature than man acting alone.   —*William Jennings Bryan*

Sayings

If you want to join the club, you have to pay your dues.

A club has to have more than one member and has to exclude more than one person; if anyone can get in, it isn't a club anymore.

A club may be judged by its choice of members, and an individual by his or her choice of clubs.

The basis of the fraternity system is that not all men are brothers.

Joke

• How does an elk make love?
    —How should I know? I'm a Shriner.

COOPERATION

A song without music is a lot like H2 without the O.   —*Ira Gershwin*

I never could understand how two men can write a book together; to me that's like three people getting together to have a baby.   —*Evelyn Waugh (attrib.)*

People of the same trade seldom meet together, even for merriment and diversion, but the conversation ends in a conspiracy against the public, or in some contrivance to raise prices.   —*Adam Smith*

When bad men combine, the good must associate; else they will fall, one by one, an unpitied sacrifice in a contemptible struggle.   —*Edmund Burke*

We must, indeed, all hang together, or most assuredly we shall all hang separately.

—*Benjamin Franklin*

No matter what accomplishments you make, somebody helps you.

—*Althea Gibson Darben*

I hand him a lyric and get out of his way.

—*Oscar Hammerstein, on partnership with Richard Rodgers*

Never get on another man's island without your own boat.

—*E. J. Applewhite*

Sayings

The gums best understand the teeth's affairs   —*West African saying*

Sticks in a bundle are unbreakable.   —*East African saying*

You are permitted in time of great danger to walk with the devil until you have crossed
the bridge.   —*Bulgarian proverb*

Jokes

• When Jones died, he descended to hell, where he saw souls seated before a banquet
of unimaginable bounty. However, a long spoon was strapped to each person's wrist,
so long that he or she was unable to bring the delicacies to his or her own mouth.
And so everyone was full of frustration and rage.

   In heaven, Jones found the same setup, except that everyone was radiantly happy.
For the people were using the long spoons to feed each other.

• The telephone operator in the tiny town received a call every single day requesting
the exact time. Finally her curiosity got the better of her and she asked her caller
why he did so.

   "I have to know the correct time," he explained, "because I have to blow the
factory whistle right at noon."

   The operator gasped. "Oh my goodness—I always set my clock by your whistle!"

• When the van pulled into the only remaining vacant campsite, everyone jumped out
and began to work at a feverish pace. After completely unloading the vehicle and
setting up the tent, two kids rushed off to gather firewood while the other two set up
the camp stove and began setting out the ingredients for dinner.

   "Gee," commented a fellow at the neighboring campsite, "you sure get some
teamwork out of your family. I never saw anything like it."

   "I have a system," the father confided. "No one gets to go to the bathroom until
camp is set up."

FRIENDSHIP

Friends are God's apology for relatives.   —*Hugh Kingsmill*

Your friend is the man who knows all about you and still likes you.

—*Elbert Hubbard*

The only reward of virtue is virtue; the only way to have a friend is to be one.
—*Ralph Waldo Emerson*

It takes your enemy and your friend, working together, to hurt you to the heart; the one to slander you and the other to get the news to you.   —*Mark Twain*

Instead of loving your enemies, treat your friends a little better.
—*Edgar Watson Howe*

True friendship is like sound health; the value of it is seldom known until it be lost.
—*Charles Caleb Colton*

Friendship is like money, easier made than kept.   —*Samuel Butler*

One loyal friend is worth ten thousand relatives.   —*Euripides*

Friendship is a single soul dwelling in two bodies.   —*Aristotle*

My best friend is the one who brings out the best in me.   —*Henry Ford*

A faithful friend is a strong defense: and he that hath found such a one hath found a treasure.   —*Ecclesiasticus 6:14*

A friend cannot be known in prosperity: and an enemy cannot be hidden in adversity.
—*Ecclesiasticus 12:8*

We are so fond of one another because our ailments are the same.
—*Jonathan Swift*

We have to learn to be our own best friends because we fall too easily into the trap of being our own worst enemies.   —*Roderick Thorpe*

Greater love hath no man than this, that a man lay down his life for his friends.
—*John 15:13*

Good friends are good for your health.   —*Irwin Sarason*

A true friend is the best possession.   —*Benjamin Franklin*

Friendships multiply joys, and divide grief.   —*Thomas Fuller*

I never considered a difference of opinion in politics, in religion, in philosophy, as cause for withdrawing from a friend.   —*Thomas Jefferson*

A friend may well be reckoned the masterpiece of nature.
—*Ralph Waldo Emerson*

We often choose a friend as we do a mistress—for no particular excellence in themselves, but merely from some circumstance that flatters our self-love.
—*William Hazlitt*

The ornament of a house is the friends who frequent it.
—*Ralph Waldo Emerson*

There are three faithful friends—an old wife, an old dog, and ready money.
—*Benjamin Franklin*

Friendship is seldom lasting but between equals, or where the superiority on one side is reduced by some equivalent advantage on the other.   —*Samuel Johnson*

Friendship is constant in all things, save in the office and affairs of love.

—*William Shakespeare*

The holy passion of friendship is of so sweet and steady and loyal and enduring a nature that it will last through a whole lifetime, if not asked to lend money.

—*Mark Twain*

A friend in need is a friend to be avoided.   —*Lord Samuel*

Anybody can sympathize with the sufferings of a friend, but it requires a very fine nature to sympathize with a friend's success.   —*Oscar Wilde*

I have lost friends, some by death . . . others by sheer inability to cross the street.

—*Virginia Woolf*

It is prudent to pour the oil of delicate politeness upon the machinery of friendship.

—*Colette*

Friends are the thermometer by which we may judge the temperature of our fortunes.

—*Marguerite, Countess of Blessington*

God gives us our relatives; thank God we can choose our friends.

—*Ethel Watts Mumford*

A devoted friendship is never without anxiety.   —*Madame de Sévigné*

Sayings

A knot in the tree spoils the ax; famine spoils friendship.   —*West African saying*

An enemy slaughters, a friend distributes.   —*West African saying*

A powerful friend becomes a powerful enemy.   —*East African saying*

An intelligent enemy is better than an ignorant friend.   —*North African saying*

Do not use a hatchet to remove a fly from your friend's forehead.   —*Chinese saying*

No man is the whole of himself. His friends are the rest of him.

A friend to everybody is a friend to nobody.

Friendship's a two-way street.

Money won't buy friendship, but a set of jumper cables will.

Books and friends should be few and good.

Friendship is the only thing in the world concerning the usefulness of which all mankind are agreed.

Jokes

• My friends all told me I'd never be anything but a failure at this business, so I decided to do something about it—I went out and made some new friends.

• Poor Hackley—half his friends deserted him the day he lost his money. The rest left as soon as they found out.

• He's really a wonderful guy. Why, if I asked him to, he'd give me the shirt off his back. After all, it's mine.

NEIGHBORS

People have discovered that they can fool the devil; but they can't fool the neighbors.
—*Edgar Watson Howe*

Once asked why he chose to live in a few small dusty rooms on the top floor of Harvard's Hollis Hall, Professor Charles Copeland replied, "It is the only place in Cambridge where God alone is above me." He paused, then added, "He's busy, but He's quiet."

Thou shalt love the Lord thy God with all thy heart, and with all thy soul, and with all thy mind. This is the first and great commandment. And the second is like unto it, Thou shalt love thy neighbor as thyself. On these two commandments hang all the law and the prophets.   —**Matthew** *22:37–40*

Do not love your neighbor as yourself. If you are on good terms with yourself, it is an impertinence; if on bad, an injury.   —*George Bernard Shaw*

Nothing makes you more tolerant of a neighbor's party than being there.
—*Franklin P. Jones*

It is easier to love humanity as a whole than to love one's neighbor.

—*Eric Hoffer*

The way to get on in the world is to be neither more nor less wise, neither better nor worse than your neighbors.   —*William Hazlitt*

No man is an island, entire of itself; every man is a piece of the continent, a part of the main; . . . any man's death diminishes me, because I am involved in mankind; and therefore never send to know for whom the bell tolls; it tolls for thee.

—*John Donne*

Good fences make good neighbors.   —*Robert Frost*

Your own safety is at stake when your neighbor's house is burning.

—*Horace*

. . . better a neighbor that is near than a brother far off.   —**Proverbs** *27:10*

In the field of world policy, I would dedicate this nation to the policy of the good neighbor.   —*Franklin D. Roosevelt*

. . . I am as desirous of being a good neighbor as I am of being a bad subject. . . .
—*Henry David Thoreau*

Sayings
We can live without our friends, but not without our neighbors.

When you have a plot of land, the best thing to cultivate is your neighbors.

Two's company; three's a neighborhood.

Jokes

• What did one Indian say to the other when they spotted the Pilgrims landing at Plymouth Rock?

"There goes the neighborhood!"

• Did you hear about the sign this guy around the corner hangs on his front door whenever he goes away on vacation? It reads: "Attention, thieves: Do not bother to go any further, as anything of value has already been borrowed by my neighbors."

REUNIONS

[We look like] a road company of the Last Supper.

—*Dorothy Parker, on her companions*
at the celebrated Algonquin Round Table

We never had a tenth-year reunion, which was just as well with me. The principal's office statute of limitations probably doesn't run out in ten years. They might have had something on me.   —*Lewis Grizzard*

Benjamin Franklin said, "Fish and visitors smell in three days," but old friends from college usually smell already.   —*P. J. O'Rourke*

It is indeed ironic that we spend our school days yearning to graduate and our remaining days waxing nostalgic about our school days.   —*Isabel Waxman*

The phenomenon of wishing to return to high school is only slightly less powerful and neurotic than the desire to return to the womb.   —*Isaac Flood*

Given the fact that most of us spent our high school days feeling ugly and unattractive, it's not surprising that reunions make such great settings for revenge-oriented horror movies.   —*Charlotte King*

You can't go home again.   —*Thomas Wolfe*

Forsake not an old friend; for the new is not comparable to him: a new friend is as new wine when it is not old, thou shalt not drink it with pleasure.

—*Ecclesiasticus 9:10*

Absence makes the heart grow fonder.   —*Sextus Propertius*

Saying

An alumni reunion is living history in the process of being rewritten.

Joke

• The wealthy old man looked around the table at his sons and daughters and their spouses gathered for a family reunion. "Not a single grandchild," he said with a sigh. "Why, I'll give a million dollars to the first kid who presents me with a little one to bounce on my knee. Now let's say grace."

When the old man lifted his eyes again, his wife was the only other person at the table.

COMMUNICATION

COMMUNICATIONS

There is nothing that can't be made worse by telling. —*Terence*

Good conversation is as stimulating as black coffee, and just as hard to sleep after.
—*Anne Morrow Lindbergh*

When he who hears does not know what he who speaks means, and when he who speaks does not know what he himself means—that is philosophy. —*Voltaire*

Professors simply can't discuss a thing. Habit compels them to deliver a lecture.
—*Hal Boyle*

My method is to take the utmost trouble to find the right thing to say, and then to say it with the utmost levity. —*George Bernard Shaw*

Words are like money; there is nothing so useless, unless when in actual use.
—*Samuel Butler*

His words leap across rivers and mountains, but his thoughts are still only six inches long. —*E. B. White*

A blow with a word strikes deeper than a blow with a sword. —*Robert Burton*

If you think before you speak, the other fellow gets in his joke first.
—*Edgar Watson Howe*

It is all right to hold a conversation, but you should let go of it now and then.
—*Richard Armour*

That which we are capable of feeling, we are capable of saying.
—*Miguel de Cervantes*

Many attempts to communicate are nullified by saying too much.
—*Robert Greenleaf*

He was as uncommunicative as a vending machine.
—*Lewis H. Lapham, on White House press secretary George E. Reedy*

I am told that I talk in shorthand and then smudge it.
—*J. R. R. Tolkien, acknowledging comments
that his conversation was difficult to understand*

Saying
The turtle lays thousands of eggs without anyone knowing, but when the hen lays an egg, the whole country is informed. —*Malay proverb*

Jokes

• "What happened?" asked the receptionist when the account executive came out of the chairman's office shaking his head.

"I'm not sure," he admitted, "but I think I've been fired."

"What do you mean, you *think* so?"

"Well, she just looked me in the eye and said, 'Morris, I don't know how we're going to get along without you, but starting a week from Monday we're going to do our best.'"

• In the interest of streamlining operations, an urgent memo was issued by the chairman of the board. It read: "We must eliminate all unnecessary duplication of communication. I cannot repeat this too many times."

• On her way back from the ladies' room, the businesswoman ran into another member of the audience. Wondering whether to reenter the lecture hall, she asked, "Has the speaker finished what he had to say yet?"

"Oh yeah, he finished that five minutes ago," came the reply, "but he's still talking."

• Sign on executive's desk: "I know you believe you understood what you think I said, but I'm not sure you realize that what you heard is not what I meant to say."

FAREWELLS AND EPITAPHS

I am always grieved when a man of real talent dies, for the world needs such men more than heaven does.   —*Georg Christoph Lichtenberg*

Good night, Mrs. Calabash, wherever you are!

—*Jimmy Durante's sign-off line,*
referring to the nickname of his late wife

And that's the way it is, March 6, 1981.
                    —*Walter Cronkite, sign-off line on his last night as television anchor*

It won't be long before we'll be writing together again. I just hope they have a decent piano up there.
                    —*Frederick Loewe, in a letter read at Alan Jay Lerner's memorial service*

This is the epitaph I want on my tomb: Here lies one of the most intelligent animals who ever appeared on the face of the earth.   —*Benito Mussolini*

When good men die, their goodness does not perish.   —*Euripides*

The general outlook is not that the person has died but that the person has lived.
                    —*William Buchanan, on obituaries*

Every time an artist dies, part of the vision of mankind passes with him.
                    —*Franklin D. Roosevelt*

The rarest quality in an epitaph is truth.   —*Henry David Thoreau*

I would rather be living in Philadelphia.

—*W. C. Fields, suggested epitaph for himself*

It's all in the greetings and the farewells. When guests arrived, Washington hostess Perle Mesta would say, "At last you're here." And as each departed, she'd remark, "I'm sorry you have to leave so soon."

Sayings

I told you I was sick, Elizabeth.   *—New England tombstone inscription*

She lived with her husband fifty years and died in the confident hope of a better life.
—Tombstone inscription

If you can't be good, be careful.

Joke

• The businesswoman ordered a fancy floral arrangement for the grand opening of her new outlet, and she was furious when it arrived adorned with a ribbon which read, "May You Rest in Peace."

Apologizing profusely, the florist finally got her to calm down with the reminder that in some funeral home stood an arrangement bearing the words "Good Luck in Your New Location."

JOURNALISM

People don't actually read newspapers. They get into them every morning, like a hot bath.   *—Marshall McLuhan*

Surprise, the stuff that news is made of.   *—William E. Giles*

It is only fair to state, with regard to modern journalists, that they always apologize to one in private for what they have written against one in public.   *—Oscar Wilde*

There is much to be said in favor of modern journalism. By giving us the opinions of the uneducated, it keeps us in touch with the ignorance of the community.
—Oscar Wilde

Journalism is literature in a hurry.   *—Matthew Arnold*

I wanted to be a sports writer, but it took me too long to turn out my stuff. I found I could become vice president faster than I could become a newspaperman.
—Richard M. Nixon

Four hostile newspapers are more to be feared than a thousand bayonets.
—Napoleon Bonaparte

All I know is what I read in the papers.   *—Will Rogers*

The press should be not only a collective propagandist and a collective agitator, but also a collective organizer of the masses.   *—V. I. Lenin*

The most important service rendered by the press is that of educating people to approach printed matter with distrust.   *—Samuel Butler*

News is a business, but it is also a public trust.   *—Dan Rather*

It's all storytelling, you know. That's what journalism is all about.

—*Tom Brokaw*

People everywhere confuse what they read in the newspaper with news.

—*A. J. Liebling*

Like officials in Washington, we suffer from Afghanistanism. If it's far away, it's news, but if it's close to home, it's sociology.   —*James Reston*

Editorial writers . . . enter after battle and shoot the wounded.

—*Neil E. Goldschmidt*

If writing must be a precise form of communication, it should be treated like a precision instrument. It should be sharpened and it should not be used carelessly.

—*Theodore M. Bernstein*

Were it left to me to decide whether we should have a government without newspapers, or newspapers without a government, I should not hesitate a moment to prefer the latter.   —*Thomas Jefferson*

Newspapers always excite curiosity. No one ever lays one down without a feeling of disappointment.   —*Charles Lamb*

I keep reading between the lies.   —*Goodman Ace*

Everything you read in the newspapers is absolutely true except for the rare story of which you happen to have first-hand knowledge.   —*Erwin Knoll*

[A device] unable . . . to discriminate between a bicycle accident and the collapse of civilization.   —*George Bernard Shaw*

In the old days men had the rack, now they have the Press.   —*Oscar Wilde*

You should always believe all you read in the newspapers, as this makes them more interesting.   —*Rose Macaulay*

Rock journalism is people who can't write interviewing people who can't talk for people who can't read.   —*Frank Zappa*

Cronyism is the curse of journalism. After many years I have reached the conclusion that it is impossible for any objective newspaperman to be a friend of a president.

—*Walter Lippmann*

[Ken] Kesey practices what has come to be known as gonzo journalism. The reporter, often intoxicated, fails to get the story but delivers a stylishly bizarre account that mocks conventional journalism.   —*R. Z. Sheppard*

I was too old for a paper route, too young for Social Security, and too tired for an affair.   —*Erma Bombeck, on beginning her humor column*

A master passion is the love of news.   —*George Crabbe*

The permanent power brokers of this town are the columnists.

—*Hugh Newell Jacobsen, about Washington, D.C.*

All day long they lie in the sun, and when the sun goes down, they lie some more.

—*Frank Sinatra, on Hollywood reporters*

Every morning I take out my bankbook, stare at it, shudder—and turn quickly to my typewriter.   *—Sydney J. Harris, on incentive as a journalist*

Sayings

Reporters are like alligators. You don't have to love them, you don't necessarily have to like them. But you do have to feed them.   *—Anonymous White House source*

Freedom of the press is a right; freedom from the press is an illusion.

Bad news travels fast.

No news is good news.

It isn't news till it's reported.

News is where you find it.

Joke

• At dinner the editor of the country paper was all smiles. "What happened today?" asked his wife. "Some piece of good luck?"

"I'll say," answered the editor. "Parson Nelson, who hasn't paid for the paper since 1978, came in and stopped his subscription today."

TELEVISION

Television is best when it has something on its mind.   *—Norman Lear*

The medium is the message.   *—Marshall McLuhan*

I have a fantasy where Ted Turner is elected president but refuses because he doesn't want to give up power.   *—Arthur C. Clarke*

Television probably has become the most evocative, widely observed signpost we have.   *—Robert McC. Adams*

All television is children's television.   *—Richard P. Adler*

If *The Scarlet Letter* took place in modern times, Hester and the Reverend Arthur Dimmesdale would appear on talk show after talk show until they had whetted themselves into a kind of telegenic sharpness.   *—Colin McEnroe*

All television is educational television. The question is what is it teaching?   *—Nicholas Johnson*

[Television executives] are afraid to advertise condoms that could save lives, but do not blush about telecasting a *National Geographic* special on President Reagan's pelvic plumbing.   *—Martin F. Nolan*

The routine promotion of condoms through advertising has been stopped by networks who are so hypocritically priggish that they refuse to describe disease control as they promote disease transmission.   *—Henry A. Waxman*

[The television] viewer who skips the advertising is the moral equivalent of a shoplifter.   *—Nicholas Jackson*

Television is business, and business is America.   —*Bill Cosby*

Imitation is the sincerest form of television.   —*Fred Allen*

Television is the bland leading the bland.   —*Murray Schumach*

Thanks to television, for the first time the young are seeing history made before it is censored by their elders.   —*Margaret Mead*

When I got my first television set, I stopped caring so much about having close relationships.   —*Andy Warhol*

Television should be kept in its proper place—beside us, before us, but never between us and the larger life.   —*Robert Fraser*

Some television programs are so much chewing gum for the eyes.

—*James Mason Brown*

Nothing is really real unless it happens on television.   —*Daniel J. Boorstin*

It is a medium of entertainment which permits millions of people to listen to the same joke at the same time, and yet remain lonesome.   —*T. S. Eliot*

The product is the delivery of the largest number of people at the least cost.

—*George Gerbner*

[Television] is like the invention of indoor plumbing. It didn't change people's habits. It just kept them inside the house.   —*Alfred Hitchcock*

The heightened public clamor resulting from radio and television coverage will inevitably result in prejudice. Trial by television is, therefore, foreign to our system.

—*Tom C. Clark*

When television is good, nothing—not the theater, not the magazines or newspapers— nothing is better. But when television is bad, nothing is worse. . . . A vast wasteland.

—*Newton H. Minow*

Television is the first truly democratic culture—the first culture available to everybody and entirely governed by what the people want. The most terrifying thing is what the people do want.   —*Clive Barnes*

All you have to do on television is be yourself, provided, that is, that you have a self to be.   —*Clive James*

I hate television, I hate it as much as peanuts. But I can't stop eating peanuts.

—*Orson Welles*

I like to talk on TV about those things that aren't worth writing about.

—*Truman Capote*

The ultimate game show will be the one where somebody gets killed at the end.

—*Chuck Barris*

Television is for appearing on, not looking at.   —*Noel Coward*

What the mass media offer is not popular art, but entertainment which is intended to be consumed like food, forgotten, and replaced by a new dish.   —*W. H. Auden*

Sayings

Everybody is an expert on television.

Veni, video, vici: I came, I appeared on television, I conquered.

TV or not TV: that is the question.

TV is the great democratizer: everyone gets a front row seat.

Television is everybody's window on the world.

Jokes

- What were the lewdest words ever spoken on TV?
  "Gee, Ward, you were kind of rough on the Beaver last night."

- A recent poll reported that the more intelligent a person is, the less he watches television. Personally, I think they have it backwards: the more a person watches television, the less intelligent he becomes.

- I just saw a movie on TV that was so old, France was on our side.

- What do television and the mind have in common?
  —When either goes blank, it's best to turn off the sound.

E D U C A T I O N

EDUCATION

I will have no intellectual training. Knowledge is ruin among my young men.
—*Adolf Hitler*

I read Shakespeare and the Bible, and I can shoot dice. That's what I call a liberal
education. —*Tallulah Bankhead*

There is one sin that slavery committed against me which I can never forgive. It robbed
me of my education. The injury is irreparable.
—*James W. C. Pennington*

I consider a human soul without education like marble in a quarry, which shows none
of its inherent beauties until the skill of the polisher sketches out the colors, makes the
surface shine, and discovers every ornamental cloud, spot, and vein that runs through
it. —*Joseph Addison*

In the 1940s a survey listed the top seven discipline problems in public schools:
talking, chewing gum, making noise, running in the halls, getting out of turn in line,
wearing improper clothes, and not putting paper in wastebaskets. A 1980s survey lists
these top seven: drug abuse, alcohol abuse, pregnancy, suicide, rape, robbery, assault.
(Arson, gang warfare, and venereal disease are also-rans.) —*George F. Will*

Four years was enough of Harvard. I still had a lot to learn, but had been given the
liberating notion that now I could teach myself. —*John Updike*

One may receive the information but miss the teaching. —*Jean Toomer*

An educated man . . . is thoroughly inoculated against humbug, thinks for himself and
tries to give his thoughts, in speech or on paper, some style.
—*Alan Simpson*

Education is the ability to listen to almost anything without losing your temper or your
self-confidence. —*Robert Frost*

My definition of an educated man is the fellow who knows the right thing to do at the
time it has to be done. . . . You can be sincere and still be stupid.
—*Charles F. Kettering*

The essence of our effort to see that every child has a chance must be to assure each
an equal opportunity, not to become equal, but to become different—to realize
whatever unique potential of body, mind, and spirit he or she possesses.
—*John Fischer*

It is always the season for the old to learn. —*Aeschylus*

It is important that students bring a certain ragamuffin, barefoot irreverence to their studies; they are not here to worship what is known, but to question it.

—*Jacob Bronowski*

In old days men studied for the sake of self-improvement; nowadays men study in order to impress other people. —*Confucius*

Only the educated are free. —*Epictetus, first century* B.C.

Education is a method by which one acquires a higher grade of prejudice.

—*Laurence J. Peter*

To the strongest and quickest mind it is far easier to learn than to invent.

—*Samuel Johnson*

. . . it was in making education not only common to all, but in some sense compulsory on all, that the destiny of the free republics of America was practically settled.

—*James Russell*

'Tis education forms the common mind: Just as the twig is bent the tree's inclined.

—*Alexander Pope*

Training is everything. The peach was once a bitter almond; cauliflower is nothing but cabbage with a college education. —*Mark Twain*

Education . . . has produced a vast population able to read but unable to distinguish what is worth reading. —*G. M. Trevelyan*

Education is an admirable thing, but it is well to remember from time to time that nothing that is worth knowing can be taught. —*Oscar Wilde*

A nation that continues to produce soft-minded men purchases its own spiritual death on the installment plan. —*Martin Luther King, Jr.*

We cannot always build the future for our youth, but we can build our youth for the future. —*Franklin D. Roosevelt*

This will never be a civilized country until we expend more money for books than we do for chewing gum. —*Elbert Hubbard*

What we want is to see the child in pursuit of knowledge, and not knowledge in pursuit of the child. —*George Bernard Shaw*

It is one thing to show a man that he is in error, and another to put him in possession of truth. —*John Locke*

Sixty years ago I knew everything; now I know nothing; education is a progressive discovery of our own ignorance. —*Will Durant*

Much learning does not teach understanding. —*Heraclitus*

Learning is its own exceeding great reward. —*William Hazlitt*

You can get help from teachers, but you are going to have to learn a lot by yourself, sitting alone in a room. —*Theodore Geisel (Dr. Seuss)*

Poverty of goods is easily cured; poverty of the mind is irreparable.

—*Michel Eyquem de Montaigne*

Poverty has many roots, but the tap root is ignorance.

—*Lyndon B. Johnson*

Human history becomes more and more a race between education and catastrophe.

—*H. G. Wells*

You don't learn to hold your own in the world by standing on guard, but by attacking and getting well hammered yourself.   —*George Bernard Shaw*

You have learned something. That always feels at first as if you had lost something.

—*George Bernard Shaw*

Learn as though you would never be able to master it; hold it as though you would be in fear of losing it.   —*Confucius*

Education is helping the child realize his potentialities.   —*Erich Fromm*

A man who has never gone to school may steal from a freight car; but if he has a university education, he may steal the whole railroad.   —*Theodore Roosevelt*

Do you know the difference between education and experience? Education is when you read the fine print; experience is what you get when you don't.

—*Pete Seeger*

Next in importance to freedom and justice is popular education, without which neither freedom nor justice can be permanently maintained.   —*James A. Garfield*

Against human nature one cannot legislate. One can only try to educate it, and it is a slow process with only a distant hope of success.   —*Bernard Berenson*

The direction in which education starts a man will determine his future in life.

—*Plato*

Education is an ornament in prosperity and a refuge in adversity.

—*Aristotle*

The gains in education are never really lost. Books may be burned and cities sacked, but truth, like the yearning for freedom, lives in the hearts of humble men.

—*Franklin D. Roosevelt*

Just as eating against one's will is injurious to health, so study without a liking for it spoils the memory, and it retains nothing it takes in.   —*Leonardo da Vinci*

I am convinced that it is of primordial importance to learn more every year than the year before. After all, what is education but a process by which a person begins to learn how to learn.   —*Peter Ustinov*

America is the only country left where we teach languages so that no pupil can speak them.   —*Alfred Kazin*

Too often we give children answers to remember rather than problems to solve.

—*Roger Lewin*

The object of education is to prepare the young to educate themselves throughout their lives.   —*Robert Maynard Hutchins*

Education is what survives when what has been learned has been forgotten.

—*B. F. Skinner*

The average Ph.D. thesis is nothing but a transference of bones from one graveyard to another.   —J. Frank Dobie

The college graduate is presented with a sheepskin to cover his intellectual nakedness.
                                                                    —Robert Maynard Hutchins

His studies were pursued but never effectually overtaken.   —H. G. Wells

The test and the use of man's education is that he finds pleasure in the exercise of his mind.   —Jacques Barzun

Experience, travel—these are as education in themselves.   —Euripides

It is no matter what you teach them first, any more than what leg you shall put into your breeches first. You may stand disputing which is best to put in first, but in the mean time your breech is bare. Sir, while you are considering which of two things you should teach your child first, another boy has learned them both.
                                    —Samuel Johnson, replying to the question of what
                                        should be the first lesson taught to children

I don't want to send them to jail. I want to send them to school.
                                    —Adlai E. Stevenson, on picketers who attacked him in Dallas

The best kind of sex education is life in a loving family.
                                                                    —Rosemary Haughton

Sayings
Instruction in youth is like engraving in stone.   —North African saying

The only thing more expensive than education is ignorance.

Jokes
- Sometimes we give kids information they're too young to understand. Like the seven-year-old who listened patiently to a lecture about the birds and the bees, then turned to his dad with a big smile. "I get it," he announced triumphantly. "Since I have a brother and a sister, you and Mom did it three times!"

- William was none too proud of his report card, on which the highest grade was a D+, but he was startled to see his father sign in the appropriate spot with an "X."
  "Why'd you do that, Dad?" asked the schoolboy.
  "Because with grades like those," his father explained, "I don't want your teacher to think you were raised by people who can read and write."

SCHOOL

Show me the man who has enjoyed his school days and I will show you a bully and a bore.   —Robert Morley

A school should not be a preparation for life. A school should be life.
                                                                    —Elbert Hubbard

A child must feel the flush of victory and the heart-sinking of disappointment before he takes with a will to the tasks distasteful to him and resolves to dance his way through a dull routine of textbooks.
—*Helen Keller*

Of making many books there is no end; and much study is a weariness of the flesh.
—**Ecclesiastes** *12:12*

You can't expect a boy to be vicious until he's been to a good school.
—*Saki (H. H. Munro)*

The world's great men have not commonly been great scholars, nor great scholars great men.
—*Oliver Wendell Holmes, Sr.*

I believe that the school is primarily a social institution. Education being a social process, the school is simply that form of community life in which all those agencies are concentrated that will be most effective in bringing the child to share in the inherited resources of the race, and to use his own powers for social ends.
—*John Dewey*

You send your child to the schoolmaster, but 'tis the schoolboys who educate him.
—*Ralph Waldo Emerson*

. . . the common school, improved and energized as it can easily be, may become the most effective and benignant of all the forces of civilization.
—*Horace Mann*

In the first place God made idiots. This was for practice. Then he made school boards.
—*Mark Twain*

In real life, I assure you, there is no such thing as algebra.
—*Fran Lebowitz*

I have never let my schooling interfere with my education.
—*Mark Twain*

As we read the school reports on our children, we realize a sense of relief that can rise to delight that—thank heaven—nobody is reporting in this fashion on us.
—*J. B. Priestley*

Saying
It costs more now to amuse a child than it used to cost to educate his father.

Jokes
• The third grader came home thrilled with that day's substitute teacher. "She only made us follow two rules," reported the little girl cheerfully. "Sit down, and shut up."

• What's the problem with a liberal arts education?—It leaves you well rounded, but not pointed in any direction.

TEACHERS AND TEACHING

A good teacher, like a good entertainer first must hold his audience's attention. Then he can teach his lesson.
—*John Hendrik Clarke*

We expect teachers to handle teenage pregnancy, substance abuse, and the failings of the family. Then we expect them to educate our children.   —*John Sculley*

Professors simply can't discuss a thing. Habit compels them to deliver a lecture.
—*Hal Boyle*

Teaching is not a lost art, but regard for it is a lost tradition.
—*Jacques Barzun*

The gift of teaching is a peculiar talent, and implies a need and a craving in the teacher himself.   —*John Jay Chapman*

A professor must have a theory as a dog must have fleas.   —*H. L. Mencken*

The city is the teacher of the man.   —*Simonides, fifth century* B.C.

What nobler employment, or more valuable to the state, than that of the man who instructs the rising generation?   —*Cicero*

This instrument [radio] can teach. It can illuminate, yes, and it can even inspire. But it can do so only to the extent that humans are determined to use it to those ends. Otherwise it's nothing but wires and lights in a box.   —*Edward R. Murrow*

The object of teaching a child is to enable him to get along without a teacher.
—*Elbert Hubbard*

A poor surgeon hurts one person at a time. A poor teacher hurts [a whole classroom].
—*Ernest Boyer*

A teacher affects eternity; he can never tell where his influence stops.
—*Henry Brooks Adams*

He who can, does. He who cannot, teaches.   —*George Bernard Shaw*

I expect to lose half of you before I'm finished. I will use every means at my disposal, fair or unfair, to trip you up, expose your weaknesses . . . as a potential aviator . . . and as a human being. Understand? The prize at the other end is a flight education worth one million dollars, but first you have to get past me.
—*Sergeant Foley, in* An Officer and a Gentleman, *screenplay by Douglas Day Stewart*

Sayings
Teachers must think for themselves if they are to help others think for themselves.
—*Carnegie Corporation*

For every person wishing to teach, there are thirty not wanting to be taught.

Jokes
• Teacher No. 1: "The school's star athlete is flunking all his courses."
  Teacher No. 2: "I hope he realizes what that means."
  Teacher No. 1: "He can see the writing on the wall, but he can't read it."

• Define teacher.
    —One who bores without striking oil, or someone who talks in other people's sleep.

COLLEGES AND UNIVERSITIES

If you feel you have both feet planted on level ground, then the university has failed you.
—*Robert F. Goheen*

Universities are full of knowledge; the freshmen bring a little in and the seniors take none away, and the knowledge accumulates.   —*Abbott Lawrence Lowell*

A university should be a place of light, of liberty, and of learning.
—*Benjamin Disraeli*

The quality of a university is measured more by the kind of student it turns out than the kind it takes in.   —*Robert J. Kibbee*

I find that the three major administrative problems on a campus are sex for the students, athletics for the alumni, and parking for the faculty.   —*Clark Kerr*

One of the benefits of a college education is to show the boy its little avail.
—*Ralph Waldo Emerson*

The idea of a college education for all young people of capacity, provided at nominal cost by their own states, is very peculiarly American. We in America invented the idea. We in America have developed it with remarkable speed.
—*Lyndon B. Johnson*

The most conservative persons I ever met are college undergraduates.
—*Woodrow Wilson*

The use of a university is to make young gentlemen as unlike their fathers as possible.
—*Woodrow Wilson*

Sayings
A college education never hurt anyone willing to learn something afterward.

A college diploma used to be a license to look for a job. Now it is a license to look for a higher degree.

College is a storehouse of learning because so little is taken away.

Adults now speak of their children as having a choice: to go to work or to go to college. When did they become opposed?

Jokes
• "What's your son going to be when he graduates from college?"
  —"Senile."

• The McKenzies were thrilled to get a letter from their daughter, who was halfway through her freshman year in college, but less than thrilled as they began reading:
  "Dear Mom and Dad:
  "Just wanted to fill you in on my plans. I've been going with a really cool guy named Lance for a couple of months now. He doesn't believe in the capitalist system, but he makes enough playing occasional gigs with an acid rock group to help support the two little children from his first marriage. As soon as his divorce comes through we want to get married, but until then I think I'm just going to move into his trailer. It's kind of far from the campus, but I was planning to drop out anyhow—maybe I'll

go back someday. I need to save money anyhow, because I think I might be pregnant."

Sweating and white-faced, the Browns turned the page:

"Mom and Dad, none of what I've written is true. *It hasn't happened.* I promise. But it *is* true that I'm failing Computer Science and barely pulling a C in Asian Studies. And it *is* true that I'm overdrawn and need $300 more to get through the semester.

"Lots of love from your darling daughter . . ."

L E I S U R E

CARS AND DRIVERS

The automobile changed our dress, manners, social customs, vacation habits, the shape of our cities, consumer purchasing patterns, common tastes, and positions in intercourse.
—John Keats

Except for the American woman, nothing interests the eye of the American man more than the automobile, or seems so important to him as an object of aesthetic appreciation.
—Alfred Barr

The wheel was man's greatest invention until he got behind it.
—Bill Ireland

A lot of friction is caused by half the drivers trying to go fast enough to thrill their girlfriends and the other half trying to go slow enough to placate their wives.
—Bill Vaughan

Some people would not hesitate to drive up to the gate of heaven and honk.
—John Andrew Holmes

The sage who said "Go West" never had to figure out how to do it on a cloverleaf intersection.
—Gladys Boblitt

The car has become a secular sanctuary for the individual, his shrine to the self, his mobile Walden Pond.
—Edward McDonagh

Mass transportation is doomed to failure in North America because a person's car is the only place where he can be alone and think.
—Marshall McLuhan

Whither goest thou, America, in thy shiny car in the night?
—Jack Kerouac

Thanks to the interstate highway system, it is now possible to travel across the country coast to coast without seeing anything.
—Charles Kuralt

No other manmade device since the shields and lances of the knights quite fulfills a man's ego like an automobile.
—William Rootes

The car trip can draw the family together, as it was in the days before television when parents and children actually talked to each other.
—Andrew H. Malcolm

When it comes to cars, only two varieties of people are possible—cowards and fools.
—Russell Baker

[A car] for every purse and purpose.

—*Alfred P. Sloan, Jr., president of General Motors*

Everything in life is someplace else, and you get there in a car.

—*E. B. White*

This is the only country that ever went to the poorhouse in an automobile.

—*Will Rogers*

More than any country, ours is an automobile society.

—*Lyndon B. Johnson*

Cursed is he that does not know the width of his car.   —*Christopher Driver*

Sayings

The car salesman waits to see who walks in; the customer waits to see what's thrown in.

The easiest way to determine someone's inner character is to put that person behind the wheel of a fast car on an open road.

Would you buy a used car from this man?

In some cities you can drive a car all day for less money a day than it costs to park it.

Drive the way you wish your children would.

Nothing depreciates your car so fast as a new model in your neighbor's garage.

Jokes

• The guy was such a bad driver, the police gave him a season ticket.

• Kermit: "Fozzie, where did you learn to drive?"
    Fozzie: "I took a correspondence course."   —*Jerry Juhl and Jack Burns*

• My car insurance is with one of those companies that questions everything. I think I've got the $100 Debatable.

• I remember when $500 was the down payment on a new car. Now it's the sales tax.

• My new car turned out to have defective brakes, so when I took it back to the dealer, I said, "Forget about standing behind this car—I want you to stand in front of it."

• How did I find out about the defective brakes? Let's just say I don't have to back out of the garage anymore.

• She never really parked the car . . . she abandoned it.

• I didn't realize how bad the smog was getting until they started making freeway signs in braille.

• When Andrew saw an ad for the shiny red Corvette he'd dreamed of owning all his life, he simply couldn't resist. But after a few months he began to have real trouble meeting the monthly installments, so he dropped into his boss's office for a little advice.
    After listening to Andrew's dilemma, his boss said matter-of-factly, "Simple enough: you'll have to sell the car or quit eating." He turned back to his work, and

when he looked up a few minutes later he was surprised to see Andrew still standing there silently. "Well?" he snapped impatiently.

"I'm thinking," responded Andrew miserably. "I'm still thinking."

• Why do women have such trouble parking cars?

—Because all their lives they've been told that this [hold hands a few inches apart] is eight inches.

COOKING

Beauty is in the eyes and mind of the eater. Even if the salmon has been dropped on the linoleum, it comes up smiling. Let the guests remain in equally smiling ignorance.

—*Madeleine Bingham*

Cooking, like unrequited love, is all in the mind. Once a girl has decided her ex-boyfriend is a fat slob, she can forget all about him. It is just the same with burned cakes.

—*Madeleine Bingham*

Cooking is a serious matter, but it should also be fun.

—*Maria Floris*

Nobody can cook as well as mother.

—*Maria Floris*

When microwave ovens didn't exist . . . did people sit around [in an emotional vacuum] saying, "Heat is so boring. I wish I could bombard a potato with mutant intergalactic energy"?

—*Colin McEnroe*

Cooking is like love. It should be entered into with abandon or not at all.

—*Harriet Van Horne*

A good cook is like a sorceress who dispenses happiness.

—*Elsa Schiaparelli*

As for butter versus margarine, I trust cows more than chemists.

—*Joan Gussow*

Cantonese will eat anything in the sky but airplanes, anything in the sea but submarines, and anything with four legs but the table.

—*Amanda Bennet*

Today's restaurant is theater on a grand scale.

—*Marian Burros*

Murder is commoner among cooks than among members of any other profession.

—*W. H. Auden*

There has always been a food processor in the kitchen, but once upon a time she was usually called the missus, or Mom.

—*Sue Berkman*

Cookery is become an art, a noble science: cooks are gentlemen.

—*Robert Burton*

The discovery of a new dish does more for human happiness than the discovery of a new star.

—*Anthelme Brillat-Savarin*

We may live without friends; we may live without books; but civilized man cannot live without cooks.

—*Edward Bulwer-Lytton*

Kissing don't last; cookery do!

—*George Meredith*

Sayings

Anyone can become a good cook by using plenty of butter.

Too many cooks spoil the broth.

Too many brews spoil the cook.

Where there's smoke, there's toast.

Jokes

• When Marilyn Monroe was married to Arthur Miller, his mother always made matzo ball soup. After the tenth time, Marilyn said, "Gee, Arthur, these matzo balls are pretty nice, but isn't there any other part of the matzo you can eat?"

• When his friend inquired as to the joys of newlywed life, George confessed that as soon as he set foot in the door at the end of the day, his wife made him feel like a god. "Because for dinner," he went on to explain, "there's always a burnt offering."

• My husband/wife has a wonderful way of keeping all the pots and pans sparkling clean—he/she never uses them!

• She's the type who does all her own canning, preserving, and baking, because she's too lazy to shop.

FASHION

I can wear a hat or take it off, but either way it's a conversation piece.

—Hedda Hopper

A fashionable woman wears clothes. The clothes don't wear her.

—Mary Quant

Fashion is not frivolous. It is part of being alive today.   —Mary Quant

"Style" is an expression of individualism mixed with charisma. Fashion is something that comes after style.   —John Fairchild

Fashion is only the attempt to realize art in living forms and social intercourse.

—Oliver Wendell Holmes, Sr.

Eat to please thyself, but dress to please others.   —Benjamin Franklin

Fashions, after all, are only induced epidemics.   —George Bernard Shaw

Every generation laughs at the old fashions, but follows religiously the new.

—Henry David Thoreau

Change in fashion is the tax which the industry of the poor levies on the vanity of the rich.   —Sébastien Chamfort

I just put on what the lady says. I've been married three times, so I've been well supervised.   —Upton Sinclair

Luxury must be comfortable, otherwise it is not luxury.

—Gabrielle (Coco) Chanel

Fashion is gentility running away from vulgarity, and afraid of being overtaken.

—*William Hazlitt*

Clothes and courage have much to do with each other.

—*Sara Jeannette Duncan*

The fashion of this world passeth away.   —*1 Corinthians 7:31*

A well-tied tie is the first serious step in life.   —*Oscar Wilde*

Fashion: A despot whom the wise ridicule and obey.   —*Ambrose Bierce*

She wears her clothes as if they were thrown on her with a pitchfork.

—*Jonathan Swift*

Isn't elegance forgetting what one is wearing?   —*Yves Saint Laurent*

All women's dresses are merely variations on the eternal struggle between the admitted desire to dress and the unadmitted desire to undress.

—*Lin Yutang*

Fashion is so close in revealing a person's inner feelings and everybody seems to hate to lay claim to vanity so people tend to push it away. It's really too close to the quick of the soul.   —*Stella Blum*

Elegance is not the prerogative of those who have just escaped from adolescence, but of those who have already taken possession of their future.

—*Gabrielle (Coco) Chanel*

Fashion is as profound and critical a part of the social life of man as sex, and is made up of the same ambivalent mixture of irresistible urges and inevitable taboos.

—*René King*

A woman's dress should be like a barbed-wire fence: serving its purpose without obstructing the view.   —*Sophia Loren*

[Perfume] is the unseen, unforgettable, ultimate accessory of fashion . . . that heralds your arrival and prolongs your departure.   —*Gabrielle (Coco) Chanel*

Only men who are not interested in women are interested in women's clothes; men who like women never notice what they wear.   —*Anatole France*

If you've got it, wear it.
    —*Louis Mountbatten, advising Prince Charles on the use of royal insignia and medals*

Women's rear ends just weren't made for pants.   —*Gabrielle (Coco) Chanel*

Don't follow fashion blindly into every dark alley. Always remember that you are not a model or mannequin for which the fashion is created.   —*Marlene Dietrich*

Women dress alike all over the world: they dress to be annoying to other women.

—*Elsa Schiaparelli*

Sayings
Clothes make the man.

It's not what you wear, it's who you are.

Jokes

- "Mom," asked the little girl, gazing up at her mother in awe, "when will I be old enough to wear the kind of shoes that kill you?"

- The policeman was pressing the bank teller, who had been robbed by the same man three times, for details about the thief. "Did you notice anything *specific* about him?"
  "Yes, as a matter of fact I did," she offered. "He seems to be better dressed each time."

- "I just *love* those adorable pumps," cooed one woman to another. "I do wish I could wear cheap shoes."

- "Now there's a woman who has suffered a great deal for what she believes," declared Irma about a mutual acquaintance.
  "Really? How so?" asked the friend she was lunching with.
  "She believes she can wear size six shoes on a size eight foot."

- The way to go from rags to riches is to start by getting a decent set of rags.

FLYING

I owned the world that hour as I rode over it . . . free of the earth, free of the mountains, free of the clouds, but how inseparably I was bound to them.
—*Charles A. Lindbergh*

The main . . . divorce routes are along the heavily traveled corridor between Boston and Washington in the Northeast and between nearby cities, such as Houston and Dallas in Texas and San Francisco and Los Angeles in California.
—*Robert Reinhold, on the increasing number of children traveling between divorced parents*

Americans have an abiding belief in their ability to control reality by purely material means. . . . Airline insurance replaces the fear of death with the comforting prospect of cash.
—*Cecil Beaton*

[Soon] the only people flying to Europe will be terrorists, so it will be, "Will you be flying in armed or unarmed?"
—*Robin Williams*

In the space age, man will be able to go around the world in two hours—one hour for flying and the other to get to the airport.
—*Neil H. McElroy*

Doc Daneeka hated to fly. He felt imprisoned in an airplane. In an airplane there was absolutely no place to go except to another part of the airplane.
—*Joseph Heller*

Flying? I've been to almost as many places as my luggage!
—*Bob Hope*

Sayings

Fly, be free.

Frequent-flier miles are the business traveler's equivalent of combat pay.

Jokes

- I just flew in from Chicago . . . and boy, are my arms tired.

• It was considered a great step forward in civil aviation when the first fully automated flight was ready for its maiden transcontinental journey. Bigwigs of every sort were shown to their seats and served champagne cocktails by cyborg hostesses, while hundreds of airline employees waved from the runway. Suddenly, the engine snapped on and the plane made a perfect takeoff into the cloudless sky.

A silky, mechanical voice came over the plane's speaker system a few minutes later. "Welcome aboard this historic flight, ladies and gentlemen, and simply press the call button if you would like more champagne to be served by one of our robot attendants. Even those of you who may have been anxious about flying in the past can now relax in the knowledge that this flight is free from the possibility of human error. Every aspect—altitude, air pressure, course setting, weather conditions—is being continuously monitored by state-of-the-art computer circuitry, so virtually nothing can go wrong . . . go wrong . . . go wrong . . .

• "Do you have a reservation, Ms. Decker?" asked the polite clerk at the airline check-in desk.

The old woman looked around her, then whispered confidentially, "To tell you the truth, flying makes me nervous as a witch."

• Did you hear that Alitalia and El Al were merging to form a new airline?
—It's going to be called Well I'll Tell Ya . . .

GAMBLING

The race is not always to the swift, nor the battle to the strong, but that's the way to bet.   —*Damon Runyon*

One should play fairly when one has the winning cards.   —*Oscar Wilde*

The only man who makes money following the races is one who does it with a broom and shovel.   —*Elbert Hubbard*

The gambling known as business looks with austere disfavor upon the business known as gambling.   —*Ambrose Bierce*

The best throw of the dice is to throw them away.   —*Austin O'Malley*

The sure way of getting nothing for something.   —*Wilson Mizner*

A woman gambling for a man is the finest player on earth. Not so in a game of chance. There she reveals exactly what she is holding.   —*Belle Livingstone*

One of the healthiest ways to gamble is with a spade and a package of garden seeds.
—*Dan Bennett*

If there was no action around, he would play solitaire—and bet against himself.
—*Groucho Marx, of his brother Chico (attrib.)*

Sayings
Don't bet on horses. Bet on jockeys.

Don't bet any more than you can afford to lose.

Don't play with scared money.

Jokes
- It's good to see that the nation's racetracks are holding the line against inflation—the $2 betting window is still the $2 window.

- Then there was the little boy who ran in the house and said, "Mommy, Mommy, Daddy took me to the zoo and one of the animals paid $52.50 across the board."

- Did you hear about the moron who lost $50 on the football game?—$25 on the game, and $25 on the instant replay.

THE GOOD LIFE

Most people spend most of their days doing what they do not want to do in order to earn the right, at times, to do what they may desire.   —*John Brown*

Enjoy your ice cream while it's on your plate—that's my philosophy.
    —*Thornton Wilder*

I am a staunch believer in having one's cake and eating it, a principle I have followed greedily throughout my life.   —*Anne Scott-James*

Variety is the soul of pleasure.   —*Aphra Behn*

Increased means and increased leisure are the two civilizers of man.
    —*Benjamin Disraeli*

A flock of blessings light upon thy back.   —*William Shakespeare*

Variety is the mother of enjoyment.   —*Benjamin Disraeli*

What nature requires is obtainable, and within easy reach. It's for the superfluous we sweat.   —*Seneca the Younger*

A man hath no better thing under the sun, than to eat, and to drink, and to be merry.
    —*Ecclesiastes 8:15*

The greatest luxury of riches is that they allow you to escape so much good advice.
    —*Arthur Helps*

It is better to live rich than die rich.   —*Samuel Johnson*

Simple pleasures are the last refuge of the complex.   —*Oscar Wilde*

When faced with a decision, I always ask, "What would be the most fun?"
    —*Peggy Walker*

How sweet it is!   —*Jackie Gleason*

Luxury must be comfortable, otherwise it is not luxury.
    —*Gabrielle (Coco) Chanel*

I have learned to seek my happiness by limiting my desires, rather than in attempting to satisfy them.   —*John Stuart Mill*

Nothing succeeds like excess.   —*Oscar Wilde*

Money is better than poverty, if only for financial reasons.   —*Woody Allen*

He who loves not wine, woman, and song, remains a fool his whole life long.
—*John Heinrich Voss (attrib.)*

The moral sense enables one to perceive morality—and avoid it. The immoral sense enables one to perceive immorality and enjoy it.   —*Mark Twain*

Happiness: A good bank account, a good cook and a good digestion.
—*Jean-Jacques Rousseau*

Happiness? A good cigar, a good meal, a good cigar and a good woman—or a bad woman; it depends on how much happiness you can handle.
—*George Burns*

Give me chastity and self-restraint, but do not give it yet.   —*St. Augustine*

You never know what is enough unless you know what is more than enough.
—*William Blake*

Bed is the perfect climate.   —*Noel Coward*

I rise from bed the first thing in the morning not because I am dissatisfied with it, but because I cannot carry it with me during the day.   —*Edgar Wilson Nye*

All real men love to eat.   —*Marlene Dietrich*

Variety's the very spice of life.   —*William Cowper*

Carpe diem. (Seize the day.)   —*Horace*

Be sure to stop and smell the flowers.   —*Walter C. Hagen*

Sayings
This is as good as it gets.

He's living the life of Riley.

If it feels good, do it.

Peel me a grape.

Jokes
• Our motto used to be "Go for it!" Now it's "Have it delivered!"

• A naive fellow boarded an ocean liner for a fancy cruise and was amazed at the grand scale of shipboard life. The ballroom was the size of a ball field, the couches seated ten couples, the banquet tables stretched for what seemed like miles. After a considerable amount to eat and drink, he asked the steward directions to the men's room, but got lost en route and fell into the Olympic-size pool. Splashing frantically toward the ladder, he screamed in a panic, "Don't flush! Don't flush!"

• What do *Penthouse* and *National Geographic* have in common?
  —Both show great places you'll probably never visit.

HOME

No matter under what circumstances you leave it, home does not cease to be home. No matter how you lived there—well or poorly.   —*Joseph Brodsky*

A man's home is his Disneyland, in the sense that there is a good deal going on behind the scenes, by way of maintenance, that he cannot even guess at as he drifts through the main attractions.   —*Colin McEnroe*

Home is where you hang your head.   —*Groucho Marx*

Domestic strife is nothing new. As Sir Edward Coke said four centuries ago, "A man's house is his hassle."   —*Fletcher Knebel*

The average American home is no longer a harbor and a haven, but rather a mere place of debarkation.   —*George Jean Nathan*

When you're safe at home you wish you were having an adventure; when you're having an adventure you wish you were safe at home.   —*Thornton Wilder*

The fellow that owns his own house is always just coming out of a hardware store.   —*Kin Hubbard*

Home is the girl's prison and the woman's workhouse.

                          —*George Bernard Shaw*

A man's house is his castle.   —*Edward Coke*

When we were finishing our house, we found we had a little cash left over, on account of the plumber not knowing it.   —*Mark Twain*

Set thine house in order.   —*2 Kings 20:1*

Home is the place where, when you have to go there, they have to take you in.

                          —*Robert Frost*

Any place I hang my hat is home.   —*Johnny Mercer*

Be it ever so humble, there's no place like home.   —*John Howard Payne*

Home, sweet home.   —*John Howard Payne*

Sayings
Home is the place where, no matter where you're sitting, you're looking at something you should be doing.

God bless our mortgaged home.

Here's to home, the place where we are treated the best, and grumble the most.

Home is where the heart is.

Jokes
• Mother (to small child who wants the light left on): "But you sleep fine in the dark at home, sweetheart."
  Child: "Yes, but at home it's my own dark."

• The homeowner got into his grubbiest clothes one Saturday morning and set about all the chores he'd been putting off for weeks. He'd cleaned out the garage, pruned the hedge, and was halfway through mowing the lawn when a woman pulled up in her car and yelled out her window, "Say, what do you get for yard work?"

The fellow thought for a minute, then answered, "The lady who lives here lets me sleep with her."

- Where all the women are strong, all the men are good-looking, and all the children are above average.

—Garrison Keillor, on Lake Woebegon, fictional town
in his radio series "Prairie Home Companion"

LEISURE

More free time means more time to waste. The worker who used to have only a little time in which to get drunk and beat his wife now has time to get drunk, beat his wife —and watch TV.   *—Robert Maynard Hutchins*

Tell me how a people uses its leisure and I will tell you the quality of its civilization.

—Maurice Maeterlinck

Leisure is the mother of philosophy.   *—Thomas Hobbes*

If all the year were playing holidays, to sport would be as tedious as to work.

—William Shakespeare

There can be no high civilization where there is not ample leisure.

—Henry Ward Beecher

We may divide the struggles of the human race into two chapters: first, the fight to get leisure; and second, what to do with our leisure when we have won it. Like all blessings, leisure is a bad thing unless it is well used.   *—James A. Garfield*

Leisure is the time for doing something useful.   *—Benjamin Franklin*

To be able to fill leisure intelligently is the last product of civilization.

—Bertrand Russell

Saying
People's worth should be judged by what they do when they don't have to be doing anything.

Jokes
- Instructed to make sure his squad got some time off, the drill sergeant lined them up and barked, "Relax—that's an order!"

- Three old friends were walking home from work through their grimy neighborhood when one of them spotted a brass lantern poking out of a garbage can. And when he gave it a rub, sure enough a genie popped out. "Three wishes are yours, gentlemen," the spirit informed them, "one for each of you—but only one, so choose your words carefully. Each of you can be a man of leisure from this moment on. What is your command?"

  He turned to the first guy, who scratched his chin thoughtfully. "Set me up in a house on a private beach on Maui with a beautiful native wife to indulge my every whim." Poof! He disappeared.

  The second guy said, "I want to be the richest man in the world and be sailing in the Caribbean on my luxurious motor yacht." Poof! He disappeared.

The third guy glumly considered his surroundings. "Gee, I'm lonely already—I wish I had my buddies back."

• You know those seed catalogs? I think the pictures are posed by professional flowers getting $50 an hour.

• I don't consider gardening so much growing flowers as burying seeds.

PETS

Cats

Cats are to dogs what modern people are to the people we used to have. Cats are slimmer, cleaner, more attractive, disloyal, and lazy. It's easy to understand why the cat has eclipsed the dog as modern America's favorite pet. People like pets to possess the same qualities they do. Cats are irresponsible and recognize no authority, yet are completely dependent on others for their material needs. Cats cannot be made to do anything useful. Cats are mean for the fun of it. In fact, cats possess so many of the same qualities as some people (expensive girlfriends, for instance) that it's often hard to tell the people and the cats apart.
—*P. J. O'Rourke*

All I need to know I learned from my cat.
—*Suzy Becker*

The only thing that prevents cats from killing us is that they're not big enough. But they'd love to.
—*Mike Royko*

I think one reason we admire cats, those of us who do, is their proficiency in one-upmanship. They always seem to come out on top, no matter what they are doing—or pretend they do. Rarely do you see a cat discomfited. They have no conscience, and they never regret. Maybe we secretly envy them.
—*Barbara Webster*

Sayings
Curiosity killed the cat.

A cat always lands on its feet.

There's more than one way to skin a cat.

Jokes
• One day two cats were sitting by a tennis court watching the ball bounce back and forth over the net.
    "Hey," said the first cat, "I didn't know you liked tennis."
    "Actually, I don't," responded the other cat. "The only reason I'm remotely interested is because my father's in the racket."

• Why did the cat eat a piece of cheese, then immediately place his mouth over a mouse hole?
    —He wanted to wait with baited breath.

Dogs

A dog teaches a boy fidelity, perseverance, and to turn around three times before lying down.
—*Robert Benchley*

Dogs laugh, but they laugh with their tails. . . . What puts man in a higher state of evolution is that he has got his laugh on the right end.   —*Max Eastman*

A dog is the only thing on this earth that loves you more than he loves himself.
                                                                          —*Josh Billings*

The dog who meets with a good master is the happier of the two.
                                                                   —*Maurice Maeterlinck*

Anybody who doesn't know what soap tastes like never washed a dog.
                                                                    —*Franklin P. Jones*

It is by muteness that a dog becomes for one so utterly beyond value; with him one is at peace, where words play no torturing tricks. . . . Those are the moments that I think are precious to a dog—when, with his adoring soul coming through his eyes, he feels that you are really thinking of him.   —*John Galsworthy*

The one absolutely unselfish friend that man can have in this selfish world, the one that never deserts him, the one that never proves ungrateful or treacherous, is his dog. A man's dog stands by him in prosperity and in poverty, in health and in sickness. He will sleep on the cold ground . . . if only he may be near his master's side. He will kiss the hand that has no food to offer, he will lick the wounds and sores that come in encounter with the roughness of the world. He guards the sleep of his pauper master as if he were a prince. When all other friends desert, he remains . . . as constant in his love as the sun in its journey through the heavens.   —*George Graham Vest*

Happiness is a warm puppy.   —*Charles M. Schulz*

Anybody who hates children and dogs can't be all bad.   —*W. C. Fields*

To his dog, every man is Napoleon; hence the constant popularity of dogs.
                                                                        —*Aldous Huxley*

Among God's creatures two, the dog and the guitar, have taken all the sizes and all the shapes, in order not to be separated from the man.   —*Andrés Segovia*

The more I see of men, the more I like dogs.   —*Madame de Staël*

Don't make the mistake of treating your dogs like humans, or they'll treat you like dogs.   —*Martha Scott*

Dog will have his day.   —*William Shakespeare*

Sayings
Dogs that bark at a distance never bite.

A dog will not howl if you beat him with a bone.

Jokes
• Sign on bulletin board: "Puppies for sale: The only love that money can buy."

• Mrs. Green had recently acquired a dog and was proudly demonstrating his good points to a friend. "I know he's not what you would call a pedigree dog," she admitted, "but if any stranger comes within fifty feet of the house, he lets us know about it."

"What does he do?" asked her friend. "Bark the house down?"
"No. . . . he crawls under the sofa."

- Two guys were walking down the street when they came across a dog sitting in the middle of the sidewalk, studiously licking its private parts.
  "Gee, would I ever like to do that," sighed one fellow enviously.
  "Go right ahead," encouraged his friend. "But if I were you, I'd pat him first."

- Why do dogs lick their private parts?
  —Because they can.

PRIVACY

The right to be let alone is indeed the beginning of all freedoms.

—*William O. Douglas*

My personality doesn't interest me.

—*Andrei A. Gromyko, refusing to answer personal questions*

Unfortunately, we're in the age of full disclosure, with celebrities blabbing about every detail of their lives to anyone who will listen.   —*Mike Royko*

Abortion doesn't belong in the political arena. It's a private right, like many other rights concerning the family.   —*Bella Abzug*

A whale is harpooned only when it spouts.

—*Henry Hillman, on why he avoids interviews*

If the First Amendment means anything, it means that a state has no business telling a man, sitting alone in his own house, what books he may read or what films he may watch. . . . Our whole constitutional heritage rebels at the thought of giving government the power to control men's minds.   —*Thurgood Marshall*

The right of the individual to conduct intimate relationships in the intimacy of his or her own home seems to me to be the heart of the Constitution's protection of privacy.

—*Harry A. Blackmun*

. . . the right to be let alone—the most comprehensive of rights, and the right most valued by civilized man.   —*Louis D. Brandeis*

. . . a man's house is his castle. . . .   —*Edward Coke*

I want to be left alone.   —*Greta Garbo (attrib.)*

A man must ride alternately on the horses of his private and his public nature.

—*Ralph Waldo Emerson*

Don't throw stones at your neighbors', if your own windows are glass.

—*Benjamin Franklin*

Sayings
Nobody's life is a totally open book.

In the computer age, it is disturbing to realize that a machine has your number.

Jokes
- I've got so many people listening in to my phone, every time I dial I get stage fright.

- The law professor was trying to convey to his first-year students the varying importance ascribed to personal privacy, depending on circumstance. "Take the IRS for example," he pointed out. "It's seldom interested in the identity of the vast majority of us who lose money gambling, but consider how hard they work to pin down the winners."

TRAVEL AND VACATIONS

Unusual travel suggestions are dancing lessons from the gods.

—Kurt Vonnegut

Americans have always been eager for travel, that being how they got to the new world in the first place.   *—Otto Friedrich*

Travel seems not just a way of having a good time, but something that every self-respecting citizen ought to undertake, like a high-fiber diet, say, or a deodorant.

—Jan Morris

Travel teaches toleration.   *—Benjamin Disraeli*

They spell it Vinci and pronounce it Vinchy; foreigners always spell better than they pronounce.   *—Mark Twain*

I have been a stranger in a strange land.   *—Exodus 2:22*

When the whistle blew and the call stretched thin across the night, one had to believe that any journey could be sweet to the soul.   *—Charles Turner*

Travel by sea nearly approximates the bliss of babyhood. They feed you, rock you gently to sleep, and when you wake up, they take care of you and feed you again.

—Geoffrey Bocca

The whole object of travel is not to set foot on foreign land. It is at last to set foot on one's own country as a foreign land.   *—G. K. Chesterton*

I should like to spend the whole of my life in traveling abroad, if I could anywhere borrow another life to spend afterward at home.   *—William Hazlitt*

To give you an idea of how fast we traveled: we left Spokane with two rabbits and when we got to Topeka we still had only two.   *—Bob Hope*

There are two classes of travel—first class, and with children.

—Robert Benchley

It is amazing how nice people are to you when they know you are going away.

—Michael Arlen

Experience, travel—these are as education in themselves.   *—Euripides*

The average American home is no longer a harbor and a haven, but rather a mere place of debarkation.   *—George Jean Nathan*

Restore human legs as a means of travel. Pedestrians rely on food for fuel and need no special parking facilities.   *—Lewis Mumford*

He who would travel happily must travel light.   —*Antoine de Saint-Exupéry*

Travel is broadening, particularly where food and drink are good. But the journey home is an exultant occasion.   —*Brooks Atkinson*

Thanks to the miles of superhighways under construction, America will soon be a wonderful place to drive—if you don't want to stop.   —*Fletcher Knebel*

Though it may be essential to the imagination, travel is not necessary to an understanding of men.   —*Freya Stark*

Traveling may be one of two things—an experience we shall always remember, or an experience which, alas, we shall never forget.   —*Rabbi Julius Gordon*

Once a place becomes special, it's no longer special.   —*Peter Storey*

There is nothing so good for the human soul as the discovery that there are ancient and flourishing civilized societies which have somehow managed to exist for many centuries and are still in being though they have had no help from the traveler in solving their problems.   —*Walter Lippmann*

The yearning of the provincial for the capital is a quite exceptional passion. It sets in early, and until it is satisfied it does not let go. It draws its subjects into a strange world where trains and hotels take on an exceptional significance. Many suffering from it become travelers, but perhaps they are aware that travel is simply an extension of that first uprooting, a desire to repeat that first incomparable shock.

—*Margaret Drabble*

I wouldn't mind seeing China if I could come back the same day.

—*Philip Larkin*

When does this place get to England?

—*Bea Lillie, aboard the* **Queen Mary**

Journeys, like artists, are born and not made. A thousand differing circumstances contribute to them, few of them willed or determined by the will—whatever we may think.   —*Lawrence Durrell*

Dress impressively like the French, speak with authority like the Germans, have blond hair like the Scandinavians, and speak of no American presidents except Lincoln, Roosevelt, and Kennedy.

—*Sylvaine Rouy Neves, on how to gain respect while traveling in Europe*

I was well acquainted with the gag that if you looked like your passport picture, you needed a trip. I was unprepared for the preponderance of thuglike pictures which I found in the course of processing passports.

—*Frances G. Knight, director, U.S. Passport Office, ruling that it is all right to smile in passport photos*

Everybody wants to be someplace he ain't. As soon as he gets there, he wants to go right back.   —*Henry Ford, on why he went into the car business*

I shall always be glad to have seen it—for the same reason Papa gave for being glad to have seen Lisbon—namely "that it will be unnecessary ever to see it again."

—*Winston Churchill, on Calcutta*

When in Rome, live in the Roman style.   *—St. Ambrose*

Sayings

Please go away.   *—Sign on a travel agency door*

He that travels far, knows much.

He who does not travel will not know the value of men.   *—North African saying*

Getting there is half the fun.

Jokes

- Clearly more interested in shopping than history, the woman climbed out of the tour bus and whined, "How long is it going to take to see Florence?"

    The immensely cultured guide replied courteously, "Madam, you can see all of Florence in a day, some of Florence in a week, and a very little bit of Florence in a month."

- After a delicious lunch in an Italian restaurant, the well-traveled businesswoman called the chef over to compliment him on the meal. "Frankly, your eggplant Parmesan was better than the one I ate in Milan last Tuesday," she told him.

    "It's not surprising," said the chef proudly. "They use domestic cheese. Here we use imported!"

- Paul Putney had planned a trip to Paris for a very long time, and the day after his retirement, he was on a plane. His old friend Herb met him at the airport, and asked, "Well, Paul, how was Paris?"

    "Oh, it was fine," replied the weary traveler, "but I wish I'd gone twenty years ago."

    "When Paris was really Paris, eh?" said Herb sympathetically.

    "No, when Paul Putney was really Paul Putney."

- The weary traveler came up to the hotel desk to check in. "Would you like the $78 room, or the $95 one?" asked the clerk politely.

    "What's the difference?" the traveler wondered.

    "In the $95 room," the clerk explained, "you get free color TV."

- My big problem was the tour guide. Every day we stopped in twenty-two souvenir shops and one rest room. Naturally. Who gets kickbacks from rest rooms?

- You remember the story of the Ark, the ship that carried a male and female of every living creature on earth? I think it was the last cruise ship that was evenly matched.

SOCIAL BEHAVIOR

ADVICE

Never eat at a place called Mom's. Never play cards with a man named Doc. And never lay down with a woman who's got more troubles than you.

—Nelson Algren

It is very good advice to believe only what an artist does, rather than what he says about his work.
—David Hockney

When we ask advice, we are usually looking for an accomplice.
—Charles Varlet de La Grange

Whatever your advice, make it brief.
—Horace

When a man comes to me for advice, I find out the kind of advice he wants—and I give it to him.
—Josh Billings

There is nothing which we receive with so much reluctance as advice.
—Joseph Addison

Advice is seldom welcome; and those who want it the most always like it the least.
—Lord Chesterfield

When we feel a strong desire to thrust our advice upon others, it is usually because we suspect their weakness; but we ought rather to suspect our own.
—Charles Caleb Colton

We may give advice, but we can't inspire conduct.
—François de La Rochefoucauld

It is always a silly thing to give advice, but to give good advice is absolutely fatal.
—Oscar Wilde

Advice is like castor oil, easy enough to give but dreadful uneasy to take.
—Josh Billings

The worst men often give the best advice.
—Philip James Bailey

In those days, he was wiser than he is now; he used frequently to take my advice.
—Winston Churchill

I don't give advice. I can't tell anybody what to do. Instead I say this is what we know about this problem at this time. And here are the consequences of these actions.
—Dr. Joyce Brothers

My job is to give the president and secretary of defense military advice before they know they need it.   —*General John W. Vessey, Jr.*

A good scare is worth more to a man than good advice.

—*Edgar Watson Howe*

Never put anything on paper, my boy, and never trust a man with a small black mustache.   —*P. G. Wodehouse*

Preachers say, Do as I say, not do as I do.   —*John Selden*

A word to the wise ain't necessary—it's the stupid ones who need the advice.

—*Bill Cosby*

Reporter: "Millions of travelers from all over the world have stayed at your fine establishments. I wonder, sir, if you have a word or two of advice to pass on to them?"
    Conrad Hilton (famous hotelier): "I do indeed. Please put the shower curtain *inside*."

Sayings
Never take your own advice.

Everybody loves to give advice, but no one likes to take it.

Jokes
- Cub reporter: "I've come for some advice on how to run a newspaper, sir."
  Editor: "You've come to the wrong place, son. Ask one of my subscribers."

- The elderly woman was utterly charmed by the suave gentleman who rang her doorbell one day and proceeded to outline the attractions of a special investment opportunity for retired persons, one that would triple her savings in five years at no risk whatsoever. She proceeded to sign over her entire pension, and when the money disappeared without a trace, she duly reported the scam to the Better Business Bureau.
    "But why didn't you come to us beforehand?" scolded the representative gently. "Didn't you know about our services?"
    "Oh, certainly I did," replied the old woman contritely, "but I was sure you'd tell me not to do it."

CHARM

A stranger loses half his charm the day he is no longer a stranger.

—*Geneviève Antoine Dariaux*

Charms strike the sight, but merit wins the soul.   —*Alexander Pope*

Do you know the difference between a beautiful woman and a charming one? A beauty is a woman you notice, a charmer is one who notices you.

—*Adlai E. Stevenson*

All charming people have something to conceal, usually their total dependence on the appreciation of others.   —*Cyril Connolly*

Charm is a way of getting the answer yes without having asked any clear question.

—*Albert Camus*

"It's all in the greetings and the farewells," confided famous Washington hostess Perle Mesta on the secret of her successful parties. When each guest arrived, she'd say, "At last you're here." And as each departed, she'd say, "I'm sorry you have to leave so soon."

Saying
What can the enemy do when the friend is cordial?   —*Persian proverb*

Jokes
• "Please don't leave," implored the lonely fellow. "Do stay for dinner—it's raining."
  "It's not raining *that* hard."

• As usual Hildegarde was the last to arrive at the dinner party; in fact she was unconscionably late. "Do forgive me, darling," she said to the host, offering her cheek for him to kiss.
  "No forgiveness is called for," replied the host smoothly. "You could never come too late."

• The very well dressed man was approached by a shabby, unkempt fellow. "Could you spare a dollar for a cup of coffee?" asked the bum.
  "A cup of coffee is only fifty cents," the man responded icily.
  "Oh I know," replied the bum breezily. "I was hoping you'd join me."

• The only charm she'll ever have is on a bracelet.

GOSSIP

When gossip grows old it becomes myth.   —*Stanislaw Lec*

The more virtuous any man is, the less easily does he suspect others to be vicious.

—*Cicero*

Hear no evil, speak no evil—and you'll never be invited to a party.

—*Oscar Wilde*

Don't talk about yourself; it will be done when you leave.   —*Wilson Mizner*

They have sharpened their tongues like a serpent; adder's poison is under their lips.

—*Psalms 140:3*

Today's gossip is tomorrow's headline.   —*Walter Winchell*

Gossip is just news running ahead of itself in a red satin dress.

—*Liz Smith*

Gossip, even when it avoids the sexual, bears around it a faint flavor of the erotic.

—*Patricia Meyer Spacks*

Of course I wouldn't say anything about her unless I could say something good. And, oh boy, is this good . . .   —*Bill King*

If you can't say something good about someone, sit right here by me.

—*Allegedly embroidered on a pillow*
in Alice Roosevelt Longworth's living room

Sayings

A gossip in a village is like a viper in a bed.

If you can't say anything nice about someone, don't say anything at all.

News does not have wings, yet it can cross the seven seas.   —*West African saying*

A chattering bird builds no nest.   —*West African saying*

Joke

- Deciding to drink his troubles away, a fellow stayed on and on until the bar closed and he was ejected onto the sidewalk. And when he woke up the next morning, who should he see walking up to him but the pastor of his church. "Oh, Reverend," he croaked, "I hate for you to see me this way."

  "Remember, Jimmy, God sees you this way too," counseled the minister gently.

  "I suppose so," groaned the fellow, "but he keeps it to himself."

HOSTS AND HOSPITALITY

The guest is always right—even if we have to throw him out.

—*Charles Ritz, hotelier*

I will gladly lecture for fifty dollars, but I'll not be a guest for less than a hundred.

—*Elbert Hubbard*

What is pleasanter than the tie of host and guest?   —*Aeschylus*

The ornament of a house is the friends who frequent it.

—*Ralph Waldo Emerson*

Fish and visitors smell in three days.   —*Benjamin Franklin*

May our house always be too small to hold all our friends.   —*Myrtle Reed*

Welcome the coming, speed the parting guest.   —*Homer*

Sayings

Mi casa es su casa (My house is your house).

The master of the house is the servant of the guest.

Jokes

- The successful host confided the following secret of seeming happy while entertaining houseguests. "It's easy to go around smiling," he explained, "when you keep thinking of how nice it will be when they leave."

- It seems to me that houses being built today have plenty of closets. It's just that the developers have a different name for them; they call them guest bedrooms.

MANNERS

Nothing is less important than which fork you use.   *—Emily Post*

Manners require time, as nothing is more vulgar than haste.

—Ralph Waldo Emerson

There is nothing settled in manners, but the laws of behavior yield to the energy of the individual.   *—Ralph Waldo Emerson*

Under bad manners, as under graver faults, lies very commonly an overestimate of our special individuality, as distinguished from our generic humanity.

—Oliver Wendell Holmes, Sr.

Fine manners need the support of fine manners in others.

—Ralph Waldo Emerson

The most difficult thing in the world is to know how to do a thing and to watch someone else doing it wrong, without commenting.   *—T. H. White*

Good manners is the art of making those people easy with whom we converse. Whoever makes the fewest persons uneasy is the best bred in the company.

—Jonathan Swift

Manners are the happy ways of doing things; each once a stroke of genius or of love, now repeated and hardened into usage.   *—Ralph Waldo Emerson*

Manners make the fortune of the ambitious youth.   *—Ralph Waldo Emerson*

Good breeding consists in concealing how much we think of ourselves and how little we think of the other person.   *—Mark Twain*

Never drink from your finger bowl—it contains only water.

—Addison Mizner

A general rule of etiquette is that one apologizes for the unfortunate occurrence, but the unthinkable is unmentionable.   *—Judith Martin (Miss Manners)*

When God sneezed, I didn't know what to say.   *—Henny Youngman*

Good manners have much to do with the emotions. To make them ring true, one must feel them, not merely exhibit them.   *—Amy Vanderbilt*

Protocol is everything.
        —François Giuliani, spokesman for the secretary-general of the United Nations

It would be a swell world if everybody was as pleasant as the fellow who's trying to skin you.   *—Kin Hubbard*

A car is useless in New York, essential everywhere else. The same with good manners.
—Mignon McLaughlin

Politeness is one half good nature and the other half good lying.

—Mary Wilson Little

The trouble with being punctual is that there's nobody there to appreciate it.

—Harold Rome

Sayings

Tact is changing the subject without changing your mind.

It's nice to be important, but it's more important to be nice.

Learn politeness from the impolite.

—*North African saying*

Social tact is making your company feel at home, even though you wish they were.

Jokes

• The tired woman boarded the crowded bus at rush hour, loaded with shopping, groceries, and a sleeping child. She stood for almost twenty minutes, until she felt a tap on her shoulder and looked down at a fresh-faced young man.
   "Pay attention at 34th Street," he whispered loudly. "That's where I get off."

• The woman was more than a little upset when her car stalled in the middle of the main street, and more so when no amount of cajoling could get it started again. As the light turned from red to green a third time and the car still failed to respond, the honking of the fellow in the car behind her grew even more insistent. Finally the woman got out and walked over to his door. "Excuse me, sir," she said politely, "if you'd like to help out by trying to get my car started yourself, I'll be glad to sit here and honk your horn for you."

• "A polite person is someone who listens with interest to things he knows all about from someone who knows little or nothing about them," the speaker told his audience at the conclusion of his talk. "Thank you for being so polite to me this afternoon."

• The story goes that George Washington and General Lafayette were talking one afternoon when an old black fellow passed them and tipped his hat. "Good mo'nin', Gen'l Washington," croaked the old fellow.
   Immediately Washington removed his hat and bowed. "Good morning to you," he replied, "and have a pleasant day."
   Lafayette was shocked. "That old man is a slave," he pointed out. "Why did you bow to him?"
   Washington smiled. "I would not allow him to be a better gentleman than I."

• Define punctuality.
   —When your watch can do an hour in forty-five minutes.

STYLE AND TASTE

In matters of grave importance, style, not sincerity, is the vital thing.

—*Oscar Wilde*

It was from Handel that I learned that style comes from force of assertion.

—*George Bernard Shaw*

Style is the hallmark of a temperament stamped upon the material at hand.

—*André Maurois*

"Camp" is a vision of the world in terms of style—but a particular style. It is the love of the exaggerated.

—*Susan Sontag*

Hair style is the final tip-off whether or not a woman really knows herself.
—*Hubert de Givenchy*

The manner in which one endures what must be endured is more important than the thing that must be endured.   —*Dean Acheson*

Style is knowing who you are, what you want to say, and not giving a damn.
—*Gore Vidal*

"Style" is an expression of individualism mixed with charisma. Fashion is something that comes after style.   —*John Fairchild*

It's no good running a pig farm badly for thirty years while saying, "Really, I was meant to be a ballet dancer." By that time, pigs will be your style.
—*Quentin Crisp*

Self-plagiarism is style.   —*Alfred Hitchcock*

No one ever went broke underestimating the taste of the American public.
—*H. L. Mencken*

I don't believe less is more. I believe that less is less, fat fat, thin thin, and enough is enough.   —*Stanley Elkin*

Do not do unto others as you would that they should do unto you. Their tastes may not be the same.   —*George Bernard Shaw*

Exuberance is better than taste.   —*Gustave Flaubert*

Ah, good taste! What a dreadful thing! Taste is the enemy of creativeness.
—*Pablo Picasso*

Bad taste is, specifically, gladioli, cut-glass flower bowls, two-tone motor cars, and doilies to hide telephones. Good taste is, frankly, what *I* think is good taste.
—*David Hicks*

To me, bad taste is what entertainment is all about.   —*John Waters*

I like corn.   —*Walt Disney*

I hate broccoli.   —*George Bush*

One man's fish is another man's *poisson.*   —*Carolyn Wells*

Isn't elegance forgetting what one is wearing?   —*Yves Saint Laurent*

Elegance is not the prerogative of those who have just escaped from adolescence, but of those who have already taken possession of their future.
—*Gabrielle (Coco) Chanel*

Elegance is innate. It has nothing to do with being well dressed. Elegance is refusal.
—*Diana Vreeland*

What is elegance: Soap and water!   —*Cecil Beaton*

One man's meat is another man's poison.   —*Oswald Dykes*

Saying
To each his own.

Jokes

• Before you criticize your mate's style, remember—they chose to be seen with you.

• "But sir, you really must try this pair," insisted the shoe salesman, showing the gentleman a sleek, narrow, pointed-toe pair of boots. "It's what *everyone's* wearing this season."

   The customer shook his head and pointed at a classic pair of oxfords, explaining politely that he was still wearing last season's feet, which came a bit wider.

• All his taste is in his mouth.

• She looks like she was poured into that dress and forgot to say when.

• When asked what he thought of his date's new dress, the fellow answered, "Nothing is more becoming to you, my dear."

   "That may be," she responded after a brief pause, "but you won't find out till after dinner."

S P O R T S

GENERAL

Show me a good loser in professional sports and I'll show you an idiot.

—*Leo Durocher*

Defeat is worse than death, because you have to live with defeat.

—*Bill Musselman*

. . . I do not in the least object to a sport because it is rough.

—*Theodore Roosevelt*

The battle of Waterloo was won on the playing fields of Eton.

—*Duke of Wellington (attrib.)*

Generally speaking, I look upon [sports] as dangerous and tiring activities performed by people with whom I share nothing except the right to trial by jury.

—*Fran Lebowitz*

Serious sport has nothing to do with fair play. It is bound up with hatred, jealousy, boastfulness, disregard of all rules, and sadistic pleasure in witnessing violence: in other words it is war minus the shooting. —*George Orwell*

Winning isn't everything. It's the only thing.   —*Vince Lombardi (attrib.)*

Competition in play teaches the love of the free spirit to excel by its own merit. A nation that has not forgotten how to play, a nation that fosters athletics, is a nation that is always holding up the high ideal of equal opportunity for all. Go back through history and find the nations that did not play and had no outdoor sports, and you will find the nations of oppressed peoples.   —*Warren G. Harding*

Nice guys finish last.   —*Leo Durocher*

In the field of sports you are more or less accepted for what you do rather than what you are.   —*Althea Gibson Darben*

Sayings

They keep saying that what really matters isn't whether you won but how well you played. The problem is that the best way to determine how well you played the game is by whether or not you won.

Good sports are seldom good at sports.

Joke
• Organized sports is the American man's favorite exercise—to sit and watch.

BASEBALL

I may not be the bestest pitcher in the world, but I sure out-cutes 'em.
—Leroy (Satchel) Paige

Ideally, the umpire should combine the integrity of a Supreme Court Justice, the physical agility of an acrobat, the endurance of Job, and the imperturbability of Buddha.   **—Time** *magazine*

You're expected to be perfect the day you start, and then improve.
—Ed Vargo, supervisor of umpires, National League

It ain't over till it's over.   *—Yogi Berra*

Hit them where they ain't.   *—Willie Keeler*

If people don't want to come out to the ball park, nobody's going to stop them.
—Yogi Berra

Baseball's very big with my people. It figures. It's the only time we can get to shake a bat at a white man without starting a riot.   *—Dick Gregory*

The secret of managing is to keep the guys who hate you away from the guys who are undecided.   *—Casey Stengel*

You gotta be a man to play baseball for a living, but you gotta have a lot of little boy in you too.   *—Roy Campanella*

And so I shall catch the fly.   *—William Shakespeare*

A hit, a very palpable hit.   *—William Shakespeare*

Strike!   *—William Shakespeare*

For the relief, much thanks.   *—William Shakespeare*

You have scarce time to steal.   *—William Shakespeare*

O hateful error.   *—William Shakespeare*

Fair is foul and foul is fair.   *—William Shakespeare*

Why do I like baseball? The pay is good, it keeps you out in the fresh air and sunshine, and you can't beat them hours.   *—Umpire Tim Hurst (attrib.)*

Sayings
As American as baseball and apple pie.

You're batting 1,000.

You're out in left field.

Jokes

- What do you do with an elephant with three balls?
  —Walk him, and pitch to the rhino.

- One thing I'll say about our baseball team is they're nonviolent. They haven't hit anything in weeks.

- When a friend came to visit from London, Mac couldn't wait to take him to that most American of pastimes, a baseball game. The Britisher tried valiantly to grasp the rudiments of the game, but appeared rather confused. In the bottom of the ninth, with two outs, the bases were loaded and the roar in the stadium grew deafening. "I say, Mac," he asked, "why is everyone getting so excited?"

  "We've got a man on every base," explained Mac, jumping up and down with excitement.

  "So I see," said the Brit, "but so does the other team."

- It was only her second date with the die-hard baseball fan, and Helene was a little nervous: it was her fault that they arrived at the stadium a full hour after the game had begun. Taking her seat, Helene glanced up at the scoreboard. It was a tight pitcher's battle, bottom of the fifth, 0-0.

  "Look, Charlie," she exclaimed in relief, "we haven't missed a thing!"

- Two old guys wonder if there's baseball in heaven, and promise each other that the first to die will somehow let the other one know. A week later, one of them dies. And a week after that, his friend recognizes his voice coming down from the clouds. "Joe, I've got some good news and some bad news," the disembodied voice reports. "The good news is that there is a baseball team in heaven. The bad news is that you're pitching on Friday."

- An American takes a foreigner to a baseball game. The foreigner is just beginning to get into cheering batters as they run to first, when a batter draws a walk.

  The foreigner starts to yell, "Run, boy, run!"

  His host, with a bemused smile, explains: "He doesn't have to run; he has four balls."

  The foreigner stands up and shouts, "Walk proudly, boy, walk proudly."

BOXING

First your legs go. Then you lose your reflexes. Then you lose your friends.

—*Willie Pep*

Boxers are not dragged into the ring, although they might sometimes be dragged out. They go voluntarily.   —*E. M. Braddock*

We've all been blessed with God-given talents. Mine just happens to be beating people up.   —*Sugar Ray Leonard*

I'll never forget my first fight . . . All of a sudden I found someone I knew in the fourth row. It was me. He hit me amongst my nose.   —*Henny Youngman*

He can run but he can't hide.   —*Joe Louis*

I'll be floating like a butterfly and stinging like a bee.
     —*Muhammad Ali, before defeating Sonny Liston for world heavyweight championship*

Honey, I forgot to duck.

—*Jack Dempsey, to his wife after losing 1926 fight to Gene Tunney*

The bigger they come, the harder they fall.

—*Bob Fitzsimmons (before his bout with heavyweight champion*
Jim Jeffries in 1897—Jeffries, the larger man, won by a knockout)

A boxing match is like a cowboy movie. There's got to be good guys and there's got to be bad guys. And that's what people pay for—to see the bad guys get beat.

—*Sonny Liston (attrib.)*

Saying
Boxing is dueling with gloves on.

Jokes
• I'm not much of a boxer—I studied it for years, but it was a correspondence course.

• I tried shadow boxing . . . but I lost.

• The manager came back to the dressing room to cheer up a boxer who'd just been mauled in the ring. "The judges didn't give you a single round, Georgie," he informed him, "but there's some good news—I got you a rematch!"

EXERCISE

I get my exercise running to the funerals of my friends who exercise.

—*Barry Gray*

We can now prove that large numbers of Americans are dying from sitting on their behinds.

—*Bruce B. Dan*

Whenever I feel like exercise, I lie down until the feeling passes.

—*Robert Maynard Hutchins*

Most of the evils of life arise from man's inability to sit still in a room.

—*Blaise Pascal*

A Chicago alderman once confessed he needed physical exercise, but didn't like jogging because in that sport you couldn't hit anyone.

—*Andrew H. Malcolm*

The only reason I would take up jogging is so that I could hear heavy breathing again.

—*Erma Bombeck*

I like long walks, expecially when they are taken by people who annoy me.

—*Fred Allen*

Sayings
Use it or lose it.

Don't let your meat loaf.

Jokes

- Mr. Universe: "Don't forget, Mr. Carson, your body is the only home you'll ever have."

    Johnny Carson: "Yes, my home *is* pretty messy. But I have a woman who comes in once a week."

- For me, exercise just doesn't make sense—like a vegetarian going to a barbecue.

FISHING

Fishing, with me, has always been an excuse to drink in the daytime.

—Jimmy Cannon

Fishing is much more than fish. . . . It is the great occasion when we may return to the fine simplicity of our forefathers.   *—Herbert Hoover*

A stream is music and motion: smooth glides, fast, turbulent riffles and deep pools, each posing a special challenge.   *—Nelson Bryant*

Luck affects everything; let your hook always be cast. In the stream where you least expect it, there will be fish.   *—Ovid*

A fishing rod is a stick with a hook at one end and a fool at the other.

—Samuel Johnson

All men are equal before fish.   *—Herbert Hoover*

Saying

Fishing philosophy:

1. The two best times to fish are when it's raining and when it ain't.
2. There ain't no property you can't fish if you know how to sit a spell with the person that owns it.
3. Any time you ain't fishing, you're fritterin' away your time.

Jokes

- The fishing party was hopelessly lost in the deep woods. The sun was going down and the mosquitoes starting to bite when one of the fishermen growled, "I thought you said you were the best damn guide in Minnesota."

    "Oh I am," replied the guide firmly, "but I'm pretty sure we're in Manitoba by now."

- The determined angler staggered up to the counter with an armload of the latest gear. As the cashier was ringing up the total, which came to several hundred dollars, he sighed and commented, "You know, you could save me an awful lot of money if you'd just start selling fish here."

FOOTBALL

Football is a game designed to keep coal miners off the streets.

—Jimmy Breslin

An atheist is a guy who watches a Notre Dame—SMU football game and doesn't care who wins.
—*Dwight D. Eisenhower*

I give the same halftime speech over and over. It works best when my players are better than the other coach's players.
—*Chuck Mills*

Pro football is like nuclear warfare. There are no winners, only survivors.
—*Frank Gifford*

Nobody is hurt. Hurt is in the mind. If you can walk, you can run.
—*Vince Lombardi*

I do believe that my best hits border on felonious assault.
—*Jack Tatum, pro football player*

In short, in life, as in a football game, the principle to follow is: Hit the line hard; don't foul and don't shirk, but hit the line hard.
—*Theodore Roosevelt*

. . . you base foot-ball player.
—*William Shakespeare*

If the FBI went back far enough, I was always suspect: I never liked football.
—*Daniel Berrigan*

Football is not a contact sport. It's a collision sport. Dancing is a good example of a contact sport.
—*Duffy Daugherty*

[Football] is committee meetings, called huddles, separated by outbursts of violence.
—*George F. Will*

If a man watches three football games in a row, he should be declared legally dead.
—*Erma Bombeck*

The football coaching legend, Paul (Bear) Bryant, had the following advice on getting his players to work as a team: "There's just three things I'd ever say:
If anything goes bad, I did it.
If anything goes semigood, then we did it.
If anything goes real good, then you did it.
That's all it takes to get people to win football games for you."

Saying
It's easy to be a Monday morning quarterback.

Jokes
• A football fan is a guy who'll yell at the quarterback for not spotting an open receiver forty-five yards away, then head for the parking lot and not be able to find his own car.

• The exercise during history class one day was for each of the students to list those they considered to be the eleven greatest Americans. After half an hour, everyone had turned in their papers except Anthony, who was still scratching his head and thinking furiously. "What's up?" asked the teacher. "Can't you come up with eleven great Americans?"

    "I've got all but one," explained Anthony hastily. "It's the quarterback I can't decide on."

GOLF

If there is any larceny in a man, golf will bring it out.

—Paul Gallico

If you break 100, watch your golf. If you break 80, watch your business.

—Joey Adams

Well, they're southern people, and if they know you are working at home, they think nothing of walking right in for coffee. But they wouldn't dream of interrupting you at golf.

—Harper Lee, on why she has done her best creative thinking while playing golf

You drive for show but putt for dough.   *—Bobby Locke*

Give me my golf clubs, fresh air, and a beautiful partner, and you can keep my golf clubs and the fresh air.   *—Jack Benny*

The uglier a man's legs are, the better he plays golf. It's almost a law.

—H. G. Wells

Golf is a good walk spoiled.   *—Mark Twain*

Sayings

Golf is not so much a sport as an insult to lawns.

One of the quickest ways to meet new people is to pick up the wrong ball on a golf course.

Jokes

• Eric: "You know what your main trouble is?"
  Ernie: "What?"
  Eric: "You stand too close to the ball after you've hit it."
                            —Eric Morecambe and Ernie Wise

• When the legendary salesman was asked his secrets of success, he gave a humble shrug. "I'm sure you all know the cardinal rules: Know your product; make lots of calls; never take no for an answer. But frankly, I owe my success to consistently missing a three-foot putt by two inches."

• Hear about the naive golf widow who wanted to surprise her husband on his birthday?
    —She went into a sporting goods store and asked the salesperson if she could see a low handicap.

• The ham-handed golfer was playing so clumsily that the turf behind him was ruined, and great hunks of sod went flying with every shot. Finally he turned to his caddy and admitted that he didn't seem to be hitting very well. "What club do you think I should use?" he asked.
    "The one in the next country?" the caddy suggested hopefully.

• Why do businessmen play golf?
    —So they can dress up like pimps.

• I don't play golf. Personally, I think there's something psychologically wrong with any game in which the person who gets to hit the ball the most is the loser.

• The prime minister of Israel invited the pope to play a game of golf, and since the pope had no idea how to play, he convened the College of Cardinals to ask their advice. "Call Jack Nicklaus," they suggested, "and let him play in your place. Tell the prime minister you're sick or something."

Honored by His Holiness's request, Nicklaus agreed to represent him on the links. The pope, again on the advice of his staff, appointed him a cardinal to make the arrangement seem more legitimate. "So how'd you do?" he asked eagerly when Nicklaus returned to the Vatican.

"I came in second," was the reply.

"Second! You mean to tell me the prime minister of Israel beat you?" howled the pope.

"No, Your Holiness," said Nicklaus. "Rabbi Palmer did."

HUNTING

Biography, like big-game hunting, is one of the recognized forms of sport, and it is [as] unfair as only sport can be.
—*Philip Guedalla*

Throughout the city [Helena, Montana] the talk now is of the kill or the near kill. Some of it may even be true.
—*Jim Robbins*

Some violent spectacle is normal in most countries.
—*Luis Gonzalez Seara, on bullfighting as compared to boxing in the United States and fox hunting in Great Britain*

It is very strange and very melancholy that the paucity of human pleasures should persuade us ever to call hunting one of them.
—*Samuel Johnson*

Saying
Support the right to arm bears.

Joke
• If God didn't want man to hunt, he wouldn't have given us plaid shirts.
—*Johnny Carson*

RUNNING

If you are not afraid to just go out and compete, then you will run your best race. But if you go out with a fear of something, even against yourself or against the clock, then you have lost the race before you start.
—*Jim Ryun*

The qualities and capacities that are important in running—such factors as willpower, the ability to apply effort during extreme fatigue, and the acceptance of pain—have a radiating power that subtly influences one's life.
—*James Fixx*

Is the quick and stoic stepper . . . going to spawn a secondary event—a maternithon for expectant mothers?
—*Bud Collins, on Joan Benoit's decision to run in the Boston Marathon while pregnant*

Mental preparation is perhaps the most neglected factor in racing.

—Bob Glover and Pete Schuder

Perseverance is not a long race; it is many short races one after another.

—Walter Elliott

Above all, do not lose your desire to walk.   *—Søren Kierkegaard*

Sayings
You can run, but you can't hide.

Running for your varsity team is athletics; running for a train is exercise; running for office is work.

Joke
• If your nose runs and your feet smell—maybe you were built upside down.

TENNIS

The serve was invented so that the net can play.   *—Bill Cosby*

People don't seem to understand that it's a damn war out there.

—Jimmy Connors

Tennis is a perfect combination of violent action taking place in an atmosphere of total tranquillity.   *—Billie Jean King*

When we have match'd our racquets to these balls, we will, in France, by God's grace play a set shall strike his father's crown into the hazard.

—William Shakespeare

My advice to young players is to see as much good tennis as possible and then attempt to copy the outstanding strokes of the former stars.   *—Bill Tilden*

Sayings
In tennis, a love match is always possible.

A sport in which even an unseeded player can flower.

Tennis is like a lawsuit: activity from across the court is often surprising.

In tennis, love means nothing.

Jokes
• One day two cats were sitting by a tennis court watching the ball bounce back and forth over the net.

"Hey," said the first cat, "I didn't know you liked tennis."

"Actually, I don't," responded the other cat. "The only reason I'm remotely interested is because my father's in the racket."

• This taught me a lesson, but I'm not sure what it is.

—John McEnroe, on losing the Ebel U.S. Pro Indoor Championships to Tim Mayotte

- Know the definition of endless love?
   —Stevie Wonder playing tennis with Ray Charles.

YACHTING

The first responsibility of a skipper is the safety of his ship and of his people.
—Charles F. Chapman

Your yachtsman would lose much of his enjoyment if he were obliged to do for pay
what he is doing for the love of the thing itself.   *—Louis D. Brandeis*

I must go down to the sea again.   *—John Masefield*

Years ago, when I was young and inexperienced, I hired a yacht myself.
—Jerome K. Jerome

I had to sink my yacht to make the guests go home.   *—F. Scott Fitzgerald*

Alone on a wide, wide sea.   *—Samuel Taylor Coleridge*

I will go back to the great sweet mother, mother and lover of men, the sea.
—Algernon Charles Swinburne

The sea never changes, and its works, for all the talk of men, are wrapped in mystery.
—Joseph Conrad

Saying
Yachting teaches humility to the mighty.

Jokes
- The Coast Guard cutter tuned in to a faint distress signal from a sinking pleasure
   craft. "What is your position? Repeat, what is your position?" shouted the radio
   operator into the microphone.
   Finally a faint reply crackled over the static: "I'm executive vice president of First
   Global Bank—please hurry!"

- Since their boss was an avid yachtsman, everyone in the office chipped in to buy him
   a sextant for a birthday present. Henderson volunteered to make the purchase, and
   when he learned the marine supply store was out of stock, he phoned the local
   sporting goods store. When he burst out laughing and hung up, a co-worker asked
   what was so funny.
   "They transferred my call," Henderson explained, "and when I asked the woman
   who answered if they had a sextant, she said they had all kind of tents and what I
   did in them was my business."

- Definition of a yacht: A floating box you throw money into.

- Definition of yachting: Standing in a cold shower tearing up hundred-dollar bills.

THE ENVIRONMENT

CONSERVATION AND ECOLOGY

We haven't too much time left to ensure that the government of the earth, by the earth, for the earth, shall not perish from the people.

—*C. P. Snow and Philip Snow*

Our ideals, laws, and customs should be based on the proposition that each generation in turn becomes the custodian rather than the absolute owner of our resources—and each generation has the obligation to pass this inheritance on to the future.

—*Alden Whitman*

Remember, this planet is also disposable.

—*Paul Palmer*

Industrialism is the systematic exploitation of wasting assets. . . . Progress is merely an acceleration in the rate of that exploitation. Such prosperity as we have known up to the present is the consequence of rapidly spending the planet's irreplaceable capital.

—*Aldous Huxley*

Perhaps our age will be known to the future historians as the age of the bulldozer and the exterminator; and in many parts of the country the building of a highway has about the same result upon vegetation and human structure as the passage of a tornado or the blast of an atom bomb.

—*Lewis Mumford*

Man is a complex being: he makes deserts bloom—and lakes die.

—*Gil Stern*

Those who warn of a population explosion picture a world of too many people and not enough food—sort of like the average cocktail party.

—*Bill Vaughan*

Ecology is boring for the same reason that destruction is fun.

—*Don DeLillo*

We've got a program to invent a new name for ecology, so we can keep it alive after it's been talked to death. We're thinking of calling it politics.

—*Harvey Wheeler*

Mining is like a search-and-destroy mission.

—*Stewart L. Udall*

We may go down in history as an elegant technological society which underwent biological disintegration through lack of economic understanding.

—*David M. Gates*

Ecological devastation is the excrement, so to speak, of man's power worship.

—*Ernest Becker*

The irony of the matter is that the future generations do not have a vote. In effect, we hold their proxy.   —*Charles J. Hitch, on the environment*

The best investment on earth is earth.   —*Louis J. Glickman*

The sun, the moon, and the stars would have disappeared long ago, had they happened to be within reach of predatory human hands.   —*Havelock Ellis*

Avarice and luxury have been the ruin of every great state.   —*Livy*

One of the weaknesses of our age is the apparent inability to distinguish our needs from our goals.   —*Don Robinson*

We won't have a society if we destroy the environment.   —*Margaret Mead*

Hurt not the earth, neither the sea, nor the trees . . .   —**Revelation 7:3**

The earth has a skin and that skin has diseases; one of its diseases is called man.
                                        —*Friedrich Wilhelm Nietzsche*

We must realize that we can no longer throw our wastes away because there is no "away."   —*William T. Cahill*

Men and nature must work hand in hand. The throwing out of balance of the resources of nature throws out of balance also the lives of men.
                                        —*Franklin D. Roosevelt*

Kill no more pigeons than you can eat.   —*Benjamin Franklin*

[We stand] today poised on a pinnacle of wealth and power, yet we live in a land of vanishing beauty, of increasing ugliness, of shrinking open space and of an overall environment that is diminished daily by pollution and noise and blight. This, in brief, is the quiet conservation crisis.   —*Stewart Udall*

Extinct is forever.   —*Kurt Benirschke*

Over increasingly large areas of the United States, spring now comes unheralded by the return of the birds, and the early mornings are strangely silent where once they were filled with the beauty of bird song.   —*Rachel Carson*

We must plant the sea and herd its animals . . . using the sea as farmers instead of hunters. That is what civilization is all about—farming replacing hunting.
                                        —*Jacques Cousteau*

Sayings
Treat the earth well. It was not given to you by your parents. It is lent to you by your children.   —*Kenyan proverb*

Save Water—Shower with a Friend.

Environment is one-tenth science and nine-tenths politics.

Enjoy the world gently, enjoy the world gently; if the world is spoiled, no one can repair it, enjoy the world gently.   —*Nigerian chant*

Jokes

- I didn't realize how bad the smog was getting until they started making freeway signs in braille.

- Help beautify our city dumps—throw something pretty away today!

- The problem used to be that bad environments bred bad people; now it's the other way around.

- I just found out where all that chemical fertilizer comes from: plastic horses.

- It's hard for me to get used to these changing times. I can remember when the air was clean and sex was dirty.   —*George Burns*

- It's not that our rivers aren't fit to drink . . . but where else can you see the fish coughing?

ENVIRONMENT

Man shapes himself through decisions that shape his environment.

—*René Dubos*

Every day we see increasing world problems because of rapidly expanding populations. Safe and effective contraception is essential in man's battle to control his environment. Thus far, the Pill remains one of the most effective weapons. Taken properly, under careful medical supervision, it is still the most reliable means of preventing unwanted pregnancy that man has yet been able to devise for wide-scale use.

—*Elizabeth Connell*

A river has no politics.   —*David E. Lilienthal*

Wildness is a benchmark, a touchstone. In the wilderness we can see where we have come from, where we are going, how far we've gone. In wilderness is the only unsullied earth sample of the forces generally at work in the universe.

—*Kenneth Bower*

You can't be suspicious of a tree, or accuse a bird or a squirrel of subversion or challenge the ideology of a violet.   —*Hal Borland*

Repetition is the only form of permanence that nature can achieve.

—*George Santayana*

One of the healthiest ways to gamble is with a spade and a package of garden seeds.

—*Dan Bennett*

Environment controls the making of man.   —*Charles Waddell Chestnutt*

Over the long haul of life on this planet, it is the ecologists, and not the bookkeepers of business, who are the ultimate accountants.   —*Stewart Udall*

The sea is the universal sewer.   —*Jacques Cousteau*

If we go on the way we have, the fault is our greed [and] if we are not willing [to change], we will disappear from the face of the globe, to be replaced by the insect.

—*Jacques Cousteau*

Secrecy is a disease, and Chernobyl its symptom, a threat both to the Soviet Union and its neighbors.   —New York Times *editorial*

Man is slightly nearer to the atom than to the star. From his central position man can survey the grandest works of nature with the astronomer, or the minutest works with the physicist.   —*Arthur Stanley*

The earth is like a spaceship that didn't come with an operating manual.
                                       —*R. Buckminster Fuller*

The American people want to preserve their American heritage, and they have the quaint belief that public lands belong to them as much as to the people of the state where the lands are located.   —*John F. Seberling*

Saying
The stream won't be advised, therefore its course is crooked.

                                       —*West African saying*

Jokes
• Pollution is so bad in New York that I saw the Statue of Liberty holdin' her nose.
                                       —*Jackie (Moms) Mabley*

• The camping expedition got lost, and spent several weeks hiking over snow-covered peaks, across flower-strewn alpine meadows, and fording sparkling, trout-filled brooks, until finally an automobile junkyard flanked by a smelly mountain of trash tires appeared around the bend. "At last," gasped the leader of the expedition, "civilization."

NATURE

Look at those cows and remember that the greatest scientists in the world have never discovered how to make grass into milk.   —*Michael Pupin*

We look too much to museums. The sun coming up in the morning is enough.
                                       —*Romare Bearden*

Nature, to be commanded, must be obeyed.   —*Francis Bacon*

What nature requires is obtainable, and within easy reach. It's for the superfluous we sweat.   —*Seneca the Younger*

To destroy is still the strongest instinct in nature.   —*Max Beerbohm*

Deviation from nature is deviation from happiness.   —*Samuel Johnson*

Nature is no spendthrift, but takes the shortest way to her ends.
                                       —*Ralph Waldo Emerson*

Nature gave men two ends—one to sit on and one to think with. Ever since then man's success or failure has been dependent on the one he used most.
                                       —*George R. Kirkpatrick*

Nature is often hidden, sometimes overcome, seldom extinguished.
                                       —*Francis Bacon*

But perhaps the universe is suspended on the tooth of some monster.

—Anton Chekhov

Individuality seems to be nature's whole aim—and she cares nothing for individuals.

—Johann Wolfgang von Goethe

In the survival of favored individuals and races, during the constantly recurring struggle for existence, we see a powerful and ever-acting form of selection.

—Charles Darwin

Natural beauty is essentially temporary and sad; hence the impression of obscene mockery which artificial flowers give us.   *—John Updike*

A hen is only an egg's way of making another egg.   *—Samuel Butler*

Knowing trees, I understand the meaning of patience. Knowing grass, I can appreciate persistence.   *—Hal Borland*

When you have seen one ant, one bird, one tree, you have not seen them all.

—Edward O. Wilson

. . . to me the outdoors is what you must pass through in order to get from your apartment into a taxicab.   *—Fran Lebowitz*

Lovers of the town have been content, for the most part, to say they loved it. They do not brag about its uplifting qualities. They have none of the infernal smugness which makes the lover of the country insupportable.   *—Agnes Repplier*

Life is an offensive, directed against the repetitious mechanism of the universe.

—Alfred North Whitehead

It is far from easy to determine whether nature has proved to man a kind parent or a merciless stepmother.   *—Pliny the Elder*

The principal task of civilization, its actual raison d'être, is to defend us against nature.   *—Sigmund Freud*

Nature works on a method of all for each and each for all.

—Ralph Waldo Emerson

It were happy if we studied nature more in natural things, and acted according to nature, whose rules are few, plain, and most reasonable.   *—William Penn*

Men and nature must work hand in hand. The throwing out of balance of the resources of nature throws out of balance also the lives of men.

—Franklin D. Roosevelt

Everything is good when it leaves the hands of the Creator; everything degenerates in the hands of man.   *—Jean-Jacques Rousseau*

. . . the laws of nature are the same everywhere. Whoever violates them anywhere must always pay the penalty.   *—Carl Schurz*

One touch of nature makes the whole world kin.   *—William Shakespeare*

Nature never did betray the heart that loved her.   *—William Wordsworth*

Nature does nothing uselessly.   *—Aristotle*

Sayings

You can't fool Mother Nature.

Nature always wins in the long run.

Nature is the greatest show on earth.

Ain't nature grand!

Joke

• "Nature is not perfect and all-knowing," pointed out the pompous old philosopher. "That is why man invented cosmetics."

"Yes, but long before cosmetics nature came up with another invention," pointed out his practical wife. "The darkness of night."

part four

Relationships

R E L A T I O N S H I P S

ANCESTRY

Remember always that all of us, and you and I especially, are descended from
immigrants and revolutionists.
—Franklin D. Roosevelt

No man can cause more grief than one clinging blindly to the voices of his ancestors.
—William Faulkner

A man who thinks too much about his ancestors is like a potato—the best part of him
is underground.
—Henry S. F. Cooper

Gentility is what is left over from rich ancestors after the money is gone.
—John Ciardi

Genealogy: Tracing yourself back to people better than you are.
—John Garland Pollard

I don't know who my grandfather was; I am much more concerned to know what his
grandson will be.
—Abraham Lincoln

The family you came from isn't as important as the family you're going to have.
—Ring Lardner

We are all omnibuses in which our ancestors ride, and every now and then one of them
sticks his head out and embarrasses us.
—Oliver Wendell Holmes, Sr.

It is certainly desirable to be well descended, but the glory belongs to our ancestors.
—Plutarch

Whoever serves his country well has no need of ancestors.
—Voltaire

. . . I agree with you that there is a natural aristocracy among men. The grounds of
this are virtue and talents. . . . There is also an artificial aristocracy, founded on
wealth and birth, without either virtue or talents; for with these, it would belong to the
first class.
—Thomas Jefferson

She's descended from a long line her mother listened to.
—Gypsy Rose Lee

Sayings
Those who inherit fortunes are often more troublesome than those who make them.
—Central African saying

Nobody got here without ancestors.

Ancestry is a hereditary condition.

You can't choose your ancestors, and neither can your descendants.

The true aristocrat is not merely a descendant of previous generations, but more particularly an improvement.

Jokes

- "I can trace my ancestors back sixteen generations," boasted the haughty grande dame over high tea.

    "Is that so?" sniffed her acquaintance. "I never felt the need, myself."

- "Oh, yes," Mrs. Squires-Thompson declared proudly. "We can trace our ancestors back to . . . to . . . Well, I don't know exactly to whom, but we've been descending for centuries."

MARRIAGE

The Positive View

Marriage is our last, best chance to grow up.

—*Joseph Barth*

Marriage has many pains, but celibacy has no pleasures.

—*Samuel Johnson*

There is no more lovely, friendly, and charming relationship, communion, or company than a good marriage.

—*Martin Luther*

Love seems the swiftest, but it is the slowest of all growths. No man or woman really knows what perfect love is until they have been married a quarter of a century.

—*Mark Twain*

There is no greater excitement than to support an intellectual wife and have her support you. Marriage is a partnership in which each inspires the other, and brings fruition to both of you.

—*Millicent Carey McIntosh*

Therefore shall a man leave his father and his mother, and shall cleave unto his wife: and they shall be one flesh.

—**Genesis** *2:24*

Look for a sweet person. Forget rich.

—*Estée Lauder*

I would like to have engraved inside every wedding band *Be kind to one another.* This is the Golden Rule of marriage and the secret of making love last through the years.

—*Randolph Ray*

It is a lovely thing to have a husband and wife developing together and having the feeling of falling in love again. That is what marriage really means: helping one another to reach the full status of being persons, responsible and autonomous beings who do not run away from life.

—*Paul Tournier*

To keep the fire burning brightly, there's one easy rule: keep the two logs together, near enough to keep each other warm and far enough apart—about a finger's breadth— for breathing room. Good fire, good marriage, same rule.

—*Marnie Reed Crowell*

What counts in making a happy marriage is not so much how compatible you are, but how you deal with incompatibility.
—*George Levinger*

Marriage is popular because it combines the maximum of temptation with the maximum of opportunity.
—*George Bernard Shaw*

. . . to have and to hold from this day forward, for better, for worse, for richer, for poorer, in sickness and in health, to love and to cherish, till death do us part.
—**The Book of Common Prayer**

The Jaundiced View

Marriage is a wonderful institution, but who wants to live in an institution?
—*Groucho Marx*

I can't mate in captivity.
—*Gloria Steinem*

It is better to marry than to burn.
—**1 Corinthians 7:9**

When two people are under the influence of the most violent, most insane, most delusive, and most transient of passions, they are required to swear that they will remain in that excited, abnormal, and exhausting condition continuously until death do them part.
—*George Bernard Shaw*

In Hollywood all marriages are happy. It's trying to live together afterwards that causes all the problems.
—*Shelley Winters (attrib.)*

When two people marry, they become in the eyes of the law one person, and that person is the husband.
—*Shana Alexander*

Marriage is the only adventure open to the timid.
—*Voltaire*

Marriage resembles a pair of shears, so joined that they cannot be separated; often moving in opposite directions, yet always punishing anyone who comes between them.
—*Sydney Smith*

Love is an ideal thing, marriage a real thing; a confusion of the real with the ideal never goes unpunished.
—*Johann Wolfgang von Goethe*

What has the women's movement learned from [Geraldine Ferraro's] candidacy for vice president? Never get married.
—*Gloria Steinem*

Don't wish me happiness—I don't expect to be happy . . . it's gotten beyond that somehow. Wish me courage and strength and a sense of humor—I will need them all.
—*Anne Morrow Lindbergh*

A man may be a fool and not know it, but not if he is married.
—*H. L. Mencken*

The fundamental error of their matrimonial union: that of having based a permanent contract on a temporary feeling.
—*Thomas Hardy*

Men marry because they are tired; women because they are curious. Both are disappointed.
—*Oscar Wilde*

Marriage may be compared to a cage: the birds outside frantic to get in and those inside frantic to get out.
—*Michel Eyquem de Montaigne*

Keep your eyes wide open before marriage, half shut afterwards.

—*Benjamin Franklin*

Happiness in marriage is entirely a matter of chance.   —*Jane Austen*

Well married, a man is winged—ill married, he is shackled.

—*Henry Ward Beecher*

A man in love is incomplete until he has married. Then he's finished.

—*Zsa Zsa Gabor*

Wedlock: The deep, deep peace of the double bed after the hurly-burly of the chaise longue.   —*Mrs. Patrick Campbell*

Whoever perpetrated the mathematical inaccuracy "Two can live as cheaply as one" has a lot to answer for.   —*Caren Meyer*

It is difficult to tell which gives some couples the most happiness, the minister who marries them, or the judge who divorces them.   —*Mary Wilson Little*

It is better to know as little as possible of the defects of the person with whom you are to pass your life.   —*Jane Austen*

A fool and his money are soon married.   —*Carolyn Wells*

Proposals make cowards of us all.   —*Carolyn Wells*

Brought up to respect the conventions, love had to end in marriage. I'm afraid it did.

—*Bette Davis*

Never go to bed mad. Stay up and fight.   —*Phyllis Diller*

Every woman should marry—and no man.   —*Benjamin Disraeli*

I never knew what real happiness was until I got married. And by then it was too late.

—*Max Kauffmann*

Marrying a man is like buying something you've been admiring for a long time in a shop window. You may love it when you get it home, but it doesn't always go with everything else in the house.   —*Jean Kerr*

Familiarity breeds contempt—and children.   —*Mark Twain*

By all means marry; if you get a good wife, you'll become happy; if you get a bad one, you'll become a philosopher.   —*Socrates*

I married beneath me. All women do.   —*Nancy Astor*

A good marriage would be between a blind wife and a deaf husband.

—*Michel Eyquem de Montaigne*

Matrimony is a process by which a grocer acquired an account the florist had.

—*Francis Rodman*

Before marriage, a man will lie awake all night thinking about something you said; after marriage, he'll fall asleep before you finish saying it.

—*Helen Rowland*

There is only one thing for a man to do who is married to a woman who enjoys spending money, and that is to enjoy earning it.   —*Edgar Watson Howe*

If you are afraid of loneliness, don't marry.   —*Anton Chekhov*

The dread of loneliness is greater than the fear of bondage, so we get married.
—*Cyril Connolly*

Remember, it's as easy to marry a rich woman as a poor woman.
—*William Makepeace Thackeray*

It destroys one's nerves to be amiable every day to the same human being.
—*Benjamin Disraeli*

Marriage must incessantly contend with a monster that devours everything: familiarity.
—*Honoré de Balzac*

A successful marriage requires falling in love many times, always with the same
person.   —*Mignon McLaughlin*

Marriage is a good deal like a circus: there is not as much in it as is represented in the
advertising.   —*Edgar Watson Howe*

As to marriage or celibacy, let a man take which he will, he is sure to repent.
—*Socrates*

Take it from me—marriage isn't a word—it's a sentence.   —*King Vidor*

We would have broken up except for the children. Who were the children? Well, she
and I were.   —*Mort Sahl*

The only thing that holds a marriage together is the husband bein' big enough to step
back and see where his wife is wrong.   —*Archie Bunker*

Sayings

A man without a wife is like a vase without flowers.   —*Cape Verde Islands saying*

Bigamy is having one wife too many. Monogamy is the same thing.

Marriage is the only war where one sleeps with the enemy.   —*Mexican proverb*

Marry in haste, repent at leisure.

Marriage is an institution run by the inmates.

Marriage may be made in heaven, but it can be hell on earth.

Marriage is the price men pay for sex; sex is the price women pay for marriage.

Jokes

• Whom God hath joined together no man shall ever put asunder; God will take care of
  that.   —*George Bernard Shaw*

• Woman to marriage counselor: "The only thing my husband and I have in common is
  that we were married on the same day."

• What's the difference between a married man and a single man?
  —The married man has a better half, while a single man gets lots of pieces.

• First guy: "I've got a big problem. I'm married to a wonderful cook, a marvelous
  lover, and the best-looking woman in town."

Second guy: "So what's the problem?"

First guy: "Having more than one wife is illegal."

• The other night I said to my wife Ruth, "Do you feel that the sex and excitement has gone out of our marriage?" Ruth said, "I'll discuss it with you during the next commercial."

—*Milton Berle*

• The wise old codger pointed out that it was impossible to judge the happiness of a married couple from observation alone. "Some couples hold hands because if they let go, they're afraid they'd kill each other."

• We sleep in separate rooms, we have dinner apart, we take separate vacations— we're doing everything we can to keep our marriage together.

—*Rodney Dangerfield*

• President and Mrs. Coolidge once visited a state fair, where the prize rooster was brought to Mrs. Coolidge's attention. "This here rooster does his duty up to eight times a day, ma'am," the proud owner informed her.

The first lady's eyes opened wide. "Please see to it that that piece of information reaches the president," she instructed crisply.

Not long after, the president's party passed through the poultry barn, and the rooster's owner dutifully informed Coolidge of the bird's prowess.

"Eight times a day, eh?" the president marveled. "With the same hen?"

"No sir—with a different hen each time."

"Pass *that* on to Mrs. Coolidge!"

• Listening to Winston Churchill expound at length on his political opinions, Lady Astor grew more and more furious. Finally, unable to contain herself, she snapped, "If you were my husband, I'd put poison in your coffee."

"And if I were your husband," returned Churchill, "I'd drink it."

• Harry Jones was a prominent member of a fraternal lodge, and one morning over breakfast he related to his wife an incident that had occurred the previous night. The president of the lodge had offered a top hat to the brother who could stand up and truthfully say that during his married life he had never kissed any woman but his own wife. "And, would you believe it, Helen?—not a one stood up?"

"Harry," his wife chided, "why didn't you stand up?"

"I was going to, honey," he explained, "but you know I'd look ridiculous in a top hat."

• On hearing that a colleague who had endured a long and unhappy marriage had just remarried for a second time, Samuel Johnson characterized his act as "the triumph of hope over experience."

• How does a Wasp propose marriage?

—He asks, "How would you like to be buried with my people?"

• Are you living a life of *quiet* desperation, or are you married?

• Harry was stunned to come home from work one evening and find his wife stuffing all her belongings into a suitcase. "What on earth are you doing?" he cried.

"I can't stand it anymore!" she shrieked. "Thirty-two years we've been married, and all we do is bicker and quarrel and ignore each other. I'm leaving!"

Stunned, Harry watched his wife close the suitcase, lug it down the stairs, and proceed to walk out of the house . . . out of his life. Suddenly he was galvanized into action. Running into the bedroom and grabbing a second suitcase, he yelled back at his wife, "Sylvia, you're right, you're absolutely right—and I can't bear it either. Wait a minute, and I'll go with you."

HUSBANDS AND WIVES

Husbands and Wives

Many a man owes his success to his first wife and his second wife to his success.
—*Red Buttons*

Wives are people who feel they don't dance enough.   —*Groucho Marx*

A man's wife has more power over him than the state has.
—*Ralph Waldo Emerson*

Men are nicer to the women they don't marry.   —*Belle Livingston*

I'm having trouble managing the mansion. What I need is a wife.
—*Governor Ella Grasso*

Basically my wife was immature. I'd be at home in the bath and she'd come in and sink my boats.   —*Woody Allen*

Saying
The longer a couple stays together, the more they begin to resemble each other.

Jokes
• An extravagance is anything you buy that is of no use to your spouse.

• A wife has no trouble buying pajamas for her husband, but a husband buying his wife a nightgown acts as guilty as an escaped convict.

Husbands

I married beneath me. All women do.   —*Nancy Astor*

A man in love is incomplete until he has married. Then he's finished.
—*Zsa Zsa Gabor*

For the first year of marriage I had a basically bad attitude. I tended to place my wife underneath a pedestal.   —*Woody Allen*

An archeologist is the best husband any woman can have: the older she gets, the more interested he is in her.   —*Agatha Christie*

I've been asked to say a couple of words about my husband, Fang. How about "short" and "cheap"?   —*Phyllis Diller*

Husbands are like fires: they go out if unattended.   —*Zsa Zsa Gabor*

A husband is what is left of the lover after the nerve has been extracted.

—Helen Rowland

Sayings
A husband must be deaf and the wife blind to have quietness.

Jealous husbands were once lewd bachelors.

When the husband drinks to the wife all would be well; when the wife drinks to the husband, all *is* well.

Jokes
• What three things can an average man do in a minute and a half?
   —Drink a beer, burp, and have sex with his wife.

• I've been reading that advice column for years, and the way I see it, the happiest husband in the world must be Mr. Abby.

Wives

My wife was too beautiful for words, but not for arguments.

—John Barrymore

There's nothing like a good dose of another woman to make a man appreciate his wife.

—Clare Boothe Luce

An occasional lucky guess as to what makes a wife tick is the best a man can hope for. Even then, no sooner has he learned how to cope with the tick than she tocks.

—Ogden Nash

It is not good that man should be alone; I will make him an help meet for him.

—Genesis 2:18

No man should have a secret from his wife—she invariably finds out.

—Oscar Wilde

I just put on what the lady says. I've been married three times, so I've been well supervised.   *—Upton Sinclair*

Edith, stifle yourself!   *—Archie Bunker*

Do you know what it means to come home at night to a woman who'll give you a little love, a little affection, a little tenderness? It means you're in the wrong house, that's what it means.   *—Henny Youngman*

Saying
Bigamy is having one wife too many. Monogamy is the same thing.

Jokes
• I made a big mistake when I put my wife on a pedestal. Now she can't reach the floor to clean.

• I don't drink to my wife. I drink because of her.

• Explaining to his doctor that his sex life wasn't all it could be, Norm asked his doctor for a pill that would enable him to perform for his wife. It so happened that the doctor had just the right medication, so Norm popped a pill and drove home, but it also happened that his wife had to work late that night. So after waiting for a while in growing discomfort, Norm finally had to jerk off.

When the doctor called to check the next day, Norm explained what had happened. "Gee, Norm," the doctor explained, "there are other women in the building, you know."

"Doctor," Norm explained in an exasperated tone, "for other women I don't need a pill."

• Noting they she and her husband made love more and more infrequently, Sandy tried everything she could think of: romantic dinners and cruises, greeting him at the door in sexy lingerie, trying out exotic paraphernalia from a sex boutique. But nothing seemed to work, and finally he yielded to her urgings that he consult a sex therapist.

To her amazement, a single visit restored her husband's ardor to honeymoon dimensions. The only quirk was that every so often during lovemaking her husband would dash into the bathroom for a minute or two. Finally her curiosity overcame her better judgment, and she followed him to the bathroom door. Looking in, she saw him peering intently into the mirror and repeating, "She's not my wife . . . she's not my wife . . ."

BABIES

A baby is an inestimable blessing and a bother.   —*Mark Twain*

Insomnia: A contagious disease often transmitted from babies to parents.

—*Shannon Fife*

I can't think why mothers love them.   —*William Faulkner*

When we are born we cry that we are come to this great stage of fools.

—*William Shakespeare*

Out of the mouth of babes and sucklings has thou ordained strength.

—*Psalms 4:8*

A baby is God's opinion that the world should go on.   —*Carl Sandburg*

You can sort of be married, you can sort of be divorced, you can sort of be living together, but you can't sort of have a baby.   —*David Shire*

Every baby born into the world is a finer one than the last.

—*Charles Dickens*

Infancy conforms to nobody; all conform to it.   —*Ralph Waldo Emerson*

Who would not tremble and rather choose to die than to be a baby again, if given such a choice?   —*St. Augustine*

When I was born, I was so surprised I couldn't talk for a year and a half.

—*Gracie Allen*

[A baby is] a loud noise at one end and no sense of responsibility at the other.

—Ronald Knox

There is two things in this life for which we are never fully prepared, and that is—twins.   *—Josh Billings*

People who say they sleep like a baby usually don't have one.

—Leo J. Burke

Sayings

You spend the first year waiting for them to walk and talk, and the next twenty waiting for them to sit down and shut up.

When the baby cries, you've got two alternatives—one at each end.

Jokes

• The meeting went on for quite a while, and toward the end the junior executive couldn't quite cover up a huge yawn. "Jones, you're never going to get ahead in this company on less than a full night's sleep," snipped the chairman.

"You're absolutely right, sir," replied the fellow wearily, "but you try getting that across to my two-month-old baby."

• After going through Lamaze, Leboyer, and La Leche classes with his expectant wife, the proud new father remained by his wife's bedside throughout labor and delivery. Wanting to be as sympathetic as possible, he took his wife's hand afterward and said emotionally, "Tell me how it was, darling, how it actually felt to give birth."

"Okay, honey," his wife replied. "Smile as hard as you can."

Beaming down beatifically at his wife and newborn child, the man commented, "That's not so hard."

She continued, "Now stick a finger in each corner of your mouth." He obeyed, smiling broadly.

"Now stretch your lips as far as they'll go," she went on.

"Still not too tough," he remarked.

"Right," she snapped. "Now pull them over your head."

CHILDREN

Our children may learn about heroes of the past. Our task is to make ourselves architects of the future.   *—Jomo Mzee Kenyatta*

Insanity is hereditary—you get it from your children.   *—Sam Levenson*

The United States in the 1980s may be the first society in history in which children are distinctly worse off than adults.   *—Daniel Patrick Moynihan*

Every child is an artist. The problem is how to remain an artist once he grews up.

—Pablo Picasso

I see the mind of the five-year old as a volcano with two vents: destructiveness and creativeness.   *—Sylvia Ashton Warner*

Children have never been very good at listening to their elders, but they have never failed to imitate them.   —*James Baldwin*

You are the bows from which your children, as living arrows, are sent forth.
                                                      —*Kahlil Gibran*

Nature makes boys and girls lovely to look upon so they can be tolerated until they acquire some sense.   —*William Lyon Phelps*

Reasoning with a child is fine, if you can reach the child's reason without destroying your own.   —*John Mason Brown*

What we want is to see the child in pursuit of knowledge, and not knowledge in pursuit of the child.   —*George Bernard Shaw*

You may give them your love but not your thoughts, for they have their own thoughts. You may house their bodies but not their souls, for their souls dwell in the house of tomorrow, which you cannot visit, not even in your dreams.
                                                      —*Kahlil Gibran*

Children need love, especially when they do not deserve it.

                                                      —*Harold S. Hubert*

Children are a great comfort in your old age—and they help you to reach it faster, too.
                                                      —*Lionel M. Kauffman*

You know children are growing up when they start asking questions that have answers.
                                                      —*John J. Plomp*

Before I got married I had six theories about bringing up children; now I have six children and no theories.   —*John Wilmot*

The real menace in dealing with a five-year-old is that in no time at all you begin to sound like a five-year-old.   —*Jean Kerr*

Our children are not going to be just "our children"—they are going to be other people's husbands and wives and the parents of our grandchildren.

                                                      —*Mary S. Calderone*

You cannot write for children . . . They're much too complicated. You can only write books that are of interest to them.   —*Maurice Sendak*

The thing that impresses me most about America is the way parents obey their children.   —*Duke of Windsor*

Our children will hate us too, y'know.   —*John Lennon*

Children are without pity.   —*Jean de La Fontaine*

How sharper than a serpent's tooth it is to have a thankless child.

                                                      —*William Shakespeare*

The childhood shows the man as morning shows the day.   —*John Milton*

Train up a child in the way he should go: and when he is old, he will not depart from it.   —**Proverbs 22:6**

Give a little love to a child, and you get a great deal back.   —*John Ruskin*

I have found the best way to give advice to your children is to find out what they want and then advise them to do it.   —*Harry S Truman*

Children begin by loving their parents. After a time, they judge them. Rarely, if ever, do they forgive them.   —*Oscar Wilde*

A child develops individuality long before he develops taste. I have seen my kid straggle into the kitchen in the morning with outfits that need only one accessory: an empty gin bottle.   —*Erma Bombeck*

Ah, the patter of little feet around the house. There's nothing like having a midget for a butler.   —*W. C. Fields (attrib.)*

Anybody who hates children and dogs can't be all bad.   —*W. C. Fields*

Ask your child what he wants for dinner only if he's buying.

—*Fran Lebowitz*

Mankind owes to the child the best it has to give. . . .
                                    —*Opening words of the United Nations' Declaration of*
                                    the Rights of the Child

Familiarity breeds contempt—and children.   —*Mark Twain*

It now costs more to amuse a child than it once did to educate his father.
                                    —*Vaughan Monroe*

The children now love luxury, they have bad manners, contempt for authority, they show disrespect for elders and love chatter in place of exercise. They no longer rise when elders enter the room. They contradict their parents, chatter before company, gobble up dainties at the table, cross their legs, and tyrannize over their teachers.
                                    —*Socrates*

If you treat a sick child like an adult and a sick adult like a child, everything usually works out pretty well.   —*Ruth Carlisle*

Sayings
The man who has a full set of tools has no children.

Children are the wisdom of the nation.   —*West African saying*

The two things children wear out are clothes and parents.

Children should be seen and not heard.

Children are poor people's riches.

The worst children are always somebody else's.

Jokes
• The door-to-door salesman rang the doorbell, and the door was opened by a nine-year-old boy puffing on a long black cigar. Trying to conceal his surprise, the salesman asked nonchalantly, "Is your mother home, sonny?"

   The boy pulled the cigar out of his mouth, flicked off the ash, and asked, "What do *you* think, mister?"

• "There's a new baby at our house," Katie informed the mailman.

"Is that so? Is he going to stay?" asked the mailman.

"I think so," replied Katie glumly. "He's got all his things off."

• I've got nothing against kids. I just follow the advice on every bottle in my medicine cabinet: "Keep Away from Children."

• The eight-year-old was talking to her grandmother, and when the subject happened to come around to spanking, the girl announced that her father didn't spank her anymore.

"And what does he do instead?" inquired Granny.

"Oh, when I'm bad he just makes a speech about it."

"And just what does he say?" pursued Granny.

"Search me," said the girl breezily. "I never listen."

• Nowadays children are getting all of the things their parents never had when they were young: ulcers, neuroses, anxiety attacks, psychotherapy. . . .

• What is a home without children? Paid for!

FAMILY

God gives us our relatives; thank God we can choose our friends.

—*Ethel Watts Mumford*

The presidency is temporary—but the family is permanent.

—*Yvonne de Gaulle, wife of the French president*

One's family is the most important thing in life. I look at it this way: one of these days I'll be over in a hospital somewhere with four walls around me. And the only people who'll be with me will be my family.   —*Robert C. Byrd*

Happiness is having a large, loving, caring, close-knit family in another city.

—*George Burns*

The families of one's friends are always a disappointment.

—*Norman Douglas*

One loyal friend is worth ten thousand relatives.   —*Euripides*

Big sisters are the crab grass in the lawn of life.   —*Charles M. Schulz*

Other things may change us, but we start and end with the family.

—*Anthony Brandt*

After all, what is a pedestrian? He is a man who has two cars—one being driven by his wife, the other by one of his children.   —*Robert Bradbury*

A family is a unit composed not only of children but of men, women, an occasional animal, and the common cold.   —*Ogden Nash*

Am I my brother's keeper?   —*Genesis 4:9*

The voice of thy brother's blood crieth unto me from the ground.

—*Genesis 4:10*

All happy families are alike, but each unhappy family is unhappy in its own way.

—*Leo Tolstoy*

A family is but too often a commonwealth of malignants.   *—Alexander Pope*

You don't choose your family. They are God's gift to you, as you are to them.
—Archbishop Desmond Tutu

To each other, we were as normal and nice as the smell of bread. We were just a family. In a family, even exaggerations make perfect sense.   *—John Irving*

A sister is both your mirror—and your opposite.   *—Elizabeth Fishel*

We are willing to spend the least amount of money to keep [an American child] at home, more to put him in a foster home, and the most to institutionalize him.
—Marian Wright Edelman

It is not observed in history that families improve with time.
—George William Curtis

Behind every successful man stands a proud wife and a surprised mother-in-law.
—Brooks Hays

Relations are simply a tedious pack of people who haven't got the remotest knowledge of how to live, nor the smallest instinct about when to die.   *—Oscar Wilde*

The family is one of nature's masterpieces.   *—George Santayana*

I do not condemn nepotism, provided the relatives really work.
—Margaret Chase Smith

. . . a family . . . is a little kingdom, torn with factions and exposed to revolutions.
—Samuel Johnson

Alcoholism isn't a spectator sport. Eventually the whole family gets to play.
—Joyce Rebeta-Burditt

Sayings
Blood will tell.

Blood is thicker than water.

You pick your friends but not your family.

Jokes
• They treated the hired girl like one of the family—so she quit.

—Elbert Hubbard

• Older man: "So, you want to become my son-in-law?"
    Younger man: "No, I don't. But since I want to marry your daughter, I don't see how I can get out of it."

• "How come the Greens have started taking French lessons?"
    "Didn't you know their adoption plans finally came through? They've gotten an adorable French baby, and they want to understand what she says when she begins to talk."

• The young lady had just been introduced to a polite young man who politely asked her to dance. By way of making conversation as they waltzed around the ballroom, she asked, "Who's that terribly ugly man sitting over there by the potted palm?"

Looking over, he exclaimed, "Why, that's my brother!"

"Oh, you must excuse me," blurted the mortified young lady. "I really hadn't noticed the resemblance."

FATHERS

Men are generally more careful of the breed of their horses and dogs than of their children.   —*William Penn*

Many a man wishes he were strong enough to tear a telephone book in half—especially if he has a teenage daughter.   —*Guy Lombardo*

He may be president, but he still comes home and swipes my socks.

—*Joseph P. Kennedy*

One father is more than a hundred schoolmasters.   —*George Herbert*

It is a wise father that knows his own child.   —*William Shakespeare*

You don't raise heroes, you raise sons. And if you treat them like sons, they'll turn out to be heroes, even if it's just in your own eyes.

—*Walter M. Schirra, Sr.*

My father was not a failure. After all, he was the father of a president of the United States.   —*Harry S Truman*

You don't have to deserve your mother's love. You have to deserve your father's.

—*Robert Frost*

He's a great kid. He hates the same way I do.

—*Joseph P. Kennedy, on his son Bobby*

Build me a son, O Lord, who will be strong enough to know when he is weak, and brave enough to face himself when he is afraid, one who will be proud and unbending in honest defeat, and humble and gentle in victory.   —*Douglas MacArthur*

Sayings
You'll never be the man your father was.

Fathers are blind to the faults of their daughters.

Dear Old Dad.

The bond between mother and child always remains slightly mysterious to the father.

A father can't help competing with his son.

Jokes
• The first-time father, beside himself with excitement over the birth of his son, was determined to follow all the rules to a T. "So tell me, Nurse," he asked as his new family headed out the hospital door, "what time should we wake the little guy in the morning?"

• After going through Lamaze, Leboyer, and La Leche classes with his expectant wife, the proud new father remained by his wife's bedside throughout labor and delivery.

Wanting to be as sympathetic as possible, he took his wife's hand afterwards and said emotionally, "Tell me how it was, darling, how it actually felt to give birth."

"Okay, honey," his wife replied. "Smile as hard as you can."

Beaming down beatifically at his wife and newborn child, the man commented, "That's not so hard."

She continued, "Now stick a finger in each corner of your mouth." He obeyed, smiling broadly.

"Now stretch your lips as far as they'll go," she went on.

"Still not too tough," he remarked.

"Right," she snapped. "Now pull them over your head."

MOTHERS

My mother had a great deal of trouble with me, but I think she enjoyed it.

—*Mark Twain*

The hand that rocks the cradle may not rule the world, but it certainly makes it a better place.   —*Margery Hurst*

I will never understand children. I never pretended to. I meet mothers all the time who make resolutions to themselves. "I'm going to . . . go out of my way to show them I am interested in them and what they do. I am going to understand my children." These women end up making rag rugs, using blunt scissors.

—*Erma Bombeck*

An author who speaks about his own books is almost as bad as a mother who talks about her own children.   —*Benjamin Disraeli*

Only mothers can think of the future—because they give birth to it in their children.

—*Maxim Gorky*

I looked on child-rearing not only as a work of love and duty but as a profession that was fully as interesting and challenging as any honorable profession in the world and one that demanded the best that I could bring it.   —*Rose Kennedy*

Oh, what a power is motherhood, possessing a potent spell. All women alike fight fiercely for a child.   —*Euripides*

As is the mother, so is her daughter.   —*Ezekiel 16:44*

You become about as exciting as your food blender. The kids come in, look you in the eye, and ask if anybody's home.   —*Erma Bombeck*

Every mother is like Moses. She does not enter the promised land. She prepares a world she will not see.   —*Pope Paul VI*

I gave her life. I can take life away.

—*Mary Beth Whitehead, on her role as surrogate mother to Baby M*

One of my children wrote in a third-grade piece on how her mother spent her time . . . "one-half time on home, one-half time on outside things, one-half time writing."

—*Charlotte Montgomery*

Men are what their mothers made them.   —*Ralph Waldo Emerson*

I really learned it all from mothers.

—*Dr. Benjamin Spock*

Clever men create themselves, but clever women, it seems to me, are created by their mothers. Women can never quite escape their mothers' cosmic pull, not their lip-biting expectations or their faulty love. We want to please our mothers, emulate them, disgrace them, oblige them, outrage them, and bury ourselves in the mysteries and consolations of their presence.

—*Carol Shields*

There's always room for improvement, you know—it's the biggest room in the house.

—*Louise Heath Leber, on being chosen Mother of the Year*

It's like being grounded for eighteen years.

—*New York City Board of Education poster warning against teenage pregnancy*

Saying
Why do grandparents and grandchildren get along so well? They have the same enemy —the mother.

Joke
• The young man staggered into the small-town bakery at the crack of dawn on a hideously cold, wet, stormy morning. "Thank God you're open," he gasped. "Do you have fresh cranberry muffins?" When the baker nodded, a huge smile broke out on the fellow's face. "It's worth the trek, then—she'll be so happy. It'll make her day."

The baker nodded understandingly. "Are these for your mother, then?" he asked.

"Would my mother send me out on a day like this?" returned the young man with an incredulous look. "And would I go?"

PARENTS

We are the people our parents warned us against.

—*Nicholas von Hoffman*

The only reason I always try to meet and know the parents better is because it helps me to forgive their children.

—*Louis Johannot*

How you lose or keep your hair depends on how wisely you choose your parents.

—*Edward R. Nida*

Being a good psychoanalyst . . . has the same disadvantage as being a good parent: the children desert one as they grow up.

—*Morton Hunt*

Romance fails us and so do friendships, but the relationship of parent and child, less noisy than all others, remains indelible and indestructible, the strongest relationship on earth.

—*Theodor Reik*

If parents would only realize how they bore their children!

—*George Bernard Shaw*

Here all mankind is equal: rich and poor alike, they love their children.

—*Euripides*

In automobile terms, the child supplies the power but the parents have to do the steering.

—*Dr. Benjamin Spock*

A man with parents alive is a fifteen-year-old boy.   *—Philip Roth*

If all parents today were as strict as I was, we wouldn't have so many brats and little vandals.   *—Dr. Benjamin Spock's mother*

A baby-sitter is a teenager who comes in to act like an adult while the adults go out and act like teenagers.   *—Harry Marsh*

I looked on child-rearing not only as a work of love and duty but as a profession that was fully as interesting and challenging as any honorable profession in the world and one that demanded the best that I could bring it.   *—Rose Kennedy*

Most of us become parents long before we have stopped being children.
                    —Mignon McLaughlin

There must be such a thing as a child with average ability, but you can't find a parent who will admit that it is his child.   *—Thomas Bailey*

If you want an intelligent child, have an intelligent wife.
                    —James D. Watson, pioneer in the field of genetics

Parenthood remains the greatest single preserve of the amateur.
                    —Alvin Toffler

[Parents] must get across the idea that "I love you always, but sometimes I do not love your behavior."   *—Amy Vanderbilt*

As we read the school reports on our children, we realize a sense of relief that can rise to delight that—thank heaven—nobody is reporting in this fashion on us.
                    —J. B. Priestley

You don't have to deserve your mother's love. You have to deserve your father's.
                    —Robert Frost

The father is always a Republican toward his son, and his mother's always a Democrat.
                    —Robert Frost

The most important thing a father can do for his children is to love their mother.
                    —Theodore M. Hesburgh

People who lose their parents when young are permanently in love with them.
                    —Aharon Appelfeld

Loving a child doesn't mean giving in to all his whims; to love him is to bring out the best in him, to teach him to love what is difficult.   *—Nadia Boulanger*

In the next year or so, my signature will appear on $60 billion of United States currency. More important to me, however, is the signature that appears on my life— the strong, proud, assertive handwriting of a loving father and mother.
                    —Katherine D. Ortega, U.S. Treasurer

This is a moment that I deeply wish my parents could have lived to share. My father would have enjoyed what you have so generously said of me—and my mother would have believed it.   *—Lyndon B. Johnson*

We never know the love of our parents for us until we become parents.
                    —Henry Ward Beecher

Men are generally more careful of the breed of their horses and dogs than of their children.
—*William Penn*

All women become like their mothers. That is their tragedy. No man does. That is his.
—*Oscar Wilde*

Honor thy father and thy mother: that thy days may be long upon the land.
—Exodus *20:12*

The first half of our lives is ruined by our parents, and the second half by our children.
—*Clarence S. Darrow*

I will never understand children. I never pretended to. I meet mothers all the time who make resolutions to themselves. "I'm going to . . . go out of my way to show them I am interested in them and what they do. I am going to understand my children." These women end up making rag rugs, using blunt scissors.
—*Erma Bombeck*

. . . parents . . . are sometimes a bit of a disappointment to their children. They don't fulfill the promise of their early years.
—*Anthony Powell*

Parentage is a very important profession, but no test of fitness for it is ever imposed in the interest of the children.
—*George Bernard Shaw*

The longer I live the more keenly I feel that whatever was good enough for our fathers is not good enough for us.
—*Oscar Wilde*

You are the bows from which your children, as living arrows, are sent forth.
—*Kahlil Gibran*

Before I got married I had six theories about bringing up children; now I have six children and no theories.
—*John Wilmot (Lord Rochester)*

Give a little love to a child, and you get a great deal back.
—*John Ruskin*

I have found the best way to give advice to your children is to find out what they want and then advise them to do it.
—*Harry S Truman*

Children begin by loving their parents. After a time, they judge them. Rarely, if ever, do they forgive them.
—*Oscar Wilde*

A Sunday school is a prison in which children do penance for the evil conscience of their parents.
—*H. L. Mencken*

You know more than you think you do.
—*Benjamin Spock, first sentence of* Baby and Child Care

There's no tragedy in life like the death of a child. Things never get back to the way they were.
—*Dwight D. Eisenhower, on the death of his first son*

. . . what law is it that says a woman is a better parent simply because of her sex? I guess I've had to think a lot about whatever it is that makes somebody a good parent: constancy, patience, understanding . . . love. Where is it written that a man has any less of those qualities than a woman?
—*Ted, in* Kramer vs. Kramer, *screenplay by Robert Benton*

Sayings
Parenthood has two stages: when your children ask all the questions, and when they think they know all the answers.

In loco parentis—Latin for "Children drive their parents crazy."

Jokes
- Did you hear about the degenerate who murdered both his parents . . . and then threw himself on the mercy of the court as an orphan?

- How many times has every wayward child heard, "When you grow up I hope you have a child just like you so you'll know what I'm going through!"

- How ambitious was Mrs. Jones when it came to her offspring? Well, when a stranger inquired as to their ages, she replied, "The doctor's in third grade and the lawyer will be starting kindergarten in the fall."

GRANDPARENTS

Just about the time a woman thinks her job is done, she becomes a grandmother.
                              —Edward H. Dreschnack

Grandchildren don't make a man feel old; it's the knowledge that he's married to a grandmother.   *—G. Norman Collie*

Was there ever a grandparent, bushed after a day of minding noisy youngsters, who hasn't felt the Lord knew what he was doing when he gave little children to young people?   *—Joe E. Wells*

Why do grandparents and grandchildren get along so well together? Perhaps the best answer is the one I heard from a psychiatrist recently: "Because they have a common enemy—the parents."   *—Sydney J. Harris*

Our children are here to stay, but our babies and toddlers and preschoolers are gone as fast as they grow up—and we have only a short moment with each. When you see a grandfather take a baby in his arms, you see that the moment hasn't always been long enough.   *—St. Clair Adams Sullivan*

Sayings
Perfect love sometimes does not come until the first grandchild.   *—Welsh proverb*

Grandchildren are God's rewards to grandparents for not shooting their children.

The best thing about grandchildren is that you're not too busy supporting them to enjoy them.

Joke
- Slow, Grandparents at Play.   *—Traffic sign in Florida mobile-home park*

MOTHERS-IN-LAW

Of all the peoples whom I have studied, from city dwellers to cliff dwellers, I always find that at least 50 percent would prefer to have at least one jungle between themselves and their mothers-in-law.

—*Margaret Mead*

A person often catches a cold when a mother-in-law comes to visit. Patients mentioned mothers-in-law so often that we came to consider them a common cause of disease in the United States.

—*Thomas Holmes*

Go not empty unto thy mother-in-law.

—*Ruth 3:17*

I haven't spoken to my mother-in-law for eighteen months—I don't like to interrupt her.

—*Ken Dodd*

Behind every successful man stands a proud wife and a surprised mother-in-law.

—*Brooks Hays*

Peter remained on friendly terms with Christ notwithstanding Christ's having healed his mother-in-law.

—*Samuel Butler*

Saying
The mother-in-law remembers not that she was a daughter-in-law.

Jokes
- First person: "I got this bottle of brandy for my mother-in-law."
  Second person: "What a great trade!"

- Over a beer one evening, Fred was going on and on about his mother-in-law: how cheap she was, how meddlesome, how petty, how overbearing, how boring. But then he leaned over and confessed that he had to give the old bird credit for one thing: there was one moment when he'd have cut his throat if it weren't for her.
  "Huh?" His buddy was startled.
  "She was using my razor."

RITES OF PASSAGE

ADOLESCENCE

You have a wonderful child. Then, when he's thirteen, gremlins carry him away and leave in his place a stranger who gives you not a moment's peace.
—*Jill Eikenberry*

Many a man wishes he were strong enough to tear a telephone book in half—especially if he has a teenage daughter.
—*Guy Lombardo*

The imagination of a boy is healthy, and the mature imagination of a man is healthy; but there is a space of life in between, in which the soul is in ferment, the character undecided, the way of life uncertain, the ambition thick-sighted: thence proceeds mawkishness.
—*John Keats*

[Adolescence is the time] when the brisk minor pants for twenty-one.
—*Alexander Pope*

Just at the age 'twixt boy and youth,/ When thought is speech, and speech is truth.
—*Sir Walter Scott*

He has quit the awkward stage; he is out of his teens.
—*Terence, 166 B.C.*

Definition of adolescence: A kind of emotional seasickness.
—*Arthur Koestler*

A boy becomes an adult three years before his parents think he does, and about two years after he thinks he does.
—*General Lewis B. Hershey*

Remember that as a teenager you are at the last stage in your life when you will be happy to hear that the phone is for you.
—*Fran Lebowitz*

When I was a boy of fourteen, my father was so ignorant I could hardly stand to have the old man around. But when I got to be twenty-one, I was astonished at how much he had learned in seven years.
—*Mark Twain*

She has her own apartment, in mine.
—*Jean Carrol, on her teenage daughter's lifestyle*

Sayings
They're either too young or too old—depending on what you want them to do.

An adolescent is a new dog learning old tricks.

First adolescent, then obsolescent.

The teenage years are the one time in life when you're thrilled to be told you look older than you are.

Teenage is a moment that seems like an eternity; a time of perpetual emotion, cured by time, which brought it on in the first place.

Jokes
- According to the latest census, the average American family now has 2.7 children. And if you've talked to a teenager lately, you know where the .7 comes from—a lot of them aren't all there.

- The hardworking father grew more and more concerned as his son passed through his teens without a single sign of responsible behavior. "When I was a boy your age," he said, confronting the irresponsible fellow one night, "I was a man."

ANNIVERSARIES

I salute my parents' anniversary. I'll celebrate anything that proves my legitimacy.
—*Andrew Frothingham*

One reason people get divorced is that they run out of gift ideas.
—*Robert Byrne*

What ought to be done to the man who invented celebrating of anniversaries? Mere killing would be too light. —*Mark Twain*

The best way you can surprise a woman with an anniversary gift is to give her just what she wanted. —*Arbuth Arundale*

Sayings
It just keeps getting better.

Some things, like fine wines, improve with age.

Jokes
- The aged farmer and his wife were leaning against the edge of the pigpen when the old woman wistfully recalled that the next week would mark their golden wedding anniversary. "Let's have a party, Homer," she suggested. "Let's kill the pig."
  The farmer scratched his grizzled head. "Gee, Elmira," he finally responded, "I don't see why the pig should take the blame for something that happened fifty years ago."

- An aspiring actor called home to announce with great pride that he'd been cast in an off-Broadway play. "It's a real opportunity, Dad," he said, "I play this guy who's been married for twenty-five years."
  "That's great, son," enthused his father. "And one of these days you'll work up to a speaking part."

- Having been invited to his friend's wedding anniversary party, the man asked which apartment he should go to.

"Go to the eleventh floor," the friend instructed, "find Apartment G, push the buzzer with your elbow, and when the door opens quickly put your foot against it."

"Why such an elaborate plan?" asked the perplexed guest.

"Well," cried the host, "you're not planning on coming empty-handed, are you?"

- Wife: "Honey, what is the meaning of this vase of flowers on the breakfast table?"

  Husband: "Today is your wedding anniversary."

  Wife: "Really! Well, do let me know when yours is so I can do the same."

BIRTHDAYS

I think it's wonderful you could all be here for the forty-third anniversary of my thirty-ninth birthday. We decided not to light the candles this year—we were afraid Pan Am would mistake it for a runway.   —*Bob Hope*

The secret of staying young is to live honestly, eat slowly, and lie about your age.

—*Lucille Ball*

I am in the prime of senility.   —*Joel Chandler Harris*

The hardest years in life are those between ten and seventy.

—*Helen Hayes*

My mother is going to have to stop lying about her age because pretty soon I'm going to be older than she is.   —*Tripp Evans*

Saying

Diplomat: Someone who remembers a woman's birthday but forgets her age.

Jokes

- Birthdays are when a man takes a day off and a woman takes a year off.

- The best way for a husband to remember his wife's birthday is to forget it once.

- It's an awful thing to grow old alone. My wife hasn't had a birthday in six years.

- When an eighty-year-old woman was asked if there were to be candles on her birthday cake, she responded curtly, "No, it's a birthday party, not a torchlight procession."

- You know you're getting old when by the time you've lit the last candle on the birthday cake, the first one has burned out.

- You know you're getting old when the heat from the candles on the birthday cake keeps you from getting close enough to blow them out.

- Husband to wife: "How do you expect me to remember your birthday when you never look older?"

GRADUATION

Nothing is as easy to make as a promise this winter to do something next summer; this is how commencement speakers are caught.   —*Sydney J. Harris*

The fireworks begin today. Each diploma is a lighted match. Each one of you is a fuse.
—*Edward I. Koch*

I am not unmindful of the fact that countless middle-aged moralists like me are rising these days on countless platforms all over the world to tell thousands of helpless young captives the score—and I suspect that all of those commencement orators are almost as uncomfortable as I am.
—*Adlai E. Stevenson*

It's not at all hard for me to remember that vivid day of my own graduation. Strangely enough, the one thing about that day that I cannot remember is what the commencement speaker had to say. My thoughts, like yours, were targeted upon my family and my friends and my plans for the summer. But of one thing I'm sure: if the speaker made a short speech, I know that I blessed him.
—*Thomas J. Watson, Jr.*

In his later years, Winston Churchill was asked to give the commencement address at Oxford University. Following his introduction, he rose, went to the podium, and said, "Never, never, never give up." Then he took his seat.

I came to the enlightened conclusion that women would not be truly emancipated until commencement speakers ignored the fact that they were women.
—*Adlai E. Stevenson, after reviewing his planned commencement address*

Commencement speakers have a good deal in common with grandfather clocks: standing usually some six feet tall, typically ponderous in construction, more traditional than functional, their distinction is largely their noisy communication of essentially commonplace information.
—*W. Willard Wirtz*

Saying
The greatest achievement of the graduate is sitting through the commencement address.

Joke
- The president of the university clambered up onto the podium and began his commencement speech with the proud claim that his school really prepared its graduates for the real world.

  "I'll say," interrupted a voice from the sea of mortarboards. "Right off the bat I'm $52,000 in debt!"

DATING AND COURTSHIP

Courtship [is] to marriage as a very witty prologue [is] to a very dull play.
—*William Congreve*

When a couple of young people strongly devoted to each other commence to eat onions, it is safe to pronounce them engaged.
—*James Montgomery Bailey*

Infatuation is when you think that he's as sexy as Robert Redford, as smart as Henry Kissinger, as noble as Ralph Nader, as funny as Woody Allen and as athletic as Jimmy Connors. Love is when you realize that he's as sexy as Woody Allen, as smart as Jimmy Connors, as funny as Ralph Nader, as athletic as Henry Kissinger and nothing like Robert Redford—but you'll take him anyway.
—*Judith Viorst*

She was a lovely girl. Our courtship was fast and furious—I was fast and she was furious.
—*Max Kauffmann*

The hardest task in a girl's life is to prove to a man that his intentions are serious.
—*Helen Rowland*

If men knew all that women think, they'd be twenty times more daring.
—*Alphonse Karr*

Whoever called it necking was a poor judge of anatomy.
—*Groucho Marx*

A youth with his first cigar makes himself sick; a youth with his first girl makes other people sick.
—*Mary Wilson Little*

Cooking, like unrequited love, is all in the mind. Once a girl has decided her ex-boyfriend is a fat slob, she can forget all about him. It is just the same with burned cakes.
—*Madeleine Bingham*

Whenever I date a guy, I think, is this the man I want my children to spend their weekends with?
—*Rita Rudner*

He spoke of love and the Supreme Court.
—*Elizabeth Black, on Hugo L. Black's marriage proposal*

Sayings

You don't have to marry every boy you go out with.

Throw yourself at a man and you'll land at his feet.

Don't marry anyone until you've seen them drunk.

You don't want to get a man by chasing him, because then he'll always remember how he was gotten.

You call *that* a kiss?

You'll get over it before you get married.

Marry in haste, repent at leisure.

Jokes

• What do you think of computer dating?
   —It's terrific if you're a computer.
—*Rita Mae Brown*

• She was another one of his near Mrs.
—*Alfred McFote*

• A man was startled to hear the young lady next to him say, "Strange, but you look like my fourth husband."
   "My God!" he exclaimed. "How many have you had?"
   "Three," she answered smugly.

• The college senior took his new girlfriend to a football game and pointed out a talented new player. "Take a good look at that guy," he advised. "I'm expecting him to be our best man next year."
   The coed cuddled right up and cooed, "That's a strange way to propose, darling, but I accept."

WEDDINGS

Music played at weddings always reminds me of the music played for soldiers before they go into battle.   —*Heinrich Heine*

When two people are under the influence of the most violent, most insane, most delusive, and most transient of passions, they are required to swear that they will remain in that excited, abnormal, and exhausting condition continuously until death do them part.   —*George Bernard Shaw*

Here's to the happy man: All the world loves a lover.

—*Ralph Waldo Emerson*

Look down, you gods, and on this couple drop a blessed crown.

—*William Shakespeare*

Never above you. Never below you. Always beside you.   —*Walter Winchell*

Sayings
A wedding ring is like a tourniquet—it reduces your circulation.

Wedlock is a padlock.

Jokes
• How did the wedding night go? Let's just say that when they came down for breakfast, they asked for separate checks.

• Is it wrong to have sex before you're married?
    —Only if it makes you late for the ceremony!

DIVORCE

It is difficult to tell which gives some couples the most happiness, the minister who marries them, or the judge who divorces them.   —*Mary Wilson Little*

The main . . . divorce routes are along the heavily traveled corridor between Boston and Washington in the Northeast and between nearby cities, such as Houston and Dallas in Texas and San Francisco and Los Angeles in California.
    —*Robert Reinhold, on the increasing number of children traveling between divorced parents*

The divorced person is like a man with a black patch over one eye: he looks rather dashing but the fact is that he has been through a maiming experience.

—*Jo Coudert*

Americans, who make more of marrying for love than any other people, also break up more of their marriages, but the figure reflects not so much the failure of love as the determination of people not to live without it.   —*Morton Hunt*

I never hated a man enough to give him his diamonds back.

—*Zsa Zsa Gabor*

No one is going to take women's liberation seriously until women recognize that they will not be thought of as equals in the secret privacy of men's most private mental parts until they eschew alimony.   —*Norman Mailer (attrib.)*

You never realize how short a month is until you pay alimony.

—*John Barrymore*

There is no fury like an ex-wife searching for a new lover.

—*Cyril Connolly*

A divorce is like an amputation. You survive, but there's less of you.

—*Margaret Atwood*

Divorces as well as marriages can fail.   —*Maurice Merleau-Ponty*

Divorce is the psychological equivalent of a triple coronary bypass. After such a monumental assault on the heart, it takes years to amend all the habits and attitudes that led up to it.   —*Mary Kay Blakely*

The happiest time of anyone's life is just after the first divorce.

—*John Kenneth Galbraith*

. . . being divorced is like being hit by a Mack truck. If you live through it, you start looking very carefully to the right and to the left.   —*Jean Kerr*

Alimony: Bounty after the mutiny.   —*Max Kauffmann*

Alimony is like buying oats for a dead horse.   —*Arthur (Bugs) Baer*

The wages of sin is alimony.   —*Carolyn Wells*

Saying
Definition of alimony: The high cost of leaving.

Jokes
• Alimony: The screwing you get for the screwing you got.

• Divorce is like coffee: Both require grounds.

T H E   S E X E S

BACHELORS

All reformers are bachelors.

—George Moore

She was another one of his near Mrs.

—Alfred McFote

A bachelor never quite gets over the idea that he is a thing of beauty and a boy forever.

—Helen Rowland

What a pity it is that nobody knows how to manage a wife but a bachelor.

—George Colman

Saying
A bachelor never makes the same mistake once.

Joke
• Being a bachelor is great. You get home-cooked meals, along with a choice of cooks.

WOMEN'S RIGHTS

If women want any rights more than they've got, why don't they just take them, and not be talking about it.

—Sojourner Truth

Women and dogs, and other impure animals, are not permitted to enter.

—Inscription on mosque entrance

Woman knows and feels her wrongs as a man cannot know and feel them, and she also knows as well as he can know, what measures are needed to redress them.

—Frederick Douglass

I became a feminist as an alternative to becoming a masochist.

—Sally Kempton (attrib.)

A white woman has one handicap to overcome: that of sex. I have two—both sex and race.

—Mary Church Terrell

Women in America too easily accept the idea of their inferiority to men—if not actually, then in order to curry favor with men, who imagine it easier to live with inferiors than with equals.

—Pearl Buck

There are very few jobs that actually require a penis or a vagina. All other jobs should be open to everybody.

—Florynce Kennedy (also attributed to Gloria Steinem)

I would even go to Washington . . . just to glimpse Jane Q. Public being sworn as the first female president of the United States, while her husband holds the Bible and wears a silly pillbox hat and matching coat.   —*Anna Quindlen*

Any woman who has a career and a family automatically develops something in the way of two personalities, like two sides of a dollar bill, each different in design. . . . Her problem is to keep one from draining the life from the other.

—*Ivy Baker Priest*

[Rape] is the only crime in which the victim becomes the accused.

—*Freda Adler*

There are only about twenty murders a year in London and not all are serious—some are just husbands killing their wives.   —*G. H. Hatherill, Scotland Yard*

A marriage license should not be viewed as a license for a husband to forcibly rape his wife with impunity. . . . A married woman has the same right to control her own body as does an unmarried woman.   —*Sol Wachter*

The testimony of a woman has only half the value of the testimony of a man.

—*Iranian penal code*

To be a housewife is . . . a difficult, a wrenching, sometimes an ungrateful job if it is looked on only as a job. Regarded as a profession, it is the noblest as it is the most ancient of the catalogue. Let none persuade us differently or the world is lost indeed.

—*Phyllis McGinley*

We are unalterably opposed to the presentation of the female body being stripped, bound, raped, tortured, mutilated, and murdered in the name of commercial entertainment and free speech.   —*Susan Brownmiller*

The Constitution requires that Congress treat similarly situated persons similarly, not that it engage in gestures of superficial equality.   —*Lewis F. Powell, Jr.*

I will not answer until I am addressed correctly.
    —*Mary Hamilton, to an Alabama prosecutor who addressed her by her first name*

Without women, we stood in space on one leg only.
                    —*Vladimir Dzanibekov, Soviet cosmonaut,
                    commenting on the first space walk by a woman*

Where I am today has *everything* to do with the years I spent hanging on to my career by my fingernails.   —*Barbara Aronstein Black, on appointment as dean of
        Columbia Law School after raising a family and returning to her studies*

Women do two thirds of the world's work. . . . Yet they earn only one tenth of the world's income and own less than one percent of the world's property. They are among the poorest of the world's poor.   —*Barber B. Conable, Jr.*

I think women are too valuable to be in combat.   —*Caspar W. Weinberger*

What has the women's movement learned from [Geraldine Ferraro's] candidacy for vice president? Never get married.   —*Gloria Steinem*

In politics, if you want anything said, ask a man. If you want anything done, ask a woman.   —*Margaret Thatcher*

I have a brain and a uterus, and I use both.   —*Patricia Schroeder*

Toughness doesn't have to come in a pinstripe suit.   —*Diane Feinstein*

The most stupendous system of organized robbery known has been that of the church toward woman, a robbery that has not only taken her self-respect but all rights of person; the fruits of her own industry; her opportunities of education; the exercise of her own judgment; her own conscience, her own will.   —*Matilda Gage*

The true aim of female education should be not a development of one or two, but all the faculties of human soul, because no perfect womanhood is developed by imperfect culture.   —*Frances Ellen Watkins Harper*

In childhood a woman must be subject to her father; in youth, to her husband; when her husband is dead, to her sons. A woman must never be free of subjugation.
                    —**Code of Manu** *(Hindu)*

Blessed be Thou, our God and Lord of Hosts, who has not created me a woman.
                    —*Traditional Jewish prayer*

No woman can call herself free until she can choose consciously whether she will or will not be a mother.
                    —*Margaret Sanger, founder of Planned Parenthood*

Some of us are becoming the men we wanted to marry.   —*Gloria Steinem*

Women are not entirely wrong when they reject the rules of life prescribed for the world, for these were established for men only, without their consent.
                    —*Michel Eyquem de Montaigne*

We do not ask man to represent us; it is hard enough in times like these for man to carry backbone enough to represent himself.   —*Elizabeth Cady Stanton*

It is a silly question to ask a prostitute why she does it. . . . These are the highest-paid "professional" women in America.   —*Gail Sheehy*

No longer is the female destined solely for the home and the rearing of the family and only the male for the marketplace and the world of ideas.
                    —*William J. Brennan*

When two people marry, they become in the eyes of the law one person, and that person is the husband.   —*Shana Alexander*

These are very confusing times. For the first time in history a woman is expected to combine: intelligence with a sharp hairdo, a raised consciousness with high heels, and an open, nonsexist relationship with a tan guy who has a great bod.
                    —*Lynda Barry*

It is hard to fight an enemy who has outposts in your head.
                    —*Sally Kempton*

No one is going to take women's liberation seriously until women recognize that they will not be thought of as equals in the secret privacy of men's most private mental parts until they eschew alimony.   —*Norman Mailer (attrib.)*

Nobody can argue any longer about the rights of women. . . . It's like arguing about earthquakes.   —*Lillian Hellman (attrib.)*

. . . Women's liberationists . . . keep on getting up on soapboxes and proclaiming that women are brighter then men. That's true, but it should be kept very quiet or it ruins the whole racket.   —*Anita Loos*

There is one thing women can never take away from men. We die sooner.

—*P. J. O'Rourke*

Whatever women do, they must do twice as well as men to be thought half as good. Luckily, this is not difficult.   —*Charlotte Whitton*

I love being under submission to my husband. . . . I believe in keeping the male ego intact.   —*Tammy Faye Bakker*

I never understood women's liberation. I always got what I wanted from men without asking.   —*Martha Graham*

Women will never be as successful as men because they have no wives to advise them.

—*Dick Van Dyke*

I would rather lie on a sofa than sweep beneath it.   —*Shirley Conran*

Women are not men's equals in anything except responsibility. We are not their inferiors, either, or even their superiors. We are, quite simply, different races.

—*Phyllis McGinley*

What this woman wants, with all due respect to S. Freud, is for men to stop asking that question and to realize that women are human beings, not some alien species. They want the same things men want.   —*Diane White*

Women want men, careers, money, children, friends, luxury, comfort, independence, freedom, respect, love, and a three-dollar pantyhose that won't run.

—*Phyllis Diller*

Women want a family life that glitters and is stable. They don't want some lump spouse watching ice hockey in the late hours of his eighteenth beer. They want a family that is so much fun and is so smart that they look forward to Thanksgiving rather than regarding it with a shudder. That's the glitter part. The stable part is, obviously, they don't want to be one bead on a long necklace of wives. They want, just like men, fun, love, fame, money, and power. And equal pay for equal work.   —*Carolyn See*

[Women want] the seemingly impossible: that men treat them with the respect and fairmindedness with which they treat most men.   —*Joyce Carol Oates*

No one should have to dance backwards all their lives.   —*Jill Ruckelshaus*

Women fail to understand how much men hate them.   —*Germaine Greer*

Now we find ourselves threatened by a new form of Puritanism called feminism, which attempts to stamp out sex by denying the fundamental and radical differences between men and women. But it is precisely the differences between male and female which create the tension and the delight.   —*Edward Abbey*

To enlist native help . . . treat natives like human beings. . . . Respect personal property, especially their women.   —*1969 U.S. Army Field Manual*

Sayings
Wouldn't it be nice to hear just one joke about the saleswoman and the farmer's son?

Some leaders are born women.

A woman needs a man like a fish needs a bicycle.

You've come a long way, baby.

A woman who strives to be like a man lacks ambition.

A woman's work is never done by men.

Jokes

• Support women's lib—make *him* sleep on the wet spot.

• Definition of a lesbian: Just another damn woman trying to do a man's job.

• Sexual harassment at work—is it a problem for the self-employed?

—*Victoria Wood*

• What's one advantage of electing a woman president of the United States?
    —We wouldn't have to pay her as much.

• What's the best thing about women's liberation?
    —It gives you gals something to do in your spare time!

MANKIND

I love mankind, it's people I can't stand.   —*Charles M. Schulz*

Men are born equal but they are also born different.   —*Erich Fromm*

No man is an island, entire of itself; every man is a piece of the continent, a part of the main; . . . any man's death diminishes me, because I am involved in mankind; and therefore never send to know for whom the bell tolls; it tolls for thee.

—*John Donne*

The propagandist's purpose is to make one set of people forget that certain other sets of people are human.   —*Aldous Huxley*

The meek shall inherit the earth.   —*Psalms 35:17*

I sometimes think that God, in creating man, somewhat overestimated his ability.

—*Oscar Wilde*

Of mankind in general, the parts are greater than the whole.   —*Aristotle*

When people are free to do as they please, they usually imitate each other.

—*Eric Hoffer*

Man spends his life in reasoning on the past, in complaining of the present, in fearing for the future.   —*Antoine Rivarol*

Man is not the creature of circumstances. Circumstances are the creatures of men.

—*Benjamin Disraeli*

Man shapes himself through decisions that shape his environment.

—*René Dubos*

The ablest man I ever met is the man you think you are.

—*Franklin D. Roosevelt*

Man is at the bottom an animal, midway a citizen, and at the top divine. But the climate of this world is such that few ripen at the top.

—*Henry Ward Beecher*

Man, unlike any other thing organic or inorganic in the universe, grows beyond his work, walks up the stairs of his concepts, emerges ahead of his accomplishments.

—*John Steinbeck*

Man is not made for defeat.

—*Heraclitus*

Man is not the sum of what he has but the totality of what he does not yet have, of what he might have.

—*Jean-Paul Sartre*

The desire to take medicine is perhaps the greatest feature which distinguishes man from animals.

—*William Osler*

I finally know what distinguishes man from the other beasts: financial worries.

—*Jules Renard*

We must, however, acknowledge, as it seems to me, that man with all his noble qualities . . . still bears in his bodily frame the indelible stamp of his lowly origin.

—*Charles Darwin*

Numberless are the world's wonders, but none more wonderful than man.

—*Sophocles*

Inasmuch as ye have done it unto one of the least of these my brethren, ye have done it unto me.

—*Matthew 25:40*

The world is a stage, but the play is badly cast.

—*Oscar Wilde*

The mass of men lead lives of quiet desperation.

—*Henry David Thoreau*

The earth has a skin and that skin has diseases; one of its diseases is called man.

—*Friedrich Wilhelm Nietzsche*

Millions long for immortality who do not know what to do with themselves on a rainy Sunday afternoon.

—*Susan Ertz*

All of the animals except man know that the principal business of life is to enjoy it.

—*Samuel Butler*

I believe that man will not merely endure. He will prevail. He is immortal, not because he alone among creatures has an inexhaustible voice, but because he has a soul, a spirit capable of compassion and sacrifice and endurance.

—*William Faulkner*

Man is not an end but a beginning. We are at the beginning of the second week. We are children of the eighth day.

—*Thornton Wilder*

There is no indispensable man.

—*Franklin D. Roosevelt*

There is no escape—man drags man down, or man lifts man up.

—*Booker T. Washington*

Mankind owes to the child the best it has to give. . . .   *—Opening words of the*
UN's Declaration of the Rights of the Child

Man is a pliable animal, a being who gets accustomed to anything.
—Fyodor Dostoyevsky

Man is the only animal that laughs and weeps; for he is the only animal that is struck
with the difference between what things are, and what they ought to be.
—William Hazlitt

The proper study of mankind is man.   *—Alexander Pope*

Man is the only animal that can remain on friendly terms with the victims he intends to
eat until he eats them.   *—Samuel Butler*

Man is the only animal that laughs, drinks when he is not thirsty, and makes love at
all seasons of the year.   *—Voltaire*

Study mankind. Learn to use men without surrendering to them. Have confidence in
those who, if necessary, are courageous enough to contradict you.
—Catherine the Great

I don't think you have to teach people how to be human. I think you have to teach
them how to stop being inhumane.   *—Eldridge Cleaver*

Sayings
He's no better than you—we all stand up naked inside our clothes.

A man can die but once.

Men, not walls, keep a city safe.

Long ago all men were divine, but mankind so abused the privilege that Brahma, the
god of all gods, decided the godhead should be taken away from them. But he had to
hide it where man would never find it again.
    "Let us bury it deep in the earth," suggested one god.
    Brahma said, "No, man will dig down until he finds it."
    "Then let us throw it into the deepest part of the biggest ocean," proposed another
god.
    "Man will learn to dive and someday come across it," insisted Brahma.
    "Then it can be hidden in the clouds atop the highest mountain of the Himalayas."
    "Man will manage to climb that high some day," Brahma pointed out. "I have a
better idea. Let us hide it where he will never think to look: inside man himself."
    —Hindu legend

Joke
• At times it helps to believe in evolution . . . so you can remember that man isn't
  finished yet.

MEN AND WOMEN

Friends are generally of the same sex, for when men and women agree, it is only in
their conclusions; their reasons are always different.   *—George Santayana*

Neither sex, without some fertilization of the complementary characters of the other, is capable of the highest reaches of human endeavor. —*H. L. Mencken*

Even the wisest men make fools of themselves about women, and even the most foolish women are wise about men. —*Theodor Reik*

Ever since Eve gave Adam the apple, there has been a misunderstanding between the sexes about gifts. —*Nan Robertson*

Behind almost every woman you ever heard of stands a man who let her down. —*Naomi Bliven*

In the sex-war thoughtlessness is the weapon of the male, vindictiveness of the female. —*Cyril Connolly*

A man falls in love through his eyes, a woman through her ears. —*Woodrow Wyatt*

Girls are born knowing everything they need to know; boys have to learn it. —*E. J. Applewhite*

They say great themes make great novels . . . but what these young writers don't understand is that there is no greater theme than men and women. —*John O'Hara*

The woman most in need of liberation is the woman in every man and the man in every woman. —*William Sloan Coffin*

Instead of this absurd division into sexes, they ought to class people as static and dynamic. —*Evelyn Waugh*

Women are never disarmed by compliments. Men always are. That is the difference between the sexes. —*Oscar Wilde*

On one issue at least, men and women agree: they both distrust women. —*H. L. Mencken (attrib.)*

God created man, and finding him not sufficiently alone, gave him a companion to make him feel his solitude more. —*Paul Valéry*

Love is the whole history of a woman's life, but it is an episode in a man's. —*Madame de Staël*

Nobody will ever win the battle of the sexes. There's too much fraternizing with the enemy. —*Henry A. Kissinger*

God made man, and then said I can do better than that and made woman. —*Adela Rogers St. John*

In our civilization, men are afraid that they will not be men enough and women are afraid that they might be considered only women. —*Theodor Reik*

Men play the game; women know the score. —*Roger Woddis*

Women are smarter than men because they listen. —*Phil Donahue*

Male and female are really two cultures and their life experiences are utterly different. —*Kate Millett*

Girls got balls. They're just a little higher up, that's all. —*Joan Jett*

Sayings

Men get wealth and women keep it.

A woman is flax, a man is fire; the devil comes and blows the bellows.

Women in mischief are wiser than men.

Woman is the confusion of man.

Joke

• Rick: "I mean, what *am* I supposed to call you? My 'Girl Friend'? My 'Companion'? My 'Roommate'? Nothing sounds quite right."
Joanie: "How about your 'Reason for Living' "?
Rick: "No, no, I need something I can use around the office."

—*Garry Trudeau*

MEN

A man's best fortune, or his worst, is his wife.   —*Thomas Fuller*

Men's minds are raised to the level of the women with whom they associate. . . .
—*Alexandre Dumas (père)*

That common cold of the male psyche, fear of commitment.
—*Richard Schickel*

His life was gentle and the elements so mixed in him that nature might stand on its feet and say to all the world—this was a man!
—*William Shakespeare, about Hamlet*

I wonder men dare trust themselves with men.   —*William Shakespeare*

Men are but children of a larger growth.   —*John Dryden*

Men become old, but they never become good.   —*Oscar Wilde*

Is there a way to accept the concept of the female orgasm and still command the respect of your foreign-auto mechanic?   —*Bruce Feirstein*

Men have a much better time of it than women; for one thing, they marry later; for another thing they die earlier.   —*H. L. Mencken*

. . . men of few words are the best men. . . .   —*William Shakespeare*

Sayings

Some men are like a brook, noisy but shallow.

Man is like a razor, the sharper for bring stropped.

Some men, like wagons, rattle most when there's nothing in them.

Men's years and their faults are always more than they are willing to own.

A good man is hard to find—and hard to keep good.

A man is like a plank of wood—soft until seasoned.

A self-made man is judged by his product.

A hard man is good to find.

A real man's man is no man's man.

Jokes

- What did the elephant say to the naked man?
  —"How do you breathe through that thing?"

- What were the first words Adam spoke to Eve?
  —"Stand back—I don't know how big this thing's gonna get!"

MEN—THE FEMALE VIEW

Women want mediocre men, and men are working hard to be as mediocre as possible.
—Margaret Mead

He was every other inch a gentleman.
—Rebecca West

Only men who are not interested in women are interested in women's clothes; men who like women never notice what they wear.
—Anatole France

Miss Doggett again looked puzzled; it was as if she had heard that men only wanted one thing but had forgotten for the moment what it was.
—Barbara Pym

I'm not denyin' the women are foolish: God Almighty made 'em to match the men.
—George Eliot, Adam Bede

It takes a woman twenty years to make a man of her son, and another woman twenty minutes to make a fool of him.
—Helen Rowland

Most women set out to try to change a man, and when they have changed him they do not like him.
—Marlene Dietrich (attrib.)

A woman has got to love a bad man once or twice in her life to be thankful for a good one.
—Marjorie Kinnan Rawlings

Women do not like timid men. Cats do not like prudent mice.
—H. L. Mencken

Any woman can fool a man if she wants to and if he's in love with her.
—Agatha Christie

Men are nicer to the women they don't marry.
—Belle Livingston

I have always wanted to be a man, if only for the reason that I would like to have gauged the value of my intellect.
—Margot Asquith

Men should only be the accessories of the strong woman.
—Marie Bashkirtseff

When a man wants to deceive you, he'll find a way of escape through the tiniest holes.
—Colette

My idea of a screamingly boring man is a chap who doesn't like the company of women.
—Anne Edwards

Men don't like independent women.   —*Shirley Chisholm*

Embryologically speaking, it is correct to say that the penis is an exaggerated clitoris.
—*Mary Jane Sherfey*

Remember, all men would be tyrants if they could.   —*Abigail Adams*

I like men to behave like men—strong and childish.   —*Françoise Sagan*

The male is a domestic animal which, if treated with firmness and kindness, can be
trained to do most things.   —*Jilly Cooper*

All real men love to eat.   —*Marlene Dietrich*

I require only three things of a man. He must be handsome, ruthless, and stupid.
—*Dorothy Parker*

I like two kinds of men: domestic and foreign.   —*Mae West*

It's not the men in my life that count; it's the life in my men.   —*Mae West*

No nice men are good at getting taxis.   —*Katherine Whitehorn*

A man's womenfolk, whatever their outward show of respect for his merit and authority,
always regard him secretly as an ass, and with something akin to pity.
—*H. L. Mencken (attrib.)*

Men are what their mothers made them.   —*Ralph Waldo Emerson*

I refuse to consign the whole male sex to the nursery. I insist on believing that some
men are my equals.   —*Brigid Brophy*

Men are too emotional to vote. Their conduct at baseball games and political
conventions shows this, while their innate tendency to appeal to force renders them
particularly unfit for the task of government. . . . Men's place is in the armory.
—*Alice Duer Miller*

Giving a man space is like giving a dog a computer. The chances are he will not use it
wisely.   —*Bette-Jane Raphael*

Macho does not prove mucho.   —*Zsa Zsa Gabor*

Some men are so macho they'll get you pregnant just to kill a rabbit.
—*Maureen Murphy*

Sayings
A man without a hearty appetite at the table won't have a good appetite for anything
else.

Behind every successful man is a woman.

A woman needs a man like a fish needs a bicycle.

Jokes
• Why did the Lord make man first and woman thereafter?
    —Because after one look at Adam, he realized man was going to need some help.

• Why did God create men?
    —Because a vibrator can't mow the lawn.

WOMEN

She turned him down like a bedspread.

—*P. G. Wodehouse*

When you civilize a man, you civilize an individual; but when you civilize a woman, you civilize a whole people.

—*Patrice Emery Lumumba*

I have some women friends but I prefer men. Don't trust women. There is a built-in competition between women.

—*Edna O'Brien*

In nine cases out of ten, a woman had better show more affection than she feels.

—*Jane Austen*

A woman, especially if she has the misfortune of knowing anything, should conceal it as well as she can.

—*Jane Austen*

Women are too imaginative to have much power of reasoning.

—*Marquise du Defand*

I'm glad I'm a woman because I don't have to worry about getting men pregnant.

—*Nell Dunn*

If I were asked . . . to what the singular prosperity and growing strength of [the Americans] ought mainly to be attributed, I should reply: To the superiority of their women.

—*Alexis de Tocqueville*

If she wants to get to the top, a woman must be prepared to work ninety percent harder than a man.

—*Margery Hurst*

A woman is like a teabag; you never know how strong she is until she gets in hot water.

—*Nancy Reagan*

Most women have all other women as adversaries; most men have all other men as their allies.

—*Gelett Burgess*

No woman should ever be quite accurate about her age. It looks so calculating.

—*Oscar Wilde*

The women of Greece count their age from their marriage, not from their birth.

—*Homer*

The whole thing about women is, they lust to be misunderstood.

—*Will Rogers*

The way to fight a woman is with your hat—grab it and run.

—*John Barrymore*

Oh, woman, woman! When to ill thy mind is bent, all hell contains no fouler fiend.

—*Homer*

There are two ways to handle a woman, and nobody knows either of them.

—*Kin Hubbard*

A woman's guess is much more accurate than a man's certainty.

—*Rudyard Kipling*

Woman was God's second mistake.   —*Friedrich Wilhelm Nietzsche*

Brigands demand your money or your life; women require both.

—*Samuel Butler*

Here's to woman! Would that we could fall into her arms without falling into her hands.

—*Ambrose Bierce*

Neither earth nor ocean produces a creature as savage and monstrous as woman.

—*Euripides*

The entire being of a woman is a secret which should be kept.

—*Isak Dinesen*

Woman understands children better than man does, but man is more childlike than woman.   —*Friedrich Wilhelm Nietzsche*

The man who discovers a woman's weakness is like the huntsman in the heat of the day who finds a cool spring. He wallows in it.   —*Jean Giraudoux*

Women give us solace, but if it were not for women we should never need solace.

—*Don Herold*

Women as a sex are sphinxes without secrets.   —*Oscar Wilde*

What is better than wisdom? Woman. And what is better than a good woman? Nothing.

—*Geoffrey Chaucer*

The female of the species is more deadly than the male.

—*Rudyard Kipling*

Women are not entirely wrong when they reject the rules of life prescribed for the world, for these were established for men only, without their consent.

—*Michel Eyquem de Montaigne*

Every woman is a rebel, and usually in wild revolt against herself.

—*Oscar Wilde*

We have no faith in ourselves. I have never met a woman who, deep down in her core, really believes she has great legs. And if she suspects that she *might* have great legs, then she's convinced that she has a shrill voice and no neck.

—*Cynthia Heimel*

Heav'n has no rage like love to hatred turn'd, nor hell a fury like a woman scorned.

—*William Congreve*

A beautiful woman who gives pleasure to men serves only to frighten the fish when she jumps in the water.   —*Kwang Tse*

The evidence indicates that woman is, on the whole, biologically superior to man.

—*Ashley Montagu*

Sayings
A woman is like a gun. Don't fool with it.

A woman is like a salad: much depends on the dressing.

Always take the advice of a woman.

A woman either loves or hates in extremes.

Women's work is never done.

Women's work is never done—by a man.

Woman's intuition.

When a woman has no answer, the sea has no salt.

It is easier for a woman to be famous for her genius than to be forgiven for it.

Jokes

• Intuition: The strange instinct that tells a woman she is right, whether she is or not.

• Why did God create women?
   —Because sheep can't cook.

• Why is a clitoris like Antarctica?
   —Because men know it's down there, but how many really care?

• How can you determine a woman's history?
   —Look at her geography.

WOMEN—THE MALE VIEW

There are only two kinds of women—goddesses and doormats.

—Pablo Picasso

Women like silent men. They think they're listening.   *—Marcel Achard*

The last thing a woman will consent to discover in a man whom she loves, or on whom she simply depends, is want of courage.   *—Joseph Conrad*

Woman will be the last thing civilized by man.   *—George Meredith*

It takes a man a lifetime to find out about one particular woman; but if he puts in, say ten years, industrious and curious, he can acquire the general rudiments of the sex.

—O. Henry

What passes for woman's intuition is often nothing more than man's transparency.

—George Jean Nathan

These impossible women! How they do get around us! The poet was right: can't live with them, or without them.   *—Aristophanes*

For a man to pretend to understand women is bad manners; for him really to understand them is bad morals.   *—Henry James*

If men knew all that women think, they'd be twenty times more daring.

—Alphonse Karr

When I was eleven, I thought that women were solid from the neck down.

—C. E. M. Joad

Women are just like elephants to me; I like to look at them, but I wouldn't want one.

—*Elbert Hubbard*

You can never get a woman to sit down and listen to a drum solo.

—*Clive James*

Despite my thirty years of research into the feminine soul, I have not been able to answer . . . the great question that has never been answered: what does a woman want?
—*Sigmund Freud*

Man has his will—but woman has her way.   —*Oliver Wendell Holmes, Sr.*

Women and people of low birth are very hard to deal with. If you are friendly with them, they get out of hand, and if you keep your distance, they resent it.

—*Confucius*

Women have more imagination than men. They need it to tell us how wonderful we are.   —*Arnold H. Glasow*

When women kiss, it always reminds one of prizefighters shaking hands.

—*H. L. Mencken*

Changeable women are more endurable than monotonous ones. They are sometimes murdered but seldom deserted.   —*George Bernard Shaw*

No matter how much a woman loves a man, it would still give her a glow to see him commit suicide for her.   —*H. L. Mencken*

I don't believe women can carry a pack, live in a foxhole, or go a week without a bath.
—*General William Westmoreland*

I hate women because they always know where things are.

—*James Thurber*

A woman's place is in the wrong.   ·   —*James Thurber*

There are three things I have always loved and never understood—art, music, and women.   —*Le Bovier de Fontenelle*

Love is based on a view of women that is impossible to those who have had any experience with them.   —*H. L. Mencken*

God settled it that one woman is enough for a man, and two is a war on your hands.
—*John Jasper*

You should not attempt to outwit a woman.   —*Alexandre Dumas (fils)*

The fickleness of the women I love is only equaled by the infernal constancy of the women who love me.   —*George Bernard Shaw*

Saying
The only reason why women go to the ladies' room in groups is so they can plot against men without being interrupted.

Jokes
• How many men does it take to mop a floor?
    —None; it's a woman's job.

- How can a real man tell when his girlfriend's having an orgasm?
  —Real men don't care.

- What do you call a woman who can suck a golf ball through fifty feet of garden hose?
  —Darling.

- A man without a woman is like a neck without a pain.

SEX

All lovers swear more performance than they are able.

—*William Shakespeare*

Male sexual response is far brisker and more automatic. It is triggered easily by things —like putting a quarter in a vending machine.   —*Alex Comfort*

The man takes a body that is not his, claims it, sows his so-called seed, reaps a harvest—he colonizes a female body, robs it of its natural resources, controls it.

—*Andrea Dworkin*

Girls who put out are tramps. Girls who don't are ladies. This is, however, a rather archaic use of the word. Should one of you boys happen upon a girl who doesn't put out, do not jump to the conclusion that you have found a lady. What you have probably found is a lesbian.   —*Fran Lebowitz*

. . . I've always gone along with the view that, first, the surest guarantee of sexual success is sexual success (you can't have one without the other and you can't have the other without the one), and, second, that the trappings of sexual success are only fleetingly distinguishable from sexual success itself.   —*Martin Amis*

For lovers, touch is a metamorphosis. All the parts of their bodies seem to change, and they become different and better.   —*John Cheever*

Too much of a good thing can be taxing.   —*Mae West*

There may be some things better than sex, and some things may be worse. But there is nothing exactly like it.   —*W. C. Fields*

Let us live and love, my Lesbia, and value at a penny all the talk of crabbed old men. Suns may set and rise again: for us, when our brief light has set, there's the sleep of perpetual night. Give me a thousand kisses.

—*Gaius Valerius Catullus*

You're not just sleeping with one person, you're sleeping with everyone *they* ever slept with.   —*Theresa Crenshaw, about AIDS*

When you look back on your life . . . what you really find out is that the only person you really go to bed with is yourself.   —*Shirley MacLaine*

You mustn't force sex to do the work of love or love to do the work of sex.

—*Mary McCarthy*

Is sex dirty? Only if it's done right.   —*Woody Allen*

It doesn't matter what you do in the bedroom as long as you don't do it in the street and frighten the horses.   —*Mrs. Patrick Campbell*

I don't want to see any faces at this party I haven't sat on.   *—Bonnie Raitt*

The zipless fuck is absolutely pure . . . and is rarer than the unicorn.

—Erica Jong

Sex—the poor man's polo.   *—Clifford Odets (attrib.)*

. . . is there any greater or keener pleasure than physical love? No, nor any which is more unreasonable.   *—Plato*

Give me chastity and continence, but not just now.   *—St. Augustine*

Is it not strange that desire should so many years outlive performance?

—William Shakespeare

Whoever called it necking was a poor judge of anatomy.   *—Groucho Marx*

If it weren't for pickpockets I'd have no sex life at all.

—Rodney Dangerfield

. . . she said, "Do you mind if I sit down, 'cause I'm pregnant?" I said, "You don't look it. How long have you been pregnant?" She said, "Only ten minutes—but doesn't it make you feel tired?"   *—Max Miller*

To err is human—but it feels divine.   *—Mae West*

[Disapproval of homosexuality cannot justify] invading the houses, hearts, and minds of citizens who choose to live their lives differently.   *—Harry A. Blackmun*

Sayings
One good turn gets most of the blankets.

The battle of the sexes has more surrenders than casualties, and a great many hand-to-hand encounters.

Remember back when we had only two sexes?

Jokes
- I'm at the age where food has taken the place of sex in my life. In fact, I've just had a mirror put over my kitchen table.   *—Rodney Dangerfield*

- It requires a lot of experience for a girl to kiss like a beginner.

- When little Susie came home from her first day of second grade, she promptly asked her mother, "What's sex?"

  Susie's mother had been expecting the question for some time, so she launched into a well-prepared speech about the birds and the bees and eggs and sperm and what happens when two people love each other very very much, and on and on. After about half an hour, noticing that her daughter's brow was still furrowed, she stopped talking. "Honey, haven't you been able to follow what I've been telling you?"

  "I have, Mom, I really have," replied Susie, pulling her school registration card out of her backpack. "But how'm I going to fit it all in this little box?"

- What's the worst thing about oral sex?
  —The view.

- Little Billy was getting old enough to be curious about the birds and bees, so when he and his father encountered two dogs going at it in an empty lot, his dad explained that they were making puppies. It was only a week later that Billy stumbled into his parents' room in the middle of the night, catching them in the act. "What are you and Mommy doing?" he asked.

"Well, Billy," the red-faced parent explained, "Mommy and I are making babies."

"Roll her over, Dad, roll her over!" yelled the little boy. "I'd rather have puppies."

part five

The World

NATIONS AND NATIONALITIES

AMERICA AND THE AMERICANS

America is the only country deliberately founded on a good idea.

—*John Gunther*

America is not like a blanket—one piece of unbroken cloth, the same color, the same texture, the same size. America is more like a quilt—many patches, many pieces, many colors, many sizes, all woven and held together by a common thread.

—*Jesse Jackson*

Violence is as American as cherry pie.　　　　　　　　　—*H. Rap Brown*

[America] is the red man's country by natural right, and the black man's by virtue of his suffering and toil.　　　　　　　　　—*Robert Purvis*

The unhealthy gap between what we preach in America and what we often practice creates a moral dry rot that eats at the very foundation of our democratic ideals and values.　　　　　　　　　—*Whitney Moore Young, Jr.*

America is just the country that shows how all the written guarantees in the world for freedom are no protection against tyranny and oppression of the worst kind. There the politician has come to be looked upon as the very scum of society.

—*Peter Kropotkin*

The American dream is, in part, responsible for a great deal of crime and violence because people feel that the country owes them not only a living but a good living.

—*David Abrahansen*

America has put a tight shoe on the Negro and now he has a callus on his soul.

—*Dick Gregory*

They'll like you because you're a foreigner. They love foreigners; it's just strangers they hate.　　　　　　　　　—*Jonathan Raban*

The popular song is America's greatest ambassador.　　　　—*Sammy Cahn*

. . . it was in making education not only common to all, but in some sense compulsory on all, that the destiny of the free republics of America was practically settled.

—*James Russell*

In the field of world policy, I would dedicate this nation to the policy of the good neighbor.　　　　　　　　　—*Franklin D. Roosevelt*

England and America are two countries separated by the same language.

—*George Bernard Shaw*

The short memories of American voters is what keeps our politicians in office.

—*Will Rogers*

The haughty American nation . . . makes the Negro clean its boots and then proves the moral and physical inferiority of the Negro by the fact that he is a bootblack.

—*George Bernard Shaw*

Our record as a righteous nation has proved so filled with error that, obviously, we must stop thanking God that we are not like other nations.

—*Reinhold Niebuhr*

In other countries, art and literature are left to a lot of shabby bums living in attics and feeding on booze and spaghetti, but in America the successful writer or picture-painter is indistinguishable from any other decent businessman.

—*Sinclair Lewis*

This is the only country that ever went to the poorhouse in an automobile.

—*Will Rogers*

More than any country, ours is an automobile society.

—*Lyndon B. Johnson*

The thing that impresses me most about America is the way parents obey their children.   —*Duke of Windsor*

My rackets are run on strictly American lines and they're going to stay that way.

—*Al Capone*

The only foes that threaten America are the enemies at home, and these are ignorance, superstition, and incompetence.   —*Elbert Hubbard*

Ours seems to be the only nation on the earth that asks its teenagers what to do about world affairs, and tells its golden-agers to go out and play.   —*Julian Gerow*

America is the country where you buy a lifetime supply of aspirin for one dollar, and use it up in two weeks.   —*John Barrymore*

Americans have always been eager for travel, that being how they got to the new world in the first place.   —*Otto Friedrich*

This continent, an open palm spread frank before the sky.   —*James Agee*

No one flower can ever symbolize this nation. America is a bouquet.
—*William Safire, regarding selection of a national flower*

America is God's Crucible, the great Melting Pot where all the races of Europe are melting and re-forming!   —*Israel Zangwill*

America is the greatest of opportunities and the worst of influences.

—*George Santayana*

We must keep America whole and safe and unspoiled.   —*Al Capone*

Here in America we are descended in blood and spirit from revolutionists and rebels— men and women who dared to dissent from accepted doctrine.

—*Dwight D. Eisenhower*

. . . not merely a nation but a nation of nations.   —*Lyndon B. Johnson*

Give me your tired, your poor, your huddled masses yearning to breathe free, the wretched refuse of your teeming shore. Send these, the homeless, tempest-tost to me, I lift my lamp beside the golden door!   —*Emma Lazarus*

America did not invent human rights. In a very real sense . . . human rights invented America.   —*Jimmy Carter*

The American idea . . . a democracy—that is, a government of all the people, by all the people, for all the people. . . .   —*Theodore Parker*

The youth of America is their oldest tradition.   —*Oscar Wilde*

Americans like fat books and thin women.   —*Russell Baker*

The American language is in a state of flux based on the survival of the unfittest.   —*Cyril Connolly*

America's dissidents are not committed to mental hospitals and sent into exile; they thrive and prosper and buy a house in Nantucket and take flyers in the commodities market.   —*Ted Turner*

America is a large, friendly dog in a very small room. Every time it wags its tail, it knocks over a chair.   —*Arnold Toynbee*

This country will not be a good place for any of us to live in unless we make it a good place for all of us to live in.   —*Theodore Roosevelt*

No one ever went broke underestimating the taste of the American public.
    —*H. L. Mencken*

America—a country that has leapt from barbarism to decadence without touching civilization.   —*John O'Hara*

Being a great power is no longer much fun.   —*David Schoenbaum*

Americans adore me and will go on adoring me until I say something nice about them.
    —*George Bernard Shaw (attrib.)*

. . . as American as English muffins and French toast.
    —*John Russell Taylor*

The business of America is business.   —*Calvin Coolidge*

An Englishman is a person who does things because they have been done before. An American is a person who does things because they haven't been done before.
    —*Mark Twain*

American women expect to find in their husbands a perfection that English women only hope to find in their butlers.   —*W. Somerset Maugham*

If I were asked . . . to what the singular prosperity and growing strength of [the Americans] ought mainly to be attributed, I should reply: To the superiority of their women.   —*Alexis de Tocqueville*

Sayings
America: love it or leave it.

Frankly, if I'd been an Indian, I'd have wished Plymouth Rock had landed on the Pilgrims.

An American believes more than anything else in the last four letters of that title: I can.

Jokes

- A Frenchman, a Swiss, and an American were having a friendly discussion of their national traits. "We French are terribly intolerant of the faults of others," the Frenchman admitted quite happily, "while you Swiss just sit back and never get involved in anything . . . but you Americans, you always think you know it all."
  Nodding, the American said, "I know."

- The average American is someone who deplores violence in the street and has seen *High Noon* five times.

- What's the difference between the American Dream and everybody else's dream?
  —Everyone else's dream is to come to America.

CANADA AND THE CANADIANS

We have achieved the most amazing things, a few million people opening up half a continent. But we have not yet found a Canadian soul except in time of war.
—*Lester B. Pearson*

Canada could have enjoyed English government, French culture, and American know-how. Instead it ended up with English know-how, French government, and American culture.   —*John Robert Columbo*

Canada is a country so square that even the female impersonators are women.
—*Richard Benner*

Living next to you [the United States] is in some ways like sleeping with an elephant. No matter how friendly and even-tempered is the beast, if I can call it that, one is affected by every twitch and grunt.
—*Pierre Trudeau, former Canadian prime minister*

In any world menu, Canada must be considered the vichysoisse of nations—it's cold, half-French, and difficult to stir.   —*Stuart Keate (attrib.)*

We have never been a melting pot. The fact is we are more like a tossed salad. We are green, some of us are oily, and there's a little vinegar injected when you get up to Ottawa.   —*Arnold Edinborough*

I accept now with equanimity the question so constantly addressed to me, "Are you an American?" and merely return the accurate answer, "Yes, I am a Canadian."
—*Lester B. Pearson*

The biggest trading partner of the United States is not West Germany or Japan. It's right here [Canada].   —*Brian Mulroney, demanding that the Reagan administration honor commitments on trade and acid rain*

Canada is useful only to provide me with furs.   —*Madame de Pompadour*

Sayings
The Great North.

It's hard to hate a Canadian.

The Royal Canadian Mounties always get their man.

Jokes
* What's a Wasp's idea of open-mindedness?
    —Dating a Canadian.

* What do you call a witty man in Canada?
    —A tourist.

* Why do Canadians do it doggie-style?
    —So both can keep watching the hockey game.

CHINA AND THE CHINESE

I wouldn't mind seeing China if I could come back the same day.

—Philip Larkin

We send missionaries to China so the Chinese can get into heaven, but we won't let them into our country.   *—Pearl Buck*

I founded Wang Laboratories . . . to show that Chinese could excel at things other than running laundries and restaurants.   *—An Wang*

Within a pitifully short time, the China that sat on the [Security] Council and was supposed to represent a billion people represented nothing but a steamy Pacific island.
    —A. M. Rosenthal, recalling the effect of the Chinese Revolution on UN representatives

China and North Vietnam are closely united to each other, like the lips and the teeth.
    —Chou En-lai

China is an attractive piece of meat coveted by all . . . but very tough, and for years no one has been able to bite into it.   *—Chou En-lai*

Man's contribution to human history is nothing more than a drop of sperm.
    —Chian Ching

Let a hundred flowers bloom.
    —Mao Tse-tung, acknowledging contradictions within Communist society

By following the concept of "One country, two systems," you don't swallow me up nor I you.   *—Deng Xiaoping, on policy regarding Hong Kong*

Cantonese will eat anything in the sky but airplanes, anything in the sea but submarines, and anything with four legs but the table.   *—Amanda Bennet*

Sayings
For all the tea in China . . .

Meant to keep people out, the Great Wall is one of the great monuments to xenophopia. It is also the only manmade artifact visible from the moon.

China's greatest natural resource is its vast population.

Jokes

* They say the Chinese are inscrutable—so how come there are over a billion of them?

* When the president visited Beijing, the zoo was one of the highlights of his tour. The premier proudly showed him to the grand cage housing a giant panda and a little lamb. "This is our peaceful coexistence exhibit," he explained proudly.

    The president was most impressed. "It certainly seems to work well," he commented politely.

    "It does, it does," the premier assured him. "Of course we have to put in a new lamb every morning."

ENGLAND AND THE ENGLISH

No one can be as calculatedly rude as the British, who amaze Americans, who do not understand studied insult and can only offer abuse as a substitute.

—Paul Gallico

An Englishman thinks he is moral when he is only uncomfortable.

—George Bernard Shaw

The British . . . are the only people who like to be told how bad things are, who like to be told the worst. *—Winston Churchill*

It was the nation and the race dwelling all round the globe that had the lion's heart. I had the luck to be called upon to give the roar. *—Winston Churchill*

We have always been, we are, and I hope that we always shall be detested in France.

—Duke of Wellington

I have a feeling that this island is uninhabitable, and therefore people have tried to make it habitable by being reasonable with one another. *—Ralf Dahrendorf*

The climate of England has been the world's most powerful colonizing impulse.

—Russell Green

The English instinctively admire any man who has no talent and is modest about it.

—James Agee

The English think incompetence is the same thing as sincerity.

—Quentin Crisp

We didn't win the war, we just refused to lose it. *—Tom Sharpe*

England is a slipshod place. The English are forever seeking amusement without finding it, whilst the French possess it without the fatigue of running after it.

—Duchess of Kingston

The English are the greatest nationalists in the world, but they're also the subtlest. They do it by convincing everyone that any other kind of nationalism is in bad taste, and they've somehow put it across. *—Winifred Ewing*

Enough scarps and rocks and countries are conveniently distributed across the face of the earth so that the sun still always shines on something British.

—Pamela Marsh

Take all your dukes and marquesses and earls and viscounts, pack them into one chamber, call it the House of Lords to satisfy their pride and then strip it of all political power. It's a solution so perfectly elegant and preposterous that only the British could have managed it.   —*Charles Krauthammer*

He [Prince Charles] is just as entitled to be underwhelmed by the prospect of reigning over a fourth-class nation as the rest of us are by the prospect of living in it.
                                                        —*Peter Jay*

An Englishman is a person who does things because they have been done before. An American is a person who does things because they haven't been done before.
                                                        —*Mark Twain*

England and America are two countries separated by the same language.
                                                —*George Bernard Shaw*

There have been many definitions of hell, but for the English the best definition is that it is a place where the Germans are the police, the Swedish are the comedians, the Italians are the defense force, Frenchmen dig the roads, the Belgians are the pop singers, the Spanish run the railways, the Turks cook the food, the Irish are the waiters, the Greeks run the government, and the common language is Dutch.
                                            —*David Frost and Antony Jay*

Sayings
It used to be said that England rules the waves; now it's said that England waives the rules.

Stiff upper lip.

Jokes
• The sun never sets on the British Empire because God doesn't trust the Brits in the dark.

• What does an Englishwoman say after sex?
   —"Feel better now, ducky?"

FRANCE AND THE FRENCH

A Frenchman must always be talking, whether he knows anything of the matter or not; an Englishman is content to say nothing when he has nothing to say.
                                                        —*Samuel Johnson*

Political thought in France is either nostalgic or utopian.   —*Raymond Aron*

The parks of Paris—the Bois de Boulogne, Parc Monceau, Vert Galant, Luxembourg, Tuileries, Buttes-Chaumont, and others of varying size and fame—symbolize man's humanity to man.   —*Landt Dennis*

I was France.
    —*Charles de Gaulle, on leadership of the Free France Resistance during World War II*

The French will only be united under the threat of danger. Nobody can simply bring together a country that has 265 kinds of cheese.   —*Charles de Gaulle*

We have always been, we are, and I hope that we always shall be detested in France.
—*Duke of Wellington*

England is a slipshod place. The English are forever seeking amusement without finding it, whilst the French possess it without the fatigue of running after it.
—*Duchess of Kingston*

The French at heart are monarchists. They like to prostrate themselves in front of the monarch, whom they now call president, and every seven years or so they guillotine him.   —*Hervé de Charette*

The French are, as a *nation*, okay; but most of those who live in Paris, to be fair about it, are pond slime. These people don't just hate the Americans, they hate the British, they despise Arabs, they loathe the Swiss, the Japanese, the Germans—they *really* hate the Germans, they hate everybody. They hate somebody from the next arrondissement, for Pete's sake.   —*Harlan Ellison*

The French are true romantics. They feel the only difference betwen a man of forty and one of seventy is thirty years of experience.   —*Maurice Chevalier*

The French are wiser than they seem, and the Spanish seem wiser than they are.
—*Francis Bacon*

Sayings
Vive la France!

Vive la différence! *(between men and women)*

France—where every person is a gourmet.

The only thing frank about the French is their currency.

A nation of lovers.

In an argument, a Frenchman will always fall back on the former glories of France.

Very few French people care a scrap about ancestry, but money is respected by everyone.

Jokes
- Three eight-year-old boys, one British, one American, and one French, met at a Caribbean resort. They were strolling past a row of cabanas when they happened to look in an open window and spot a couple making love.
  "I say, what are they doing?" asked the British lad.
  "They're making love," said the American boy.
  The young Frenchman added, "Yes—and badly."

- Two Frenchmen were strolling along a boulevard when one of them gasped, "*Mon Dieu*—here comes my wife *and* my mistress!"
  "*Sacre bleu!*" exclaimed his friend. "I was about to say the same thing."

GERMANY AND THE GERMANS

One German makes a philosopher, two a public meeting, three a war.

—*Robert D. MacDonald*

Whenever the literary German dives into a sentence, that is the last you are going to see of him till he emerges on the other side of his Atlantic with his verb in his mouth.

—*Mark Twain*

I married a German. Every night I dress up as Poland and he invades me.

—*Bette Midler*

All of us, whether guilty or not, whether old or young, must accept the past. . . . It is not a case of coming to terms with the past. That is not possible. . . . Seeking to forget makes exile all the longer; the secret of redemption lies in remembrance.

—*Richard von Weizsacker*

Sayings
He who is afraid of doing too much always does too little.   —*German proverb*

The Germans—good people, with horrible taste in leaders.

Jokes
• A German call girl—what a frightening thought. Like, when she calls, you listen!

• . . . German—a language . . . which was developed solely to afford the speaker the opportunity to spit at strangers under the guise of polite conversation.

—**The National Lampoon Encyclopedia of Humor**

• Did you hear about the German-Chinese restaurant?
   —An hour after you eat, you're hungry for power.

IRELAND AND THE IRISH

Other people have a nationality. The Irish and the Jews have a psychosis.

—*Brendan Behan*

God made the grass, the air, and the rain; and the grass, the air, and the rain made the Irish; and the Irish turned the grass, the air, and the rain back into God.

—*Sean O'Faolain*

In some parts of Ireland, the sleep which knows no waking is always followed by the wake which has no sleeping.   —*Mary Wilson Little*

The Irish people do not gladly suffer common sense.

—*Oliver St. John Gogarty*

The problem with Ireland is that it's a country full of genius but with absolutely no talent.

—*Hugh Leonard*

The Irish have got gab but are too touchy to be humorous.   —*Edna O'Brien*

Sayings
The luck of the Irish.

May the roof above us never fall in, and may we friends gathered below never fall out.
—*Irish blessing*

Jokes
• The Irish are always talking about the wee people. The wee people? I don't know if that's a leprechaun or a kidney problem.

• What do the Irish say during foreplay?
   —"Brace yourself, Bridget."

ISRAEL AND THE ISRAELIS

Men and nations do behave wisely, once all other alternatives have been exhausted.
—*Abba Eban*

A land flowing with milk and honey.
—**Exodus 3:8**

If you ever forget you're a Jew, a Gentile will remind you.
—*Bernard Malamud*

Other people have a nationality. The Irish and the Jews have a psychosis.
—*Brendan Behan*

In Israel, in order to be a realist you must believe in miracles.
—*David Ben Gurion*

The civilian is a soldier on eleven months' annual leave.
—*General Yigael Yadin*

The Holocaust is a central event in many people's lives, but it also has become a metaphor for our century. There cannot be an end to speaking and writing about it. Besides, in Israel, everyone carries a biography deep inside him.
—*Aharon Appelfeld*

Leading the Jewish people is not easy—we are a divided, obstinate, highly individualistic people who have cultivated faith, sharp-wittedness and polemics to a very high level.
—*Lester B. Pearson*

We have always said that in our war with the Arabs we had a secret weapon—no alternative.
—*Golda Meir*

Above all this country is our own. Nobody has to get up in the morning and worry what his neighbors think of him. Being a Jew is no problem here.
—*Golda Meir*

A Jew's religious obsession is not to attain salvation but to make this a better world.
—*Rabbi Myer S. Kripke*

Sayings
A flower blooming in the desert.

The Promised Land.

An act of contrition by the world for centuries of oppression.

Jokes

• An American, a Russian, an Iraqi, and an Israeli were walking down the street when a man came up to them and said, "Excuse me. I'm with the Gallup Organization and we're conducting a public opinion poll about the meat shortage—"
The Russian said, "What's meat?"
The American said, "What's a shortage?"
The Iraqi said, "What's public opinion?"
And the Israeli said, "What's excuse me?"

• Is it true if you get lost in the desert in Israel, you're rescued by a big dog carrying a keg of seltzer?

• Abbreviations mean different things in different countries. A sign in front of an American motel saying "TV" means television. In Israel, it means "Tourists Velcome."

• If you liked the book, you'll love the country.
                              —*Israeli Tourist Bureau, referring to the Old Testament*

• How many Wasps does it take to plan a trip to Israel?
   —Two; one to ask where, and one to ask why.

• Heard about the Japanese-Jewish restaurant?
   —It's called So-Sue-Me.

ITALY AND THE ITALIANS

Rome was a poem pressed into service as a city.   —*Anatole Broyard*

She said that all the sights in Rome were called after London cinemas.
                                              —*Nancy Mitford*

Rome is unquestionably the lunch capital of the world.   —*Fran Lebowitz*

I want to talk to these people because they stay in power and you change all the time.
                              —*Nikita S. Khrushchev, asking to meet with*
                              Italian businessmen instead of government officials

Italian virtues of fantasy, passion, drama, creativity, color, and perspective have informed both the cuisine and the arts of that nation.   —*Fred Plotkin*

When you are in Paris, live in the Roman style.   —*St. Ambrose*

Sayings

Italians change governments as often as they change their clothes.

Words do not make flour.   —*Italian proverb*

Joke

- Clearly more interested in shopping than history, the woman climbed out of the tour bus and whined, "How long is it going to take to see Florence?"

  The immensely cultured guide replied courteously, "Madam, you can see all of Florence in a day, some of Florence in a week, and a very little bit of Florence in a month."

JAPAN AND THE JAPANESE

Japan is a great nation. It should begin to act like one.

—*John C. Danforth*

To hear the Japanese plead for free trade is like hearing the word *love* on the lips of a harlot.   —*Lane Kirkland*

If the person is over forty years old, I tell him he should do something because it is first good for Japan, good for the company, good for his family, and finally good for him. If the person is under forty, I tell him he should do it because first it is good for him, good for his family, good for the company, and finally good for Japan.

—*Ken Hayashibara*

Good son, good student, good soldier: The young pilot of the kamikaze special unit was less the martyr of a fanatic faith than of his own good heart and good will.

—*Maurice Pinguet*

Is forbidden to steal towels, please. If you are not person to do such is please not to read notice.   —*Sign in Tokyo hotel*

Sayings

Land of the Rising Sun.

As Japanese as Rockefeller Center.

The United States won the war; Japan won the peace.

A culture based on hot wine and raw fish.

Jokes

- If the Japanese are such technological giants, why do they still eat with sticks?

- I just bought a rather unusual tree. Twenty-four feet high, cost a fortune. It's a bonsai sequoia.

THE SOVIET UNION AND THE SOVIETS

The best thing we can do if we want the Russians to let us be Americans is to let the Russians be Russian.   —*George F. Kennan*

Abortion, which destroys life, is inadmissible in any country. Soviet woman has the same rights as Soviet man, but that does not absolve her from the great and honorable duty imposed on her by nature: she is to be a mother. She is to bear life. And this is certainly not a private matter but a public matter of great social significance.

—**Trud** *(official Soviet trade union paper)*

Russia, Russia—unwashed, backward, appealing Russia, so ashamed of your own backwardness, so orientally determined to conceal it from us by clever deceit.

—*George F. Kennan*

Comrades, this man has a nice smile, but he has iron teeth.

—*Andrei Gromyko on Mikhail Gorbachev*

The most unpredictable thing in the USSR is the past.   —*Georgi Arbatov*

Without glasnost there is not, and there cannot be, democratism, the political creativity of the masses and their participation in management.

—*Mikhail Gorbachev*

Tell the premier that for a party of mine, no one needs to carry a card. Just an invitation.   —*Elsa Maxwell*

I cannot forecast to you the action of Russia. It is a riddle wrapped in a mystery inside an enigma.   —*Winston Churchill*

Ideas in modern Russia are machine-cut blocks coming in solid colors; the nuance is outlawed, the interval walled up, the curve grossly stepped.

—*Vladimir Nabokov*

Saying
The greatness of Russia resides in the soul of its people, not in its politics.

Jokes
- A passerby watched the progress of two workmen down a Leningrad street. One stopped every twenty feet to dig a hole, the second filled it in as soon as he was done, and they moved on to the next site. Finally, overcome by curiosity, the observer asked what in heaven's name they were doing. "You certainly aren't accomplishing anything," she pointed out.

  "You don't understand at all," protested one worker indignantly. "We are usually a team of three: I dig the hole, Sergei plants the tree, and Vladimir packs the dirt back in. Today Sergei is home with the flu, but that doesn't mean Vladimir and I get to stop working, does it?"

- First Russian: "Hear the terrible news? The coach of our Olympic skiing team died after they lost the gold medal to the Americans."

  Second Russian: "Nyet! When did he die?"

  First Russian: "Tomorrow."

SPAIN AND THE SPANISH

Spain is a land of mystery where the dust of isolation has often settled on men's work and obscured their lives.   —**Time** *magazine*

The Spanish enjoy teasing domestic animals, not only bulls, but other barnyard creatures as well. They think it's quite merry if you kick their dogs, throw stones at their burros, and chase their chickens around with a stick.

—P. J. O'Rourke

Oh, lovely Spain! renown'd romantic land!   *—George Gordon, Lord Byron*

There actually were some nifty cities in Western Europe in 1000 A.D., but they were in southern Spain, and Spain was not really part of Europe at all, having fallen to the Moslems in the eighth century like overripe fruit from a tree.

—Gail Collins and Dan Collins

Sayings

A country known by its colonies.

The most exotic country in Europe.

A country at war with itself.

Jokes

• The Spaniard didn't do too well in school—he always reported his grades as "Si-si."

• The ignorant tourist didn't want to go see the flamenco dancers . . . he preferred to see birds fly.

CIVILIZATION

CIVILIZATION

Civilization is a movement and not a condition, a voyage and not a harbor.
—*Arnold Toynbee*

Civilization begins with order, grows with liberty, and dies with chaos.
—*Will Durant*

It is so stupid of modern civilization to have given up believing in the devil when he is the only explanation of it. —*Ronald Knox*

You can't say civilizations don't advance . . . for in every war they kill you a new way.
—*Will Rogers*

Civilization is nothing else but the attempt to reduce force to being the last resort.
—*José Ortega y Gasset*

An Englishman who was wrecked on a strange shore and wandering along the coast came to a gallows with a victim hanging on it, and fell down to his knees and thanked God that he at last beheld a sign of civilization. —*James Garfield*

Animals have these advantages over man: they have no theologians to instruct them, their funerals cost them nothing, and no one starts lawsuits over their wills.
—*Voltaire*

The civilized man has built a coach, but has lost the use of his feet. He is supported on crutches, but lacks so much support of muscle. He has a fine Geneva watch, but he fails of the skill to tell the hour by the sun. —*Ralph Waldo Emerson*

The whole history of civilization is strewn with creeds and institutions which were invaluable at first and deadly afterward. —*Walter Bagehot*

The true test of civilization is not the census, not size of cities, but the kind of man that the country turns out. —*Ralph Waldo Emerson*

Civilization and profits go hand in hand. —*Calvin Coolidge*

Increased means and increased leisure are the two civilizers of man.
—*Benjamin Disraeli*

We must plant the sea and herd its animals . . . using the sea as farmers instead of hunters. That is what civilization is all about—farming replacing hunting.
—*Jacques Cousteau*

A nation or civilization that continues to produce soft-minded men purchases its own spiritual death on the installment plan. —*Martin Luther King, Jr.*

There is nothing so good for the human soul as the discovery that there are ancient and flourishing civilized societies which have somehow managed to exist for many centuries and are still in being though they have had no help from the traveler in solving their problems.   —*Walter Lippmann*

For at least two million years, men have been reproducing and multiplying on a little automated spaceship called Earth.   —*R. Buckminster Fuller*

Sayings
Civilization is a process whereby those who have already experienced it impose it on others.

Civilization is always our way of doing things, compared to theirs.

Jokes
• When asked what lesson he had learned from civilization, the old Navajo replied, "Ingratitude."

• The camping expedition got lost, and spent several weeks hiking over snow-covered peaks, across flower-strewn alpine meadows, and fording sparkling, trout-filled brooks, until finally an automobile junkyard flanked by a smelly mountain of discarded tires appeared around the bend. "At last," gasped the leader of the expedition, "civilization."

CULTURE

When I hear the word culture, I reach for my revolver.
                                                —*Hermann Goering*

Culture is a little like dropping an Alka-Seltzer into a glass—you don't see it, but somehow it does something.   —*Hans Magnus Enzensberger*

There are three things I have always loved and never understood—art, music, and women.   —*Le Bovier de Fontenelle*

Culture, the acquainting ourselves with the best that has been known and said in the world, and thus with the history of the human spirit.   —*Matthew Arnold*

Launch your boat, blessed youth, and flee at full speed from every form of culture.
                                                        —*Epicurus*

If you want to get rich from writing, write the sort of thing that's read by persons who move their lips when they're reading to themselves.   —*Don Marquis*

Now we sit through Shakespeare in order to recognize the quotations.
                                                        —*Orson Welles*

Sayings
He's a culture vulture.

Culture is what separates us from the beasts.

Jokes
* The only difference between California and yogurt is that yogurt has active culture.
—*Woody Allen*

* Soon after the great crash of '29, a deeply shaken broker sat down with his wife to discuss ways to economize. "I'm afraid you've just got to cut back on expenses, darling," he said gently.

    Sighing deeply, his wife said, "Well, I suppose we can give up our subscription to the ballet . . . and the Shakespeare Festival . . . and our season tickets to the opera."

    The broker brightened visibly, and murmured, "Maybe there's a bright side to the crash after all."

HISTORY

I have but one lamp by which my feet are guided, and that is the lamp of experience. I know of no way of judging of the future but by the past.   —*Patrick Henry*

History is written by the winners.   —*Alex Haley*

The most unpredictable thing in the USSR is the past.   —*Georgi Arbatov*

Legend remains victorious in spite of history.   —*Sarah Bernhardt*

You only understand the present when it is past.   —*Han Suyin*

We are not makers of history. We are made by history.

—*Martin Luther King, Jr.*

There is a way to look at the past. Don't hide from it. It will not catch you if you don't repeat it.   —*Pearl Bailey*

The only thing new in this world is the history that you don't know.

—*Harry S Truman*

The essential matter of history is not what happened but what people thought or said about it.   —*Frederic William Maitland*

The tapestry of history has no point at which you can cut it and leave the design intelligible.   —*Dorothea Lynde Dix*

Someone said: "The dead writers are remote from us because we know so much more than they did." Precisely, and they are that which we know.   —*T. S. Eliot*

Historic continuity with the past is not a duty, it is only a necessity.

—*Oliver Wendell Holmes, Jr.*

History is the sole consolation left to the people, for it shows them that their ancestors were as unhappy as they are, or even more so.   —*Sébastien Chamfort*

Persistent prophecy is a familiar way of assuring the event.

—*George Robert Gissing*

We are the children of our age, but children who can never know their mother.

—*Logan Pearsall Smith*

If a man could say nothing against a character but what he could prove, history could not be written.
—*Samuel Johnson*

The history of the world is but the biography of great men.
—*Thomas Carlyle*

Very few things happen at the right time, and the rest do not happen at all; the conscientious historian will correct these defects.
—*Herodotus*

Throughout history it has been the inaction of those who could have acted, the indifference of those who should have known better, the silence of the voice of justice when it mattered most, that has made it possible for evil to triumph.
—*Haile Selassie*

Men and nations do behave wisely, once all other alternatives have been exhausted.
—*Abba Eban*

Whether you like it or not, history is on our side. We will bury you!
—*Nikita S. Khrushchev, to Western ambassadors*

The past is a foreign country. They do things differently there.
—*L. P. Hartley*

. . . what's past is prologue. . . .
—*William Shakespeare*

Why doesn't the past decently bury itself, instead of sitting waiting to be admired by the present?
—*D. H. Lawrence*

History does not treat kindly those societies that diagnose their structural weaknesses only after those weaknesses have become irreversible.
—*William J. Abernathy, Kim B. Clark, and Alan M. Kantrow*

History is more or less bunk. It's tradition. We don't want tradition. We want to live in the present and the only history that is worth a tinker's damn is the history we make today.
—*Henry Ford*

The history of the world is the history of a privileged few.
—*Henry Miller*

Human history becomes more and more a race between education and catastrophe.
—*H. G. Wells*

History repeats itself; historians repeat each other.
—*Philip Guedalla*

History is a set of lies agreed upon.
—*Napoleon Bonaparte*

We learn from history that we learn nothing from history.
—*Georg Wilhelm Friedrich Hegel*

Those who cannot remember the past are condemned to repeat it.
—*George Santayana*

. . . a page of history is worth a volume of logic.
—*Oliver Wendell Holmes, Jr.*

An era can be said to end when its basic illusions are exhausted.
—*Arthur Miller*

Winston Churchill is reported to have been confident that history would deal kindly with him. When asked upon what he based this confidence, Churchill replied, "Because I intend to write it."

Sayings
History repeats itself.

History is the past imperfect.

History is not simply what happened, but the way what happened is remembered.

Jokes
* The diligent tourist read the inscription over the State Archives Building which read, "What is Past is Prologue." Turning to the young tour guide, he asked, "What does that mean?"

    She replied brightly, "It means you ain't seen nothing yet."

* In a museum in Havana there are two skulls of Christopher Columbus, "one where he was a boy and one when he was a man."   —Mark Twain

LANGUAGE

Violence of language leads to violence of action. Angry men seldom fight if their tongues do not lead the fray.   —Charles Victor Roman

I have sometimes looked with wonder on the jargon of our times wherein those whose minds reside in the past are called "progressive" while those whose minds are vital enough to challenge and to mold the future are dubbed "reactionary."
                                                    —Jomo Mzee Kenyatta

Correct English is the slang of prigs.   —George Eliot

I have received memos so swollen with managerial babble that they struck me as the literary equivalent of assault with a deadly weapon.   —Peter Baida

Corporate identity specialists . . . spend their time rechristening other companies, [conducting] a legal search [and] a linguistic search to ensure that the name is not an insult in another language.   —Lisa Belkin

Two-tier tender offers, Pac-Man and poison-pill defenses, crown-jewel options, greenmail, golden parachutes, self-tenders—all have become part of our everyday business.   —Felix G. Rohatyn

Nothing surely is more alive than a word.   —J. Donald Adams

England and America are two countries separated by the same language.
                                                    —George Bernard Shaw

Without knowing the force of words, it is impossible to know men.
                                                    —Confucius

The American language is in a state of flux based on the survival of the unfittest.
                                                    —Cyril Connolly

If the Romans had been obliged to learn Latin, they would never have found time to conquer the world.
                                                                                    —*Heinrich Heine*

Language is the archives of history.
                                                                        —*Ralph Waldo Emerson*

By its very looseness, by its way of evoking rather than defining, suggesting rather than saying, English is a magnificent vehicle for emotional poetry.
                                                                                    —*Max Beerbohm*

Ours is a precarious language, as every writer knows, in which the merest shadow line often separates affirmation from negation, sense from nonsense, and one sex from the other.
                                                                                    —*James Thurber*

Slang is a language that rolls up its sleeves, spits on its hands, and goes to work.
                                                                                    —*Carl Sandburg*

Our language is funny—a fat chance and a slim chance are the same thing.
                                                                                    —*J. Gustav White*

The difference between the right word and the almost right word is the difference between lightning and the lightning bug.
                                                                                    —*Mark Twain*

Man does not live by words alone, despite the fact that sometimes he has to eat them.
                                                                                    —*Adlai E. Stevenson*

Language is living, kicking, growing, fluttering, evolving reality, and the teacher should spontaneously reflect its vibrant and protean qualities.
                                                                                    —*John A. Rassias*

Music is the only language in which you cannot say a mean or sarcastic thing.
                                                                                    —*John Erskine*

The pen is mightier than the sword.
                                                                                    —*Edward Bulwer-Lytton*

Sayings
Language sometimes gets in the way of communication.

Talk is cheap.

Choose your words, or your words will keep you from being chosen.

Speak softly and sweetly; later you may have to eat your words.

Jokes
• Two men got into a discussion, which turned into a difference of opinion, which turned into a violent disagreement. Despite the abundance of argument going back and forth, neither was having much success getting his point across, and finally one let loose and punched his opponent in the face.
    "Geez," said the fellow on the ground, rubbing his chin, "why didn't you say that in the first place?"

• "Merrill," asked the teacher, "what's a synonym?"
    "A synonym, Miss Cripps, is a word you use when you can't spell or pronounce the other one."

- After concluding an impassioned sales spiel for the latest model, the car salesman paused to let it sink in. "Any questions?" he asked.

  "Actually, yes," replied the prospect. "How come the $26,000 sticker price you're asking is *modest,* and the $400 rebate you're offering is *substantial?*"

- First neighbor: "How come the Hansingers have started taking French lessons?"
  Second neighbor: "Didn't you know their adoption plans finally came through? They've gotten an adorable French baby, and they want to understand what the little tyke says when he begins to talk."

TRADITION

Tradition is the dead hand of human progress.   —*Kelly Miller*

The great enemy of the truth is very often not the lie—deliberate, contrived, and dishonest—but the myth—persistent, persuasive, and unrealistic.
                                                                     —*John F. Kennedy*

Imagination continually frustrates tradition; that is its function.
                                                                     —*John Pfeiffer*

Tradition means giving votes to that obscurest of classes, our ancestors. It is the democracy of the dead.   —*W. H. Auden*

. . . when you live in a place you've always lived in, where your family has always lived, you get to see things not only in space but in time.   —*Shirley Grau*

Tradition does not mean that the living are dead but that the dead are living.
                                                                     —*G. K. Chesterton*

Saying
Innovative societies have a tradition of ignoring traditions.

Joke
- When I was fifteen, I got talked into attending a formal party. My mother made me promise to observe tradition in my apparel. I looked up the rules, which said I had to wear black tie or a full-dress uniform. I went as an admiral.

J U S T I C E

CENSORSHIP

I shall not today attempt further to define the kinds of material [pornography] . . . but I know it when I see it.
—Potter Stewart

Burn the libraries, for all their value is in the Koran.
—Caliph Omar

Secrecy is a disease, and Chernobyl its symptom, a threat both to the Soviet Union and its neighbors.
—New York Times *editorial*

Vietnam was the first war ever fought without any censorship. Without censorship, things can get terribly confused in the public mind.
—General William Westmoreland

Personally, I don't like pornography. But not because I fear it will turn me or someone else into a raging fiend. I dislike it because it is tasteless, embarrassing, and boring. But that's no reason to ban it. If being tasteless or embarrassing or boring was a crime, we'd have to get rid of 90 percent of the TV shows and hit records, close down most of the franchise food joints, muzzle the politicians, and prohibit any preacher from talking more than ninety seconds.
—Mike Royko

To limit the press is to insult a nation; to prohibit reading of certain books is to declare the inhabitants to be either fools or slaves.
—Claude-Adrien Helvétius

If we value the pursuit of knowledge, we must be free to follow wherever that search may lead us. The free mind is no barking dog to be tethered on a ten-foot chain.
—Adlai E. Stevenson

We don't want to censor your songs. What we want to do is change your song. You're the younger generation; you believe in change.
—Rocco Laginestra, RCA Records president

You have not converted a man because you have silenced him.
—John Morley

Books won't stay banned. They won't burn. Ideas won't go to jail. In the long run of history, the censor and the inquisitor have always lost. The only sure weapon against bad ideas is better ideas.
—A. Whitney Griswold

Censorship, like charity, should begin at home; but, unlike charity, it should end there.
—Clare Boothe Luce

Censorship is more depraving and corrupting than anything pornography can produce.
—Tony Smythe

I am . . . mortified to be told that, in the United States of America . . . a question about the sale of a book can be carried before the civil magistrate. . . . Are we to have a censor whose imprimatur shall say what books may be sold, and what we may buy? . . . Whose foot is to be the measure to which ours are all to be cut or stretched? . . . Shall a layman, simple as ourselves, set up his reason as the rule for what we are to read? . . . It is an insult to our citizens to question whether they are rational beings or not.   —*Thomas Jefferson*

If all mankind, minus one, were of one opinion, and only one person were of the contrary opinion, mankind would be no more justified in silencing that one person, than he, if he had the power, would be justified in silencing mankind.

—*John Stuart Mill*

The moment we begin to fear the opinions of others and hesitate to tell the truth that is in us, and from motives of policy are silent when we should speak, the divine floods of light and life no longer flow into our souls.   —*Elizabeth Cady Stanton*

If a man is pictured chopping off a woman's breast, it only gets an R rating; but if, God forbid, a man is pictured kissing a woman's breast, it gets an X rating. Why is violence more acceptable than tenderness?   —*Sally Struthers*

If the First Amendment means anything, it means that a state has no business telling a man, sitting alone in his own house, what books he may read or what films he may watch. . . . Our whole constitutional heritage rebels at the thought of giving government the power to control men's minds.   —*Thurgood Marshall*

If art is to nourish the roots of our culture, society must set the artist free to follow his vision wherever it takes him.   —*John F. Kennedy*

Freedom is absolutely necessary for progress in science and the liberal arts.

—*Benedict Spinoza*

For better or worse, editing is what editors are for: and editing is selection and choice of material. That editors—newspapers or broadcast—can and do abuse this power is beyond doubt, but that is no reason to deny the discretion Congress provided.

—*Warren E. Burger, in the Supreme Court majority ruling that allowed radio and TV stations to refuse to sell time for political or controversial advertisements*

We can't duck our responsibilities and permit the government to subsidize slime and sleaze.   —*Jesse Helms*

Assassination is the extreme form of censorship.   —*George Bernard Shaw*

Sayings
You can't tell a book by its cover.

The noncontroversial dies, but the banned plays on.

What you don't know can hurt you.

Joke
• Having obtained a seat on the crowded bus, the citizen looked up at the big fellow looming over him. "Are you a member of the Communist party?" he asked.

"No, I'm not," answered the standing man.

"Are you perhaps in the military?"
"No, I'm not."
"So I can assume you do not work for the government in any capacity?"
He shook his head.
"Then get the hell off my foot!"

FREEDOM AND LIBERTY

A hungry man is not a free man.   *—Adlai E. Stevenson*

Freedom of opinion can only exist when the government thinks itself secure.
                                                                  —Bertrand Russell

Better to starve free than be a fat slave.   *—Aesop*

Freedom suppressed and again regained bites with deeper fangs than freedom never
endangered.   *—Cicero*

You can only protect your liberties in this world by protecting the other man's freedom.
You can only be free if I am free.   *—Clarence S. Darrow*

. . . you cannot separate peace from freedom, because no one can be at peace unless
he has his freedom.   *—Malcolm X*

Free discussion is the only necessary constitution—the only necessary law of the
constitution.   *—Richard Carlile*

The tree of liberty grows only when watered by the blood of tyrants.
                                                        —Bertrand de Barère de Vieuzac

Freedom lies in being bold.   *—Robert Frost*

If a nation values anything more than freedom, it will lose its freedom; and the irony of
it is that if it is comfort or money that it values more, it will lose that too.
                                                              —W. Somerset Maugham

Necessity is the plea for every infringement of human freedom. It is the argument of
tyrants; it is the creed of slaves.   *—William Pitt*

Freedom in general may be defined as the absence of obstacles to the realization of
desires.   *—Bertrand Russell*

No woman can call herself free until she can choose consciously whether she will or
will not be a mother.   *—Margaret Sanger, founder of Planned Parenthood*

Free speech carries with it some freedom to listen.   *—Warren E. Burger*

A right is not what someone gives you; it's what no one can take from you.
                                                                   —Ramsey Clark

Give me the liberty to know, to utter, and to argue freely according to conscience,
above all liberties.   *—John Milton*

The right to be heard does not automatically include the right to be taken seriously.
                                                              —Hubert H. Humphrey

Liberty, when it begins to take root, is a plant of rapid growth.

—*George Washington*

A country can get more real joy out of just hollering for their freedom than they can if they get it.   —*Will Rogers*

Every law is an infraction of liberty.   —*Jeremy Bentham*

Liberty is obedience to the law which one has laid down for oneself.

—*Jean-Jacques Rousseau*

He that would make his own liberty secure must guard even his enemy from oppression.   —*Thomas Paine*

Let my people go.   —Exodus 5:1

Liberty has never come from the government. Liberty has always come from the subjects of it. The history of liberty is a history of resistance. The history of liberty is a history of limitations of governmental power, not the increase of it.

—*Woodrow Wilson*

Liberty without obedience is confusion, and obedience without liberty is slavery.

—*William Penn*

Is life so dear or peace so sweet as to be purchased at the price of chains and slavery? Forbid it, Almighty God! I know not what course others may take, but as for me, give me liberty, or give me death.   —*Patrick Henry*

If liberty means anything at all, it means the right to tell people what they do not want to hear.   —*George Orwell*

In fact, a fundamental interdependence exists between the personal right to liberty and the personal right to property.   —*Potter Stewart*

Liberty unregulated by law degenerates into anarchy, which soon becomes the most horrid of all despotism.   —*Millard Fillmore*

Let every nation know, whether it wishes us well or ill, that we shall pay any price, bear any burden, meet any hardship, support any friend, oppose any foe to assure the survival and success of liberty.   —*John F. Kennedy*

Liberty means responsibility. This is why most men dread it.

—*George Bernard Shaw*

Liberty: one of imagination's most precious possessions.   —*Ambrose Bierce*

. . . the sole end for which mankind are warranted, individually or collectively, in interfering with the liberty of action of any of their number, is self-protection. That the only purpose for which power can be rightfully exercised over any member of a civilized community, against his will, is to prevent harm to others. His own good, either physical or moral, is not a sufficient warrant.   —*John Stuart Mill*

The state has no business in the bedrooms of the nation.   —*Pierre Trudeau*

Only free men can negotiate; prisoners cannot enter into negotiations. Your freedom and mine cannot be separated.

—*Nelson Mandela, refusing to bargain for freedom after twenty-one years in prison*

Intellectual liberty is the air of the soul, the sunshine of the mind, and without it, the world is a prison, the universe a dungeon.   —*Robert G. Ingersoll*

I, who wish to be free, cannot be so, because around me are men who do not yet desire freedom, and, not desiring it, become, as opposed to me, the instruments of my oppression.   —*Mikhail Bakunin*

Many politicians are in the habit of laying it down as a self-evident proposition that no people ought to be free till they are fit to use their freedom. The maxim is worthy of the fool in the old story who resolved not to go into the water till he had learned to swim.   —*Thomas Babington Macaulay*

They that can give up essential liberty to obtain a little temporary safety deserve neither liberty nor safety.   —*Benjamin Franklin*

The only freedom which deserves the name is that of pursuing our own good in our own way, so long as we do not attempt to deprive others of theirs, or impede their efforts to obtain it. Each is the proper guardian of his own health, whether bodily, or mental and spiritual.   —*John Stuart Mill*

. . . the vile habits often acquired in a state of servitude are not easily thrown off. . . .
                    —*Richard Allen*

It seems almost incredible that the advocates of liberty should conceive the idea of selling a fellow creature to slavery.   —*James Forten*

A man is either free or not. There cannot be any apprenticeship for freedom.
                    —*Imamu Amiri Baraka*

We have to talk about liberating minds as well as liberating society.
                    —*Angela Davis*

We know the road to freedom has always been stalked by death.
                    —*Angela Davis*

Freedom always entails danger.   —*W. E. B. Du Bois*

We, the free, must set about our unfinished tasks of freeing others.
                    —*William Tecumseh Vernon*

Either we must attain freedom for the whole world or there will be no world left for any of us.   —*Walter Francis White*

Freedom is a hard-bought thing.   —*Paul Robeson*

Freedom belongs to the strong.   —*Richard Wright*

. . . it's a poor kind of man that won't fight for his own freedom.
                    —*Alice Childress*

. . . after you get your freedom, your enemy will respect you.
                    —*Malcolm X*

Freedom is not constituted primarily of privileges but of responsibilities.
                    —*Albert Camus*

Sayings
Your freedom to swing your arms stops at the tip of my nose.

The blessings of liberty are most appreciated when they have been lost.

Freedom of speech means that even a donkey has the right to bray.

The truth will set you free.

Joke
• What's so great about a country that promotes freedom?
   —Everyone has a right to state their opinions, but no one is forced to listen to them.

JUSTICE AND INJUSTICE

Justice is truth in action.
—*Benjamin Disraeli*

Justice, sir, is the great interest of man on earth. It is the ligament which holds civilized beings and civilized nations together.
—*Daniel Webster*

Delay in justice is injustice.
—*Walter Savage Landor*

We only want that which is given naturally to all peoples of the world, to be masters of our own fate, not of others, and in cooperation and friendship with others.
—*Golda Meir*

Whatsoever a man soweth, that shall he also reap.
—*Galatians 6:7*

Injustice is relatively easy to bear; what stings is justice.
—*H. L. Mencken*

One man's justice is another man's injustice.
—*Ralph Waldo Emerson*

The love of justice in most men is only the fear of suffering injustice.
—*François de La Rochefoucauld*

Judging from the main portions of the history of the world, so far, justice is always in jeopardy.
—*Walt Whitman*

Justice has nothing to do with expediency.
—*Woodrow Wilson*

. . . moderation in the pursuit of justice is no virtue.
—*Barry M. Goldwater*

With what measure ye mete, it shall be measured to you again. And why beholdest thou the mote that is in thy brother's eye, but considerest not the beam that is in thine own eye?
—*Matthew 7:3*

That only a few, under any circumstances, protest against the injustice of long-established laws and customs, does not disprove the fact of the oppressions, while the satisfaction of the many, if real, only proves their apathy and deeper degradation.
—*Elizabeth Cady Stanton*

Eye for eye, tooth for tooth.
—*Exodus 21:24*

Sayings
Once the game is over, the king and the pawn go back into the same box.
—*Italian saying*

Justice is like fire; if one covers it with a veil, it still burns.   *—Madagascan saying*

Justice is blind.

Justice often satisfies neither side.

Justice has different faces for different people.

Jokes

* Requesting the judge's attention, the jury foreman said, "Your Honor, in the course of our deliberations, a question of law has come up: what is justice?"

    "That is not a question of law," responded the judge gravely. "It's a question of judgment."

* After a while the baker came to suspect that the farmer from whom he bought his butter was shorting him on his order. So for an entire week he carefully weighed the butter at home, and sure enough his suspicions were confirmed. Irate, he had the farmer arrested.

    A hearing was scheduled without delay. "I assume you use the standard weights when measuring out your goods?" the judge asked the farmer sternly.

    "As a matter of fact, I don't," responded the farmer evenly.

    "Well then, how do you do your measuring?"

    "You see, Your Honor, when the baker began buying butter from me, I decided to buy his bread," explained the farmer. "And I measure out his butter by placing his one-pound loaf of bread on the other side of the scale."

LAW AND ORDER

It's a poor rule that won't work both ways.   *—Frederick Douglass*

Human law may know no distinction among men in respect of rights, but human practice may.   *—Frederick Douglass*

Mob law is the most forcible expression of an abnormal public opinion; it shows that society is rotten to the core.   *—Timothy Thomas Fortune*

To make a new concept fit into an old statute makes tortured law with tortured results.
    —Harvey R. Sorkow, ruling that the Baby M surrogacy contract was a valid contract

What a cage is to the wild beast, law is to the selfish man.

—Herbert Spencer

Law: An ordinance of reason for the common good, made by him who has care of the community.   *—St. Thomas Aquinas*

I favor capital punishment. It saves lives.   *—Nancy Reagan*

When I came back to Dublin, I was courtmartialed in my absence and sentenced to death in my absence, so I said they could shoot me in my absence.

—Brendan Behan

It is the very merit of the death penalty that its bark is worse than its bite.

—Lord Quickswood

A successful lawsuit is one worn by a policeman.   *—Robert Frost*

Laws are like spiders' webs in that if anything small falls into them they ensnare it, but large things break through and escape.   —*Solon*

Morality cannot be legislated, but behavior can be regulated. Judicial decrees may not change the heart, but they can restrain the heartless.

—*Martin Luther King, Jr.*

The law is silent during war.   —*Cicero*

The law, in its majestic equality, forbids the rich as well as the poor to sleep under bridges.   —*Anatole France*

There is no better way of exercising the imagination than the study of law. No poet ever interpreted nature as freely as a lawyer interprets the truth.

—*Jean Giraudoux*

The legal system is often a mystery, and we, its priests, preside over rituals baffling to everyday citizens.   —*Henry G. Miller*

Common sense often makes good law.   —*William O. Douglas*

The layman's constitutional view is that what he likes is constitutional and that which he doesn't like is unconstitutional.   —*Hugo L. Black*

Anyone who takes it on himself, on his own authority, to break a bad law, thereby authorizes everyone else to break the good ones.   —*Denis Diderot*

Law is not self-executing. Unfortunately, at times its execution rests in the hands of those who are faithless to it. And even when its enforcement is committed to those who revere it, law merely deters some human beings from offending, and punishes other human beings for offending. This does not make men good. This task can be performed only by ethics or religion or morality.   —*Samuel J. Ervin, Jr.*

There are not enough jails, not enough policemen, not enough courts to enforce a law not supported by the people.   —*Hubert H. Humphrey*

. . . a strict observance of the written laws is doubtless *one* of the high duties of a good citizen, but it is not the *highest*. The laws of necessity, or self-preservation, of saving our country when in danger, are of higher obligation.

—*Thomas Jefferson*

Ye shall have one manner of law, as well for the stranger as for one of your own country.   —*Leviticus 24:22*

Whenever law ends, tyranny begins.   —*John Locke*

Ignorance of the law excuses no man; not that all men know the law, but because 'tis an excuse every man will plead, and no man can tell how to confute him.

—*John Selden*

To make laws that man cannot, and will not obey, serves to bring all law into contempt.   —*Elizabeth Cady Stanton*

The more laws, the more offenders.   —*Thomas Fuller*

Law cannot persuade where it cannot punish.   —*Thomas Fuller*

The law must be stable, but it must not stand still.   —*Roscoe Pound*

When you punish someone, you pay for it later. There was a time when pickpockets were publicly hanged, but other pickpockets took advantage of the crowds attracted to the execution to ply their trade. —*J. Hopps Baker*

The police must obey the law while enforcing the law. —*Earl Warren*

Distrust all in whom the impulse to punish is powerful.
—*Friedrich Wilhelm Nietzsche*

A policeman's lot is not a happy one. —*W. S. Gilbert*

Law is order, and good law is good order. —*Aristotle*

Of all the tasks of government, the most basic is to protect its citizens from violence.
—*John Foster Dulles*

Law enforcement cannot succeed without the sustained—and informed—interest of all citizens. —*Lyndon B. Johnson*

There is no greater wrong in our democracy than violent, willful disregard of law.
—*Lyndon B. Johnson*

There is no grievance that is a fit object of redress by mob law.

—*Abraham Lincoln*

So long as governments set the example of killing their enemies, private individuals will occasionally kill theirs. —*Elbert Hubbard*

Nothing is illegal if a hundred businessmen decide to do it, and that's true anywhere in the world. —*Andrew Young*

When I was a kid, one cop could have taken care of the whole neighborhood. Now, one cop wouldn't be *safe* in the neighborhood. —*Mike Royko*

I don't want to send them to jail. I want to send them to school.
—*Adlai E. Stevenson, about picketers who attacked him in Dallas*

Necessity hath no law. —*Oliver Cromwell*

Sayings
A government of law is a government of lawyers.

The practice of medicine occurs even in primitive society, but law accompanies civilization.

A bad compromise beats a good lawsuit.

Law and order are not necessarily partners.

When you read the riot act, be prepared to enforce it.

Jokes
• Storming the jail, the lynch mob insisted on the release of a much feared criminal into their hands. Standing firmly in their path, the sheriff pointed out that if they took the law into their own hands, it ceased to be the law. "Nobody owns the law," he pointed out calmly.

"Oh yeah?" bellowed the leader of the mob. "You're sure acting like you own it." The sheriff shook his head. "Nope. The law owns me."

• The visiting dictator engaged the president in a discussion of civil liberties. "How can you maintain law and order and still be a democracy?" he asked.

"See, it all depends on who orders the law," replied the president.

COURTS

Judges . . . rule on the basis of law, not public opinion, and they should be totally indifferent to pressures of the times.   —*Warren E. Burger*

The efficiency of our criminal system is only marred by the difficulty of finding twelve men every day who don't know anything and can't read.   —*Mark Twain*

The heightened public clamor resulting from radio and television coverage will inevitably result in prejudice. Trial by television is, therefore, foreign to our system.
                                                                            —*Tom C. Clark*

A judge is a law student who marks his own examination papers.

                                                                            —*H. L. Mencken*

The detective series on TV always end at precisely the right moment—after the criminal is arrested and before the court turns him loose.   —*Robert Orben*

The trial of a case [is] a three-legged stool—a judge and two advocates.

                                                                            —*Warren E. Burger*

Judges ought to remember that their office is *ius dicere* and not *ius dare*: to interpret law and not to make law, or give law.   —*Francis Bacon*

Agree, for the law is costly.   —*William Camden*

When a judge puts on his robes he puts off his relations to any, and, like Melchisedech, becomes without pedigree.   —*Thomas Fuller*

A good and faithful judge prefers what is right to what is expedient.

                                                                            —*Horace*

I have always thought, from my earliest youth till now, that the greatest scourge an angry heaven ever inflicted upon an ungrateful and sinning people was an ignorant, a corrupt, or a dependent judiciary.   —*John Marshall*

If one man sin against another, the judge shall judge him.   —*1 Samuel 2:25*

A jury consists of twelve persons chosen to decide who has the better lawyer.

                                                                            —*Robert Frost (attrib.)*

I don't want a lawyer to tell me what I cannot do; I hire him to tell me how to do what I want to do.   —*J. P. Morgan*

For certain people, after fifty, litigation takes the place of sex.

                                                                            —*Gore Vidal*

Saying
It's called jury *duty*, not jury inconvenience. It is an obligation, not an interruption.

Joke
• When charged with breaking and entering Richards vehemently delared his innocence. Nevertheless he was indicted on the basis of his car having been observed parked that night outside the scene of the crime.

As soon as he was released on bail, Richards parked his car overnight outside the church in the center of town and called a policeman as his witness. "If you think I'm guilty of the crime," he declared, "you now have equal proof that I have repented."

part six

Science and Technology

SCIENCE AND TECHNOLOGY

COMPUTERS

The book is here to stay. What we're doing is symbolic of the peaceful coexistence of the book and the computer.

—*Vartan Gregorian, on computerization of the New York Public Library card catalog*

The mind can store an estimated 100 trillion bits of information—compared with which a computer's mere billions are virtually amnesiac. —*Sharon Begley*

Men are going to have to learn to be managers in a world where the organization will come close to consisting of all chiefs and one Indian. The Indian, of course, is the computer. —*Thomas L. Whisler*

Computers are useless. They can only give you answers. —*Pablo Picasso*

Not even computers will replace committees, because committees buy computers.

—*Edward Shepherd Mead*

If you put tomfoolery into a computer, nothing comes out but tomfoolery. But this tomfoolery, having passed through a very expensive machine, is somehow ennobled and no one dares criticize it. —*Pierre Gallois*

Computers can figure out all kinds of problems, except the things in the world that just don't add up. —*James Magary*

In a few minutes a computer can make a mistake so great that it would take many men many months to equal it. —*Merle L. Meacham*

The new electronic independence recreates the world in the image of a global village.

—*Marshall McLuhan*

The real danger is not that computers will begin to think like men, but that men will begin to think like computers. —*Sydney J. Harris*

The more data banks record about each one of us, the less we exist.

—*Marshall McLuhan*

. . . man is still the most extraordinary computer of all.

—*John F. Kennedy*

The presence of humans, in a system containing high-speed electronic computers and high-speed accurate communications, is quite inhibiting.

—*Stuart Luman Seaton*

Immunity to boredom gives computers the edge. —*Alan Lakein*

The computer is more than a tool, it is a medium. Just as the typeface standardized information—changing us from a society where information was at the mercy of monks busy with hand copying into a fact-loving society where nonfiction outsells fiction—so the computer will change the way we look at the world.   —*John Sculley*

Sayings

To err is human, but to really screw up requires a computer.

In the computer age, it is disturbing to realize that a machine has your number.

A company we know is encountering so many errors it's thinking of buying a computer to blame them on.

The computer is only a fast idiot—it has no imagination; it cannot originate action. It is, and will remain, only a tool to man.

The computer is down.

Jokes

• "I hate this darn machine," complained an office worker about his newly automated work station. "It never does what I want it to do, only what I tell it."

• I don't see why religion and science can't cooperate. What's wrong with using a computer to count our blessings?   —*Robert Orben*

• Smith was a man of cold facts, a scientist, a computer jock, and a confirmed atheist. He became somewhat obsessed with the desire to prove the truth. So he mortgaged his house and sold his car in order to put a down payment on the most powerful computer commercially available. Then Smith plugged it into every data bank in the world, accessed every library in the United States and Europe, and had the machine scan every book published since the invention of the printing press.

  Finally Smith sat down at the console, took a deep breath, and typed, "Is there a God?"

  The monitor flickered, the hard drives clicked, and up on the screen came the words "There is now."

• From then on, when anything went wrong with a computer, we said it had bugs in it.
    —*Grace Murray Hopper, on the removal of a two-inch-long moth from an experimental computer at Harvard in 1945*

• How do they know computers existed in biblical times?
    —Because Eve had an Apple, and Adam had a Wang.

• How can you spot a secretary who's a slow learner?
    —He's the one with Wite-Out all over his screen, and the one who Xeroxes floppies in order to copy files.

THE NUCLEAR ISSUE

It is ironical that in an age when we have prided ourselves on our progress in the intelligent care and teaching of children we have at the same time put them at the mercy of new and most terrible weapons of destruction.   —*Pearl Buck*

Man has wrested from nature the power to make the world a desert or to make the deserts bloom. There is no evil in the atom; only in men's souls.

—Adlai E. Stevenson

We have genuflected before the god of science only to find that it has given us the atomic bomb, producing fears and anxieties that science can never mitigate.

—Martin Luther King, Jr.

We turned the switch, saw the flashes, watched for ten minutes, then switched everything off and went home. That night I knew the world was headed for sorrow.

—Leo Szilard, describing the 1939 experiment which confirmed that the atom could be split

Atoms for peace. Man is still the greatest miracle and the greatest problem on this earth.

—David Sarnoff; first message sent with atomic-powered electricity, January 27, 1954

An optimist, in the atomic age, is a person who thinks the future is uncertain.

—Russell Crouse and Howard Lindsay

What was gunpowder? Trivial. What was electricity? Meaningless. The atomic bomb is the Second Coming in wrath.

—Winston Churchill

The atomic bomb . . . made the prospect of future wars unendurable. It has led us up those last few steps to the mountain pass: and beyond there is a different country.

—J. Robert Oppenheimer

I thought it might have a practical use in something like neon signs.

—Harold C. Urey, on developing heavy water, vital to the atomic bomb

One hopes to achieve the zero option, but in the absence of that we must achieve balanced numbers.

—Margaret Thatcher

I feel impelled to speak today in a language that in a sense is new—one which I, who have spent so much of my life in the military profession, would have preferred never to use. That new language is the language of atomic warfare.

—Dwight D. Eisenhower

[President John F.] Kennedy said that if we had nuclear war we'd kill 300 million people in the first hour. [Secretary of Defense Robert S.] McNamara, who is a good businessman and likes to save, says it would be only 200 million.

—Norman Thomas

One cannot fashion a credible deterrent out of an incredible action.

—Robert S. McNamara

[Nuclear weapons are] like having a cobra in the nursery with your grandchildren. . . . You get rid of the cobra or you won't have any grandchildren.

—Theodore M. Hesburgh

There is a silent enemy lurking there.

—Robert Peter Gale, bone-marrow specialist, regarding radiation levels near Chernobyl

A world without nuclear weapons would be less stable and more dangerous for all of us.

—Margaret Thatcher

Saying
We'll end up paying for nuclear power on a "pay as you glow" basis.

Jokes
• Trying to cover up an accident on a nuclear-powered submarine, the admiral stated firmly, "We've been getting glowing reports."

• Heard the new recipe for Chicken Kiev?
    —First you preheat the oven to 400,000 degrees.

• Heard about the recent batch of Ukrainian babies?
    —They've all got blue hair and blond eyes.

PROGRESS

Nothing happens until something is sold.   *—Arthur H. (Red) Motley*

In a world where the time it takes to travel (supersonic) or to bake a potato (microwave) or to process a million calculations (microchip) shrinks inexorably, only three things have remained constant and unrushed: the nine months it takes to have a baby, the nine months it takes to untangle a credit card dispute, and the nine months it takes to publish a hardcover book.   *—Andrew Tobias*

In just twenty years terrorism, communications, the jet plane, and the increase of wealth and knowledge have forced, to varying degrees, world leaders into a haunted and secret peerage whose links with the people they guide are meticulously cleansed and staged.   *—Hugh Sidey*

Our ability to create has outreached our ability to use wisely the products of our invention.   *—Whitney Moore Young, Jr.*

Tradition is the dead hand of human progress.   *—Kelly Miller*

Martyrs are needed to create incidents. Incidents are needed to create revolutions. Revolutions are needed to create progress.   *—Chester Bomar Himes*

The simplest schoolboy is now aware of truths for which Archimedes would have given his life.   *—Ernest Renan*

The book is here to stay. What we're doing is symbolic of the peaceful coexistence of the book and the computer.
    —Vartan Gregorian, on computerization of the New York Public Library card catalog

To make a new concept fit into an old statute makes tortured law with tortured results.
    —Harvey R. Sorkow, ruling that the Baby M surrogacy contract was a valid contract

It is the customary fate of new truths to begin as heresies and to end as superstitions.
                          —Thomas Henry Huxley

One doesn't discover new lands without consenting to lose sight of the shore for a very long time.   *—André Gide*

The vast majority of human beings dislike and even actually dread all notions with which they are not familiar. . . . Hence innovators . . . have generally been persecuted, and always derided as fools and madmen.   *—Aldous Huxley*

As soon as we are shown the existence of something old in a new thing, we are pacified.
—*Friedrich Wilhelm Nietzsche*

No man can cause more grief than one clinging blindly to the voices of his ancestors.
—*William Faulkner*

Doubt begins only at the last frontiers of what is possible.
—*Giovanni Giacomo Casanova*

Discontent is the first step in the progress of a man or a nation.
—*Oscar Wilde*

The reason men oppose progress is not that they hate progress, but that they love inertia.
—*Elbert Hubbard*

Progress is not an accident, but a necessity. . . . It is part of nature.
—*Herbert Spencer*

Progress is a nice word. But change is its motivator and change has its enemies.
—*Robert F. Kennedy*

The aim of an argument or discussion should not be victory, but progress.
—*Joseph Joubert*

The art of progress is to preserve order amid change and to preserve change amid order.
—*Alfred North Whitehead*

It was luxuries like air conditioning that brought down the Roman Empire. With air conditioning their windows were shut, they couldn't hear the barbarians coming.
—*Garrison Keillor*

The first undertakers in all great attempts commonly miscarry, and leave the advantages of their losses to those that come after them.
—*Samuel Butler*

You could not step twice into the same river, for other waters are ever flowing on to you.
—*Heraclitus*

The world is moving so fast these days that the man who says it can't be done is generally interrupted by someone doing it.
—*Elbert Hubbard*

The Wright brothers flew right through the smoke screen of impossibility.
—*Charles F. Kettering*

The distance between the present system and our proposal is like comparing the distance between a Model T and the space shuttle. And I should know: I've seen both.
—*Ronald Reagan*

All progress is based upon a universal innate desire of every organism to live beyond its income.
—*Samuel Butler*

What we call "Progress" is the exchange of one nuisance for another nuisance.
—*Havelock Ellis*

The reasonable man adapts himself to the world: the unreasonable one persists in trying to adapt the world to himself. Therefore all progress depends on the unreasonable man.
—*George Bernard Shaw*

Anybody who feels at ease in the world today is a fool.
—*Robert Maynard Hutchins*

In the 1940s a survey listed the top seven discipline problems in public schools: talking, chewing gum, making noise, running in the halls, getting out of turn in line, wearing improper clothes, and not putting paper in wastebaskets. A 1980s survey lists these top seven: drug abuse, alcohol abuse, pregnancy, suicide, rape, robbery, assault. (Arson, gang warfare, and venereal disease are also-rans.)   —*George F. Will*

The civilized man has built a coach, but has lost the use of his feet. He is supported on crutches, but lacks so much support of muscle. He has a fine Geneva watch, but he fails of the skill to tell the hour by the sun.   —*Ralph Waldo Emerson*

I just invent, then wait until man comes around to needing what I've invented.
—*R. Buckminster Fuller*

The longer I live the more keenly I feel that whatever was good enough for our fathers is not good enough for us.   —*Oscar Wilde*

Change is not progress.   —*H. L. Mencken*

Perversity is the muse of modern literature.   —*Susan Sontag*

A man has been arrested in New York for attempting to extort funds from ignorant and superstitious people by exhibiting a device which he says will convey the human voice any distance over metallic wires so that it will be heard by the listener at the other end. He calls the instrument a telephone. Well-informed people know that it is impossible to transmit the human voice over wires.
—*News item in an 1868 New York paper*

We'd hate to shuffle off before we see how civilization wriggles out of this one.
—**Cottage Grove** *(Oregon)* **Sentinel**

That's one small step for man, one giant leap for mankind.
—*Neil A. Armstrong, message to Earth from the first man to walk on the moon, July 20, 1969*

Saying
Never look back unless you are planning to go that way.

Jokes
- I tell you, this world is getting too complicated. Someone just gave me a battery-operated paperweight.

- The bathtub was invented in 1850. The telephone was invented in 1875. Do you realize that made twenty-five years when you could've sat in the bath without having the phone ring?

- It seems to me that houses being built today have plenty of closets. It's just that the developers have a different name for them; they call them guest bedrooms.

TECHNOLOGY

Remember, nothing that's good works by itself, just to please you. You've got to make the damn thing work.   —*Thomas Alva Edison*

One machine can do the work of fifty ordinary men. No machine can do the work of one extraordinary man.
—*Elbert Hubbard*

The drive toward complex technical achievement offers a clue to why the United States is good at space gadgetry and bad at slum problems.
—*John Kenneth Galbraith*

You on the cutting edge of technology have already made yesterday's impossibilities the commonplace realities of today.
—*Ronald Reagan*

Technology . . . is a queer thing. It brings you great gifts with one hand, and it stabs you in the back with the other.
—*C. P. Snow*

Big machines are the awe-inspiring cathedrals of the twentieth century.
—*Daniel Kleppner*

We have become a people unable to comprehend the technology we invent.
—*Association of American Colleges report on weakness of undergraduate programs*

Look at those cows and remember that the greatest scientists in the world have never discovered how to make grass into milk.
—*Michael Pupin*

Copying has become the national disease.
—*Donald G. Adams*

Life was better before telephones became common. Back then, if some nuisance wanted to say something stupid to you, he had to sit down and write a letter or get on a streetcar and ride several miles to your home.
—*Mike Royko*

When *Consumer Reports* begins to describe the potential for dire calamity that lies behind most everyday activities, my hands tremble, my vision blurs, and I have to go lie quietly for a while.
—*Colin McEnroe*

When microwave ovens didn't exist . . . did people sit around (in an emotional vacuum) saying "Heat is so boring. I wish I could bombard a potato with mutant intergalactic energy"?
—*Colin McEnroe*

The difference between machines and human beings is that human beings can be reproduced by unskilled labor.
—*Arthur C. Clarke*

A refrigerator runs by converting the dust behind it into a peculiar mutant, reptilian substance.
—*Colin McEnroe*

There has always been a food processor in the kitchen, but once upon a time she was usually called the missus, or Mom.
—*Sue Berkman*

When I got my first television set, I stopped caring so much about having close relationships.
—*Andy Warhol*

In a few minutes a computer can make a mistake so great that it would take many men many months to equal it.
—*Merle L. Meacham*

The presence of humans, in a system containing high-speed electronic computers and high-speed accurate communications, is quite inhibiting.
—*Stuart Luman Seaton*

With the jawbone of an ass . . . have I slain a thousand men.
—*Judges 15:16*

The new electronic independence recreates the world in the image of a global village.
—*Marshall McLuhan*

Technology is so much fun, but we can drown in our technology. The fog of information can drive out knowledge.
—*Daniel J. Boorstin*

Xerox: A trademark for a photocopying device that can make rapid reproductions of human error, perfectly.
—*Merle L. Meacham*

Today even our *clocks* are not made of clockwork.
—*Ian Stewart*

Ours is the age which is proud of machines that think and suspicious of men who try to.
—*H. M. Jones*

I'm not convinced that the world is in any worse shape than it ever was. It's just that in this stage of almost instantaneous communication, we bear the weight of problems our forefathers only read about after they were solved.
—*Burton Hillis*

Sayings

Women are flooding the work force so they can afford the labor-saving devices that make it possible for them to go to work.

If we can put a man on the moon, why can't we figure out how to . . .

Jokes

- The metalworker was very proud when his son went off to college. He came to tour the school on Parents' Day, and observed his son hard at work in the chemistry lab. "What are you working on?" he asked.
  "A universal solvent," explained the son, "a solvent that'll dissolve anything."
  The metalworker whistled, clearly impressed, and asked, "What'll you keep it in?"

- How do you explain counterclockwise to a kid who grew up with a digital watch?

- The young woman fresh out of agricultural college looked the whole farm over and then pronounced the farmer's methods of cultivation hopelessly out-of-date and inefficient. "Why, I'd be amazed if you got even ten pounds of apples off that tree," she concluded decisively, pointing at a gnarled old fruit tree.
  "It'd sure surprise me too," commented the old farmer. "It's a pear tree."

- A sad thing happened at the museum the other day. They replaced that statue *The Thinker*—with a computer.

- It was considered a great step forward in civil aviation when the first fully automated flight was ready for its maiden transcontinental journey. Bigwigs of every sort were shown to their seats and served champagne cocktails by cyborg hostesses, while hundreds of airline employees waved from the runway. Suddenly, the engine snapped on and the plane made a perfect takeoff into the cloudless sky.
  A silky, mechanical voice came over the plane's speaker system a few minutes later. "Welcome aboard this historic flight, ladies and gentlemen, and simply press the call button if you would like more champagne to be served by one of our robot attendants. Even those of you who may have been anxious about flying in the past can now relax in the knowledge that this flight is free from the possibility of human error. Every aspect—altitude, air pressure, course setting, weather conditions—is

being continuously monitored by state-of-the-art computer circuitry, so virtually nothing can go wrong . . . go wrong . . . go wrong . . ."

- When the phone rang at the small electronics manufacturer at 7:30 in the morning, the only person there was the night watchman. It was Commander Ratchet at the naval base, who barked, "I need some information and I need it ASAP. What's the resistance rating and total inverse payload of your model RS476-KY-4719 unit?"

  Silence on the line.

  "You there," bellowed the officer, "don't you know anything about your own equipment?"

  "Listen, Commander," the guard responded at last, "you found out everything I know about electronics when I picked up the phone."

- Mrs. Jenkins prided herself on being an innovative, progressive mother, and one of her daughter's particularly annoying habits was to request the same goodnight story, night after night after night. So she was delighted by a sudden brainstorm. That night she recorded her rendition of "Cinderella," and the following night simply directed her daughter's attention to the Play switch.

  This worked for several nights, but then Lindsay thrust the storybook firmly into her mother's hands.

  "Now sweetheart, you know how to work the tape recorder," Mrs. Jenkins reminded her.

  "Yes I do," said Lindsay, "but I can't sit on its lap."

SCIENCE

Man is slightly nearer to the atom than to the star. From his central position man can survey the grandest works of nature with the astronomer, or the minutest works with the physicist.
—*Arthur Stanley*

Look at those cows and remember that the greatest scientists in the world have never discovered how to make grass into milk.
—*Michael Pupin*

Science cannot stop while ethics catches up . . . and nobody should expect scientists to do all the thinking for the country.
—*Elvin Stackman*

Death is just a low chemical trick played on everybody except sequoia trees.
—*J. J. Furnas*

The scientific theory I like best is that the rings of Saturn are composed entirely of lost airline luggage.
—*Mark Russell*

Is ditchwater dull? Naturalists with microscopes have told me that it teems with quiet fun.
—*G. K. Chesterton*

Every great advance in science has issued from a new audacity of imagination.
—*John Dewey*

Freedom is absolutely necessary for progress in science and the liberal arts.
—*Benedict Spinoza*

Every great advance in natural knowledge has involved the absolute rejection of authority.
—*Aldous Huxley*

Science is the great antidote to the poison of enthusiasm and superstition.

—*Adam Smith*

The investigator should have a robust faith—and yet not believe.

—*Tristan Bernard*

Science will never be able to reduce the value of a sunset to arithmetic. Nor can it reduce friendship or statesmanship to a formula.   —*Louis Orr*

A good scientist is a person in whom the childhood quality of perennial curiosity lingers on. Once he gets an answer, he has other questions.

—*Fredrick Seitz*

When a man sits with a pretty girl for an hour, it seems like a minute. But let him sit on a hot stove for a minute—and it's longer than any hour. That's relativity.

—*Albert Einstein*

The great tragedy of science—the slaying of a beautiful hypothesis by an ugly fact.

—*Thomas Henry Huxley*

Mathematics is the only science where one never knows what one is talking about nor whether what is said is true.   —*Bertrand Russell*

[Scientists are] peeping Toms at the keyhole of eternity.   —*Arthur Koestler*

Science has not yet mastered prophecy. We predict too much for the next year and yet far too little for the next ten.   —*Neil A. Armstrong*

I cannot conceive of any condition which would cause this ship to founder. I cannot conceive of any vital disaster happening to this vessel. Modern shipbuilding has gone beyond that.   —*E. J. Smith, captain of the* Titanic

Nine tenths of modern science is in this respect the same: it is the produce of men whom their contemporaries thought dreamers—who were laughed at for caring for what did not concern them—who, as the proverb went, "walked into a well from looking at the stars"—who were believed to be useless, if anyone could be such.

—*Walter Bagehot*

I simply ignored an axiom.   —*Albert Einstein (attrib.), on relativity*

Science may have found a cure for most evils; but it has found no remedy for the worst of them all—the apathy of human beings.   —*Helen Keller*

Science is the record of dead religions.   —*Oscar Wilde*

Men love to wonder, and that is the seed of our science.

—*Ralph Waldo Emerson*

. . . science can not only make man richer—but science can make man better.

—*Lyndon B. Johnson*

The simplest schoolboy is now aware of truths for which Archimedes would have given his life.   —*Ernest Renan*

Man is an animal with primary instincts of survival. Consequently, his ingenuity has developed first and his soul afterward. Thus the progress of science is far ahead of man's ethical behavior.   —*Charlie Chaplin*

The whole of science is nothing more than a refinement of everyday thinking.

—*Albert Einstein*

Science is organized knowledge.

—*Herbert Spencer*

We must, however, acknowledge, as it seems to me, that man with all his noble qualities . . . still bears in his bodily frame the indelible stamp of his lowly origin.

—*Charles Darwin*

Sayings

A drug is a substance that when injected into a guinea pig produces a scientific paper.

Science is the ascertainment of facts and the refusal to regard facts as permanent.

To err is human; to try to prevent recurrence of error is science.

Science is forever rewriting itself.

Jokes

• The physics teacher began the class with a rudimentary lesson. "For every action, there is an equal and opposite reaction," he began ponderously. "For example, which of you can tell me what happens when you get in the bathtub."

An eager student in the front row stuck up her hand and replied confidently, "The phone rings."

• Michael Faraday, a pioneer in the field of electricity, was demonstrating the tremendous potential of his new invention, the dynamo, to the British Royal Scientific Society. A young politician in the audience, William Gladstone, grew bored, finally saying, "I'm sure this is all very interesting, Mr. Faraday, but what in God's earth good is it?"

"Someday," replied the brilliant inventor dryly, "you politicians will be able to tax it."

• He has left his body to science—and science is contesting the will.

—*David Frost*

OUTER SPACE

Space: The final frontier.

—*Captain James T. Kirk*

Man has always been an explorer. There's a fascination in thrusting out and going to new places. It's like going through a door because you find the door in front of you. I think that man loses something if he has the option to go to the moon and does not take it.

—*Neil A. Armstrong*

Man, the cutting edge of terrestrial life, has no rational alternative but to expand the environmental and resource base beyond earth.

—*Krafft A. Ehricke*

America is now a space-faring nation . . . a frontier good for millions of years. The only time remotely comparable was when Columbus discovered a whole new world.

—*James S. McDonnell*

Put three grains of sand inside a vast cathedral, and the cathedral will be more closely packed with sand than space is with stars.   —*Sir James Jeans*

The fault, dear Brutus, is not in our stars but in ourselves.

—*William Shakespeare*

[Space travel] is an extravagant feat of technological exhibitionism.

—*Lewis Mumford*

The drive toward complex technical achievement offers a clue to why the United States is good at space gadgetry and bad at slum problems.

—*John Kenneth Galbraith*

What if Columbus had been told, "Chris, baby, don't go now. Wait until we've solved our number-one priorities—war and famine; poverty and crime; pollution and disease; illiteracy and racial hatred. . . ."   —*William Gates*

The message from the moon which we have flashed to the far corners of this planet is that no problem need any longer be considered insoluble.

—*Norman Cousins*

The most important fact about Spaceship Earth: an instruction book didn't come with it.   —*R. Buckminster Fuller*

Saying
The bigger our discoveries about space, the smaller we become.

Jokes
• It just goes to show you. They call the lunar landscape bleak and desolate. In Arizona, it's called a chance to invest in the future.

• The scientific theory I like best is that the rings of Saturn are composed entirely of lost airline luggage.   —*Mark Russell*

• I knew Venus was uninhabited the first time we sent a space probe past it—it didn't ask for foreign aid.

• I really envy those astronauts who can walk in space. Ever since they started showing movies on planes, I've wanted to do the same.

• I understand that there's a great new restaurant on the moon.
     —Great food; no atmosphere.

• Hear about the Albanian space program that plans to travel to the sun?
     —So that they don't burn to a crisp, they're planning to travel by night.

THE FUTURE

I object to people running down the future. I intend to live the rest of my life there.
                    —*Charles F. Kettering*

We read the future by the past.   —*Alexander Crummell*

Where there is no future before a people, there is no hope.

—*Edward Wilmot Blyden*

Our children may learn about heroes of the past. Our task is to make ourselves architects of the future.   —*Jomo Mzee Kenyatta*

There is no future for a people who deny their past.

—*Adam Clayton Powell, Jr.*

Each generation must, out of relative obscurity, discover its mission, fulfill it, or betray it.   —*Frantz Fanon*

Happiness, like youth and health, is rarly appreciated until it is past.

—*Marguerite, Countess of Blessington*

If we tried to sink the past beneath our feet, be sure the future would not stand it.

—*Elizabeth Barrett Browning*

Are we going to be a services power? The double-cheeseburger-hold-the-mayo kings of the whole world?   —*Lee Iacocca*

Celestis is a postcremation service. . . . We further reduce and encapsulate them, identify each by name, Social Security number, and a religious symbol, and place them into the payloader.

—*John Cherry, describing a plan to send human remains into permanent orbit 1,900 miles above the earth*

These doomsday warriors look no more like soldiers than the soldiers of the Second World War looked like conquistadors. The more expert they become, the more they look like lab assistants in small colleges.   —*Alistair Cooke*

Neither a wise man nor a brave man lies down on the tracks of history to wait for the train of the future to run over him.   —*Dwight D. Eisenhower*

We cannot always build the future for our youth, but we can build our youth for the future.   —*Franklin D. Roosevelt*

No date on the calendar is as important as tomorrow.   —*Roy W. Howard*

Science has not yet mastered prophecy. We predict too much for the next year and yet far too little for the next ten.   —*Neil A. Armstrong*

Future shock [is] the shattering stress and disorientation that we induce in individuals by subjecting them to too much change in too short a time.   —*Alvin Toffler*

The new electronic independence recreates the world in the image of a global village.

—*Marshall McLuhan*

There is nothing like a dream to create the future.   —*Victor Hugo*

The danger of the past was that men became slaves. The danger of the future is that men may become robots.   —*Erich Fromm*

We hope that, when the insects take over the world, they will remember with gratitude how we took them along on all our picnics.   —*Bill Vaughan*

Omen: A sign that something will happen if nothing happens.

—*Ambrose Bierce*

The more data banks record about each one of us, the less we exist.

—*Marshall McLuhan*

Future, *n*.: That period of time in which our affairs prosper, our friends are true, and our happiness is assured.   —*Ambrose Bierce*

I like the dreams of the future better than the history of the past.

—*Thomas Jefferson*

He that fears not the future may enjoy the present.   —*Thomas Fuller*

The best preparation for good work tomorrow is to do good work today.

—*Elbert Hubbard*

Never let the future disturb you. You will meet it, if you have to, with the same weapons of reason which today arm you against the present.

—*Marcus Aurelius Antoninus*

Only mothers can think of the future—because they give birth to it in their children.

—*Maxim Gorky*

I never think of the future. It comes soon enough.   —*Albert Einstein*

Never look down to test the ground before taking your next step; only he who keeps his eye fixed on the far horizon will find the right road.

—*Dag Hammarskjöld*

Who controls the past controls the future; who controls the present controls the past.

—*George Orwell*

. . . it is all too obvious that if we do not abolish war on this earth, then surely, one day, war will abolish us from the earth.   —*Harry S Truman*

The future never just happened. It was created.   —*Will and Ariel Durant*

The future isn't what it used to be.   —*Yogi Berra*

The universe grows smaller every day, and the threat of aggression by any group—anywhere—can no longer be tolerated. There must be security for *all*—or not one is safe.

—*Klaatu, in* The Day the Earth Stood Still, *screenplay by Edmund H. North*

I have sometimes looked with wonder on the jargon of our times wherein those whose minds reside in the past are called "progressive" while those whose minds are vital enough to challenge and to mold the future are dubbed "reactionary."

—*Jomo Mzee Kenyatta*

Sayings
He who does not look ahead remains behind.   —*Spanish proverb*

The best thing about the future is that it comes one day at a time.

Joke
• Optimist: "Why are you always so depressed about the future?"
  Pessimist: "I keep considering the past."

A F T E R W O R D

If you have a favorite quote, saying, or joke, or the original source of one of our sayings, we'd love to add it to our collection. Please send it to *And I Quote,* % St. Martin's Press, 175 Fifth Avenue, NY, NY 10010.

I N D E X